D1609875

JURIES IN IRELAND

IN THIS SERIES*

1 Daire Hogan and W.N. Osborough (eds), *Brehons, serjeants and attorneys: studies in the history of the Irish legal profession* (1990)
2 Colum Kenny, *King's Inns and the kingdom of Ireland: the Irish 'inn of court', 1541–1800* (1992)
3 Jon G. Crawford, *Anglicizing the government of Ireland: the Irish privy council and the expansion of Tudor rule, 1556–1578* (1993)
4 W.N. Osborough (ed.), *Explorations in law and history: Irish Legal History Society discourses, 1988–1994* (1995)
5 W.N. Osborough, *Law and the emergence of modern Dublin: a litigation topography for a capital city* (1996)
6 Colum Kenny, *Tristram Kennedy and the revival of Irish legal training, 1835–1885* (1996)
7 Brian Griffin, *The Bulkies: police and crime in Belfast, 1800–1865* (1997)
8 Éanna Hickey, *Irish law and lawyers in modern folk tradition* (1999)
9 A.R. Hart, *A history of the king's serjeants at law in Ireland: honour rather than advantage?* (2000)
10 D.S. Greer and N.M. Dawson (eds), *Mysteries and solutions in Irish legal history: Irish Legal History Society discourses and other papers, 1996–1999* (2000)
11 Colum Kenny, *King's Inns and the battle of the books, 1972: cultural controversy at a Dublin library* (2002)
12 Desmond Greer and James W. Nicolson, *The factory acts in Ireland, 1802–1914* (2003)
13 Mary Kotsonouris, *The winding-up of the Dáil courts, 1922–1925: an obvious duty* (2004)
14 Paul Brand, Kevin Costello and W.N. Osborough (eds), *Adventures of the law: proceedings of the 16th British Legal History Conference, Dublin 2003* (2005)
15 Jon G. Crawford, *A star chamber court in Ireland: the court of castle chamber, 1571–1641* (2005)
16 A.P. Quinn, *Wigs and guns: Irish barristers and the Great War* (2006)
17 N.M. Dawson (ed.), *Reflections on law and history: Irish Legal History Society discourses and other papers, 2000–2005* (2006)
18 James Kelly, *Poynings' Law and the making of law in Ireland, 1660–1800* (2007)
19 W.E. Vaughan, *Murder trials in Ireland, 1836–1914* (2009)
20 Kevin Costello, *The Court of Admiralty of Ireland, 1575–1893* (2010)
21 W.N. Osborough, *An island's law: a bibliographical guide to Ireland's legal past* (2013)
22 Felix M. Larkin and N.M. Dawson (eds), *Lawyers, the law and history: Irish Legal History Society discourses and other papers, 2005–2011* (2013)
23 Daire Hogan and Colum Kenny (eds), *Changes in practice and law: a selection of essays by members of the legal profession to mark twenty-five years of the Irish Legal History Society* (2013)
24 W.N. Osborough, *The Irish stage: a legal history* (2015)
25 Thomas Mohr, *Guardian of the Treaty: the Privy Council appeal and Irish sovereignty* (2016)
26 Joseph C. Sweeney, *The life and times of Arthur Browne in Ireland and America, 1756–1805* (2017)
27 Niamh Howlin, *Juries in Ireland: laypersons and law in the long nineteenth century* (2017)

ALSO AVAILABLE

The Irish Legal History Society (1989)

* Volumes 1–7 are published by Irish Academic Press

Juries in Ireland

Laypersons and Law in the Long Nineteenth Century

NIAMH HOWLIN

FOUR COURTS PRESS

in association with

THE IRISH LEGAL HISTORY SOCIETY

Typeset in 10.5pt on 12.5pt EhrhardtMt by
Carrigboy Typesetting Services for
FOUR COURTS PRESS LTD
7 Malpas Street, Dublin 8, Ireland
www.fourcourtspress.ie
and in North America for
FOUR COURTS PRESS
c/o ISBS, 920 N.E. 58th Avenue, Suite 300, Portland, OR 97213.

A catalogue record for this title is available
from the British Library.

ISBN 978-1-84682-621-4

Printed in England,
by CPI Antony Rowe, Chippenham, Wilts.

Contents

Illustrations

Plates appear between pages 150–1

Abbreviations

Abr.	abridgement
Ad. & E.	Adolphus & Ellis' Queen's Bench Reports
Amer. Hist. Rev.	*American Historical Review*
Amer. J. Leg. Hist.	*American Journal of Legal History*
App.	appendix
B. & Ald.	Barnewall & Alderson's King's Bench Reports
B. & C.	Barnewall & Cresswell's King's Bench Reports
B. & S.	Best & Smith's Queen's Bench Reports
Bar. N.	Barnes' Notes of Practice, Common Pleas Reports
Bl. D. & O.	Blackham, Dundas & Osborne's Irish Nisi Prius Reports
Bos. & Pul.	Bosanquet & Puller's Common Pleas Reports
Brit. J. Criminology	*British Journal of Criminology*
Bulletin Ir. Georgian Soc.	*Bulletin of the Irish Georgian Society*
C.B.	Common Bench
C.C.	Crown Cases
C.C.R.	Crown Cases Reserved
C.L.	Common Law
Camb. L. J.	*Cambridge Law Journal*
Car. & K.	Carrington & Kirwan's Nisi Prius Reports
Car. & P.	Carrington & Payne's Nisi Prius Reports
Chit. Rep.	Chitty's Reports
Circ. Ca.	Circuit Cases
Colum. L. Rev.	*Columbia Law Review*
Comp. Leg. Hist.	*Comparative Legal History*
Cr. & Dix	Crawford and Dix
Crim. Jus. Hist.	*Criminal Justice History*
Crim. L. Rev.	*Criminal Law Review*
Cro. Jac.	Croke's King's Bench Reports
D. & B.	Dearsley & Bell's Crown Cases Reserved
DCA	Dublin City Archives
Den.	Denison & Pearce's Crown Cases Reserved
Dick.	Dicken's Chancery Reports
DJA	Dublin Jurors Association
Dub. Hist. Rec.	*Dublin Historical Record*

Dub. Rev.	*Dublin Review*
Dub. U.J.	*Dublin University Journal*
E.R.	English Reports
East.	East's Term Reports, King's Bench
Eng. Hist. Rev.	*English Historical Review*
Eq.	Equity
Exch.	Exchequer
F. & F.	Foster & Finlayson's Nisi Prius Reports
Fortnightly Rev.	*Fortnightly Review*
French Hist. Stud.	*French Historical Studies*
HC	House of Commons
Hist. Ire.	*History Ireland*
Hist. J.	*Historical Journal*
HL	House of Lords
How. St. Tr.	Howell's State Trials
Hud. & Br.	Hudson & Brooke's Irish King's Bench Reports
I.C.L.R.	Irish Common Law Reports
I.H.S.	*Irish Historical Studies*
I.L.T. & S.J.	*Irish Law Times and Solicitor's Journal*
I.L.T.R.	Irish Law Times Reports
Ir. Circ. Ca.	Irish Circuit Cases
Ir. Circ. Rep.	Irish Circuit Reports
Ir. Jur.	Irish Jurist
Ir. L.R.	Irish Law Reports
Irish J. Leg. Stud.	*Irish Journal of Legal Studies*
J.	judge
J. Comp. L.	*Journal of Comparative Law*
J. Dub. Stat. Soc.	*Journal of the Dublin Statistical Society*
J. Leg. Hist.	*Journal of Legal History*
J.S.S.I.S.I.	*Journal of the Social and Statistical Inquiry Society of Ireland*
Jebb & B.	Jebb & Burke's Queen's Bench Reports
Jebb & S.	Jebb & Symes' Queen's Bench Reports
JP	justice of the peace
Keb.	Keble's King's Bench Reports
L. & Contemp. Problems	*Law and Contemporary Problems*
L. & Hist. Rev.	*Law and History Review*
L.J.	Law Journal (reports)
L. M. & P.	Lowndes, Maxwell & Pollock's Reports
L. Q. Rev.	*Law Quarterly Review*
L. Rev.	*Law Review*
L.R. Ir.	Law Reports Ireland
Law Rec.	Law Recorder

LCJ	lord chief justice
Leach	Leach's Crown Cases
Leon.	Leonard's Reports
Lev.	Levinz's King's Bench and Common Pleas Reports
Lew.	Lewin's Crown Cases Reserved
Lord Ray.	Raymond's Reports
M. & W.	Meeson & Welsby's Exchequer Reports
Medical Hist.	*Medical History*
Mod. L. Rev.	*Modern Law Review*
Moo. P.C.	Moore's Privy Council Cases
MP	member of parliament
MS	manuscript
N.I.L.Q	*Northern Ireland Legal Quarterly*
n.s.	new series
NA	National Archives (UK)
NAI	National Archives of Ireland
NI	Northern Ireland
NLI	National Library of Ireland
NUI	National University of Ireland
o.s.	old series
Ox. J. Leg. Stud.	*Oxford Journal of Legal Studies*
para.	paragraph
PRO	Public Record Office
PRONI	Public Record Office of Northern Ireland
Q.B.	queen's bench
R.	*regina / rex*
R. & M.	Ryan & Moody's Nisi Prius Reports
R. & R.	Russell & Ryan's Crown Cases Reserved
Rev. Eng. Stud.	*Review of English Studies*
Ridg. Lap. & Scho.	Ridgeway, Lapp & Schoale's Reports
Rowe	Rowe's Reports of Interesting Cases
Salk.	Salkeld's King's Bench Reports
Sid.	Siderfin's King's Bench Reports
St. Tr.	State Trials
T. Jones	T. Jones' King's Bench and Common Pleas Reports
T.L.R.	Times Law Reports
U. Chic. L. Rev.	*University of Chicago Law Review*
Vent.	Ventris' King's Bench Reports
W.S.C.	Wide-Streets Commission
Wm. Bl.	William Blackstone's King's Bench Reports
Y. & J.	Younge & Jervis's Exchequer Reports
Yel.	Yelverton's King's Bench Reports

Acknowledgments

THIS BOOK HAS HAD A LONG GESTATION. Over the past decade or so, my research interests have pulled me in several directions, but my interest in the nineteenth-century jury has drawn me back again and again, and it is with no small sense of relief that I have finally completed this volume.

The staffs of various libraries and archives have been immensely helpful in putting together this book, in particular, the staffs of the National Archives of Ireland, the Public Record Office of Northern Ireland, the Dublin City Archives and the British National Archives, and the librarians of the British Library, the Senate House Library, the Royal Irish Academy, University College Dublin, Trinity College Dublin, Cambridge University, Lincoln's Inn Library, Queen's University Belfast, the Irish Architectural Archive and the National Library of Ireland.

I am particularly indebted to Mary Broderick of the National Library of Ireland for her assistance in compiling the illustrations for this book. The staff of the Irish Architectural Archive and the Dublin City Archives have been most helpful in allowing me to use images from their collections. I would also like to thank Dearbhla Kelly for providing the cover image, which depicts a jury of matrons deliberating.

Many terrific colleagues and former colleagues have provided moral support, expertise and advice that helped to shape this book, including Prof. Norma Dawson, Prof. Sally Wheeler, Dr Karen Brennan, Dr Heather Conway, Prof. Brice Dickson, Sir Tony Hart, Mr Robert Marshall, Dr Sara Ramshaw, Mr Felix M. Larkin, Dr Robin Hickey, Prof. Colin Scott, Prof. Joe McMahon, Dr Thomas Mohr, Dr Kevin Costello, Prof. Imelda Maher, Ms Ruth Crawley, Mr Aengus Fallon, Dr Cliona Kelly, Dr Donal Coffey, Dr Maebh Harding, Dr Conor Hanly, Prof. Heikki Pihlajamäki, Dr Liam Thornton, Dr Noel McGrath, Dr Eoin Daly, Prof. Ian O'Donnell, Prof. Suzanne Kingston and Dr Mark Coen. I am especially grateful to Prof. Des Greer for his insightful comments on an earlier draft.

My interest in Irish legal history was originally sparked by Professor Nial Osborough, who has inspired and encouraged many scholars to pursue research in this field. The Irish Legal History Society has also been extremely supportive of this project. I would also like to express my thanks to Sam Tranum at Four Courts Press, and to Julitta Clancy for the excellent indexing.

I am also particularly grateful to the Sutherland School of Law in UCD for supporting this publication and allowing me a period of research leave in which to focus on it.

Finally, I thank my wonderful husband Robert and my extended family and friends for their support and encouragement over the past decade.

CHAPTER ONE

Introduction

A WOMAN UNDER SENTENCE OF DEATH for a capital felony claims to be pregnant, in the hope of a reprieve. A Dublin landlord learns that his properties are to be compulsorily purchased as part of a city improvement scheme. Two farmers squabble over a right of way. A body is discovered in suspicious circumstances. A baker sells adulterated bread at a city market. A man claims that his sister is insane and cannot manage her own affairs. Another man is on trial for his life for committing violent outrages in the name of nationalism.

What all of these disparate situations had in common in the eighteenth and nineteenth centuries was that they were all resolved, one way or another, by a panel of laypersons rather than by a professional judge or magistrate.[1] Juries were used in many situations, adding a modicum of community sanction to decision-making. Numerous categories of jury survived into the nineteenth century,[2] some with adjudicative powers and others with powers of presentment, valuation, inspection or seizure. A broad distinction can be drawn between juries of inquiry and presentment (such as grand juries or juries on coroners' inquests), and juries of issue and assessment (such as trial juries and juries on lunacy commissions).

Broadly speaking, grand juries indicted prisoners who subsequently went on to be tried by petty juries. Most criminal cases were tried by common juries, while commercial civil cases tended to be tried before special juries. Juries *de medietate linguae* determined civil and criminal cases involving aliens, while leet and baron juries decided minor cases in local manorial courts. Market juries regulated fairs and markets, coroners' juries conducted inquests on dead bodies, and juries of matrons determined pregnancy in specific criminal and civil cases. Lunacy juries determined whether persons were of sound mind and wide-street juries conducted valuations on properties that were to be compulsorily purchased. Although many categories of jury fell into abeyance or were abolished during the nineteenth century, as late as 1913 a parliamentary committee observed:

1 In this book, the terms 'lay' and 'professional' are ascribed meanings similar to those given by Dawson. He considers a 'professional' to be someone who 'applies a substantial part of his time and energy, with some degree of continuity, to the task at hand. In most instances this specialization is rewarded by paid income'. A lay judge, by contrast, is 'drawn from his community at random, is in no way distinguished from others by his tenure of an office, and works without continuity', John Dawson, *A history of lay judges* (Cambridge, MA, 1960), pp 3–4.

2 See, e.g., J. Brown, *The dark side of trial by jury* (London, 1859), p. 7.

> The purposes for which a jury may be called together are far more numerous than might be supposed, and many of them can be known to few but lawyers. Such are, for example, presentments whereon to found the Sovereign's title to land or goods, presentments declaring what debts are due to the Sovereign, presentments as to lands or tenements of a judgment debtor under writs of elegit, presentments under special acts and customs, verdicts after inquisitions held under the Lunacy Acts, &c. To a jury is also entrusted the assessment of damages before the sheriff under a writ of enquiry and of compensation before the Lands Clauses Consolidation Act 1845, and similar statutes.[3]

Although called 'juries', many of these were not juries as a twenty-first-century lawyer would recognise them. The term is used throughout this book to refer to the many bodies or panels of laypersons that had legally recognised decision-making powers. In a broader sense, the zeal in Ireland for involving laypersons in the administration of justice never quite matched that in England, mainly because of Ireland's specific political, economic and social situation.[4] But juries, and the idea of lay decision-making, were firmly entrenched, and juries were used to decide a wide range of civil, criminal and administrative issues.

In a sense, the appetite for lay decision-making has gone full circle. As Dzur observes, 'the use of jury-like procedures to address complex problems of urban planning, environmental protection, biotechnology, and more has become increasingly attractive to academics and public officials'.[5] However, while Dzur characterises these modern uses of lay decision-making as democratically inspired attempts to re-engage citizens with policymaking, it will be seen that there was little emphasis on democracy or civic engagement underlying juries in the eighteenth and nineteenth centuries.

This book is not a detailed examination of the role of the jury in eighteenth- and nineteenth-century Irish criminal justice. It is, rather, a broader examination of the role of laypersons in decision-making during this period, in both the civil and criminal spheres. As such, it is not possible to provide extensive coverage of the operation of nineteenth-century criminal juries. To some extent, many of these issues have been addressed elsewhere by this author and others.[6] A full-length

3 *Report on juries* [C-6817] 1913, xxx, 403.

4 As has been discussed elsewhere, professionalism was preferred over amateurism in areas such as prosecution, policing and magistracy. See N. Howlin, 'Nineteenth-century criminal justice: uniquely Irish or simply "not English"?', *Irish J. Leg. Stud.*, 3:1 (2013), 67–89.

5 Albert Dzur, *Punishment, participatory democracy and the jury* (Oxford, 2012), p. 107. Dzur describes the use of 'citizens' juries' and deliberative polls in the United States and Canada. A comparison may be drawn with the relatively recent Convention on the Constitution, described as 'a new venture in participative democracy in Ireland' (www.constitution.ie, accessed 22 Nov. 2016). This was a forum of 100 persons: 66 randomly selected citizens, 33 parliamentarians and a chairman. The group convened periodically between 2012 and 2014 to deliberate upon the continued relevance of, and potential amendments to, aspects of the Irish constitution.

6 See, for example, David Johnson, 'Trial by jury in Ireland, 1860–1914', *J. Leg. Hist.*, 17:3 (1996),

treatment of the Irish criminal jury is a worthy project for another time, and perhaps another author.

In many ways the popularity of lay decision-making in Ireland echoed developments in other European countries at the time. The end of the eighteenth century and the aftermath of the French Revolution had seen the rise of ideas about popular sovereignty, and in 1781 trial by jury for criminal offences was transplanted to France.[7] The criminal jury was extended to Belgium at the time of its foundation in 1830,[8] and throughout the nineteenth century it spread to other European countries, including Switzerland, Portugal, Germany, Austria, Denmark and Hungary, forming part of the liberal agenda in many countries.[9] Meanwhile, some Nordic countries had had juries, or bodies resembling them, firmly entrenched since the Middle Ages.[10] As Antal observes, '[i]n Europe the golden age of the criminal jury was in the second part of the nineteenth century: it spread to almost every "civilized state" with the exception of Spain and the Netherlands – even to Russia'.[11] In the common-law world, by the nineteenth century, versions of the jury trial were well-established in the United States, Australia, Canada, New Zealand, India and many other colonies in Africa and elsewhere.[12] Reforms to

270–91; David Johnson, 'The trials of Sam Gray: Monaghan politics and nineteenth century Irish criminal procedure', *Ir. Jur.* (n.s.), 20 (1985), 109–34; John McEldowney, 'The case of *The queen v. McKenna* and jury packing in Ireland', *Ir. Jur.* (n.s), 12 (1977), 339–54; John McEldowney, 'Stand by for the crown: an historical analysis', *Crim. L. Rev.* (1979), 272–83; and William E. Vaughan, *Murder trials in Ireland, 1833–1914* (Dublin, 2009).

7 See, e.g., James M. Donovan, *Juries and the transformation of criminal justice in France in the nineteenth and twentieth centuries* (Chapel Hill, NC, 2010); William Savitt, 'Rethinking the nineteenth-century French jury', *Colum. L. Rev.*, 96:4 (1996), 1019–61; and James M. Donovan, 'Magistrates and juries in France, 1791–1952', *French Hist. Stud.*, 22:3 (1999), 379–420.

8 See generally Phillip Traest, 'The jury in Belgium', *Revue Internationale de Droit Pénal*, 72:1 (2001), 27–50.

9 For Switzerland, see Francis William O'Brien, 'Switzerland questions the jury', *Saskatchewan L. Rev.*, 32:1 (1967), 31–44; see generally Arnd Koch, 'C.J.A. Mittermaier and the nineteenth century debate about juries and mixed courts', *Revue Internationale de Droit Pénal*, 72:1 (2001), 347–53; for Austria see, e.g., Greg Taylor, 'Jury trial in Austria', *New Criminal L. Rev.*, 14:2 (2011), 281–325, p. 286 and Antonio Padua Schioppa, *The trial jury in England, France, Germany, 1700–1900* (Berlin, 1987); for Denmark see Stanley Anderson, 'Lay judges and jurors in Denmark', *Am. J. Comp. L.*, 38:4 (1990), 839–64; and for Hungary see Tamás Antal, 'The codification of the jury procedure in Hungary', *J. Leg. Hist.*, 30:3 (2009), 279–97.

10 See, e.g., Heikki Pihlajamäki, 'From compurgators to mixed courts: reflections on the historical development of Finnish evidence law and court structure', *Revue Internationale de Droit Pénal*, 72:1 (2001), 159–74.

11 Antal, 'Codification', 280; Samuel Kucherov, 'The jury as part of the Russian judicial reform of 1864', *American Slavic & East European Rev.*, 9:2 (1950), 77–90; and Marina Nemytina, 'Trial by jury: a western or a peculiarly Russian model?', *Revue Internationale de Droit Pénal*, 72:1 (2001), 365–70.

12 For Australia see, e.g., J.M. Bennett, 'The establishment of jury trials in New South Wales', *Sydney L. Rev.*, 3 (1959–61), 463–85; Alex Low, 'Sir Alfred Stephen and the jury question in Van Diemen's Land', *University of Tasmania L. Rev.*, 21 (2002), 72–119; M. Chesterman, 'Criminal trial juries in Australia: from penal colonies to a federal democracy' in Neil Vidmar (ed.), *World*

England's juries were often followed (albeit with modifications) throughout its empire.[13]

Lay participation in the legal process also took the form of lay justices and magistrates.[14] Local courts were originally administered by unpaid amateurs known as justices of the peace (JPs),[15] the office having its origins in a statute of 1327.[16] They exercised their jurisdiction either individually or in threes, at the quarter sessions, and were described as not having been 'educated for the law; nor have they received any training for the duties which that office imposes on them'.[17] McDowell cites some of the 'obvious difficulties' in appointing justices of the peace,[18] who in Ireland tended to be drawn from a slightly lower social class than in England. The office of justice of the peace was brought into disrepute in the early nineteenth century, and efforts to reform it included the establishment of petty sessions, which curbed the arbitrariness of single JPs sitting alone.[19]

jury systems (Oxford, 2000). For Canada, see Graham Parker, 'Trial by jury in Canada', *J. Leg. Hist.*, 8 (1987), 179–89; and Robert Blake Brown, *A trying question: the jury in nineteenth-century Canada* (Toronto, 2009). For New Zealand, see N. Cameron, S. Potter and W. Young, 'The New Zealand jury', *L. & Contemp. Problems*, 62 (1999), 103–40. For India, see Richard Vogler, 'The international development of the jury: the role of the British empire', *Revue Internationale de Droit Pénal*, 72:1 (2001), 525–50 at 542–8. For Africa, see J.H. Jeary, 'Trial by jury and trial with the aid of assessors in the superior courts of British African territories, I-III', *J. African L.*, 4:3 (1960); 5:1 (1961), 133–46; 5:2 (1961), 36–47; E.V. Mittlebeeler, 'Race and jury in Nigeria', *Howard L.J.*, 18 (1973–5), 88–106; R. Howman, 'Trial by jury in southern Rhodesia', *Rhodes-Livingstone J.*, 7 (1949), 41–66; R. Knox-Mawer, 'The jury system in British colonial Africa', *J. African L.*, 2 (1958), 160–3; E. Kahn, 'Restore the jury? Or "Reform? Reform? Aren't things bad enough already?" I-III', *South African L.J.*, 108 (1991), 672–87; 109 (1992), 82–111; and 109 (1992), 307. P.R. Spiller, 'The jury system in early Natal (1846–1874)', *J. Leg. Hist.*, 8:2 (1987), 129–47; S.A. Strauss, 'The jury in South Africa', *U. Western Australia L. Rev.*, 11 (1973–4), 133–9; and *Committee on Africa (Western Coast)*, HC 1865 (412–I) i, 499, paras 543–5 (Henry St. George Ord, colonel in the Royal Engineers and governor of Bermuda); paras 3176–9 (Sir Benjamin Pine, former chief justice of Sierra Leone and government administrator in Natal and Gold Coast); paras 8244–9 (William A. Ross, colonial secretary). For other colonies see, e.g., J.J. Cremona, 'The jury system in Malta', *American J. Comp. L.*, 13 (1964), 570–82; *Report of commissioners on Malta, part III*, HC 1839 (140) xvii, 753, pp 107–8; and R. Deosaran, 'The jury system in a post-colonial multi-racial society: problems of bias', *Brit. J. Criminology*, 21:4 (1981), 305–23.

13 See generally Vogler, 'International development'.

14 Dawson, for example, regards justices of the peace more as lay than as professional decision-makers. Dawson, *Lay judges*, p. 3.

15 See Hamilton Smythe, *The office of justice of the peace in Ireland* (Dublin, 1841). For a history of justices of the peace in Ireland see E.A. Comerton, *A handbook of the Magistrates' Courts Act (NI) 1964* (Belfast, 1968), p. xxxviii.

16 John McEldowney, 'Lord O'Hagan and the Irish Jury Act 1871' (PhD, Cambridge University, 1981), p. 35.

17 Smythe, *Justice of the peace*, p. iii.

18 R.B. McDowell, 'The Irish courts of law, 1801–1914', *I.H.S.*, 10:40 (1957), 363–91 at 371.

19 Petty Sessions Act (Ireland), 1827 (7 & 8 Geo. IV, c. 67). This divided counties into petty sessions districts and provided for the renting of suitable premises.

Although they were originally laypersons, without formal legal training, and were arguably drawn from the same social classes as some types of juror, justices of the peace are distinguishable from lay juries in a number of respects. Instead of being drawn from a pool, they were appointed individually. Their appointments were official and for a longer term, rather than ad hoc. There was not a large pool of potential magistrates to choose from. They were appointed by act of parliament or by commission under the great seal.[20] Their appointment lay in the hands of the Irish lord chancellor on the recommendation of the lords lieutenant of counties,[21] rather than the cess collectors, sheriffs and crown solicitors who between them determined who sat on a lay jury. Instead of reaching decision as part of a panel of twelve (or six), they either made decisions alone, or in much smaller groups of two or three.

Moreover, these lay judges were supplemented with professionals from the late eighteenth century, evidencing a move away from the use of amateurs in this regard. Paid professionals, who were to be barristers of six years' standing, were first introduced for some counties in 1787.[22] In 1796 these assistant barristers were introduced in every county.[23] The assistant barristers could dispose of civil bills, and their status and salary were raised in the 1850s.[24] Another category of magistrates was created in 1814 – these were salaried resident magistrates.[25]

Eighteenth- and nineteenth-century juries were not representative in a modern sense. Eligibility was limited by class, income, profession, gender and, in eighteenth-century Ireland, religion. The limitations on jury membership were always contentious, even despite significant reforms in the nineteenth century that broadened the jury franchise. Those in the majority in the general population tended to be in the minority on juries, thus reinforcing for many a sense of oppression, unfairness and unrepresentativeness. Dicey wrote in the late nineteenth century that the jury was 'for preserving harmony between the action of the law and the sentiment of the people', but that '[w]herever and whenever the class from whom juries are taken do not sympathise with the law, the system leads to an utter failure in the attempt to enforce punishment'.[26] It could also, as will be seen, lead to failures in civil justice, corruption and disillusionment.

20 Constantine Molloy, *Justice of the peace for Ireland: a treatise on the powers and duties of magistrates in Ireland in cases of summary jurisdiction in the prosecution of indictable offences and in other matters* (Dublin, 1890), p. 3. He notes that '[o]f justices pointed by act of parliament, some are appointed directly under the provisions of some particular statute', while 'others act as justices by virtue of some office which they hold'.

21 McEldowney, 'Lord O'Hagan', p. 36.

22 Peace Preservation Act, 1787 (27 Geo. III, c. 40), ss 15, 16.

23 Administration & Justice Act, 1796 (36 Geo. III, c. 25), s. 2.

24 Civil Bills and Quarter Sessions (Ireland) Act, 1851 (14 & 15 Vic., c. 57). Their title was later changed to chairman of the quarter sessions and eventually to county court judge: see McDowell, 'The Irish courts of law', p. 373.

25 Ibid.

26 A.V. Dicey, 'How is the law to be enforced in Ireland?', *Fortnightly Rev.* (n.s.), 179 (1881), 537–52 at 549.

However, despite its shortcomings, Ireland had a functioning and extensive system of juries, broadly defined, which reached its peak in the late eighteenth century and early nineteenth century. Jury laws and procedures were revised more frequently in Ireland than in England because they more often came under intense public scrutiny, commonly after perceived failures of justice. As will be seen, the unique social and political conditions prevailing in nineteenth-century Ireland, along with waves of unrest and criminality throughout the century, profoundly affected the evolution and operation of the justice system generally, and the jury trial in particular.

CONTEXT: THE ADMINISTRATION OF JUSTICE IN IRELAND

Ireland's legal system in the eighteenth and nineteenth centuries was not markedly different to England's.[27] Both were common-law systems and adhered to the same basic principles of justice. By the nineteenth century the structure and hierarchy of courts were not wholly dissimilar, with the royal courts of king's bench, common pleas, chancery and exchequer existing alongside various prerogative courts.[28] In Ireland, criminal prosecutions and civil disputes were generally dealt with at a local level. Several times a year the judges from the superior courts in Dublin travelled around on circuit to preside at county assizes to hear important civil and criminal cases. The judges would also travel to disturbed counties on an ad hoc basis under special commissions if there were a large number of criminal cases arising between assizes. This generally happened during times of political unrest and violence. At a lower level, the quarter sessions[29] were held four times a year or more, if necessary. They were presided over by justices of the peace, and dealt with less serious criminal offences and civil cases of relatively low value.[30] Below these were the local courts, including both borough courts (known as tholsel courts) and manorial courts (the courts baron and leet).[31] These dealt with criminal offences and some civil transactions.

27 See generally F.H. Newark, 'Notes on Irish legal history', *N.I.L.Q.*, 7 (1946–8), 121–39; and W.J. Johnston, 'The first adventure of the common law', *L. Q. Rev.*, 36 (1920), 9–30.

28 Until the late seventeenth century, these had included the court of castle chamber, broadly equivalent to the English court of star chamber. See Jon Crawford, *A star chamber court in Ireland: the court of castle chamber, 1571–1641* (Dublin, 2005).

29 See R.B. McDowell, *The Irish administration, 1801–1914* (1st ed., London, 1964), pp 116–18; John F. McEldowney, 'Some aspects of law and policy in the administration of criminal justice in nineteenth-century Ireland' in John McEldowney and Paul O'Higgins (eds), *The common law tradition: essays in Irish legal history* (Dublin, 1990), p. 132; Neal Garnham, *The courts, crime and criminal law in Ireland, 1692–1760* (Dublin, 1996), p. 77; and P.J. McKenna, 'On the criminal jurisdiction of quarter sessions in Ireland', *J.S.S.I.S.I.*, 1 (1856), 276–85.

30 Jurors who tried cases at quarter sessions tended to be socially inferior to those trying cases at assizes: *Select committee on juries (Ireland)*, HC 1873 (283) xv, 389, para. 8 (Charles Hemphill, chairman of the Kerry quarter sessions).

31 See McDowell, *The Irish administration*, p. 115; Richard McMahon, 'Manor courts in the west of Ireland before the Famine' in D.S. Greer and N.M. Dawson (eds), *Mysteries and solutions in Irish legal history* (Dublin, 2001); and Richard McMahon, 'The court of petty sessions and society in

In terms of administration and enforcement, it is clear that the justice systems of England and Ireland differed on several counts; for example, Ireland had a centralised constabulary and a comprehensive system of public prosecutors at an earlier stage than England.[32] The fact that justice was administered at parish level in England and at county level in Ireland further impacted on the development of legal practice. Criminal cases were disposed of differently in the two countries, with conviction rates lower in Ireland for all categories of offences.[33] Between 1855 and 1864 the average conviction rate in Ireland was around 50 per cent. It reached a ten-year high of almost 59 per cent in 1864, but this was still much lower than the rate in England, which was at about 76.5 per cent.[34]

Social differences between the two countries also affected the way jury trial developed and was experienced. For example, the structure of rural society in Ireland[35] did not lend itself to the existence of an extensive pool of middle-class landowners who could sit as trial jurors.[36] Especially in the early part of the century, there was a large rural population of subsistence farmers, many of whom were Catholic, who did not hold freehold or long-leasehold interests in the land they farmed, partially as a result of the penal laws.[37] While, broadly speaking, those at the lower end of the socio-economic scale tended to be Roman Catholic, members of the ruling elite were more likely to be Protestant, further dividing the ruling and working classes.[38] Over the course of the eighteenth century, the Irish population doubled from around two million to four million.[39] By the eve of the great Famine, the population of Ireland was just over eight million, of which almost six and a half million were Roman Catholic, representing roughly 80 per cent of the total population.[40] Ten per cent belonged to

pre-Famine Galway' in Raymond Gillespie (ed.), *The remaking of modern Ireland, 1750–1950: Beckett Prize essays in Irish history* (Dublin, 2004).

32 See William H. Dodd, 'The preliminary proceedings in criminal cases in England, Ireland, and Scotland, compared', *J.S.S.I.S.I.* (1878), 201–9; John McEldowney, 'Crown prosecutions in nineteenth-century Ireland' in Douglas Hay and F. Snyder (eds), *Policing and prosecution in Britain, 1750–1850* (Oxford, 1989), p. 428. See also John H. Langbein, 'The origins of public prosecution and common law', *Amer. J. Leg. Hist.*, 17 (1973), 313–35.

33 Johnson, 'Trial by jury in Ireland, 1860–1914', 275. He also demonstrates, 276, that conviction rates were lower in rural areas than in urban ones.

34 *Judicial statistics. 1864. Ireland. Part I. Police – criminal proceedings – prisons. Part II. Common law – equity –civil and canon law* [C-8563] HC 1864 (52) lii, 657.

35 See, generally, William E. Vaughan, *Landlords and tenants in mid-Victorian Ireland* (Oxford, 1994).

36 It was less difficult to secure jurors for coroners' inquests, as there were less prescribed qualifications. See p. 81. It should also be added that the lack of a substantial middle class did not materially affect the ability to appoint grand jurors, who were generally drawn from a higher social class; see pp 37–40.

37 See J.C. Brady, 'Legal developments, 1801–79' in William Vaughan (ed), *A new history of Ireland, v: Ireland under the Union, 1801–1870* (Oxford, 1989).

38 See generally David Hempton, *Religion and political culture in Britain and Ireland from the Glorious Revolution to the decline of empire* (Cambridge, 1996) and Sean J. Connolly, *Religion and society in nineteenth century Ireland* (Dundalk, 1985).

39 K.H. Connell, *The population of Ireland, 1750–1845* (Oxford, 1950), p. 5.

40 *Return of population for 1841*, HC 1843 (354) li, 321. Note that the estimations as to the numbers belonging to each religion dated from 1834.

the Church of Ireland and the remaining 10 per cent mainly comprised Presbyterians and other Protestant dissenters. By 1881, the population had dropped to roughly five million, of which approximately 77 per cent were Roman Catholic. Differences in religious affiliation were in some parts of the country accompanied by a language barrier; in the poorer areas in the west of the country, Irish was the language spoken.[41] All of these issues added to the tensions that afflicted the Irish justice system in the nineteenth century.

There were other differences in the ways that lay participation in the administration of justice manifested itself in England and Ireland. Regulation of markets, for example, was not delegated to market jurors to the same extent in England as in Ireland.[42] At the same time, there were other bodies of laypersons, such as annoyance juries, which carried out some market-regulation functions, such as inspection of weights and measures.[43] Juries were also used in the context of property valuations, street maintenance and disputes surrounding compulsory purchase in England, but not necessarily in a manner identical to the way such bodies were used in Ireland.

AN OVERVIEW OF IRISH JURY DEVELOPMENTS

There was a considerable body of eighteenth-century legislation that dealt with juries of various types. In the early years of the century, efforts were made to improve the administration of justice by means of a series of parliamentary acts prescribing the processes and procedures relating to civil jury trials.[44] Some legislation also explicitly excluded Roman Catholics from sitting on juries.[45] At the same time, legislation also provided for the use of juries to fulfil a range of functions, including land valuations in the context of economic improvement[46] and

41 See Aiden Doyle, *A history of the Irish language from the Norman invasion to independence* (Oxford, 2015), pp 81–105; and Nicholas M. Wolf, *An Irish-speaking island: state, religion, community and the linguistic landscape in Ireland, 1770–1870* (Madison, WI, and London, 2014), pp 149–80.

42 See Douglas Hay, 'The state and the market in 1800: Lord Kenyon and Mr Waddington', *Past and Present*, 162 (1999), 101–62. In England, clerks of the market had wide-ranging powers relating to weights and measures, although by the eighteenth century their position was becoming increasingly peripheral: Julian Hoppit, 'Reforming Britain's weights and measures, 1660–1824', *Eng. Hist. Rev.*, 108:426 (1993), 82–104 at 88–9. Blackstone observed that the court of the clerk of the market was 'the most inferior court of criminal jurisdiction in the kingdom'. W. Blackstone, *Commentaries on the laws of England*, 4 vols (Oxford, 1766–9), iv, p. 272. Hoppit observes, p. 89, that there was overlap between the roles of the clerk of the market and the justice of the peace in England.

43 See pp 71–2.

44 E.g. Advancement of Justice Act, 1707 (6 Anne, c. 10); Regulation of Juries Act, 1735 (9 Geo. II, c. 3); Regulation of Juries (Amendment) Act, 1739 (13 Geo. II, c. 5); Regulation of Juries (Amendment) Act, 1747 (21 Geo. II, c. 6); Regulation of Juries Act, 1755 (29 Geo. II, c. 6).

45 E.g. Popery Act, 1703 (2 Anne, c. 7); Papist Solicitors Act, 1707 (6 Anne, c. 6); Popery (Amendment) Act, 1709 (8 Anne, c. 3); Regulation of Galway Act, 1717 (4 Geo. I, c. 15).

46 E.g. Bog Act, 1715 (2 Geo. I, c. 12); Lighthouses Act, 1717 (4 Geo. I, c. 7); Mines Act, 1723 (10 Geo. I, c. 5); Bog (Amendment) Act, 1749 (25 Geo. II, c. 10).

street maintenance.[47] By the mid-eighteenth century, as the Irish economy improved,[48] juries were regularly being used for a range of valuation and improvement schemes, including mining and the building and repair of streets, roads, bridges and canals.[49] This continued until the end of the century, alongside legislative attempts to improve and reform special juries[50] and market juries,[51] among others.

After the union of Great Britain and Ireland, the Irish justice system functioned under increasingly difficult conditions. The Catholic emancipation movement sought to improve the legal, political and civil position of Catholics, and the dismantling of lingering discriminations under the eighteenth-century penal laws. This included better representation of Catholics on various types of jury. In the 1820s and '30s, waves of crime, many of which were associated with political or agrarian agitation, saw increased activity by secret societies, which sought at times to control jury verdicts by the use of threats or violence.[52] The first decades of the nineteenth century saw little legislative activity in relation to jurors,[53] but in 1825 a major piece of reforming and consolidating legislation was passed by Robert Peel in England. The English Juries Act, 1825 introduced a range of reforms – for example, it altered the qualifications for jurors.[54] It typified what Oldham describes

47 E.g. Dublin Pavements Act, 1717 (4 Geo. I, c. 11); Paving Act, 1719 (6 Geo. I, c. 15).
48 See generally L.M. Cullen, *An economic history of Ireland since 1660* (London, 1972).
49 E.g. Wide Streets (Dublin) Act, 1757 (31 Geo. II, c. 19). Baal's-Bridge Act, 1757 (31 Geo. II, c. 20); Lighting Act, 1759 (33 Geo. II, c. 18); Wide Streets (Amendment) Act, 1759 (33 Geo. II, c. 15); Regulation of Cork Act, 1765 (5 Geo. III, c. 24); Timber Act, 1767 (7 Geo. III, c. 23). Regulation of Cork Act, 1771–2 (11 & 12 Geo. III, c. 18); Grand Canal Act, 1771–2 (11 & 12 Geo. III, c. 31); Paving and Lighting (Dublin) Act, 1773–4 (13 & 14 Geo. III, c. 22); Roads Act, 1773–4 (13 & 14 Geo. III, c. 32); Paving and Lighting (Dublin) (Amendment) Act, 1775–6 (15 & 16 Geo. III, c. 20); Cork Police Act, 1777–8 (17 & 18 Geo. III, c. 38); Dublin Wide Streets Act, 1781–2 (21 & 22 Geo. III, c. 17); Dundalk Road Act, 1783–4 (23 & 24 Geo. III, c. 27); Dublin Wide Streets (Amendment) Act, 1783–4 (23 & 24 Geo. III c. 31); Waterford Police Act, 1783–4 (23 & 24 Geo. III, c. 52); River Lee Act, 1786 (26 Geo. III, c. 28); Dublin Turnpike Act, 1787 (27 Geo. III, c. 59); Dublin Wide Streets (Amendment) Act, 1790 (30 Geo. III, c. 19); Royal Canal Act, 1790 (30 Geo. III, c. 20); Londonderry Act, 1790 (30 Geo. III, c. 31); Kilkenny Turnpike Act, 1790 (30 Geo. III, c. 44); Kinnegad Turnpike Act, 1790 (30 Geo. III, c. 46); Limerick and Cork Roads Act, 1790 (30 Geo. III, c. 47); Dublin Paving Act, 1790 (30 Geo. III, c. 42); Merrion Square Act, 1791 (31 Geo. III, c. 45); Inland Navigation Act, 1792 (32 Geo. III, c. 15); Mines Act, 1792 (32 Geo. III, c. 24); Royal Canal Act, 1792 (32 Geo. III, c. 26); Kilkenny Turnpike Act, 1792 (32 Geo. III, c. 39); Newry Navigation Act, 1793 (33 Geo. III, c. 10); Castlecomber Act, 1793 (33 Geo. III, c. 19); Cork Turnpike Act, 1799 (39 Geo. III, c. 52); Dublin Wide Streets Act, 1799 (39 Geo. III, c. 53); Dublin Wide Streets (Amendment) Act, 1800 (40 Geo. III, c. 61).
50 Special Juries Act, 1777–8 (17 & 18 Geo. III, c. 45).
51 E.g. Market Juries Act, 1787 (27 Geo. III, c. 46).
52 For an examination of the relationship between sectarianism and homicide in the early nineteenth century see Richard McMahon, '"The madness of party": sectarian homicide in Ireland, 1801–1850', *Crime, History and Societies*, 11:1 (2007), 83–112. On political violence in Ireland, see C. Townshend, *Political violence in Ireland: government resistance since 1848* (Oxford, 1983).
53 E.g. Jury Act, 1800 (40 Geo. III, c. 72).
54 English Juries Act 1825 (6 Geo. IV, c. 50), later known as the County Jurors Act.

as 'the reform sentiment characteristic of the era'.[55] Some thought was given to extending the provisions of this act to Ireland, but for various reasons this was not immediately done. There followed a decade of lobbying for Irish jury reforms along similar lines.[56] This came to a head in 1833, against the background of a parliamentary committee examining problematic aspects of the administration of justice in Ireland.[57] Daniel O'Connell introduced an unsuccessful jury bill in March,[58] and some months later a bill by Louis Perrin was introduced and circulated to the Irish judges.[59] This was done at the same time that coercive legislation was passed.[60] Unlike O'Connell's bill, Perrin's was aimed at standardising the laws of England and Ireland by consolidating existing laws along the lines of Peel's 1825 act.[61] The legislation finally passed as the Juries (Ireland) Act, 1833,[62] although it was not brought into force until 1835. It abolished the distinction between civil and criminal juries, but introduced a new distinction between counties at large and counties of cities and towns.[63] Far from being revolutionary, however, this act essentially consolidated the existing rules and practices as expressed in the patchwork of eighteenth-century legislation.

The Juries (Ireland) Act, 1833 was problematic in several respects, not the least of which was the degree of discretion allowed to sheriffs and other officials in the preparation of trial jury lists, and the unrepresentative nature of the juries empanelled. As McEldowney observes, '[i]t was not long before the act was heavily criticised'.[64] Many of these criticisms were aired before a parliamentary committee in 1839.[65] Several high-profile controversies highlighted the deficiencies of the Irish jury system, including the trial of Daniel O'Connell and others by a 'packed' jury in 1844.[66]

55 James C. Oldham, 'Special juries in England: nineteenth century usage and reform', *J. Leg. Hist.*, 8 (1987), 148–66 at 152. See also David Cairns, *Advocacy and the making of the adversarial criminal trial, 1800–1865* (Oxford, 1998), ch. 1. Carins describes, p. 1, the period from the 1820s as being decades of 'progressive rationalisation of law and procedure'.

56 E.g. *Juries (Ireland) bill*, HC 1826–7 (451) i, 623; *Juries (Ireland) bill*, HC 1828 (98) iii, 363; *Juries (Ireland) bill*, HC 1828 (202) iii, 393; see *Hansard 3*, xi, 1248 (3 Apr. 1832); *Juries (Ireland) bill*, HC 1830 (108) i, 455; *Juries (Ireland) bill*, HC 1831 (132) ii, 385.

57 *Report on the state of Ireland*, HC 1831–2 (677) xvi, 1.

58 *Hansard 3*, xvi, 344 (7 Mar. 1833).

59 See *Letter regarding the jury bill 1833, from the judges of Ireland to E.G. Stanley, Feb. 1833* (NAI, OP/1833/14).

60 An Act for the more effectual suppression of local disturbances and dangerous associations in Ireland, 1833 (3 & 4 Will. IV, c. 4), also referred to as the Peace Preservation Act, 1833.

61 McEldowney, 'Lord O'Hagan', p. 84.

62 3 & 4 Will. IV, c. 91.

63 McEldowney, 'Lord O'Hagan', p. 85.

64 Ibid., p. 90.

65 *Report on the state of Ireland in respect of crime*, HC 1839 (486) xi, xii, 1.

66 *R v. O'Connell and others* (1844) 11 Cl. & F. 155; 8 E.R. 1061; (1843–6) 1 Cox C.C. 379; (1844) 8 Ir. L.R. 261; and *R v. O'Connell:* J. Flanedy (ed.), *A special report of the proceedings in the case of the queen against Daniel O'Connell, esq., M.P.* (Dublin, 1844). See also I. Holloway, '*O'Connell v. The queen*: a sesquicentennial remembrance', *N.I.L.Q.*, 46 (1995), 63–71. The following year, further

Frequent calls for reform were made, including recommendations made by another parliamentary committee in 1852.[67] Several bills were introduced in attempts to address the problems facing juries,[68] but none were successful. McEldowney is of the view that the reason for so many abortive bills between 1852 and 1871 was 'because no parliamentary time was found for debate'.[69] He considers it difficult to give reasons for the failures, but notes that 'the bills were introduced with little or no parliamentary support to ensure their passage into law, and the government seemed apathetic about the whole question of jury reform'.[70] So it was indifference, rather than strong opposition, which prevented these bills from becoming law. However, the question of jury reform was very much alive in Irish circles, and members of the Dublin Statistical Society delivered several papers on the issue during this period.[71] McEldowney also notes that three papers on jury reform were read at the National Association for the Promotion of Social Science conference in Belfast in 1867.[72] In 1869 the case of *R v. McKenna* brought the issue of jury packing in Ireland to the fore, and McEldowney considers this case to have been the catalyst for change.[73]

A major overhaul of the Irish jury system was eventually passed by Lord Thomas O'Hagan in 1871. He had been appointed the first Catholic lord chancellor of Ireland since the reign of James II, following the passing of the Office and Oaths Act, 1867.[74] By the time of his appointment in 1868, O'Hagan had been an active law reformer for decades, primarily through his membership of the Dublin Statistical Society.[75] He was also particularly interested in jury reform from an early date, and had been personally involved in the abovementioned trial of Daniel O'Connell, infamous for its packed jury. His Benthamite utilitarian view of the law was that, in the words of McEldowney, 'law reform should be used to bring people into greater harmony with the law and that the law should remedy existing

amending legislation was passed: Regulation of Jurors' books (Ireland) Act, 1845 (8 & 9 Vic., c. 67). See pp 22–4.

67 *Report on outrages (Ireland)*, HC 1852 (438) xiv, 1.

68 *Juries bill (Ireland)*, HC 1854 (114) iii, 295; *Juries bill (Ireland)*, HC 1854–5 (2) iii, 407; *Juries bill (Ireland) No. 2*, HC 1854–5 (6) iii, 435; *Juries bill (Ireland)*, HC 1856 (19) iv, 451; *Juries bill (Ireland)*, HC 1857–8 (44) ii, 621; *Juries bill (Ireland) No. 2*, HC 1857–8 (131) ii, 643; *Juries bill (Ireland)*, HC 1859 (25) i, 807; *Petit juries bill (Ireland)*, HC 1866 (41) iv, 43; *Petit juries bill (Ireland)*, HC 1867 (46) iv, 571; and *Petit juries bill (Ireland)*, HC 1867–8 (70) iv, 21.

69 McEldowney, 'Lord O'Hagan', p. 95.

70 Ibid.

71 E.g. Arthur Houston, 'Observations on trial by jury, with suggestions for the amendment of our present system', *J. Dub. Stat. Soc.*, 3 (1861), 100–9; and Constantine Molloy, 'Observations on the law relating to the qualification and selection of jurors, with suggestions for its amendment', *J.S.S.I.S.I.*, 4:39 (1865), 186–93.

72 McEldowney, 'Lord O'Hagan', p. 95.

73 Ibid., p. 104. See also John McEldowney, 'The case of *The queen v. McKenna* and jury packing in Ireland', *Ir. Jur.* (n.s.), 12 (1977), 339–54. See further chapter 10.

74 30 & 31 Vic., c. 75. The English equivalent was the Lord Chancellor (Tenure of Office and Discharge of Ecclesiastical Functions) Act, 1974.

75 McEldowney, 'Lord O'Hagan', p. 1.

distress'.[76] O'Hagan was also critical of Catholic disabilities and the exclusion of Catholics from the administration of public affairs.

O'Hagan's Juries (Ireland) Act, 1871[77] wrought radical change to the ways in which jury trials operated. It had three aims: to broaden jury participation by introducing a rateable valuation qualification; to introduce summoning by alphabetical rotation; and to abolish the sheriff's discretion when it came to summoning jurors.[78] The act introduced a new basis for jury qualification, which had the effect of including large numbers of Catholics and small farmers for the first time. As will be seen, the act had unintended consequences, and was criticised from the moment it came into effect in 1873. A select committee was appointed in that year to examine the act's operation,[79] and there followed a series of amending statutes in the 1870s.[80] Problems persisted into the 1880s, when difficulties were encountered in securing convictions in agrarian or political cases.[81] Controversy dogged the criminal jury system throughout the 1880s, which saw attempts to limit trial by jury in cases related to the Land War agitation. Such attempts met strong resistance from judges and lawyers, as well as the general population.

Despite such controversies, as will be seen, juries in Ireland long enjoyed a degree of popular support, and the notion of lay decision-making was firmly embedded in the public consciousness. Discourse around juries and jury service was common, whether the focus was the non-representation of Catholics, the poor state of jury lists, or the discomforts associated with jury service. Such was the public awareness of some of these issues, in fact, that in 1875 the Dublin Jurors Association was established.[82] Comprising 'the most prominent and energetic members of [Dublin's] mercantile community',[83] it saw its role as looking out for the interests of Dublin jurors. Among their concerns was the frequency with which they were summoned, the physical discomfort involved in jury service, and the impact of being away from their businesses. They became actively involved in the revision of jury lists, claiming exemptions for their members where appropriate, and agitated for jury reform. Representatives from the DJA began to appear in court on behalf of members, both at the revision sessions and when individuals had been summoned.[84] At first, their position in making such representations was

76 Ibid.

77 Juries (Ireland) Act, 1871 (34 & 35 Vic., c. 65).

78 McEldowney, 'Lord O'Hagan', p. i.

79 *First, second, and special reports from the select committee on juries (Ireland)*, HC 1873 (283) xv, 389. See also *Report from the select committee on the working of the Irish jury system, together with the proceedings of the committee, minutes of evidence, and appendix*, HC 1874 (244) ix, 557.

80 Juries (Ireland) (Amendment) Act, 1873 (36 & 37 Vic., c. 27); Juries Qualification (Ireland) Act, 1876 (39 & 40 Vic., c. 21) and Juries (Procedure) Ireland Act, 1876 (39 & 40 Vic., c. 78).

81 *Report from the select committee of the house of lords on Irish jury laws*, HC 1881 (430) xi, 1. See also A.V. Dicey, 'How is the law to be enforced in Ireland?', *Fortnightly Rev.* (n.s.), 179 (1881), 537–52.

82 *Freeman's Journal*, 30 Jan. 1875.

83 Ibid., 25 June 1875.

84 The Dublin recorder in 1877 described the association as 'a most useful body', but questioned

doubtful, but the body was soon recognised by the courts as having standing. It met regularly, advertised in the *Freeman's Journal* and other newspapers, and continued to function into the twentieth century.[85] A Waterford Jurors Association was also later established, and appears to have essentially been an imitation of the Dublin operation, though perhaps not as visible and organised.[86]

THIS BOOK'S CONTRIBUTION

Why write a book about lay decision-making in the long nineteenth century? The jury was a fundamental element of the administration of justice in Ireland until its decline in the twentieth century. The late eighteenth and early nineteenth centuries in particular were the heyday of Irish juries, at a time when other European countries were similarly adopting versions of lay participation in their justice systems. Within the common-law world, trial by jury has arguably been one of England's greatest exports, with the jury in the United States still firmly embedded in both the civil and criminal justice systems. Even as twenty-first-century jury systems in England, Ireland and other common-law countries are in decline, emerging democracies in Asia and Eastern Europe seek to introduce elements of lay participation, and are looking to the common-law world for inspiration.

The changing role of the trial jury in civil cases was an important development in the nineteenth century, and is intertwined with the significant doctrinal changes in areas such as tort and contract. Swain, for example, has examined the role of civil juries in shaping contract law doctrine,[87] while Lobban considers their role in the development of tortious principles in the nineteenth century.[88] The gradual erosion of the jury's power over the eighteenth and nineteenth centuries is evident, and has been written about elsewhere.[89] However, as Polden warns, '[t]he nineteenth-century civil jury was an institution in decline, but neither the extent of the decline nor its rapidity should be overstated'.[90] The decline was more evident in some areas than in others. Swaine points out that while '[b]efore the

whether its representatives could hand in letters of excuse from men who had been summoned as jurors: *Irish Times*, 3 Oct. 1877.

85 The association was reportedly attending revision sessions as late as 1917: *Irish Times*, 3 Oct. 1917.

86 The hon. sec. of the DJA, Thomas Edmondson, did not consider the Waterford Jurors Association to be 'any formal association': *Report on Irish jury laws*, HC 1881 (430) xi, 1, para. 491.

87 Warren Swaine, *The law of contract, 1670–1870* (Cambridge, 2015).

88 Michael Lobban, 'Tort' in John Baker, *The Oxford history of the laws of England* (Oxford, 2004–10), p. xii.

89 See e.g. Michael Lobban, 'The strange life of the English civil jury, 1837–1914' in J.W. Cairns and G. McLeod (eds), *'The dearest birth right of the people of England': the jury in the history of the common law* (Oxford, 2002); and Conor Hanly, 'The decline of civil jury trial in nineteenth-century England', *J. Leg. Hist.*, 26:3 (2005), 253–78.

90 Patrick Polden, 'The superior courts of common law' in Baker (ed.), *History of the laws of England*, xi, p. 595.

eighteenth century, the assessment of damages had, on the face of it, been rather an unprincipled exercise',[91] jury discretion as to the award of damages was eroded by the mid-nineteenth century.[92] By contrast, Lobban notes that 'in tort law, juries continued to have a good deal of discretion in awarding damages'.[93] Civil juries continued to play an important part in the settling of disputes in the Irish courts during the period in question.

Rather than concentrating on either the criminal or civil trial jury, this book considers a wide range of lay decision-making bodies, including the trial jury, the coroner's jury, the grand jury, the special jury, the manor court jury, and some lesser-known types of jury such as the market jury, the lunacy jury, the jury of matrons, the mixed jury, the wide-streets jury and the valuation jury. The reasons for this are to demonstrate the role of the lay decision-maker in the administration of justice at a time when most power lay in the hands of the élite, and to explore how lay decision-making operated in practice. Who were the men (or women) qualified to serve on these various tribunals? How did these qualifications change over time? This book is concerned not only with the extent and reach of lay juries, but also with their operation. How were their members chosen, managed and treated? It outlines the procedures involved in empanelling Irish juries – how were lists of qualified and suitable persons drawn up, and how could these people be compelled to come to court when summoned? It considers their experiences of the justice system, and the extent to which they were compensated for their time and effort. The book also looks at some of the problems facing the jury system, including the intimidation of jurors; bribery and corruption; jurors delivering verdicts against the weight of evidence and jurors refusing to carry out their duties. How did trial juries of the nineteenth century differ from those of the twenty-first? What powers did they have beyond the delivery of a binary verdict?

Another question this book addresses is, how did the various types of juror behave or misbehave, and how did they interact with one another and with other court actors? The public perception of juries was (and remains) important, and the book considers some of the controversies associated with the Irish jury system during the period. It considers what, if anything, the impact of these lay juries was. Did they really bring an element of community sanction to decisions, or did they in many cases merely prop up established interests? Was there anything truly democratic about these so-called juries? Were they revolutionary or merely reactive? What was the value placed on 'lay' knowledge? It will be seen, for example, that the value of lay knowledge in relation to certain medical issues declined during this period. This can be considered in the broader context of debates around knowledge, power, agency and representation.

The right (or obligation) to sit on a jury is sometimes considered alongside the right to vote. Indeed, the drafters of the Juries (Ireland) Act, 1871 gave

91 Swaine, *The law of contract*, p. 101.
92 Ibid., p. 274.
93 Lobban, 'Tort', p. 900.

consideration to the question of whether parliamentary voter lists could be used to populate jurors' books and lists. If the electoral list became the basis for jury qualification then arguably the mechanics of summoning a jury would be greatly simplified. Such a proposal was ultimately rejected by the drafters, who reasoned that 'the list of voters did not provide information on the age, title, business or occupation of voters and this was required for jury qualification'.[94] Furthermore, as McEldowney points out, voters qualified on the basis of occupation, or possession or ownership of a freehold or leasehold interest, and not on the basis of residence, which was important for jury qualification. There were also practical and logistical problems to do with the timing of the drawing up of the electoral lists.[95] Finally, the drafters also pointed out that 'while voting was a privilege, from which persons could disqualify themselves by non-payment of rates, jury service was an obligation, from which escape ought not to be easy.'[96] This points to a fundamental difference between voting and jury service: the former was a privilege, while the latter was a duty – although in the nineteenth century it was frequently considered a right by those who were excluded from it.

Chapter 2 considers some of the practicalities around compiling lists of suitable and qualified jurors. Its main focus is civil and criminal trial juries, but consideration is also given to the formation of lists and panels for other categories of jury. It will be seen that there was a good deal of incompetence, laziness and corruption associated with drawing up of lists of jurors. Controversy, unsurprisingly, was never far away.

The five subsequent chapters consider the composition and operation of various categories of jury. Common juries, which tried civil and criminal cases, are considered in chapter 3, along with grand juries, which had powers of both indictment and presentment. Chapter 4 is dedicated to the special jury, which was at times a source of considerable controversy in nineteenth-century Ireland as its composition could be more easily controlled. Juries with valuation powers are considered in chapter 5, with a particular focus on wide-streets juries. Chapter 6 considers three types of jury – the coroner's jury, the jury of matrons and the jury *de lunatico inquirendo* – all of which may be loosely termed 'medico-legal'. Chapter 7 then considers other categories, including the market jury, which had powers of inspection and seizure, and juries in local manor courts.

The remaining chapters are broader in outlook, and deal with various themes and issues arising out of the operation of juries in Ireland. The nature of jurors' oaths is considered in chapter 9. Ireland's tumultuous nineteenth century is the background to chapter 10, which looks at frequent allegations of jury packing and the use of jury challenges and stand-aside procedures, mainly in criminal trials. Related to these issues was the problem of juror intimidation, considered in

94 McEldowney, 'Lord O'Hagan', p. 151, quoting from the *Draft preliminary and explanatory report*, 2 Mar. 1871, PRONI, O'Hagan Papers, D27777/7/n/1/50, p. 10.
95 McEldowney, 'Lord O'Hagan', p. 151.
96 Ibid., p. 152.

chapter 11. Various means were adopted to counteract the intimidation of jurors, not only in criminal trials but also in other contexts. These included changing the venues of both civil and criminal trials, for example. Chapter 12 explores the extent to which Irish jurors were active participants in legal proceedings, rather than passive observers. Chapter 13 attempts to penetrate jury deliberations, decision-making and verdicts, both in the jury room and beyond.

Although the main focus of this book is the nineteenth century, it has been necessary to consider the evolution of Irish juries during the eighteenth century and into the twentieth century, in order to provide clarity and context for the various rules and practices. Thus the time span for this book could be said to be the 'long nineteenth century'. In piecing together a history of various types of jury, use has been made of a wide variety of sources. Considerable use has been made of case law – reports found in bound and published collections, cases reported in newspapers, and pamphlets that deal with individual cases in depth. Close study of relatively uncontroversial cases, routinely reported without significant comment, helps to clarify what was routine and typical. However, the terse nature of such reports does little to assist the legal historian seeking nuance and wishing to consider legal rules and practice in context. By contrast, high-profile cases were commented on in parliament, in the press and in pamphlets. They were atypical, but generated analysis and commentary that run-of-the-mill cases could not hope to attract. Focusing solely on such cases would not paint a representative picture of the Irish justice system, but this book's combined analysis of high-profile and mundane cases facilitates consideration of the everyday workings of the justice system in the context of contemporary comment and opinion. The book also utilises legislation (both bills and acts), parliamentary papers, official records, newspapers, pamphlets, letters, treatises on Irish law and practice and contemporary legal commentary. Finally, reliance is of course placed on the works of others who have made forays into the various topics covered by this book.

I hope this book will make a modest contribution to the growing body of literature on world jury systems, especially as many of the issues experienced in Ireland were later replicated (albeit in different guises) elsewhere in both the common-law and the civil-law worlds. Indeed, many of the core principles and problems with lay participation are common to all justice systems – issues such as representativeness, legitimacy, logistics, expense, defining the limits of the jury's power and its relationship with the professional judiciary. I also hope to move beyond consideration of criminal juries and to broaden understandings of 'juries', provoking scholars elsewhere to consider lay participation in the administration of justice more widely. Finally, I hope this book will add another layer to our ever-increasing understanding of Ireland's complex legal history, for which a huge debt is owed to the Irish Legal History Society and its work over the past three decades.

CHAPTER TWO

Jury lists, books and panels

FOR WHATEVER PURPOSE A JURY was to be empanelled, officials needed to have an authoritative and up-to-date list of all those in the district who were qualified to sit on the relevant type of jury. This chapter considers the procedures involved in preparing the lists, books and panels of civil and criminal trial jurors.[1] First, there was a considerable amount of preparatory work to be done to compile and revise baronial jury lists and county jurors' books. The sheriff then selected names from the jurors' books and returned these as the panels for particular cases or entire assizes or sessions. Once the panels were drawn up, jurors were summoned – either in person or by post – and when they appeared they were excused, challenged or sworn in. The differences between England and Ireland in the administration of justice manifested themselves in many ways; for example, different personnel were involved in the drawing-up of jurors' lists and books, and in Ireland considerable autonomy lay in the hands of such officials as high and under-sheriffs, baronial constables, cess collectors, clerks of the crown and peace, and poor-law guardians. There were also different rituals and practices around the swearing-in of jurors.

JURY BOOKS AND JURY LISTS

A 1725 act set out a system for the preparation of jury lists and books.[2] It required that the sheriff in each county 'diligently enquire by the oath of twelve or more honest men', and make a list of all freeholders worth more than 40*s*. in each barony. These were supposed to be returned to the justices at quarter sessions, and then delivered by the clerk of the peace to each of the four superior courts in Dublin. However, it was observed that although '[t]his Law continue[d] unrepealed upon the Statute book', it appeared never to have been complied with.[3] Further legislation in the early eighteenth century prescribed how the books and lists were to be compiled.[4] Under a

1 With regard to non-trial juries, the specific procedures are outlined in the chapters dealing with each category.

2 Regulating Sheriffs Act, 1725 (12 Geo. I, c. 4), s. 6.

3 The judges of the superior courts noted in a letter from 1825 that 'after enquiries in our respective Courts we have not yet been able to discover any trace or tradition of its having been acted upon', *Letter regarding the jury bill 1833* (NAI, OP/1833/14).

4 Regulation of Juries Act, 1735 (9 Geo. II, c. 3), s. 2; Regulation of Juries (Amendment) Act, 1739 (13 Geo. II, c. 5); Regulation of Juries (Amendment) Act, 1745 (19 Geo. II, c. 10).

1735 act, twenty days before Michaelmas each year, the high constables of baronies were to affix lists of qualified jurors for two or more Sundays 'upon the door of every church, in which divine service shall be celebrated within their respective precincts'. They were also required to leave copies of the list with the officiating ministers of each parish, who then had to read them out at the end of divine service on one of the Sundays. The high constables then had to return to the local justices the list of persons qualified as jurors. A duplicate was given to the sheriff or under-sheriff by mid-February, and then the clerk of the peace entered the lists into a book in alphabetical order. This was known as the county jurors' book. Sheriffs, clerks or constables could be fined between 40*s*. and £10 for failing to carry out their duties. The 1730s legislation was amended in 1747[5] because 'the high constables of baronies ... frequently neglected to return the names of persons qualified to serve on juries'. This was partly due to the fact that in several counties there was no Michaelmas session of the peace. There were therefore no panels of freeholders to be given to the clerks of the peace. The 1747 act provided that if there was no grand panel of freeholders, then a justice of one of the superior courts could cause the panel to be drawn up from the list of freeholders. Procedures remained largely unchanged for the remainder of the eighteenth century, although an act of 1755 noted that there were 'many evil practices' in the compilation of jury lists.[6]

By the nineteenth century, there was still an expectation that the jurors' book would be updated annually, but indifference, laziness, bias and incompetence conspired to make it difficult to compose and maintain accurate lists of qualified jurors. In fact, it was observed in 1826 that there had been no jurors' book drawn up in Ireland since the eighteenth century.[7] The county jurors' book was a composite of jury lists compiled for each barony within the county, and the names in it were arranged either in order of status or in alphabetical order. As part of Robert Peel's general push for reform, the English jury system had been radically overhauled by the Juries Act, 1825.[8] This provided that jury lists were to be drawn

5 Regulation of Juries (Amendment) Act, 1747 (21 Geo. II, c. 6).

6 Regulation of Juries Act, 1755 (29 Geo. II, c. 6).

7 *Fifteenth report on salaries*, HC 1826 (310) xvii, 29, p. 20. It was noted in the Juries Regulation (Amendment) Act, 1747 (21 Geo. II, c. 6) that 'high constables of baronies have frequently neglected to return the names of persons qualified to serve on juries; and it hath also happened, that no sessions of the peace hath been held in Michaelmas in several counties; and by means of such neglect no pannel of the freeholders, and other persons qualified to serve on juries, could be given by the clerks of the peace of such counties to the respective sheriffs of the same'.

8 6 Geo. IV, s. 50. Although often referred to in the nineteenth century as the 'County Juries Act', it dealt with more than simply county juries. The Short Titles Act, 1896 (59 & 60 Vic., c. 4) referred to it as the 'Juries Act 1825', as will the remainder of this book, with the prefix 'English' to avoid confusion where necessary: *Report on juries* [C-6817] 1913, xxx, 403. For analysis of the general debates over the use and role of juries during the 1820s and '30s, see Conor Hanly, 'The decline of civil jury trial in nineteenth-century England', *J. Leg. Hist.*, 26:3 (2005), 253–78; and Michael Lobban, 'The strange life of the English civil jury, 1837–1914' in J.W. Cairns and Grant McLeod (eds), *'The dearest birth right of the people of England': the jury in the history of the common law* (Oxford, 2002).

up by churchwardens and overseers of the poor, but it was impossible to replicate these reforms in Ireland because the latter did not exist in that part of the United Kingdom and the former comprised only members of the established church.[9] Several bills were introduced in attempts to reform Irish jury laws.[10] One such bill[11] was sent to the Irish judges for their consideration.[12] Finally the Juries (Ireland) Act, 1833 was passed.[13]

This act prescribed how jurors' books and lists were to be created, maintained and revised for civil and criminal trials, and was by and large a restatement of the various eighteenth-century acts. Every summer, the clerk of the peace in each county was to issue and deliver a precept[14] to the baronial constable or cess collectors, requiring them, within one month, to prepare a list of all qualified men within their districts.[15] The list was to be in alphabetical order, detailing each juror's name, address, title, business, quality or calling.[16] The drawing up of the list fell to the high constables and cess collectors because, as noted, Ireland did not have overseers of the poor. The cess collectors and high constables were appointed annually at assizes by the grand jury on the payment of a security,[17] and generally served for a number of years. They were paid by presentment from the grand jury and were responsible for collecting the county cess, which was a rate levied by the grand jury on occupiers, rather than the owners, of land.[18] The office was generally bestowed as a matter of 'patronage by influential gentlemen in the county'.[19]

When the 1830s legislation was being reconsidered, some thought was given to whether the cess collectors and high constables ought to continue to carry out this function. Neither were held in particularly high regard. For example, the baronial constables were described as 'irresponsible',[20] with 'very humble qualifications'[21] and 'very likely to leave out [their] friends, and put on others'.[22] In some counties they were replaced every year.[23] Cess collectors were rumoured to accept bribes from persons who did not wish their names to be returned on the lists.[24]

9 See *Hansard 2*, xiv, 433 (16 Feb. 1826) (William Plunket, attorney general for Ireland).

10 *Juries bill (Ireland)*, HC 1826–27 (451) i, 623; *Juries bill (Ireland)*, HC 1828 (98) iii, 363; *Juries bill (Ireland)*, HC 1828 (202) iii, 393; see *Hansard 3*, xi, 1248 (3 Apr. 1832); *Juries bill (Ireland)*, HC 1830 (108) i, 455; *Juries bill (Ireland)*, HC 1831 (132) ii, 385.

11 *Juries bill (Ireland)*, HC 1831–2 (13) ii, 365.

12 See *Letter regarding the jury bill 1833* (NAI, OP/1833/14), and *Hansard 3*, xviii, 1231–4 (25 June 1833).

13 3 & 4 Will. IV, c. 91. See *Hansard 3*, xi, 1248–53 (3 Apr. 1832).

14 Sch. A. 15 S. 4. 16 S. 7.

17 Grand Juries (Ireland) Act, 1836 (6 & 7 Will. IV, c. 116). Amended by the Grand Jury Cess (Amendment) (Ireland) Act, 1848 (11 & 12 Vic., c. 26) and the County Cess (Ireland) Act, 1848 (11 & 12 Vic., c. 32).

18 Virginia Crossman, *Local government in nineteenth-century Ireland* (Belfast, 1994), p. 28.

19 *Report on outrages (Ireland)*, HC 1852 (438) xiv, 1, para. 2546 (James Major, chairman of Monaghan quarter sessions).

20 Ibid., para. 806 (Edward Golding, a Monaghan magistrate).

21 Ibid., para. 2260 (Major). 22 Ibid., para. 806 (Golding).

23 For example in Monaghan; ibid., para. 806.

24 Ibid., para. 2264 (Major). This was nothing new however; throughout the eighteenth century

McEldowney observes that, 'In Ireland cess collectors were unreliable officials who often summoned whoever they wanted with no reference to the official register of jurors.'[25] Perrin J. was said to have ordered the salary of one cess collector to be stopped when he was informed that names of qualified men were being left off the lists.[26] One commentator expressed a desire to 'sweep them away altogether, as regards the selection of jurors'.[27] The Irish judges in an 1833 letter to E.G. Stanley, chief secretary for Ireland, had commented that neither the constables nor the collectors were 'persons of an order to render them … capable or likely to discharge the duty effectually or impartially'.[28]

Despite the criticisms, these officers continued to be entrusted with the drawing up of jury lists. They were often denigrated for failing to carry out their duties under the 1833 act; for example, one year there was no jurors' book in Tipperary,[29] because the cess collector had failed to make the proper returns, and the magistrates had done nothing to force him to do so.[30] It was also said that sometimes cess collectors employed men under them to collect the cess, thus adding to the confusion surrounding the lists.[31] However, not all complaints about them were entirely justified, as it was often impossible for them to acquire the necessary information for the preparation of the jurors' lists. A witness before the 1852 committee on outrages explained that the cess collector:

> makes his return to the clerk of the peace of the persons who he supposes to be qualified; but in truth it is merely conjecture; he has no means of ascertaining it, and I do not believe he takes the trouble of ascertaining it; he returns a great number of names, and I should say that probably not one-third of the persons he returns come within the description of the qualifications of the [1833 Act].[32]

'How is it possible', the same witness asked, 'for one of those persons to know whether an estate is held in fee simple, or in tail, or for life, or the amount of it?'[33]

legislators had grappled with the problem of how to punish officials for accepting bribes from would-be jurors. E.g. Regulation of Juries Act, 1735 (9 Geo. II, c. 3), s. 3; and Regulation of Juries Act, 1755 (29 Geo. II, c. 6), s. 2.

25 John McEldowney, 'Lord O'Hagan and the Irish Jury Act 1871' (PhD, Cambridge University, 1981), p. 99.

26 *Report on outrages 1852*, para. 4206 (Burton Brabazon, sub-sheriff of Co. Louth).

27 Ibid., para. 2496 (Major).

28 *Letter regarding the Jury Bill 1833*. Maxwell Hamilton, crown solicitor on the north-east circuit, told the 1852 committee that the cess collectors were not to be trusted: *Report on outrages 1852*, para. 1535.

29 *Report on the state of Ireland*, HC 1839 (486) xi, xii 1, para. 6906 (William Kemmis, crown solicitor).

30 Ibid., paras 6910–2.

31 *Report on outrages 1852*, para. 4327 (Brabazon).

32 Ibid., paras 2258–9 (Major).

33 *Report on the state of Ireland*, 1839, para. 2263. The same point was made in relation to barony constables: para. 15,002 (Robert Smith, Monaghan clerk of the peace).

The completed lists were delivered to the clerk of the peace, who kept them in his office for three weeks so that anyone who wished could examine them.[34] By the nineteenth century there was no provision for displaying the lists on church doors[35] as there had been in the eighteenth century, and as continued to be the case in England.[36]

From time to time disputes arose as to who bore the responsibility for preparing jury lists. For example, in 1867 the Belfast clerk of the peace, one William Cunningham, complained to the law officers in Dublin that no jurors' list had been made for the barony of upper Belfast. The duty of making the lists in this borough had devolved from the high constable to the cess collectors; however, under a local act of 1865, the county cess had been replaced by a general-purposes rate, payable to the Belfast Town Council.[37] The law officers were unequivocal; the collectors of this rate were obliged to make the lists: section 4 of the Juries (Ireland) Act, 1833 stated clearly that 'the clerk of the peace in every county shall issue his precept to the high constables and collectors of grand jury cess in each barony, or other district of collection, and to the collectors of other cess or assessment, where no grand jury cess is levied, requiring the collectors to prepare lists, etc.'. Cunningham replied that '[a]ll jurors for Belfast were left off the list for this year', and that while he had issued precepts to the high constable and the rate collectors, he feared they would not be complied with, and that 'the same inconvenience [would] be experienced next year'. The law officers, however, warned that the collectors of the general purposes rate would be proceeded against under section 35 of the 1833 act, and that '[t]hey should however receive full notice in due time that this course will be taken in order to leave them no excuse'.[38] The same month, at the Antrim assizes, O'Hagan J. referred to 'the very unsatisfactory state of the jury panel, and the great inconvenience which had resulted from the exclusion of Belfast jurors during the present assizes'.[39] 'He hoped some steps would be at once taken to remedy this inconvenience, and that the town council would apply for a bill to have the grievance redressed.'[40]

The Juries (Ireland) Act, 1833 remained the principal piece of jury legislation until the 1870s. By this time, Ireland had a functioning poor law,[41] and Lord O'Hagan's Juries (Ireland) Act, 1871[42] took the task of preparing the jurors' list

34 Juries (Ireland) Act, 1833 (3 & 4 Will. IV, c. 91), s. 8.

35 But see Regulation of Juries Act, 1735 (9 Geo. II, c. 3), s. 2. Major told the 1852 committee that they may have been publicized in police stations: *Report on outrages 1852*, para. 2553.

36 English Juries Act, 1825 (6 Geo. IV, s. 50, s. 9). This practice appears to have continued into the twentieth century: see *Report on juries* [C-6817] 1913, xxx, 403, para. 88.

37 The County of Antrim and Belfast Borough Act, 1865 (28 & 29 Vic., c. clxxxiii).

38 *In re jurors' list for Belfast* (NAI, CCS/1867/242).

39 *Belfast Newsletter*, 13 Aug. 1867.

40 Ibid. However, he was urged to make no such recommendation to the town council, 'lest they should go to parliament next session for their thirteenth bill, in order to oppress the poor citizens of Belfast'. The newspaper report states: 'the subject then dropped'.

41 Poor Law (Ireland) Act, 1838 (1 & 2 Vic., c. 56). See further chapter 3.

42 34 & 35 Vic., c. 65.

from the cess collectors and entrusted it to the clerk of each poor-law union,[43] except in Dublin, where it was issued to the collector general of rates.[44] Unions were geographically small, composed of electoral divisions made up of townlands; thus the personnel of each union were likely to have detailed knowledge of the local inhabitants.[45] Over the nineteenth century, the powers and responsibilities of the poor-law boards had expanded dramatically until they became 'an increasingly important branch of local government'.[46] The clerk of the union made 'due inquiry' with the assistance of the poor-rate collector or collectors, in order to accurately draw up the lists.[47] The completed lists were then sent to the clerk of the peace,[48] as before, who kept them in his office for three weeks so that anyone who wished could examine them.

Under both the 1833 and 1871 legislation, at the October quarter sessions the justices fixed a date for the holding of special sessions[49] for the purposes of revising the lists. Those responsible for drawing up the lists were expected to attend, as well as the justices, to ensure that unqualified men were expunged from the list, and those who had been incorrectly left off were included. Patchy and inaccurate local information, coupled with lazy or corrupt officials often meant that jury lists were imprecise. The drafters of the 1871 Juries Act estimated that approximately 6 per cent of jurors summoned were not legally qualified.[50] Under the 1833 act, revision sessions were often inefficient and ineffective.[51] No name could be struck off the list without notice having been served in advance,[52] but the legislation was silent as to who was obliged to serve such notice. Thus, as seen below, attempts to reform the lists were at times frustrated. Furthermore, sometimes the sessions simply were not held, so amending legislation was passed in 1839 to allow the lord lieutenant to appoint special sessions for the purpose of revising the lists.[53]

Revision sessions were publicised in the local and national press, and by means of flyers and bills posted around the county. These sessions were not without controversy and were frequently the focus of attention amid allegations of bias and non-representativeness.[54] For example, when nationalist leader Daniel O'Connell

43 S. 8. 44 S. 10. Crossman, *Local government*, p. 46.
45 Poor Law (Ireland) Act, 1838 (1 & 2 Vic., c. 56).
46 Crossman, *Local government*, pp 49–52. 47 34 & 35 Vic., c. 65, s. 9.
48 On the roles and responsibilities of clerks of the peace and clerks of the crown, see generally Leonard MacNally, *The justice of the peace for Ireland: containing the authorities and duties of that officer, as also of the various conservators of the peace*, 2 vols (Dublin, 1808). The offices of clerk of the crown and clerk of the peace were amalgamated by the County Officers and Courts (Ireland) Act, 1877 (40 & 41 Vic., c. 56), s. 8.
49 Juries (Ireland) Act, 1833 (3 & 4 Will. IV, c. 91), s. 9; and Juries Act (Ireland), 1871 (34 & 35 Vic., c. 65), s. 12.
50 McEldowney, 'Lord O'Hagan', p. 152. 51 Ibid., p.153.
52 S. 9; see *Report on outrages 1852*, paras 2348–9 (Major) and para. 804 (Golding).
53 Juries (Ireland) Amendment Act, 1839 (2 & 3 Vic., c. 48).
54 See *Revision of jurors' lists – Wicklow 1862* (NAI, CCS/1862/223). A dispute arose in Wicklow as to the responsibility for preparing and amending jury lists and serving the requisite notices.

and a number of others were arrested and charged with conspiracy in 1843, they sought to have the trial commence on 1 February 1844 – after the revision of the special jury lists.[55] As the lists currently stood, there was an overwhelming majority of Protestants, which, according to O'Connell and his co-accused, made it unlikely that they would receive a fair trial. On the 1843 Dublin special jury lists, there were 388 names, at least 70 of whom ought to have been disqualified for one reason or another.[56] Of the 388, only 53 were Roman Catholic, and 30 of these were exempted because they were town councillors or magistrates, leaving only 23. Pierce Mahony, one of the traversers' attorneys, was of the view that there were at least 300 Roman Catholics in the city of Dublin who qualified as special jurors. Mahony applied unsuccessfully to George Pounder, the Dublin sub-sheriff, for a copy of the jurors' book and the list of special jurors for 1843. Further investigations at the office of the clerk of the peace appeared to show that the jury lists for the year were deficient; some 408 persons were not listed who ought to have been.[57] The recorder sat for several days in November to revise the lists, and 'the proceedings … excited for several days more attention than even the proceedings in the queen's bench'.[58] Among those in attendance were counsel and agents on behalf of O'Connell and the others. On one of the lists, 15 names had been omitted, 13 of whom were Roman Catholics. The list was found in an inner office of the clerk of the peace, under a desk.

After many discussions, objections and applications, the revised lists were completed in late November. After signing them, the recorder ought to have formed one general list from the twenty parish lists, but in this instance there was considerable delay. He merely delivered the twenty lists to George Magrath, deputy clerk of the peace, to be collated, and left the country before this was done. It was not until around 28 or 29 December that the completed general list was sent to the sheriff, and there were numerous omissions, with at least twenty-four qualified special jurors left off.[59] Although 2 January 1844 was set as the day for striking the special jury, it was not until 4 January that counsel for the traversers received the panel,[60] and the trial began on 16 January. The array was challenged on the ground that the jury book had not been compiled in accordance with the legislation,[61] but the challenges were disallowed for being insufficient in law, and the jury sworn in convicted the traversers.[62] O'Connell sought to have this verdict set aside and a *venire de novo* granted, on the ground that the jury lists, and thus the jurors' book, 'were fraudulently dealt with for the purpose of prejudicing [him] in his defence'.[63] Perrin J. in the court of queen's bench was of the view that the challenge to the array ought to have been allowed, but that these were insufficient

55 *R v. O'Connell and others* (1844) 11 Cl. & F. 155; 8 E.R. 1061 (1843–6) 1 Cox C.C. 379.
56 J. Flanedy (ed.), *A special report of the proceedings in the case of the queen against Daniel O'Connell, esq., M.P.* (Dublin, 1844), p. 71.
57 Ibid. 58 Ibid., p. 92. See *Freeman's Journal,* 24 Nov. 1843.
59 *R v. O'Connell* (1844) 8 Ir. L.R. 261, 273. 60 Flanedy, *Special report*, p. 95.
61 See p. 139. 62 *R v. O'Connell* (1844) 8 Ir. L.R. 261, p. 267. 63 Ibid., p. 268.

grounds for a motion for a new trial. Crampton J., on the other hand, held that O'Connell et al. had failed to establish either that the 1844 jury list had been fraudulently made up in order to prejudice them, or that they had in fact been prejudiced.[64] He considered it 'remarkable' that although fraud was alleged, there was 'not an individual in existence against whom fraud in this matter is charged, much less proved'. There could be no imputation of fraud on behalf of the recorder – he had left the country – and the crown solicitor was unconnected with the preparation of the list. The clerks of the peace were acquitted; Magrath and his clerks denied the fraud and were not accused. Thus, in the words of Crampton J., 'the matter of fraud is rested upon the general allegation that somebody committed it'. The mistakes in the jurors' list were not, according to him, attributable to the clerk of the peace or the sheriff, but it was clear that a mistake had been made in compiling the recorder's general list. He concluded that it was probably attributable to 'negligence in some of the clerks in the office of the recorder's acting registrar',[65] but that there was 'no fraud whatever in the transaction'. The year after O'Connell's trial, legislation was passed that allowed any improper inclusions or exclusions on both special and common jurors' lists to be corrected by a judge of the queen's bench.[66] It also required, rather than merely authorising, the high constables and cess collectors to have copies of the lists printed.[67]

Because of the much-publicised (and much-criticised) changes to jury composition as a result of the Juries (Ireland) Act, 1871,[68] a special effort was made in revising the lists the year it came into force. In October a circular was sent from Dublin Castle to the clerks of the peace in each county, requesting the revision of jury lists and stating that the inspector general of the Royal Irish Constabulary (RIC) was 'requested to instruct the force under his command to furnish to the sessional crown solicitors any information in their power which the solicitors may deem useful to them for the purposes of the revision'.[69] The RIC would use their considerable local knowledge to assist in determining who was eligible to be a juror.[70]

Persons whose names appeared on the baronial lists could attend the revision sessions and make representations as to why their names ought to be removed.[71] From the mid 1870s, officers of the Dublin Jurors Association[72] attended the Dublin revision sessions to make representations on behalf of members. In 1877, the status of the DJA in making such representations was unclear; Baron Deasy

64 Ibid., p. 288. 65 Ibid., pp 289–90.

66 Regulation of Jurors' books (Ireland) Act, 1845 (8 & 9 Vic., c. 67). 67 S. 5.

68 See pp 46–50. 69 NAI, CCS/1881/682.

70 In some years a high proportion of jurors were struck off the lists at the revision sessions. For example, in 1888, 41,358 names were struck of, representing 38% of the 41,358 names on the general jurors' lists for that year. Fifty-six names were added. As for special juries, 4,021 were struck off, representing around a quarter of the 15,981. *Criminal and judicial statistics, Ireland, 1888. Report on the criminal and judicial statistics of Ireland for the year 1888, with tables* [C-5795] HC 1889 lxxxv, 241, p. 53.

71 Grand jury lists were also revised at these sessions. See *Revision of jurors' lists – Dublin 1863* (NAI, CCS/1863/223) and *Irish Times*, 3 Oct. 1877. 72 See pp 11–13.

commented that while it was a 'most useful body', he was unsure whether its clerk could hand in letters and make excuses on behalf of others.[73] A week later, W.G. Edmonds, the association's assistant secretary, attended the revision of the city jurors' lists and explained that the DJA wanted the lists to be correct and for jurors' interests to be protected. There was no objection to his securing permission to attend and assist with the revision.[74] Having established that their representations would be heard, the association promptly advertised in the *Freeman's Journal* the following day, informing members that the revision court was now sitting, and that those who had been incorrectly summoned the previous year, or claiming an exemption, should contact Edmonds.[75] This was no doubt an excellent way to increase membership of the association. Over the next few days, the DJA made numerous representations on behalf of members at the revision sessions.[76] The following month, it took out another advertisement in the *Journal*, advising all persons whose names appeared on both the city and county jurors' lists for Dublin to contact Edmonds, particularly if they had been unduly fined or incorrectly summoned to join.[77] So zealous did the DJA appear to be when it came to revising the lists, that Chief Justice Morris commented some months later that 'there was some jurors association in existence, but it appeared they paid more attention to removing names from the list than to making practical suggestions'.[78]

After the jurors' lists had been revised, the justices were supposed to have a consolidated list drawn up, with the names arranged in order of rank and property, and delivered to the clerk of the peace.[79] The clerk of the peace then copied the names, in the same order, into a book known as the county jurors' book. The book was delivered to the sheriff or his deputy[80] and was brought into use at the start of January each year.[81] Although procedures were set out in the legislation for preparing separate general and special jurors' books, the practice in some counties seemed to have been to have a single jurors' book with those who were qualified as special jurors marked or highlighted.[82] The term 'book' was also fairly loosely understood by some clerks, as in many cases the book was simply the loose collection of baronial jury lists.

JURY PANELS

Before any assizes or other court sessions where there were civil or criminal issues to be tried by jury, a writ of *venire facias juratores* was issued, directing the sheriff

73 *Freeman's Journal*, 3 Oct. 1877 and *Irish Times*, 3 Oct. 1877.

74 *Freeman's Journal*, 9 Oct. 1877. 75 Ibid., 10 Oct. 1877.

76 *Freeman's Journal*, 11, 12, 16, 18, 19 Oct. 1877 and *Irish Times*, 11 Oct. 1877.

77 *Freeman's Journal*, 14 Nov. 1877. The DJA similarly attended the revision sessions the following year: *Irish Times*, 18 Oct. 1878, and regularly after that.

78 *Freeman's Journal*, 17 Apr. 1878. 79 Juries (Ireland) Act, 1833 (3 & 4 Will. IV, c. 91), s. 9.

80 34 & 35 Vic., c. 65, s. 11. 81 34 & 35 Vic., c. 65, s. 9.

82 E.g. *City of Waterford general jurors' book 1880* (NLI, MS 11,290).

to return 'twelve good and lawful men from the body of his county'.[83] The sheriff returned the writ with a panel containing the names, abodes and appellations or professions of 'a competent number of jurors'.[84] He prepared separate panels for civil and criminal cases. In practice, there were more than twelve names on the panel, in order to ensure that a full jury of twelve could be sworn in. In civil cases, legislation specified that there were usually to be between 36 and 60 jurors listed, unless the assizes or session judge ordered that there be a greater or lesser number.[85] For criminal trials the practice was to summon many in order to accommodate the challenges.[86] The number of names to be returned for other types of jury varied. Some legislation dealing with valuation juries[87] required the sheriff to return 'a sufficient jury', leaving the actual number of jurors to his discretion.[88] Other acts were more prescriptive; for example, the Dublin Wide Streets Act, 1786[89] obliged the sheriff to return between 36 and 60 jurors, and other legislation specified 24 jurors, with 12 sworn to conduct the valuation.[90]

The men returned on the civil or criminal panel were competent to try all the relevant issues at the next assizes or sessions.[91] The sheriff kept copies of the panels in his office for seven days[92] before the court sat, for the parties to inspect if they wished.[93] Witnesses testifying before the 1852 committee on outrages were critical of the practice of having separate civil and criminal panels,[94] with Sir Matthew

83 Regulation of Juries Act, 1735 (9 Geo. II, c. 3), s. 6; Regulation of Juries Act, 1755 (29 Geo. II, c. 6), s. 3; Juries Act (Ireland), 1833 (3 & 4 Will. IV, c. 90), s. 10. See also 34 & 35 Vic., c. 65, s. 13.

84 Juries Act (Ireland), 1833 (3 & 4 Will. IV, c. 90), s. 11. According to Coke, a panel was a 'little piece of parchment': J.H. Thomas, *A systematic arrangement of Lord Coke's first institute of the laws of England*, 3 vols (Philadelphia, 1826–7), iii, p. 508 (3 Co. Inst. 158b).

85 Regulation of Juries Act, 1735 (9 Geo. II, c. 3), s. 6; Regulation of Juries (Amendment) Act, 1747 (21 Geo. II, c. 6), s. 2; Regulation of Juries Act, 1755 (29 Geo. II, c. 6); Juries Act (Ireland), 1833 (3 & 4 Will. IV, c. 90), s. 12.

86 Matthew Dutton, *The office and authority of sheriffs, under-sheriffs, deputies, county-clerks, and coroners in Ireland* (Dublin, 1721), p. 352. There was controversy in 1906 when the Sligo sheriff summoned 200 jurors to try nine cases at the winter assizes. The high sheriff considered this necessary in order to allow for challenges, jurors who did not turn up, etc. *Hansard 4*, cxlvii, 150 (11 Dec. 1906) (HC).

87 See pp 72–4.

88 E.g. Limerick and Cork Roads Act, 1790 (30 Geo. III, c. 47), s. 12; Kilkenny Roads Act, 1793 (33 Geo. III, c. 19), s. 9; Lighthouses Act, 1717 (4 Geo. I, c. 7), s. 1.

89 Dublin Wide Streets Act, 1786 (26 Geo. III, c. 32) provided for distress and sale.

90 E.g. Londonderry Act, 1790 (30 Geo. III, c. 31), s. 26; and Lands Clauses Consolidation Act, 1845 (8 & 9 Vic., c. 18), s. 41.

91 S. 12. Except trials at bar or trials by special 'struck' juries.

92 Jury Panels Act, 1368 (42 Ed. III, c. 11) provided that panels were to be arrayed at least four days in advance. Jury Panels Act, 1427 (6 Hen. VI, c. 2) increased this to eight days.

93 S. 14. Concern had been expressed in parliament at publicizing the panel, which might leave the jurors open to potential pre-trial intimidation and coercion by interested parties: see *Hansard 3*, xi, 1249, 1252 (3 Apr. 1832) (Lords Wynford and Ellenborough).

94 *Report on outrages 1852*, para. 1277 (Henry John Brownrigg, deputy inspector-general of constabulary); paras 1716–8 (Hamilton); para. 2285 (Major); para. 4280 (Brabazon) and para. 4665 (William Kirk, an Armagh magistrate).

Barrington describing the situation as 'quite absurd'.[95] For civil cases the jurors' names were drawn from the list directly below the names of the twenty-three grand jurors, thus ensuring that civil cases were tried by higher-ranking men. As one witness observed, 'not nearly so respectable a class of persons is returned on the crown side as is returned on the civil side'.[96] Jurors for criminal cases were drawn from lower down the list, and were mainly small farmers and small shopkeepers. Sometimes, on the specific request of a judge, a single panel might be returned for an assize,[97] or a criminal case might be tried by the 'better class of jurors' on the civil panel.[98] The 1852 parliamentary committee recommended the merging of the civil and criminal panels.[99] This was the only one of its recommendations to be immediately implemented, by the Common Law Procedure Amendment Act (Ireland), 1853.[100]

Under the 1871 act[101] there was no writ of *venire facias*, but the sheriff's duties in this regard were essentially the same. Before a court requiring a jury was to sit, he had to procure all precepts 'necessary for commanding the return of jurors before the court'. The sheriff had to select from the relevant jurors' book a 'number of names' sufficient to allow twelve jurors to be sworn after jury challenges and absentees were taken into account. A written or printed panel containing the jurors' names, addresses and so on, as well as whether they had previously been summoned as a juror in the past two years, was prepared by the sheriff seven days before the date mentioned in the precept.[102] A printed copy of this panel was to be made available, upon the payment of a fee, to any party requiring it.

The Juries (Ireland) Act, 1833 gave the sheriff complete discretion in selecting the names from the jurors' book for the panel. This inevitably led to allegations of bias and calls were made for the power to be curbed.[103] High sheriffs were 'the principal representative[s] of central government in the county in relation to the execution of the law'.[104] Appointed by the lord lieutenant, they were predominantly wealthy Protestant landowners, and were seen as upholders of the interests of the landowning classes.[105] Most of their functions, however, were delegated to sub-sheriffs or under-sheriffs, who tended to come from legal backgrounds.[106] While

95 Ibid., para. 4821. 96 Ibid., para. 804 (Golding).

97 Ibid., para. 4825 (Matthew Barrington, Munster crown solicitor).

98 Ibid., paras 505–8 (Golding).

99 It also recommended the introduction of a rating qualification, and greater impartiality in the construction of the jury panel. The proposed rating qualification was to replace the leasehold qualification, which produced an insufficient number of jurors, which varied between counties. See also McEldowney, 'Lord O'Hagan', p. 93.

100 16 & 17 Vic., c. 113, s. 109. 101 34 & 35 Vic., c. 65. 102 34 & 35 Vic., c. 65, s. 18.

103 E.g. *Select committee on Westmeath*, HC 1871 (147) xiii, 547.

104 Crossman, *Local government*, p. 7.

105 Adam Pole, 'Sheriffs in Victorian Ireland' in Felix M. Larkin and N.M. Dawson (eds), *Lawyers, the law and history* (Dublin, 2013), p. 180.

106 Ibid., p. 183.

high sheriffs were appointed annually by the judges on the recommendation of the grand jury,[107] under-sheriffs tended to serve for much longer periods and generally had better local knowledge. In many districts the under-sheriff was a figure of mistrust,[108] and was thought to exploit his position for financial gain.[109] Crossman points out that sheriffs' and under-sheriffs' powers were 'notoriously abused',[110] and a parliamentary commission in 1825 identified various irregular practices and abuses that obstructed and perverted the administration of justice.[111] The commission noted that there was 'no department of the sheriff's office in the city of Dublin calling more loudly for correction than that connected with the summoning of juries'.[112] However, there was '[n]othing to show … that incorrectness [on the part of sub-sheriffs] … prevailed in the counties at large'.[113]

Some observers claimed that sheriffs returned panels in accordance with their own political or religious allegiances, and allegations of bias in drawing up the panel were often the basis for challenging the array of jurors at a trial.[114] It was said in 1871, for example, that a sheriff was 'almost irresponsible. If [he] chooses to return a jury that he thinks will suit the purposes of the crown, he can do it; and if he chooses to return a jury that he thinks will suit the purposes of the prisoner, he can do it.'[115] Some sheriffs gained reputations for particular biases; for example, it was said of the Fermanagh sub-sheriff in the 1820s that in four years he had never returned a Catholic freeholder to serve on any jury.[116] Others simply repeatedly summoned the men who lived closest to the courthouse, knowing them to be more likely to turn up. It was alleged in 1839 that when Keough was appointed sheriff of Co. Carlow in 1837, he returned juries almost exclusively composed of Catholics 'of the lowest grade in society'. 'Respectable Protestants' were said to be excluded until a new high sheriff, Ponsonby, appointed in 1838, sought to 'remedy the evil'.[117] Allegations of bias made against the Armagh under-sheriff in 1861 led to his explaining and defending in court his practice in compiling jury panels:

107 A controversy arose in 1863 when Deasy and Fitzgerald J.J. rejected the grand jury's nomination for Co. Tyrone and instead preferred Lt-Col Hugh Edwards, a liberal whose appointment was sought by Attorney General Maziere Brady. *Larcom Papers* (NLI, MS 7584).

108 Francis McBryan and other prisoners charged with murder at Macken, Co. Fermanagh, in 1830 complained that the Fermanagh sub-sheriff, Paul Dane, was 'a young boy, about seventeen or eighteen years of age only; that he has not profession, no knowledge or experience whatever in the business of the office of sheriff'. He had been appointed to the post merely because his uncle, Daniel Auchinleck, had been sub-sheriff for the previous four years: *Fermanagh sub-sheriff*, HC 1830 (150) xxvi, 301, p. 2.

109 Crossman, *Local government*, p. 9. 110 Ibid.

111 *Fifteenth report on salaries, 1826*.

112 Ibid., p. 66. 113 Ibid., p. 20. 114 Ibid.

115 *Report on Westmeath 1871*, para. 2050.

116 *Report on juries (Ireland)*, HC 1873 (283) xv, 389, para. 54 (Charles Hemphill, chairman of the Kerry quarter sessions); *Fermanagh sub-sheriff*, p. 2.

117 *Report on the state of Ireland*, 1839, paras 8181–2 (Thomas Harris Carroll, editor and proprietor of the *Carlow Sentinel*).

> When I receive the jury book, generally in the month of December in each year, I examine it first, and take out those whom I consider to be special jurors under the act – wholesale merchants, traders, and others of that class. From these I make up my special panel. When I receive the precept for the assizes, I send for the bailiffs, and along with them examine the books carefully, calling over the names, for the purpose of seeing whether any new names have come on in each district. I then proceed to have the district list made out for each bailiff. I have these lists made out, the name of the party, his residence, and the place for the service to be marked in by the bailiff. The summonses are then filled up according to the lists, and are signed by me, and handed to each bailiff for his district ... I have never made religion of any kind an element in preparing the panel. I have always endeavoured to put on fair and correct men, who are capable of discharging their duty.[118]

Infamous examples of corrupt sheriffs and under-sheriffs included Sam Gray in Monaghan, William Auchinleck in Fermanagh and Thomas Coote and William Mitchell in Cavan.[119]

A controversy over Armagh juries in the 1860s provides a good case study of how the composition of jurors' lists, books and panels could become the focus of attention during periods of unrest. In 1861, a group of Catholics sought a *certiorari* from the queen's bench against the Armagh justices and clerk of the crown.[120] They wished to have all orders made at the previous jury list revision sessions brought to the court of queen's bench, and quashed if found to be erroneous. If the lists were quashed then special sessions would be convened at which proper jury lists would be drawn up. A solicitor named Cochrane swore that of the 95 names on the list for the barony of Turenny, 74 were unqualified – and that 11 qualified persons had been left off the list. He had attended the revision of the special jury lists and represented a number of men who wanted their names to be added, or who objected to the lists as they currently stood.[121] The justices, however, refused to alter the lists, which were then consolidated into the jurors' book. At another barony within the county, however, upon similar objections being made, around half of the 200 names were struck off the lists. In delivering judgment, Fitzgerald J., a liberal Catholic who was a strong supporter of the jury system,

118 Anon., *The plot discovered: digest of the action for libel, Hardy v. Sullivan, tried before the lord chief justice of the queen's bench, Dublin, in November, 1861* (Armagh, 1862), p. 19.

119 For Sam Gray, see pp 145–7 and David Johnson, 'The trials of Sam Gray: Monaghan politics and nineteenth century Irish criminal procedure', *Ir. Jur.* (n.s.), 20 (1985), 109–34 at 133; for William Auchinleck, see *Second report on Orange lodges, associations or societies in Ireland*, HC 1835 (475) (476) xv, xvi, 501, 1. In one case he devolved the returning of the jury to the 'the gaoler or some persons about the dock' while he was absent, acting as the Tyrone clerk of the peace, p. 80; for Thomas Coote and William Mitchell, see John McEldowney, 'The case of *The queen v. McKenna* (1869) and jury packing in Ireland', *Ir. Jur.* (n.s.), 12 (1977), 339–54.

120 *Belfast Newsletter*, 21 Jan. 1861.

121 Including Thomas McCann and Francis Vallely, 'respectable merchants' from the town of Armagh. *Belfast Newsletter*, 21 Jan. 1861.

expressed that it was 'impossible to overstate the importance of the case'. He held that the lists ought to be brought to the queen's bench and, instead of quashing them, the court would remove the names of the unqualified persons and otherwise leave the list intact.[122] This might have the effect of invalidating the sheriff's jurors' book, but in that case recourse ought to be had to the previous year's book. Ever a champion of the jury system, he described the case as relating to 'the selection of those constitutional judges of fact by whom questions relating to life, liberty and property were decided – a tribunal which was the envy and admiration of all civilized nations'. While O'Brien J., another liberal Catholic, concurred with Fitzgerald, conservative Protestants Lefroy C.J. and Hayes J. were unconvinced that the court had jurisdiction to issue the *certiorari*, with Hayes J. warning that if the motion were granted, 'it would convulse every county in Ireland'.[123] The chief justice considered it to be 'novel and experimental' and 'utterly nugatory … mischievous … unnecessary'.[124] The result was 'no rule' on the motion. In an editorial in the *Belfast Newsletter*, the case was described as providing a clear illustration to the government 'of the impropriety, if not the absolute danger, of permitting a majority of our judges to be gentlemen of the Roman Catholic persuasion', observing that in cases 'where there is any party question involved, the Roman Catholic judge is naturally led away by his private convictions and his personal feelings, and the constitution is endangered'.[125]

These proceedings related to a clash known as the Derrymacash affray. On 12 July 1860, a riot had broken out during an illegal Orange march at Derrymacash, Co. Armagh.[126] Sixteen men were wounded and one was killed during the firing.[127] It was in anticipation of ensuing trials at the 1861 spring assizes that the Catholics of Armagh had sought to alter the composition of the jury lists. There had long been a sense that an Armagh Protestant would never be convicted for a sectarian offence, because the probability was that he would be tried by an all-Protestant jury. Led by the Catholic liberal attorney general, O'Hagan, and tried before Fitzgerald J., however, these prosecutions would be different. O'Hagan wrote to the crown solicitor instructing him to exclude from the jury box all members of the Orange Order, as well as anyone residing in the immediate vicinity who might 'be affected by prejudice or prepossession on either side'.[128] Maddox describes the events at the assizes as 'a very public stand-off … between the Orangemen and a Catholic member of the judiciary'.[129] There were three trials in total. At the first,

122 Ibid., 30 Jan. 1861. 123 Ibid. 124 Ibid., 31 Jan. 1861. 125 Ibid.

126 See the extensive reports in *Freeman's Journal*, 18, 19, 20, 21, 25, 28 July and 10 Aug. 1860 and *Belfast Newsletter*, 11 Aug. 1860. See also N. Maddox, 'A melancholy record: the story of the nineteenth-century Irish Party Processions Acts', *Ir. Jur.* (n.s.), 29 (2004), 242–73 at 256; and *Informations on Derrymacash*, HC 1861 (315) lii, 505; and *Shorthand writers' notes of trials*, HC 1861 (315) lii, 315.

127 This resulted in the passing of the Party Emblems Act to amend the Party Processions Act; see Maddox, 'Melancholy record', p. 256.

128 *Hansard 3*, clxi, 1988 (14 Mar. 1861) (Edward Cardwell).

129 Maddox, 'Melancholy record', p. 256.

the trial of Protestant Samuel Tait for murder,[130] 315 jurors' names were called over, with 130 answering.[131] Nineteen (all Protestant) were set aside by the crown,[132] and seven were challenged by the prisoner.[133] The jury consisted entirely of Protestants and although charged with murder, Tait was found guilty of manslaughter and sentenced to fifteen months.[134] At the next trial, *R v. Wright*, for firing and wounding, the crown set aside thirteen jurors, the prisoner again challenged seven, and three were excused for having served on the Tait jury.[135] Wright was acquitted by a jury composed largely of 'decent farmers'.[136] At the third trial, that of William McKeown and others for illegal procession, fifteen jurors were set aside,[137] and those who had served on the previous juries were excused by the judge. Because this was a misdemeanour, the defendants were not entitled to peremptory challenges. Counsel for the defence, McMeeham, sought to have a number of Catholics[138] challenged for cause on the grounds that they had 'entered a conspiracy to get Roman Catholics on the jurors' list, and to strike off Conservatives for the purposes of this trial'.[139] Fitzgerald J. strongly resisted this and insisted on the challenge being submitted in writing. Just as McMeeham was about to formally submit his challenge he withdrew it, realising that the challenge would be tried by the two jurors previously sworn in – both of whom happened to be Catholic.[140] The swearing in of both Catholic and Protestant jurors continued, and the final jury consisted of ten Roman Catholics and two Protestants.[141] Twelve of the prisoners were convicted of misdemeanours while three were acquitted. Although there had been no murder conviction, and the offences for which the convictions were secured were relatively minor, with light sentences, the convictions were met with surprise on all sides, and were discussed and analysed at length in the newspapers[142] and in parliament.[143] The attorney general came in

130 His name was variously spelled 'Tait' or 'Tate' in reports.

131 *Belfast Newsletter*, 6 Mar. 1861.

132 See pp 147–50.

133 These included McCann and Vallely, the Catholics who had been involved in the *certiorari* case in January. The number of challenges can be compared with those in cases analysed in chapter 10.

134 *Shorthand writers' notes*, p. 72.

135 A fourth was excused for deafness: ibid., p. 74. See also *Belfast Newsletter*, 8 Mar. 1861.

136 *Belfast Newsletter*, 9 Mar. 1861. Neither the shorthand-writer's report nor the newspaper accounts specify the religious composition of Wright's jury, but the *Belfast Newsletter* suggests that the crown's challenges focused on town dwellers and Protestants.

137 It was made known that all jurors from the town of Lurgan were going to be challenged by the crown: *Hansard 3*, clxi, 1985 (14 Mar. 1861).

138 These included McCann and Vallely, as well as James Wynn, John Small, James McCourt and Michael O'Toole.

139 *Shorthand writers' notes*, p. 113.

140 See p. 137 for an explanation of how jury challenges were tried.

141 *Hansard 3*, clxi, 1986 (14 Mar. 1861).

142 See in particular *Belfast Newsletter*, 22, 27, 28 Mar.; 1, 11, 16, 17, 18, 19, 20, 24, 29 Apr.; 6, 14, 18 May; 19, 23 July 1861. *Freeman's Journal*, 12 Mar. 1861, observed that the convictions had 'maddened the Orange party' and were completely unexpected.

143 E.g. *Hansard 3*, clix, 2262–73 (20 July 1860); *Hansard 3*, clxi, 1981–96 (14 Mar. 1861).

for severe criticism from the Orange lodges,[144] but liberal Protestant opinion appeared to be in favour of the convictions.[145]

The fallout from the Derrymacash affair continued for some time. Several Protestants were to be tried at the 1861 summer assizes, but pleaded guilty,[146] and in October of that year a number of Protestants commenced proceedings at Lurgan petty sessions against 9 Catholics who had been involved in the affray.[147] Simultaneously, true bills were found against 18 other Catholics by the grand jury at the Lurgan quarter sessions.[148] Further proceedings were taken against 36 Protestants in November.[149] In July 1861, following the Armagh summer assizes, a letter was published in the *Morning News* accusing William Hardy, the under-sheriff, of 'juggling the jury panel', and claiming that '[t]he Catholics of Armagh have been for the last twenty years virtually excluded from the jury box'.[150] The letter alleged that the Armagh sub-sheriff, acting within the law, had summoned around 15 Catholics from a panel of 200, despite their accounting for about half of the population of the county. The letter, signed 'A Catholic', was generally understood to have been written by the paper's proprietor, Alexander Martin Sullivan. A libel action was tried before a special jury[151] in the court of queen's bench.[152] Sullivan sought to justify his statements by proving that there was not a 'fair representation' of Catholics in the Armagh jurors' book. Summing up the defence, the Armagh Protestant Association[153] wrote:

> They had a 'national tribute' for their defence; they had every facility to prove the libel; they had an array of priests in court, and two of their own persuasion on the jury, one of whom is reported to have a kind of connexion with the *Morning News*; they toiled day and night, and apportioned the swearing on the strict principle of the division of labour; yet they have proved nothing against Mr Hardy, for he obtained damages and costs. All

144 Commentary in *Freeman's Journal*, 19 Apr. 1861.

145 Maddox, 'Melancholy record', p. 258. Subsequently, the jurors who had convicted Tait sent a memorial to the lord lieutenant seeking to have Tait's prosecution investigated, claiming that while they had convicted on the evidence before them, they had since become aware of additional testimony that would have exonerated Tait. *Belfast Newsletter*, 22 Mar. 1861. The lord lieutenant commuted Tate's sentence and he was discharged, having been in prison for nine months; *Belfast Newsletter*, 27 Mar. 1861. The other men convicted similarly petitioned the lord lieutenant: *Belfast Newsletter*, 31 Mar. 1861.

146 *Freeman's Journal*, 23, 24 July 1861 and *Belfast Newsletter*, 24, 25 July 1861.

147 See *Belfast Newsletter*, 2, 12, 14, 19 Oct. and 12 Nov. 1861, and *Freeman's Journal*, 12, 14, 18, 19 Oct. 1861. The cases were sent forward to the quarter sessions: *Belfast Newsletter*, 12 Nov. 1861; and the chairman of the sessions sent them to be tried at the next assizes: ibid., 7 Jan. 1862.

148 Ibid., 15 Oct. 1861. 149 Ibid., 21 Nov. 1861. 150 *Morning News*, 31 July 1861.

151 On which there were at least two Catholics.

152 See *Freeman's Journal*, 21 Nov. 1861 and the pamphlet published by the Armagh Protestant Association: Anon., *The plot discovered: digest of the action for libel, Hardy v. Sullivan, tried before the lord chief justice of the queen's bench, Dublin, in Nov, 1861* (Armagh, 1862).

153 The association had been established in the winter of 1860 in the aftermath of the Derrymacash affair. *Hardy v. Sullivan* (1862), p. i.

> that they did prove is that they are a miserable fraction in Armagh, without property qualification not being able to muster 200 men rated at £200 a-year, in a population numbering 189, 382; that a fair proportion of these 200 were summoned; that some of them begged to be excused from serving on juries; and that the object of one person at least was to convict Tate of a murder he never committed.[154]

It became apparent that while Catholics formed a large proportion of the population of the county, there were few who had sufficient property to sit on juries. John McKinstry, deputy clerk of the peace for Armagh, testified that there were around two hundred Catholics on the Armagh book, and:

> of those a large number come from the mountain districts, and are illiterate persons. I should say on the whole that two-thirds are totally unfitted to be put on any jury panel by any sheriff exercising their discretion, and I should say that the Protestant jurors, being of a better class, are better qualified to discharge the duties of jurors.[155]

It seemed that Catholics were more likely to serve on sessions juries than at the assizes – in other words, on cases of lesser significance or value.[156] However, the sheriff defended this by saying that he endeavoured to divide the labour so that the same men were not asked to serve at both sessions and assizes.[157]

Despite such high-profile controversies, not all sheriffs were corrupt, and some made a point of being as impartial as possible in the drawing-up of panels. Around the time of the Derrymacash affair, the sub-sheriff of Co. Tyrone was criticized for his mode of making up panels, which was to ensure that they were comprised of half Catholics and half Protestants. In a letter to the *Daily Mail*, he wrote:

> This, I admit, was an act of justice and straightforwardness which gave dire offence in a county from the jury panel of which Roman Catholics were in all preceding time almost entirely excluded. It ensured impartial trials and, no doubt, struck terror into such evildoers as calculated on immunity from punishment from political sympathizers in the jury box. But the well-disposed of every class and creed approved my conduct.[158]

He defended his practice, claiming 'the head and front of my offending is that I recognised the civil rights and political equality of my co-religionists in a county where, though an overwhelming majority, their existence was heretofore, in all judicial matters, practically ignored'.[159]

154 Ibid., p. iv. 155 Ibid., p. 5.
156 Ibid. See the testimony of William Murray, p. 6; Patrick Vallely, p. 8 and Patrick McGeogh, p. 9.
157 *Hardy v. Sullivan* (1862), p. 19.
158 *Daily Mail*, 1 Feb. 1864; reproduced in the Larcom Papers (NLI, MS 7584).
159 *Daily Mail*, 3 Feb. 1864.

As has been demonstrated in this chapter, there was a web of personnel responsible for the creation of jury lists, books and panels, including cess collectors, clerks of unions, constables and bailiffs. It is disingenuous to attribute all instances of biased or exclusive juries to sheriffs, as evidently many of the problems with the jury list were attributable to the cess collectors. The deputy clerk of the peace for Armagh, for example, stated in 1862 that the lists he produced were 'those returned by the cess collectors, and revised by the magistrates; the sheriff has nothing to say to them'.[160] Similarly, a witness told the 1873 parliamentary committee on Irish juries that the sub-sheriff had no control over the jurors' book.[161] His influence was limited to the framing of the panel. Furthermore, the crown solicitor's right to order jurors to stand by could have an even greater impact on jury composition,[162] and many controversies concerning jury representativeness centred on the role of crown solicitors.

Taking into account the frequent allegations of biased sheriffs, however, and the recommendations from his drafters,[163] O'Hagan's Act obliged the sheriff to take the names from the book 'in a regular alphabetical series', taking one name from each letter of the alphabet and going through the alphabet as many times as necessary when drawing up the panel.[164] Although this meant that the sheriff had less discretion in the framing of the jury panel, it did at times give rise to other problems; the sheriff might find that all letters had been exhausted except 'M' or 'O', for example. This might mean that surnames beginning with these letters, which were very common in certain parts of Ireland, might dominate a jury panel. The Tipperary crown solicitor, George Bolton, commented in 1874 that at one of the upcoming assizes in Tipperary 'we shall have only Ryans on the panel'.[165] Lewis Mansergh Buchanan, the Tyrone clerk of the peace, similarly told the 1881 parliamentary committee that at the recent spring assizes in his county, in one case 'all the jurors were Macs and ten out of twelve were Catholics'.[166]

160 *Hardy v. Sullivan* (1862), p. 5.
161 *Report on Irish juries*, 1873, para. 52 (Hemphill).
162 See pp 148–9.
163 The drafters suggested that chairmen of counties be empowered to scrutinise the jury lists, and that this would make sheriffs less likely to abuse their power. They recommended the use of a rotation system for summoning jurors, and the imposition of a fine on a sheriff for summoning a juror out of rotation. McEldowney, 'Lord O'Hagan', p. 155.
164 34 & 35 Vic., c. 65, s. 19. There was no equivalent provision in English legislation, and until the twentieth century the sheriff was free to compile panels in whatever manner he chose. A parliamentary committee in 1913 found considerable variation around England and Wales in the manner of preparing panels: *Report on juries, 1913*, p. 18.
165 *Report on the Irish jury system*, HC 1874 (244) ix, 557, para. 1533.
166 *Report on Irish jury laws*, HC 1881 (430) xi, 1, para. 334. See also paras 329–33, and the comments of Constantine Molloy, who had drafted the 1871 act, para. 643.

CONCLUSION

Many of the practices and procedures outlined in this chapter lent themselves to abuse as a result of excessive autonomy for some officials, a lack of clear information as to who qualified as jurors, and the ad hoc development of some practices. The whole process of creating and maintaining lists of qualified jurors was fraught with opportunities for error or fraud, and, unsurprisingly, did not escape the general move towards revision and reform that was evident throughout the nineteenth century.[167] As the century progressed, legislative reforms tended to be detailed and prescriptive, and, unfortunately, in many instances gave rise to new abuses. As will be seen in chapter 10, irregularities in compiling and revising the baronial jury lists, creating the general and special jurors' books and returning the jury panel frequently formed the basis for challenges to the array of the jury panel.

167 As discussed in chapter 1, before O'Hagan's Act of 1871 was passed, there had been a number of attempts to reform the Irish jury procedure.

CHAPTER THREE

Grand juries and common juries

THIS AND THE FOLLOWING FOUR CHAPTERS seek to demonstrate the extent of lay participation in the nineteenth-century administration of justice, by examining in turn the operation, composition and purpose of various categories of lay jury. The involvement of laypersons or amateurs in administering justice in Ireland was generally more limited than it was in England,[1] except when it came to juries. In Ireland, the plethora of juries could broadly be categorised either as juries of inquiry and presentment, or juries of issue and assessment. While many categories of jury flourished during the late eighteenth and early nineteenth centuries, not all of them survived the nineteenth century. Some fell into abeyance and were statutorily abolished as part of the rationalisation of the machinery of justice, their functions taken out of the hands of laypersons as an increasing emphasis on professionalization took hold.[2] This chapter examines the grand jury, which was a jury of presentment, and the common jury, which was the most commonly used type of trial jury. The focus is mainly, but not exclusively, the criminal justice system.

THE GRAND JURY

Although arguably the main function of the Irish grand jury related to local government,[3] it also played an important role in criminal trials. At the beginning of an assizes or quarter session, the grand jury decided whether the bills of

1 See R.B. McDowell, 'The Irish courts of law, 1801–1914', *I.H.S.*, 10:40 (1957), 363–91 at 373–45 (professional magistrates); John McEldowney, 'Crown prosecutions in nineteenth-century Ireland' in Douglas Hay and Francis Snyder (eds), *Policing and prosecution in Britain, 1750–1850* (Oxford, 1989), p. 420 (professional prosecutors); Stanley Palmer, 'The Irish police experiment: the beginnings of modern police in the British Isles, 1785–95'; and Ian Bridgeman, 'The constabulary and the criminal justice system in nineteenth-century Ireland' in I. O'Donnell and F. McAuley (eds), *Criminal justice history* (Dublin, 2003) (professional police).
2 See Conor Hanly, 'The decline of civil jury trial in nineteenth-century England', *J. Leg. Hist.*, 26:3 (2005), 253–78.
3 This has generally been the primary focus of scholars: see Virginia Crossman, *Local government in nineteenth century Ireland* (Belfast, 1994), pp 25–41; Thomas King, 'Local government administrators in Carlow – from grand jury to county council', *Carloviana: J. Old Carlow Soc.*, 47 (1999), 77–8; Tom Donovan, 'Miscellanea: some records of Limerick assizes', *North Munster Antiquarian Journal*, 45 (2005), 151–4; and David Broderick, *Local government in nineteenth-century County Dublin: the grand jury* (Dublin, 2007).

indictment against accused persons were 'true bills' – in other words, whether the prosecutor had made a *prima facie* case.[4] Garnham has examined the percentage of true bills returned by late eighteenth-century grand juries in Ireland, and determines that they tended overall to be more lenient than their English counterparts.[5] In the mid-nineteenth century, Irish grand juries at assizes appear to have returned true bills in around 70 per cent of cases sent to them.[6]

Dutton wrote in 1721 that nobody could be:

> convicted or attainted, or have judgment of life or member, upon any criminal accusation, but there must be two juries pass upon him, at least twenty-four persons, the one a grand jury … to present the offence fit for a trial; the other a petit or lesser jury … to try the truth of that presentment. The grand jury coming from all parts of the county, the other jury … of the very neighbourhood where the offence was committed.[7]

The grand jury consisted of 'gentlemen of the best figure of the county',[8] selected and appointed by the high sheriff at the assizes or quarter sessions.[9] As with petty juries, the sheriff could select whomever he chose for the grand jury. Traditionally there was no ballot procedure – the sheriff had discretion to choose from those who attended, having been summoned. Garnham notes that 'ties of patronage, kin, and mutual interest were vitally important in jury selection', and that selection could be chaotic: in one eighteenth-century instance in Co. Down,

4 See W. Huband, *A practical treatise on the law relating to the grand jury in criminal cases, the petty jury and the coroner's jury* (rev. ed., Dublin, 1911), pp 123–208 for details of the operation of grand juries in Ireland. See also W.R. Cornish, *The jury* (London, 1968), p. 62; W.E. Vaughan, *Murder trials in Ireland* (Dublin, 2009); and G. O'Carroll, *Mr Justice Robert Day (1746–1841): the diaries and the addresses to grand juries, 1793–1829* (Tralee, 2004), p. 3. Legislation in the late seventeenth and early eighteenth century empowered grand juries to bypass the safeguards and procedures of arraignment, indictment and conviction when it came to vagrants and vagabonds: they could be immediately imprisoned and then transported to the colonies on the mere suspicion that they posed a threat. These provisions are considered in detail in N. Garnham, 'The limits of English influence on the Irish criminal law' in M. Brown and S. Donlan (eds), *The laws and other legalities of Ireland, 1689–1850* (Surrey, 2011), pp 100–5.

5 Garnham, 'The limits of English influence', pp 108–9.

6 Between February 1850 and April 1851, there were 7,459 bills of indictment sent to assizes grand juries, and 5,230 of these were found to be true bills. *Bills of indictment (Ireland)*, HC 1851 (328) l, 317.

7 Matthew Dutton, *The office and authority of sheriffs, under-sheriffs, deputies, county-clerks, and coroners in Ireland* (Dublin, 1721), p. 347.

8 W. Blackstone, *Commentaries on the laws of England*, 4 vols (London, 1791), iv, p. 299. Garnham, however, notes that membership of the eighteenth-century Irish grand jury was not always reserved for members of the Ascendancy: Neal Garnham, 'Local elite creation in early Hanoverian Ireland: the case of the county grand jury', *Hist. J.*, 42:3 (1999), 623–42 at 629.

9 See Leonard MacNally, *The justice of the peace for Ireland: containing the authorities and duties of that officer, as also of the various conservators of the peace*, 2 vols (Dublin, 1808), ii, p. 48; and the Grand Jury (Ireland) Act, 1836 (6 & 7 Will. IV, c. 116). Huband, *Treatise*, pp 2–22, traces the origins and development of the grand jury in the context of criminal prosecutions.

'the choosing of jurors from the individuals summoned to the assizes devolved into a shoving and shouting match, as potential jurors vied for selection'.[10] One critic described the selection of grand jurors as follows:

> The high sheriff … summonses a panel of country gentlemen giving precedence as a matter of courtesy to the county representatives, who are generally absent on parliamentary duty; selecting after them certain customary baronial representatives; and then such landed proprietors as favour, friendship, political influence, or relationship, may induce him to prefer.[11]

Another commentator observed that the sheriff, 'being virtually, though not ostensibly, appointed by influential members of a sitting grand jury is bound to return the same panel (varied by some two or three names at the fag-end of the list) for the ensuing year'.[12]

At common law, grand jurors were to be freeholders,[13] and barrister John Leslie Foster (later Baron Foster) wrote in 1816 that the value of the freehold was 'immaterial', and that a penny per annum would suffice.[14] However, the freehold requirement was not always strictly complied with,[15] and did not apply in cities.[16] The Grand Juries (Ireland) Act, 1838[17] allowed leaseholders worth £100 to sit on grand juries, as well as freeholders worth £50. In practice, the legislative qualifications for special jurors came to be applied to grand jurors at assizes also.[18] The Juries (Ireland) Act, 1871[19] stated that the sheriff was to select the grand jurors from the special jurors' book, or from the jurors marked as special on the general jurors' book. If there were an insufficient number of special jurors available then the sheriff could select such common jurors as were necessary.

Under the penal laws, no Catholics were to serve on grand juries in any courts unless a sufficient number of Protestants could not be had.[20] While this was repealed by the Roman Catholic Relief Act in 1793,[21] Scully observed in 1808 that

10 Garnham, 'Local elite creation', p. 631.
11 George Orme Malley, 'On the expediency of the total abolition of grand juries in Ireland', *J.S.S.I.S.I.*, 6:40 (1871), 11–19 at 11.
12 Bernard Mullins, *Observations upon the Irish grand jury system* (Dublin, 1831), p. 9.
13 Huband, *Treatise*, p. 16.
14 *Letter from J.L. Leslie Foster to Thomas Foster* (PRONI, T2519/4/1985).
15 E.A. Hackett, *The Irish grand jury system: with a note on the Irish poor law system, 1898* (London, 1898), p. 12; R.B. McDowell, *Ireland in the age of imperialism and revolution* (Oxford, 1976), p. 107; and Garnham, 'Local elite creation', pp 634–5.
16 Huband, *Treatise*, p. 151; *R v. Sheridan and Kirwan* (1811) 31 How. St. Tr. 543; and *R v. Duffy* (1848) 1 Ir. Jur. 81.
17 6 & 7 Will. IV, c. 116.
18 *R v. Duffy* (1848) 1 Ir. Jur. 81. Note that the judge who made this point was Louis Perrin, who had drafted the 1833 act.
19 34 & 35 Vic., c. 65.
20 Papist Solicitors Act, 1707 (6 Anne, c. 6), s. 5.
21 33 Geo. III, c. 21.

'its principle continue[d] to be acted upon, in a great degree, throughout Ireland – and particularly in cities and towns'.[22] Catholic representation on grand juries was certainly patchy, and varied around the country. A number of commentators in 1825 described how Catholics continued to be under-represented on grand juries.[23] William Francis Finn, from Kilkenny, for example, noted that while increasing amounts of land were being bought by Catholics, and a number of industries had shifted from Protestant to Catholic hands,[24] there were still only between three and six Catholic grand jurors in the county.[25] Sir John Newport MP similarly told the committee that there were between three and five Roman Catholics on the grand jury in Waterford,[26] and Reverend Michael Collins estimated that there were three Catholic grand jurors in Cork.[27] By contrast, the bishop of Derry stated that there were no Catholics in his diocese who would have sufficient property to qualify as grand jurors or magistrates.[28]

Religious composition was not the only problem when it came to grand juries. In 1835 the commission on municipal corporations observed that in most cities, 'the majority of grand jurors is empanelled from the members of the governing corporate bodies ... the composition of the grand juries, which ought to be generally and impartially taken from the inhabitants at large, is thus directly and effectively that of the corporations'.[29] The 1838 act[30] excluded certain persons from the grand jury, including the coroner, high constable, cess collectors, clerks of the crown and peace, and stipendiary magistrates. Sheriffs often served as grand jurors,[31] and coroners were known to serve also, despite the fact that the coroner's salary was presented by the grand jury.[32]

There was a difference between grand juries at assizes and grand juries at quarter sessions, with the latter having fewer powers of presentment,[33] and including men slightly lower in the social pecking order. A witness before the 1873 committee on the Irish jury system pointed out that the grand jury at the quarter sessions was drawn from the special jurors' list.[34] Another witness proposed the

22 Denys Scully, *A statement of the penal laws which aggrieve the Catholics of Ireland: with commentaries* (2nd ed., Dublin, 1812), p. 219.
23 *Minutes of evidence on the state of Ireland*, HL 1825 (521) ix, 249.
24 Ibid., p. 253.
25 Ibid., p. 254. He opined that part of the reason for this was that Catholics were less likely to be sufficiently well-connected to be recommended for the grand jury panel, and that furthermore, those who were placed on the panel rarely served because of their position quite low down the panel. According to Finn, many Catholics complained 'that there are men who ought to be on the grand jury who are not'.
26 Ibid., p. 285.
27 *State of Ireland (minutes of evidence)*, HL 1825 (20) vii, 1, p. 327. He considered this to be an under-representation of Cork landowners.
28 *Minutes of evidence on the state of Ireland, 1825*, p. 280.
29 *First report on municipal corporations in Ireland*, I [C-23–28] HC 1835 xxvii, xxviii, 51, 79, 199, p. 37.
30 6 & 7 Will. IV, c. 116, s. 32.
31 Broderick, *Local government*, pp 8–9.
32 *Ex parte Nowlan* (1839) 2 Ir. LR 7.
33 Garnham, 'Local elite creation', pp 627–8.
34 *Report on juries (Ireland)*, HC 1873 (283) xv, 389, para. 5.

abolition of the use of grand jurors at quarter sessions.[35] Under the Juries Qualification (Ireland) Act, 1876,[36] the qualifications for grand jurors at general session of the peace were the same as those for petty jurors, outlined below. Briefly, they had to hold freehold land to the value of £10 annually or leasehold to the value of £15 annually, or to be rated for the poor with respect to lands of a specified annual value.[37] By the 1870s, some commentators were questioning the need for grand jurors at quarter sessions; as one witness before the 1874 committee on Irish juries observed:

> it seems to me the greatest absurdity to bring twenty-three men forty miles from their work, to say whether a man shall be tried for stealing a pair of brogues, or striking a man on the head, when it is clear from the information that the bench has to read, that it is a case to be tried.[38]

As noted above, grand jurors were traditionally taken from the whole county and not just the neighbourhood where the alleged offence was committed.[39] The procedure under the Grand Jury (Ireland) Act, 1838[40] was that the sheriff was to select someone from each barony in the county who had freehold worth £50 per annum or leasehold worth £100 per annum. These were then combined to make the grand jury panel for the county.[41]

Under the Grand Juries (Ireland) Act, 1836 the sheriff was to summon grand jurors between one and five days before the sessions or assizes, and could empanel

35 Ibid., para. 2456 (James Murland, crown solicitor for County Down).

36 39 & 40 Vic., c. 21, s. 2.

37 A parliamentary committee on juries in England and Wales noted in 1913 that while the qualifications for grand jurors at quarter sessions were to be the same as those for petty jurors, there were no specific qualifications for grand jurors at assizes, other than the requirement that they be freeholders. In practice, however, grand juries at county assizes were usually magistrates whose names were drawn from the general jurors' book: *Report on juries 1913*, p. 10.

38 *Report on the Irish jury system*, HC 1874 (244) ix, 557, para. 1040 (Henry West, chairman of Co. Wexford).

39 Under common law, a defendant could not be indicted by a grand jury in a county other than the county where the alleged offence took place. See Matthew Hale, *The history of the pleas of the crown*, 2 vols (London, 1736), ii, p. 163. The Special Juries and Trials (Ireland) Act, 1825 (6 Geo. IV, c. 51), s. 3, allowed offences to be presented by grand juries in adjoining counties. See *R v. Freeman* (1875) I.R. 9 C.L. 527. Difficulties sometimes arose where an offence was committed on the border between two counties, such as a river: e.g. *R v. King* (1865) 16 Ir. C.L.R. 50 (C.C.R.) and *Noon's case* (1841) Ir. Cir. Ca. 110. Until the 1870s winter assizes were only held in certain counties – those with more than just one or two prisoners awaiting trial. Unless there were enough cases to justify braving the bad weather and poor roads, judges were loathe to hold an assizes in every county. Under the Winter Assizes Act, 1876 (39 & 49 Vic., c. 57), where it appeared that by reason of the small number of prisoners it was inexpedient to hold separate winter assizes for any county, adjoining counties could be united by an order of the lord lieutenant in November of any year. This meant that offences committed in one county were of necessity presented and tried in another county where the assizes were to take place.

40 6 & 7 Will. IV, c. 116, s. 31.

41 See *Re Garvey* (1841) Ir. Circ. Rep. 113.

up to 23 grand jurors with agreement of at least 12 required for a true bill to be found.[42] They could be fined for non-attendance where they had been duly summoned.[43] The grand jury sat in private and only heard testimony from prosecution witnesses.[44] This secrecy was justified to prevent a criminal defendant from learning about the crown's case against him and preparing a 'corrupt defence'.[45] In *R v. O'Connell*, it was claimed (unsuccessfully) that the witnesses ought to have been sworn in open court.[46] Grand juries were often regarded with mistrust by the local population, as a result of both the secrecy of their deliberations and their composition.[47] The fact that the same men were continually re-elected as grand jurors, it was claimed, led to complacency and a monopolisation of power.[48]

THE COMMON JURY

Petty juries, which tried criminal and civil cases, could either be special or common. Originally, the qualifications for common jurors were minimal; they were to be men who were 'free and lawful, impartial and disinterested, neither the enemies nor the too close friends of either litigant'.[49] Coke outlined the common-law requirements for common jurors as follows:

> He that is of a jury must be *liber homo*, that is, not only a freeman and not bond, but also one that hath such freedom of mind as he stands indifferent as he stands unsworn. Secondly, he must be *legalis*. And by the law, every juror that is returned for the trial of any issue or cause, ought to have three properties. First, he ought to be dwelling most near to the place where the question is moved. Secondly, he ought to be most sufficient both for

42 6 & 7 Will. IV, s. 29. On summoning jurors, see Hackett, *The Irish grand jury*, p. 12. On empanelling up to 23 jurors, see Charles H. Foot, *The grand jury laws of Ireland* (2nd ed., Dublin, 1884), p. 34. For minimum number of jurors, see Huband, *Treatise*, p. 184, which notes that '[a] finding by less than twelve grand jurors is erroneous'. See also Hale, *Pleas*, ii, p. 161. Any twelve jurors could agree to the bill; it was not necessary that the foreman be one of them: *In re grand jury for county of Down* (1845) 3 Cr. & Dix C.C.

43 6 & 7 Will. IV, c. 116, s. 36.

44 The Grand Jury (Ireland) Act, 1816 (56 Geo. III, c. 87), ss 1–3 provided that no bills of indictment could be found without examining witnesses.

45 Thomas Spring-Rice, *An inquiry into the effects of the Irish grand jury laws: as affecting the industry, the improvement, and the moral character of the people of Ireland* (London, 1815), p. 36.

46 (1844) 11 Cl. & F. 155.

47 Malley, 'Expediency', 18.

48 Ibid., 12. The Courts of Justice Act, 1924, s. 27, abolished the grand jury's role in considering indictments. Grand juries were abolished in Northern Ireland by the Grand Jury (Abolition) Act (Northern Ireland), 1969.

49 F. Pollock and F.W. Maitland, *A history of English law before the time of Edward I*, 2 vols (2nd ed., Cambridge, 1898, repr. 1911), ii, p. 621. See also J.H. Thomas, *A systematic arrangement of Lord Coke's first institute of the laws of England*, 3 vols (Philadelphia, 1836), iii, p. 365 (3 Co. Inst. 155b).

understanding, and competency of estate. Thirdly, he ought to be least suspicious, that is, to be indifferent as he stands unsworn.

It was not until the fifteenth century that a specified value was attached to jurors' freehold property. An English act passed in 1414[50] provided that jurors in cases concerning homicide, disputes concerning land or disputes over the value of 40*s*., had to hold lands or tenements of a yearly value of 40*s*. or more.[51] Powell points out that this implies that a lower qualification sufficed for lesser offences.[52] Although there were further increases to the property requirement for jurors in England,[53] it was not until 1735 that the Irish qualification was raised.[54]

Writing about the sixteenth and seventeenth centuries, Lawson describes several different qualifications for jurors: 'the age qualification, the legal or moral qualification, the residential qualification, and the property qualification'.[55] During the medieval period, local residence was the 'crucial qualification', but as the role of the jury evolved, this became less important than the property requirement. The problem with almost all property qualifications for securing sufficient numbers of competent jurors was, according to Oldham, 'ineffective enforcement and obsolescence'.[56] The eighteenth century saw an ever-increasing amount of legislation dealing with juror qualification in both England and Ireland, mainly focusing on property values, though there were other requirements such as residence.[57] As the Irish judges observed in 1832, '[i]t has been the principle of our

50 Jurors Qualifications Act, 1414 (2 Hen. V, stat. 2, c. 3). This stated that such cases were being tried by 'common jurors, and others that have but little to live upon but by such inquests, and which have nothing to lose because of their false oaths'.

51 Another statute passed in the same year provided that jurors on inquests into heresy were to 'have within the realm an hundred shillings of lands, tenements, or rent by year': 2 Hen. V, stat. 1, c. 7.

52 Edward Powell, 'Jury trial at gaol delivery in the late Middle Ages' in J.S. Cockburn and Thomas A. Green (eds), *'Twelve good men and true': the criminal trial jury in England, 1200–1800* (Princeton, 1988), p. 83.

53 James C. Oldham, 'The origins of the special jury', *U. Chic. Law Rev.*, 50 (1983), 137–211, app., has a useful table of all legislation dealing English with juror qualifications, from the Magna Carta until 1730. Jurors Act, 1585 (27 Eliz., c. 6), s. 1, raised the qualification from 40*s*. to £4, noting that in return for payment, sheriffs and other officers 'oftentimes do spare at home the most able and sufficient freeholders, and return the poorer and simpler sort, least able to discern the causes in question, and most unable to bear the charges of appearance and attendances in such cases'. Jurors Act, 1664 (16 & 17 Chas. II, c. 3) provided that jurors were to have £20 in England and £8 in Wales. This expired in 1677. Reviving and Continuing Act, 1692 (4 & 5 Will. & Mar., c. 24), s. 15, lowered the qualification to £10 for jurors in England and £6 for jurors in Wales. However, this statute noted that the existing qualifications, under the 1664 act, were £10 and £4. This suggests that the legislators may have been mistaken and thought that they were merely continuing the existing qualification rather than lowering it.

54 Regulation of Juries Act, 1735 (9 Geo. II, c. 3). The 40*s*. qualification was restated in 1725: Regulation of Sheriffs Act, 1725 (12 Geo. I, c. 4), s. 16.

55 P.G. Lawson, 'Lawless juries? The composition and behaviour of Hertfordshire juries, 1573–1624' in Cockburn and Green (eds), '*Twelve good men*', p. 121.

56 Oldham, 'Origins', 147.

57 John H. Langbein, 'The English criminal trial jury on the eve of the French Revolution' in

law as far back as it can be traced, that property is only one of the qualifications by which the fitness of a juror is to be decided. Character, intelligence, exemption from imputation are by the same law considered equally indispensable.'[58] However, legislators continued to focus on property qualifications throughout the nineteenth century.

Until the eighteenth century, the Irish property qualification was always lower than the English one, which Garnham attributes to the inadequate supply of suitable men.[59] The Regulation of Juries Act, 1735 provided that persons qualified to sit on juries had to have freehold worth £5 per annum, except in cities and towns.[60] In addition, certain Protestant leaseholders were also qualified if they had a lease for a term of years, with ten years left unexpired; or a lease for sixty-one years or more, determinable on life or lives, 'with a clear profit rent of not less than fifteen pounds per annum'. In 1755 the freehold requirement was raised to £10 per annum for jurors in civil cases, except in cities and towns.[61] Protestant leaseholders now had to have fifteen years unexpired; or a lease for sixty-one years or more, with £15 rent profit per annum. These acts also prohibited Catholics from sitting on juries to try cases arising between Protestants and Catholics.[62]

In addition, there was frequently legislation passed that regulated the qualifications of jurors in specific towns and cities. For example, the lack of freeholders in the cities of Cork and Waterford led to legislation allowing any person 'possessed of or worth the sum of fifty pounds over and above all his just debts' to serve as a juror.[63] Special provision also had to be made for the city of Galway, as a result of the penal laws. A 1703 act had provided that no Catholics were permitted to live in Galway city unless they paid a surety for their fidelity to the crown.[64] A 1709 act provided that only 'known Protestants' could settle property disputes between

A. Schioppa (ed.), *The trial jury in England, France, Germany, 1700–1900* (Berlin, 1987), pp 24–5. Jurors (Inhabitant) Act, 1495 (10 Hen. VII, c. 7) provided that only continual inhabitants of towns or men who were prentices therein could be jurors.

58 *Letter regarding the jury bill 1833* (NAI, OP/1833/14).

59 Neal Garnham, *The courts, crime and criminal law in Ireland, 1692–1760* (Dublin, 1996), p. 135. In the sixteenth century, legislation provided that affinity beyond the fifth degree was not a ground to challenge a juror, because the king's subjects were so few in number, and were prohibited from marrying the Irish, so they 'of necessity must marry themselves together'. It noted that many trials and inquests 'hath been greatly hindred, put to costes and delayed sometime' because of such challenges: Consanguinity Act, 1542 (33 Hen. VIII, c. 4).

60 9 Geo. II, c. 3. This was continued and amended in the Regulation of Juries Act, 1739 (13 Geo. II, c. 5).

61 Regulation of Juries Act, 1755 (29 Geo. II, c. 6), s. 1. Sometimes referred to as the Balloting Act.

62 9 Geo. II, c. 3, s. 13; 29 Geo. II, c. 6, s. 12.

63 Regulation of Cork Act, 1765 (5 Geo. III, c. 24), s. 6; An Act for better regulating the police of the city of Waterford, 1783–4 (23 & 24 Geo. III, c. 52), s. 47.

64 Popery Act, 1703 (2 Anne, c. 7), s. 24. Seamen, fishermen and day labourers were excluded. For a discussion of the immediate impact of this act and subsequent events in Galway, see James Mitchell, 'The Catholics of Galway 1708–13: a commentary on a report by Don Giovanni Donato Mezzafalce', *Journal of the Galway Archaeological and Historical Society*, 61 (2009), 79–106.

Catholics and Protestants.[65] However, it was noted in 1717 that 'great numbers of papists by the notorious neglect of the magistrates have been, and still are, permitted to inhabit [Galway] contrary to law'.[66] There were therefore insufficient numbers of Protestant freeholders in the town to try Catholics in criminal cases, or to try disputes involving Protestants. This led to many Catholics settling in the town and being effectively sheltered from prosecution. The 1717 legislation noted that 'justice is obstructed, many criminals are protected contrary to law'. It provided that henceforth sheriffs could summon forty-shilling Protestant freeholders of the county of Galway 'to attend and serve on any grand jury or petty jury for the trial of issues' in the city of Galway.[67]

As well as revising procedural aspects of the jury system,[68] the Juries Act, 1825 also reformed the qualifications for English jurors, with common jurors in all civil and criminal cases henceforth qualifying on the basis of the poor-law rateable value of their lands.[69] The lack of a poor-law system in Ireland meant that such a basis of qualification could not be introduced.[70] Instead, the Juries (Ireland) Act, 1833 essentially consolidated existing legislation as to juror qualifications, with some relatively minor additions.[71] It retained the separate civil and criminal panels but abolished the distinction between qualifications for criminal and civil juries, and £10 freeholders and £15 leaseholders now qualified, regardless of religion.[72] It introduced a new distinction between counties at large and counties of cities and towns. Resident merchants, freemen, or householders in towns, with an annual value of £20 also qualified, as did resident merchants, freemen or householders in cities and towns with personal estate to the value of £100. There were always categories of person who were exempted from sitting on trial juries, despite having sufficient property.[73] The 1833 act exempted such groups as peers, persons connected with the administration of justice, clergymen and members of certain professions, including surgeons, apothecaries and postmasters.[74] McEldowney observes that this was merely codifying existing practice.[75] It also lowered the age limit for jurors from 70 to 60 years.[76]

65 Popery Act, 1709 (8 Anne, c. 3), s. 30. 66 Regulation of Galway Act, 1717 (4 Geo. I, c. 15), s. 1.
67 4 Geo. I, c. 15, s. 1. 68 See p. 44. 69 6 Geo. IV, c. 50.
70 See R.B. McDowell, *The Irish administration, 1801–1914* (London, 1964), pp 175–90.
71 3 & 4 Will. IV, c. 91. See *Hansard 3*, xxi, 1054 (4 Mar. 1834) (HC) (Daniel O'Connell).
72 Most of the eighteenth-century legislation discussed above dealt with civil juries, while qualification for criminal juries was largely regulated by the common law.
73 While such exemptions usually stemmed from legislation, at times they could be granted by the crown: see the English case of *R v. Perceval and others* (1659) Sid. 243; 82 E.R. 1083. In 1721, Dutton listed the following as exempt: 'Barons, and all above them in degree, tenants in ancient demesne, councellors, attornies, bailiffs, coroners, stewards or any servant of theirs, clerks and other ministers in the king's courts, officers of the sheriff, infants under the age of fourteen years, and such as are exempted by the king's charter … also clergymen.' Dutton, *Office and authority*, pp 352–3. 74 3 & 4 Will. IV, c. 91, s. 2.
75 John McEldowney, 'Lord O'Hagan and the Irish Jury Act 1871' (PhD, Cambridge University, 1981), p. 85. 76 S. 1.

Although the qualifications had not dramatically changed, commentators in the decades following nevertheless complained vociferously about the standard of jurors empanelled under the act. For example, in 1845 the agent to Lord Clements, the earl of Leitrim, despaired of the standard of petty jurors at recent assizes, and implored the earl to:

> use your influence with [the sheriff] to get the highest cess payers and most respectable people called upon the petit juries in the criminal court ... If [he] could be persuaded to summon the class I allude to, we might easily write private letters to them specially requesting them to attend and serve.[77]

There was a common perception that the jurors were now of a lower social class and of lesser quality than those empanelled before 1833.[78] In part this can be attributed to the lack of care taken with the preparation of jury lists, discussed in chapter 2. Cess collectors simply could not know who was qualified as regards freeholds and leaseholds.

The issue of Catholic representation on trial juries came to the fore in the early decades of the nineteenth century. Despite the repeal of many of the penal laws by the late eighteenth century,[79] Catholics continued to be prevented from serving on juries by various means; they might not hold property in their own names, or they might only hold leases, because of the penal laws. As their names might not be returned on the list of qualified freeholders,[80] they might not be selected by a sheriff for a panel, or they might be challenged or set aside by the parties or the crown.[81] All of this gave rise to claims of jury packing,[82] and the Catholic emancipation movement, under Daniel O'Connell, began to agitate for more Catholic representation on juries. Even after the passing of the Catholic Relief Act in 1829,[83] some inequalities persisted, and Catholics continued to be under-represented.[84] The altered qualifications under the Juries (Ireland) Act, 1833, increased the proportion of Catholics on juries.[85] Inevitably complaints were made about the act's effect on the trials of Protestants. For example, Chief Constable Hatton told the 1839 committee on the state of Ireland that Roman Catholics were now much more confident of receiving a fair trial; Protestants less so.[86] William

77 *Letter from John Robert Godley to W.S. Clements*, 20 Mar. 1845: NLI, MS 36,060/3. Lord Clements, however, was uncomfortable with this: 'I should not feel myself authorised to give [the sheriff] any advice respecting the formation of the jury list, unless he were to ask me.' *Letter from W.S. Clements to John Godley*, 26 Mar. 1845 (NLI, MS 36,060/3).

78 *Report on the state of Ireland*, HC 1839 (486) xi, xii, 1, para. 1072 (George Warburton, retired Irish Constabulary officer) and para. 2258 (Hill Wilson Rowan, a Co. Down R.M.).

79 The Roman Catholic Relief Act, 1793 (33 Geo. 3, c. 21). See Eamon O'Flaherty, 'Ecclesiastical politics and the dismantling of the penal laws in Ireland, 1774–82', *I.H.S.*, 26:101 (1988), 33–50.

80 McEldowney notes that some tenants were denied leases by their landlords, and could not therefore qualify as jurors: John McEldowney, 'Lord O'Hagan', p. 93.

81 See pp 147–50. 82 See pp 136–56. 83 10 Geo. IV, c. 7.

84 See pp 45–6 and *State of Ireland (minutes of evidence)*, HL 1825 (20) vii, 1.

85 *Report on the state of Ireland*, HC 1839 (486) xi, xii, 1. 86 Ibid., paras 3037–9.

Kemmis, a crown solicitor, observed that Catholics in criminal cases now thought they had a better chance of acquittal.[87]

During the post-Famine period the 1833 act became 'virtually obsolete'.[88] Irish juror qualifications were increasingly out of step with England's, and the introduction of the Irish poor law in 1838 made this difficult to justify.[89] Coroners' jurors qualified on the basis of the poor-law rating of their land from 1846,[90] and the years following saw repeated calls to extend this basis of qualification to petty jurors, notably from the 1852 committee on outrages.[91] Thomas O'Hagan,[92] the liberal Catholic lord chancellor, sought to abolish the old qualifications[93] and widen the jury franchise.[94] With his act he proposed to 'put an end to existing qualifications and to substitute a simple and uniform qualification',[95] thus finally giving effect to the recommendations of the 1852 committee.[96] Under the Juries (Ireland) Act, 1871,[97] jurors in all cases were now to be rated for the relief of the poor with respect to lands of a specified annual value. The required rateable annual value of the property was adjusted to take into account variations in land values around the country.[98] In most counties the specified value was £20,[99] though it went as low as £12 in some districts. For example, in Antrim the qualification for common jurors was £20 in the countryside and £12 in cities and towns, while in the towns of Drogheda and Galway it was slightly higher at £15. The qualification in Leitrim was £12 in both urban and rural areas. Section 6 of the act 'absolutely freed and exempted' certain groups from jury service. While the list was similar to

87 Ibid., para. 7228.

88 *Report on Irish jury laws*, HL 1881 (430) xi, 1, para. 5. See also David Johnson, 'Trial by jury in Ireland 1860–1914', *J. Leg. Hist.*, 17:3 (1996) 270–91 at 271.

89 Poor Law (Ireland) Act, 1838 (1 & 2 Vic., c. 56).

90 Coroners (Ireland) Act, 1846 (9 & 10 Vic., c. 37), s. 23.

91 *Report on outrages (Ireland)*, HC 1852 (438) xiv, 1.

92 See John McEldowney, 'Lord O'Hagan (1812–1885): a study of his life and period as lord chancellor of Ireland (1868–1874)', *Ir. Jur.* (n.s.), 14 (1979), 360–77. See also John McEldowney, 'The case of *The queen v. McKenna* and jury packing in Ireland', *Ir. Jur.* (n.s.), 12 (1977), 339–54; Daire Hogan, 'Arrows too sharply pointed: the relations of Lord Justice Christian and Lord O'Hagan, 1868–1874' in John McEldowney and Paul O'Higgins (eds), *The common law tradition: essays in Irish legal history* (Dublin, 1990); F.E. Ball, *The judges in Ireland, 1221–1921* (London, 1926), p. 302; and E.J. Moore, 'Lord O'Hagan', *I.L.T. & S.J.*, 42 (1908), 255–6.

93 *Hansard 3*, ccvi, 1031 (19 May 1871) (HL).

94 O'Hagan proceeded in the aftermath of the McKenna scandal, at which the sub-sheriff of Monaghan had systematically excluded Catholics and inserted unqualified Protestants on the panel, to the extent that only 30 of the 150 jurors on the panel were legally qualified. McEldowney describes this case as a catalyst for reform: see McEldowney, '*The queen v. McKenna*'.

95 Ibid. 96 *Report on outrages 1852*, pp iii–iv. 97 34 & 35 Vic., c. 65, s. 5.

98 34 & 35 Vic., c. 65, sch. 4.

99 Before the Act came into effect, there was some confusion among officials as to how the lists were to be drawn up. See, e.g., Juries Act (Ireland), 1871: general list of jurors for the county of the city of Dublin. *Case on behalf of the crown submitted to the law officers 19 Sept. 1871* (NAI, CCS 1871 262).

those exempted under the Juries (Ireland) Act, 1833, some newly exempted groups were MPs, masters of vessels and licensed pilots, civil engineers, public notaries, actuaries, professors, schoolmasters and teachers. One group who lost their exemption were justices of the peace.[100] Others were barred from sitting on juries; these included outlaws and persons suffering from a disease or disability.

When the 1871 act came into effect at the 1873 spring assizes it was hit by a tidal wave of controversy and criticism. The newly qualified jurors were inexperienced, and, in the eyes of many, unfit for jury service. The *Freeman's Journal*, for example, commented on the 'ludicrous occurrences' at assizes around the country.[101] The *Tralee Chronicle* remarked that the operation of the act 'was not calculated to impress the public mind with a high opinion of this new palladium of liberty'.[102] It went on to describe the scene at the Clare assizes:

> The 'bold peasantry' crowded into the box, and for thirty minutes the occupants of the court were kept almost in continuous laughter, which was even indulged in by the sedate and serious judge, by the stupid blundering of the jurors, some of whom persisted in answering for others and hardly could know their own names. After a great deal of endless confusion, when the traversers were arraigned, it was discovered that the foreman could neither read nor write, and that others never spoke except in the old Celtic tongue, and not being adept in the language, his lordship could not of course address them.[103]

Aside from providing spectators with entertainment, a more troubling characteristic of the new jurors was their apparent reluctance to convict in criminal cases. This could be attributed to the fact that jurors were now drawn from the same social class as many criminal defendants. Antipathy towards the criminal justice system, coupled with their inexperience and confusion about their role, also appear to have contributed to this. There was certainly a strong public perception that the new jurors would not convict. The *Daily Express* reported for example that 'criminals have enjoyed a jubilee since the passing of the act'.[104] Stories about incompetent jurors were reported widely, along with tales of jurors who refused to convict even in the face of clear evidence. The relative poverty of the new jurors was also remarked upon by a number of judges: Whiteside C.J. described the jurors of Clonmel, Co. Tipperary as 'very ill-dressed and poor looking persons',[105] and Fitzgerald J. commented that some of the jurors in Cork were 'of great poverty', while others were infirm, or 'plainly in that position in life that ought not to have been upon the jurors' book at all'.[106] Barry J. described his experience thus:

100 They had previously been allowed to sit on juries except at any sessions of the peace within their own jurisdiction (3 & 4 Will. IV, c. 91, s. 38).
101 *Freeman's Journal*, 8 Mar. 1873. 102 *Tralee Chronicle*, 25 Feb. 1873.
103 The judge at the assizes was O'Brien J. 104 *Daily Express*, 28 Feb. 1873.
105 *Report on juries (Ireland)*, HC 1873 (283) xv, 389, para. 4230. 106 Ibid., para. 3222.

> When I went into court I was amazed at the crowd in court of, apparently, a very inferior class of peasants … I asked who were all those men, and I was told that they were the jurors. I was really aghast. Without saying anything disparaging, you had nothing to do but look at the men to see that they were of a class entirely unfit to cope …[107]

The *Daily Express* derided the new jurors as 'utterly illiterate' and 'even deficient in common intelligence'.[108] The perceived lack of intelligence of the new jurors stemmed from their low levels of experience, literacy and, in some cases, proficiency in the English language. For example, at one assize, a juror was reported to be confused by the term 'gaol delivery', and thought it was his duty to release all prisoners from gaol.[109] At another trial, a defendant was convicted of perjury and the following day five jurors called on the judge and said they had not agreed to the verdict. When asked why they had not expressed their dissent when the verdict was delivered, they said 'that they understood neither the nature of the case nor the question put to the foreman'.[110] In the words of R.W. Ireland, writing about Welsh juries around this period, it was 'difficult to believe that a poor man might be clever'.[111] A typical observation was that 'their minds are not sufficiently trained for the delicate discrimination and weighing of evidence'.[112] In the face of such complaints, more optimistic commentators such as O'Hagan himself and Fitzgerald J. were firmly of the view that the national school system would eventually ensure certain basic literacy levels for all jurors.[113] Although a prominent Catholic, the enfranchisement of Catholics as jurors had not been O'Hagan's sole motivation in introducing this legislation. As president of the Statistical Society, he was a social reformer. He was motivated by a desire to see those who had 'suffered perpetual exclusion' given the chance, as he saw it, to benefit from 'that moral and political training which has been of such profit to the English race, from their continual opportunities of taking a public and responsible part in the administration of justice'.[114]

Although one of O'Hagan's aims had been to broaden the jury franchise and introduce greater diversity in the jury box, in fact in many instances the act had the opposite effect, and resulted in quite homogenous juries. The demographic spread, coupled with the rating qualification, meant that in most counties, the jurors from rural areas generally outnumbered those from towns. Evidence presented to the 1873 committee demonstrated that there had been a sharp increase in the

107 *Report on Irish jury laws, 1881*, para. 1463 (Barry J.).
108 *Daily Express*, 7 Mar. 1873. 109 *Freeman's Journal*, 8 Mar. 1873.
110 *Daily Express*, 11 Mar. 1873.
111 R.W. Ireland, 'Putting oneself on whose county? Carmarthenshire juries in the mid-nineteenth century' in T.G. Watkin (ed.), *Legal Wales: its past, its future* (Cardiff, 2001), p. 74.
112 *Report on juries*, 1873, para. 3100 (Charles Kelly, the chairman of Co. Clare).
113 Ibid., para. 3224 (Fitzgerald), and T. O'Hagan, 'Legal, educational and social reforms in Ireland' in T. O'Hagan, *Occasional papers and addresses* (London, 1884), p. 355.
114 O'Hagan, 'Legal, educational and social reforms', p. 354.

proportion of farmers on some assizes panels; for example, the proportion of farmers on the panel for the Limerick assizes increased from just under 50 per cent to just over 90 per cent between spring 1872 and summer 1873.[115] In Cork, the jump was from about 11 per cent to over 70 per cent.[116] However, these figures may not have been representative, as in some other counties the overall percentage of farmers on the jurors' books did not significantly increase. For example, a study of the books for Co. Carlow demonstrates that the percentage of farmers in 1870 was already high at 86 per cent,[117] and there was no change in 1873, though it dropped slightly to 83 per cent in 1874.[118] Although the proportion of farmers may not have altered in some places, the farmers now serving were likely to have more modest holdings than previously, because of the low rating qualification. So in the mid-1870s, farmers represented the vast majority of jurors in most counties, making it likely that the interests of farmers would be strongly upheld in the courts in both civil and criminal contexts.

One of the more welcome effects of the 1871 act was the overall increase in the number of men qualified to sit on juries. In the country as a whole, the number of men qualified to sit on juries rose by about 38,000.[119] Some areas saw significant increases: the number of jurors in Co. Antrim increased from an average of 5,285 to 7,836.[120] In King's County (Offaly) there was a fourfold increase from 365 to 1527. Areas with lower land values such as Cavan, Monaghan and Sligo tended to see the most dramatic increases. However, the change was less perceptible in other areas. The Co. Clare jurors' book remained steady at 1,100 names in 1870, 1,096 in 1873 and 1015 in 1875.[121] In Co. Carlow, there were 1,155 jurors in 1870 and 1,223 in 1873 – only a slight increase.[122]

Regardless of regional variations, the general increase in the number of farmers serving on juries was somewhat unfortunate. Although it was seen as a positive development in terms of securing convictions for larceny and damage to property,[123] the timing of the change to jurors' qualifications could not have been worse.[124] As O'Hagan himself later admitted, it 'had gone before its time';[125]

115 *Report on juries*, 1873, para. 3223 (Fitzgerald).

116 At the 1872 summer assizes there were 22 farmers out of a total of 189 jurors, while in spring 1873 there were 174 out of 240. *Report on juries, 1873*, para. 3223.

117 In Co. Clare, similarly, farmers comprised 88% of the jurors' book in 1870.

118 *Carlow jurors' books, 1870–5* (NAI, 1C-12–87).

119 Data taken the *Report on juries*, 1873, app. 1, p. 691: 'Return, by the clerks of the peace, of the number of jurors on the "jurors' book" for the last three years, and for the present year.'

120 Ibid. 121 *Clare general and special jurors' books, 1868–75* (NAI, 1D-34–64).

122 *Carlow jurors' books, 1870–5* (NAI, 1C-12–87).

123 *Report on jury laws, 1874*, para. 9 (James Hamilton, chairman of Co. Sligo). He said 'jurors are willing enough to convict in petty larceny cases. They are principally farmers, and if a person is indicted for stealing a sheep or a cow, they are very willing to convict indeed.'

124 See W.E. Vaughan, *Murder trials in Ireland* (Dublin, 2009), p. 141.

125 David Johnson, 'The trials of Sam Gray: Monaghan politics and nineteenth century Irish criminal procedure', *Ir. Jur.* (n.s.), 20 (1985), 109–34, 133.

circumstances were 'greatly unfavourable' to the working of the new system, and the 'waves of popular passion' would have 'strained any system, whatever might have been its form or substance'.[126] It was this factor more than any other that made O'Hagan's reforms virtually unworkable. O'Hagan's speech to the Social Sciences Congress in 1881 betrays some bitterness in his defence of the act. He pointed to the many failed bills introduced in the 1850s and '60s by successive law officers. His own bill, he said, had been sent down to the house of commons 'after the fullest opportunity for deliberation, and after it had been circulated throughout Ireland for a considerable time. No single objection [he said] was made in parliament or by the press to any of its provisions', and it was scarcely amended in the house of commons. 'It passed, apparently, with universal assent.'[127] But afterwards, 'a great outcry was raised against it'.[128]

In the face of ridicule and the 'ostentatious parading'[129] of the shortcomings of the act, a committee was appointed to inquire into its operation.[130] Almost immediately, this committee issued a preliminary report, stating that the rating qualification had 'placed on the jurors' books the names of persons who are not qualified in point of intelligence to serve as jurors'.[131] The committee's recommendations were given expression in a temporary act of 1873.[132] This raised the rating qualification for jurors in rural areas to £30,[133] and exempted persons who could not read and write the English language, as well as persons suffering disabilities such as deafness or blindness.[134] Unsurprisingly, the number of qualified jurors plummeted in some areas: in Carlow, the general jury list was halved from 1,223 to just 626 names in 1874.[135]

Although the general opinion was that the 1873 act had helped to improve the standards of juries, further amendment was still desirable, as the jurors were still considered 'quite inadequate to discharge their duties'.[136] The parliamentary committee was re-appointed, and its final report in 1874 concluded that the rating qualifications introduced in 1871 were too low, and that some of the sums fixed by the 1873 act also needed to be raised.[137] The various recommendations were eventually embodied in two acts of 1876 – the Juries (Procedure) Ireland Act[138] and

126 O'Hagan, 'Legal, educational and social reforms', p. 355.
127 Ibid., p. 353. 128 Ibid., p. 354. 129 *Report on juries, 1873*, para. 556 (de Moleyns).
130 See Anon., 'Irish juries', *I.L.T. & S.J.*, 7 (1873), 284. 131 *Report on juries 1873*, p. iii.
132 Juries (Ireland) (Amendment) Act, 1873 (36 & 37 Vic., c. 27).
133 36 & 37 Vic., c. 27, sch. 1. The rating in towns ranged from £12 to £20.
134 S. 1. It also altered the upper age limit for jury service, lowering it from 65 to 60 years as part of the attempt to increase the number of suitable jurors: Juries (Ireland) Act, 1873 (36 & 37 Vic., c. 27), s. 3. See Anon., 'The bill to amend the law relating to juries', *I.L.T. & S.J.*, 6 (1872), 326–7. In England, the upper age limit for jurors was 60 from 1825 onwards: the Juries Act, 1825 (6 Geo. IV, s. 50), s. 1; this was not altered by the Juries Act, 1870 (33 & 34 Vic., c. 77).
135 *Carlow jurors' books, 1870–5* (NAI, 1C-12-87).
136 *Report on jury system, 1874*, para. 3 (Hamilton).
137 As expressed by Anon., 'The Jury Act', *I.L.T. & S.J.*, 7 (1873), 167, '[t]he principle involved in it is right, but the qualification is, for the minute, too low'.
138 39 & 40 Vic., c. 78.

the Juries (Qualification) Ireland Act.[139] The latter raised the rating qualification for lands in rural areas from £30 to £40, and reduced the qualifications for private homes, offices and curtilage from £12 or £20[140] to either £6 or £10.[141] The act distinguished between cities and counties: in Dublin, Cork, Limerick and Waterford, the new rating was £20, while in the towns of Kilkenny, Carrickfergus, Drogheda and Galway it was £15. In most instances, the qualification for urban dwellers was reduced, while for those in the countryside it was increased. This was generally welcomed as excluding inexperienced and incompetent jurors.[142] The lowering of the qualification from £12 to £10 in towns was not, however, met with such unreserved approval.[143]

The Juries (Procedure) Ireland Act, 1876 also adjusted the exemptions from jury service. Overall, the exemptions under the 1871 act had been extensive, and in the view of some, excessive.[144] When proposals were made to raise the rating qualification for jurors in 1873, it was also suggested that this be accompanied by a narrowing of the exempted categories, so as to maintain a sufficient pool of jurors. The Juries (Procedure) Ireland Act, 1876, however, introduced new categories of exempted persons, such as 'persons who cannot read or write the English language', practising pharmaceutical chemists and small publicans.[145] This was largely in response to the moral panic over the constitution of juries following the 1871 act; however, it exacerbated the difficulties in securing sufficient numbers of jurors, particularly those from the wealthier classes. The exemptions in Ireland were not nearly as numerous as those in England, probably because to exempt too many would have further depleted the pool of qualified jurors.[146] Nevertheless, there was a general feeling that the 1876 legislation had gone too far. Witnesses before the 1881 parliamentary committee complained that the number of exempt classes was too great, and called for a limitation,[147] but the Juries (Procedure) Ireland Act, 1876 remained unamended and was the principal piece of legislation governing the qualifications for jurors until the twentieth century.[148] The Juries Act, 1927 retained the property rating as the basis for jury qualification, and it was not until the 1970s that this was abolished in favour of qualification based on citizenship.

139 39 & 40 Vic., c. 21. 140 36 & 37 Vic., c. 27, sch.1. 141 39 & 40 Vic., c. 21, sch. 2.

142 *Report on Irish jury laws, 1881*, paras 305, 321 (Lewis Mansergh Buchanan, clerk of the peace for Co. Tyrone).

143 Ibid., paras 1532–3 (William Edward Whelan, a Portadown R.M.).

144 See, e.g., Anon., 'The bill to amend the law relating to juries', *I.L.T. & S.J.*, 6 (1872), 326–7.

145 39 & 40 Vic., c. 78, s. 20.

146 Under the English Juries Act, 1870 (33 & 34 Vic., c. 77), the schedule of exempt persons was considerably longer than that contained in the Juries Procedure (Ireland) Act, 1876 (39 & 40 Vic., c. 78), and specifically listed, inter alia, judges, Roman Catholic priests, Jewish rabbis, certified conveyancers, special pleaders, coroners and gaolers. Another controversial group exempted in England were the income-tax commissioners.

147 *Report on Irish jury laws, 1881*, para. 2982 (Fitzgerald) and para. 790 (John Byrne, collector general of rates in Dublin).

148 39 & 40 Vic., c. 78.

CONCLUSION

Grand and common juries were the principal categories of jury determining the majority of civil and criminal matters in the Irish courts. They were frequently the subject of discussion, derision and reform – more so in Ireland than in England. As later chapters will demonstrate, common juries often operated under difficult conditions, and it could be challenging to ensure that sufficient numbers of qualified men participated in jury service. This was in marked contrast to conditions enjoyed by grand juries, which generally had well-appointed rooms and a prominent position in local society and politics.

CHAPTER FOUR

The special jury

IN ADDITION TO THE COMMON JURY, a second category of petty jury was the special jury. Its origins are somewhat obscure,[1] with some commentators considering it to have evolved from trials at bar, which will be discussed below. Although the practice of using specialised juries had long existed, the first express statutory reference to the special jury as understood here was in England in 1696.[2] It is clear that special juries were well established by the eighteenth century,[3] and were frequently used by Lord Mansfield in commercial cases in London.[4] Analogies can be drawn between special juries and attaint juries, which were generally of higher standing than juries that were the subject of attaint proceedings.[5] The practice of using jurors of high standing or social class can also be seen with the trial of peers. Oldham points out that a special jury might satisfy any of the following definitions: 'a jury of individuals of a higher class than usual; a jury of experts; and a "struck jury"'.[6] In the 1820s a Dublin solicitor observed that he usually preferred 'an intelligent and well informed jury', and 'these were likely to be got by applying for a special jury'.[7]

1 See *R v. Edmonds* (1821) 4 B. & Ald. 476; 106 E.R. 1009; and J. Thayer, *A preliminary treatise on evidence at the common law* (London, 1898), p. 94. The special jury appears to have its roots in the grand assizes, and it has been pointed out that the recognitors of the grand assizes bore a 'strong resemblance' to the nineteenth-century method of striking a jury, though 'crude in form': W. Huband, *Practical treatise* (rev. ed., Dublin, 1911), p. 96. The importance of the dispute in question meant that it was to be tried by a group of knights, as this rank implied ownership of land valued at not less than £40 per annum. See C. Flower (ed.), *Introduction to the curia regis rolls, 1199–1230 A.D.* (London, 1943), p. 130. See also G.D.G. Hall (ed.), *The treatise on the laws and customs of the realm of England commonly called Glanvill* (London, 1965), pp 10–12; and S. Thorne (ed.), *Bracton on the laws and customs of England*, 4 vols (London, 1977), f. 331b.

2 Ease of Jurors Act, 1702 (7 & 8 Will. III, c. 32).

3 See the Juries Regulation Act, 1755 (29 Geo. II, c. 6), and the Special Juries Act, 1777–8 (17 & 18 Geo. III, c. 45). In England, the Regulation of Juries Act, 1730 (3 Geo. II, c. 35) indicated that special juries were well-established.

4 See James C. Oldham, *The Mansfield manuscripts and the growth of English law in the eighteenth century* (Chapel Hill, NC, 1992).

5 James C. Oldham, 'The origins of the special jury', *U. Chic. L. Rev.*, 50 (1983), 137–211 at 162.

6 Oldham, 'Origins', 139. By the early eighteenth century, the term 'special jury' had become synonymous with 'struck jury'.

7 *Fifteenth report on salaries*, HC 1826 (310) xvii, 29, p. 540.

QUALIFICATIONS

Special jurors' qualifications always differed somewhat to those of common jurors, although this was often a matter of practice rather than legislation.[8] As well as meeting the £10 freehold or £15 leasehold qualification, the Juries (Ireland) Act, 1833 stated that the following men qualified:

> sons of peers ... baronets, knights, magistrates, persons who have served or been returned to serve as sheriff or grand juror at assize, and ... all bankers and wholesale merchants who do not exercise retail trades, and ... all trades who are possessed of personal property of the value of five thousand pounds, and the eldest sons of such persons respectively.[9]

These additional categories were at the suggestion of the judiciary.[10] The act also provided that if there were insufficient persons matching these descriptions on the general jurors' book, then the sheriff could return the names of a number of other persons, 'consideration being had of the rank and property of such persons'.

Because of the perennial problem of the lack of a substantial middle class in Ireland, there were more categories of person who qualified as special jurors than there were in England. In England, a special juror was 'a man ... described in the jurors book ... as an esquire or person of higher degree, or as a banker or merchant'.[11] When the 1833 act was being drafted, there was a view expressed by the Irish judges that the term 'esquire' was not properly understood or used in Ireland, and its application was 'nearly arbitrary and indiscriminate'.[12] There was overlap between the two countries when it came to bankers and merchants, but it was deemed necessary in the Irish act to stipulate that the merchants could not carry out any retail trade. There were also differing interpretations of what was meant by 'merchant' generally.[13]

As with common juries, a rateable qualification was introduced for special juries by the Juries Act (Ireland), 1871.[14] It set out different rateable qualifications for different counties and towns.[15] Account was taken of the variations in land values between counties. In most counties a special juror had to have rateable property to

8 For example, the Special Juries Act, 1777–8 did not mention specific qualifications for special juries (17 & 18 Geo. III, c. 45).

9 3 & 4 Will. IV, c. 91, s. 24.

10 *Letter regarding the jury bill, 1833* (NAI, OP/1833/14).

11 6 Geo. IV, c. 50, s. 31. This legislation formalized existing practice when it came to special jurors' qualifications.

12 *Letter regarding the jury bill, 1833* (NAI, OP/1833/14).

13 See, for example, *Index to the report on special and common juries*, HC 1867–8 (401) (401–I) xii, 677, 759, p. 47 (Erle).

14 The English Juries Act, 1870 (33 & 34 Vic., c. 77), s. 6, also introduced special juror qualifications based on the rateable value of property. Esquires, bankers or merchants could still qualify in accordance with the English Juries Act, 1825 (6 Geo. IV, c. 50).

15 See Juries (Ireland) Act, 1871 (34 & 35 Vic., c. 65), sch. iv.

the value of £50 or £100, whereas in towns such as Drogheda and Carrickfergus, and cities such as Galway and Kilkenny, the value was £30.[16] The Juries (Ireland) (Amendment) Act, 1873 raised the qualifications for special jurors in most counties to £150, and in most towns to between £50 and £100.[17] The qualifications were further amended in 1876, with even greater distinctions between and within counties; for example, in Meath and Kildare a special juror had to have £150 rateable property, while in counties such as Monaghan and Sligo the qualification was £70 in rural areas and £50 in urban areas.[18] Towns such as Waterford, Carrickfergus and Drogheda retained their £30 qualification.

Who were the special jurors? An examination of some individual special jurors' books indicates that they were drawn from a wide variety of trades and professions. For example, the 1844 Dublin special jurors' book included pawnbrokers, booksellers, haberdashers, bonnet makers, innkeepers, tanners, publicans, bakers, dentists and druggists. There were coal, cloth and tea merchants, as well as manufacturers of shoes, coaches, cabinets, clocks and guns. Less than a quarter were designated 'gentleman' or 'esquire'.[19] Dublin special jurors by mid-century were not necessarily drawn from the upper echelons of society, but represented the middle-class businessmen and tradesmen of the city. While there were different qualifications and procedures, and special jurors were paid for their service,[20] socially and financially there may not have been great differences between special and common jurors by the mid-nineteenth century. For example, the Dublin general jurors' book for 1852 contains a similar cross section of professions and businesses, such as bootmakers, pawnbrokers and merchants, alongside men of lesser means such as soap boilers, weavers and coopers.[21]

The very wealthy were usually exempted from jury service altogether, as discussed in chapter 3, and in 1873 most special jurors were rated for less than £200. Table 4.1 shows the spread of special jurors in each county in 1873, based on figures presented to the 1873 select committee on the Irish jury laws. There were

16 Under the English Juries Act, 1870 (33 & 34 Vic., c. 77), in England and Wales the property qualification was higher. Persons living in a town of 20,000 inhabitants had to occupy a private dwelling house rated at not less than £100. For smaller towns, the requirement was £60. Farms were to be valued at £500, and other premises were to be at £20.

17 36 & 37 Vic., c. 27, sch. 2. The exceptions to this were Leitrim, where the value was just £50, and Cavan, Donegal, Fermanagh, Kerry, Longford, Louth, Mayo, Monaghan, Sligo and Tyrone, where it was £70.

18 See Jurors Qualification (Ireland) Act, 1876 (39 & 40 Vic., c. 21), sch. i.

19 Lobban writes that in England, wealthy men of business who wished to avoid jury service generally described themselves as 'gentlemen', so that they would instead be listed as common jurors. Michael Lobban, 'The strange life of the English civil jury, 1837–1914' in John W. Cairns and Grant McLeod, *The dearest birth right of the people of England: the jury trial in the history of common law* (Oxford, 2002), p. 201. Only merchants, esquires and bankers qualified as special juries under the English Juries Act, 1825. Because the common jury list was so much larger, they were less likely to be called upon to serve. This practice would not have worked in Ireland because the various categories of special jury included gentlemen, but reluctant jurors may have engaged in something like it.

20 See pp 120–1. 21 *Dublin jurors' list*, 1852 (NLI, MS 3103).

Table 4.1 Number of qualified special jurors in each county in Ireland, 1873

	Rateable property									
	£30	£30–40	£40–50	£50–80	£80–100	£100–150	£150–200	£200+	Other	Total
Antrim				935	282	314	141	310	n/a	1,982
Armagh				452	88	97	34	47	n/a	718
Carlow	1	2	1	214	63	66	46	52	30	475
Carrickfergus		32	15	19	9	12	3	5		95
Cavan				166	41	51	16	24	n/a	296
Clare				300	62	96	466	68	n/a	572
Cork						439	185	191	n/a	815
Cork City				169	45	34	15	25	24	312
Donegal	1	4	2	243	57	65	27	19	27	445
Down										
Drogheda		13	5	3	2	1	3	1	3	31
Dublin										
Dublin City										48
Fermanagh				48	48	46	13	20		175
Galway				224	74	116	82	159	38	693
Galway Town		37	13	27	8	15	5	14	21	140
Kerry				329	69	66	19	20	18	521
Kildare						164	75	158	n/a	397
Kilkenny				572	146	182	71	74		1,045
Kilkenny City		23	9	18	4	3			9	66
King's Co.				221	62	90	53	72	32	440
Leitrim	3	132	57	82	13	18	5	14	23	347
Limerick	1			4	3	237	116	107	67	535
Limerick City		2	44	63	12	17	3	7	2	150
Londonderry		1	1	345	95	96	33	45	36	652
Longford				134	36	39	21	24		254
Louth			2	142	39	64	31	61	n/a	339
Mayo		1	1	141	38	56	43	50	62	192
Meath						208	100	285	57	650
Monaghan			2	167	455	36	11	19	22	302
Queen's Co.				254	72	114	47	63	33	583
Roscommon				119	31	55	25	64	41	335
Sligo		2		141	40	29	22	42	33	309
Tipperary						286	138	217		636
Tyrone				318	84	64	21	26	n/a	513
Waterford	1	3	3	550	181	206	83	57	7	1,091
Waterford City		38	37	21	7	14	4	8		133
Westmeath						124	53	96	55	328
Wexford				542	146	179	53	65	72	1,057
Wicklow				211	61	87	72	55	n/a	486

These figures are taken from the *Report on juries, 1873*, app. 1, p. 692 [288]: 'Return by sheriffs of the number of jurors on "special jurors' book"'. There were no figures available for Dublin, Dublin City or Co. Down. 'Other' refers to special jurors who qualified by reason other than the property qualification introduced in 1871. These were the sons of peers, baronets, knights, magistrates; there was no information on jurors in this category in Antrim.

few special jurors rated at more than £150 and relatively few with less than £30, with the majority drawn from the middle section. There were only seven special jurors in the whole country rated for less than £30, and 290 rated between £30 and £40.

It is also evident from these statistics that the number and proportion of special juries in each county or town varied considerably. Antrim had the highest total number of special jurors, at 1,982. This represented around 0.5 per cent of the total population for the county.[22] Fermanagh had only 175 special jurors, representing around 0.2 per cent of the county's total population.[23] There was also variation when it came to towns and cities. Drogheda had 31 special jurors for a population of over 16,000, which similarly represented roughly 0.2 per cent of the town's population.[24] Waterford city had 133 special jurors, which represented roughly 0.4 per cent of the population.[25] By 1880 the number of special jurors had fallen to 102 in Waterford, which was still a high proportion of the total number of jurors for the city. It represented around one-third of the 282 qualified jurors.[26] The decrease in population in the city meant that special jurors now represented roughly 0.7 per cent of the population.[27] This possibly meant a reduction of the burden of service for qualified special jurors, something that will be further discussed in chapter 8.

THE USE OF SPECIAL JURIES

From the mid-eighteenth century to the mid-nineteenth century, special juries became increasingly popular,[28] to the extent that an act passed in 1800 noted that they were 'frequently applied for in small or trivial cases'.[29] In a twelve-month period in the second decade of the nineteenth century there were twenty-seven special juries summoned in Dublin.[30] Civil actions such as libel, bribery, assumpsit and ejectment were often tried by such juries,[31] and in some civil actions there was

22 *Census of Ireland, 1881* [C-2931] HC 1881 xcvi, 159. The total population for Co. Antrim in 1871 was 404,015.
23 Ibid. The population of Fermanagh in 1871 was 92,174.
24 Ibid. The population of Drogheda in 1871 was 16,165.
25 Ibid. The population of the city of Waterford in 1871 was 29,979.
26 City of Waterford general jurors' book 1880 (NLI, MS 11,290).
27 The population of the city of Waterford in 1881 was 28,952. *Census of Ireland for the year 1881*.
28 James C. Oldham, 'Special juries in England: nineteenth century usage and reform', *J. Leg. Hist.*, 8 (1987), 148–66 at 152.
29 Jury Act, 1800 (40 Geo. III, c. 72), s. 6.
30 *Returns of writs lodged and fees received*, HC 1818 (417) xvi, 429.
31 Libel: *Hughes v. Shirley* (1866) 16 I.C.L.R. app. 6; *Spong v. Fahy* (1855) 5 I.C.L.R. 353; and *Barrett v. Long* (1851) 3 HL 395; 10 E.R. 154. Bribery: *M'Lester v. Fegan* (1859) 9 I.C.L.R. app. 44; 5 Ir. Jur. (n.s.) 70; *Magee v. Mark* (1860) 5 Ir. Jur. (n.s.) 131; *Hempton v. Humphries* (1866) 11 Ir. Jur. (n.s.) 416. Assumpsit: *Dowdell v. Kelly* (1854) 6 Ir. Jur. (n.s.) 303. Ejectment: *Jack v. M'Intyre* (1845) 12 Cl. & F. 150; 8 E.R. 1356.

a statutory right to such a jury.[32] In many cases it was the perceived necessity of having jurors with a higher level of intelligence and understanding that led litigants in complex civil cases to seek special juries.[33] Sometimes a party applied for a special jury with the sole aim of delaying the trial, though by the nineteenth century this came to be regarded as an abuse of process.[34] The 1871 act provided, in response to the perceived abuse, that if a judge believed that a special jury was being sought merely for the purpose of delay, he could order that the case be tried by a common jury.[35]

On the criminal side, there generally could not be a special jury in cases of felony or treason – it was usually only available for misdemeanours.[36] The reason lay in the accused person's right to peremptory challenges in treason or felony trials.[37] However, coercive legislation dealing with crimes associated with agrarian disturbances during the Land War specifically provided for the use of special juries in felonies. In the aftermath of the Phoenix Park murders, the Prevention of Crimes (Ireland) Act, 1882 provided for the trial of certain criminal cases by special juries.[38] Further provision for trial of offences in proclaimed districts by special juries was made in 1887 by the Criminal Law and Procedure (Ireland) Act, and both of these acts will be considered further in chapters 10–13.[39]

Special juries were usually empanelled for trials at bar.[40] These were civil or criminal actions that were considered important enough to be tried by a panel of judges and a jury in one of the superior courts in Dublin instead of in the county

32 E.g. the Railways Act (Ireland), 1851 (14 & 15 Vic., c. 70), s. 26; see *Kehoe v. Great Southern and Western Rail Co.* (1886) 20 I.L.T.R. 27. See also the Railways Act (Ireland), 1864 (27 & 28 Vic., c. 71), s. 2; and the Lands Clauses Consolidation Act, 1845 (8 & 9 Vic., c. 18).

33 E.g. *Hirsch v. Beet Sugar Company* (1854) 6 Ir. Jur. (o.s.) 291 and *Harrison v. Lynch* (1854) 3 I.C.L.R. 256.

34 *First report on the superior courts of common law*, HC 1851 (1289) xxii, 567, p. 44.

35 Juries (Ireland) Act, 1871, s. 35. See *Gubba v. McKenna* (1838) 1 Jebb & S. 62 and *Cradock v. Davies* (1819) 1 Chit. Rep. 176.

36 E.g. *R v. Parnell* (1881–1882) 8 L.R. Ir. 17, *R v. Rowlands* (1851) 2 Den. 364; 169 E.R. 540. T. Purcell, *A summary of the criminal law of Ireland* (Dublin, 1848), p. 161.

37 As will be discussed in chapter 10, the defendant in a felony trial was entitled to 35 or, after 1828, 20 peremptory challenges: Criminal Law (Ireland) Act, 1828 (9 Geo. IV, c. 54). In criminal special-jury cases, 48 jurors were brought before the master, and he struck off 24. If treason or a felony were to be tried by a special jury, this would deny the defendant the advantage of peremptorily challenging. In misdemeanours, however, there was only a right to 6 peremptory challenges, which could be accommodated within the framework of the special jury procedure. A practice later arose of restricting peremptory challenges to capital cases.

38 45 & 46 Vic., c. 25, s. 4. The Phoenix Park murders were the murders of Lord Frederick Cavendish, the chief secretary, and his undersecretary, T.H. Burke, by the Invincibles in the Phoenix Park on 6 May 1882. A number of cases were tried under these provisions, including *The trials of William Ryan, Thomas Ryan, Thomas Bradley, John Downey, Richard Phelan and James Phelan and others for riotious assembly and forcible taking of cattle (of Richard Mooney) and taking possession of houses and land, and expelling Mooney with force and violence at the Leinster winter assize, 1882* (NAI, CCS/1890/1).

39 50 & 51 Vic., c. 20, s. 9.

40 E.g. *R v. Fitzpatrick* (1813) 31 How. St. Tr. 1170.

where the action arose. According to Blackstone, special juries 'were originally introduced in trials at bar, when the causes were of too great nicety for the discussion of ordinary freeholders; or where the sheriff was suspected of partiality'.[41] Trials at bar were comparatively rare, and 'allowed only in cases of great magnitude and particular difficulty'.[42] From 1809 to 1819, for example, there were seven trials at bar on the crown side of the king's bench and seven in the common pleas.[43] The attorney general could demand a trial at bar in any case where the crown had an interest in the outcome. Such interest could result from the crown being 'a party to the action or proceeding, or because the matter in litigation affects the revenues or property of the crown, or because one of the officers of the crown has been sued for acts done by him as such officer'.[44] In trials at bar, the jurors could either be summoned from the county where the cause of action arose, or from another county in order to ensure their impartiality.[45] Either way, additional costs would be incurred to cover their expenses. There were perceived advantages of having a case heard by several judges instead of just one; the *Freeman's Journal* observed in 1843 that:

> in addition to the manifest advantage accruing to both prosecutors and the prosecuted from having a full court and not an individual judge to decide upon the admissibility or non-admissibility of the evidence offered, there is in a trial at bar the no less important advantage of the three judges acting as a check to the impetuosity of the charging chief, or should he in his charge to the jury be too lenient to the accused, each of the three judges has it in his power to correct the impression his address was calculated to make by separately charging the jury, or expressing his reasons for dissenting from the views of the chief.[46]

It must have been quite difficult for jurors in these situations to reconcile the clashing views and directions coming from the bench.

In Ireland, many high-profile political prosecutions took place at bar,[47] including the trials of Archibald Hamilton Rowan for seditious libel; William Drennan for

41 W. Blackstone, *Commentaries on the laws of England*, 4 vols (London, 1791), iii, p. 358.

42 *The seventh report on salaries*, HC 1819–20 (33) iii, 51, p. 38.

43 Ibid., apps 54 and 55.

44 W.G. Huband, *A practical treatise on the law relating to the grand jury in criminal cases, the coroner's jury and the petty jury in Ireland* (Dublin, 1896), p. 296.

45 *Attorney general v. The primate* (1837) 2 Jones 362 was tried at the bar of the court of exchequer in 1832 before a Cavan special jury. See *Court of exchequer, Ireland*, HC 1833 (4437) xxxi, 463. *Lord Sherborne v. Naper* was tried before special juries from both Westmeath and Dublin: see W. Hooper, *The birth of the law of illegitimacy: a treatise on the law affecting persons of illegitimate birth, with the rules of evidence in proof of legitimacy and illegitimacy, and an historical account of the bastard in mediaeval law* (London, 1911), pp 142–3.

46 *Freeman's Journal*, 24 Nov. 1843.

47 High-profile English trials at bar included the trial in 1903 of Australian Arthur Lynch, a Galway MP, for pro-Boer activities during the Boer war; the trial of Sir Leander Starr Jameson in 1896

sedition; Justice Robert Johnson for libel; Daniel O'Connell for conspiracy; and Charles Stewart Parnell.[48] Parnell was arrested and charged with conspiracy in 1881 for inciting tenants to refuse to pay rents, causing 'a major political sensation'.[49] Within days the Land League launched its 'no rent' manifesto, and less than a week later the league was suppressed as an illegal organisation.[50] The trial took place at bar before a special jury of the city of Dublin, struck under the 'old system',[51] and Parnell was acquitted. In 1886, a number of MPs – including John Dillon, Daniel Crilly and others – were arrested and were charged with soliciting tenants not to pay their rents under the Plan of Campaign.[52] The defendants sought a trial at bar, claiming that the matters arising in the case were of 'grave public importance'. If the trial at bar were granted, the case would be tried by a special jury struck under the old system and both sides would have the opportunity of striking off twelve jurors; if the trial took place before a common jury, then the crown could exercise its power to order numbers of jurors to 'stand by', and this might be to the defendants' disadvantage. The application was refused.

Civil cases could also be tried at bar, for example the well-known case of *Craig d. Annesley v. Earl of Anglesey*,[53] the facts of which formed the basis for Rudyard Kipling's *Kidnapped* (1886). Other examples of civil trials at bar include *Lloyd v. Trimlestown* and *Attorney general v. The primate*, an action to recover lands in Co. Cavan claimed to be crown property.[54] In 1855 a dispute over the legitimacy of the

following the Jameson Raid in South Africa, and the trial of the *Tichborne* case: see Douglas Woodruff, *The Tichborne claimant: a Victorian mystery* (London, 1957) and Edward Kenneally, *The trial at bar of sir Roger C.D. Tichborne, bart., in the court of queen's bench at Westminster, before Lord Chief Justice Cockburn, Mr Justice Mellor, & Mr Justice Lush, for perjury* (London, 1875).

48 Archibald Hamilton Rowan, *A full report of the trial at bar, in the court of king's bench, in which the rt. hon. Arthur Wolfe, his majesty's attorney general, prosecuted, and A.H. Rowan, esq., was defendant* (Dublin, 1794). Rowan was a founding member of the Society of United Irishmen; John Francis Larkin (ed.), *The trial of William Drennan on a trial of sedition, in the year 1794 and his intended defence* (Dublin, 1991); Anon., *Report of the trial at bar of the hon. Mr. Justice Johnson, one of the judges of his majesty's court of common pleas in Ireland, for a libel* (London, 1806). *R v. O'Connell and others* (1844) 11 Cl. & F. 155; 8 E.R. 1061 (1843–6) 1 Cox C.C. 379, see *Freeman's Journal*, 24 Nov. 1843; I. Holloway, *'O'Connell v. The queen:* a sesquicentennial remembrance' *N.I.L.Q.*, 46 (1995) 63–71; and Myles Dungan, *Conspiracy: Irish political trials* (Dublin, 2009), pp 96–121; *R v. Parnell and others* (1881–2) 8 L.R. Ir. 17.

49 See Anon., 'Mr Parnell's arrest', *I.L.T. & S.J.*, 15 (1881), 566; quotation from F.S.L. Lyons, *Charles Stewart Parnell* (London, 1977), p. 170.

50 Lyons, *Charles Stewart Parnell*, p. 177.

51 This term is explained in the next section.

52 See *R v. John Dillon (Habeas Corpus)* 6 Aug. 1888 in Anon., *Judgments of the superior courts in Ireland in cases under the Criminal Law and Procedure (Ireland) Act, 1887*, p. 181, and chapter 11.

53 (1743) Dick. 90; 21 E.R. 202, 17 St. Tr. 1139. The case was tried at the bar of the Irish court of exchequer. See also L. de la Torre, 'New light on Smollett and the Annesley Cause', *Rev. Eng. Stud.*, 22:87 (1971), 274–81.

54 John Hatchell, *Report of the trial of an issue, directed by the lord high chancellor of Ireland, wherin Maj. General Evan Lloyd, and Alicia Baroness Trimlestown, his wife, Peter Count Dalton, and Rosalic Countess*

heir to the late earl of Kilkenny was refused a trial at bar, with Pennefather B. noting that, 'It is always very objectionable to grant such a motion unless very special reasons are offered.'[55] It was not enough that there were to be numerous witnesses;[56] to secure a trial at bar, it was necessary that the legal matters concerned be in some way complex or difficult.[57] From the late eighteenth century, trials at bar were criticised for being expensive, lengthy and cumbersome.[58] In 1832 it was said that such trials made it 'impossible to dispose of the general business of the court'.[59] By the late nineteenth century, the use of trials at bar had waned, and in 1911 Huband noted that they were 'of comparatively rare occurrence'.[60]

SPECIAL JURY PROCEDURES

Until 1853, empanelling a special jury involved a specific procedure. When a party to a civil action requested such a jury, forty-eight names were selected by the sheriff from the special jurors' book. Each party then struck twelve names off this list;[61] thus this type of jury was sometimes known as a 'struck' jury. The parties were generally afforded a number of days to make enquiries as to the men listed, before choosing who to reject, and on a day appointed by the sheriff, they attended his office and the list was reduced to twenty-four.[62] These twenty-four were then returned for the trial, and the first twelve who answered when their names were called out, or who were not challenged, were sworn in as the jury for the trial. This procedure was replicated for every special jury case to be tried at the assizes or sessions.

These procedures remained in place until the Common Law Procedure (Amendment) Act Ireland, 1853 was passed.[63] This provided that instead of forty-

Dalton, his wife, were the plaintiffs, and the rt. hon. Thomas Lord Baron Trimlestown, was the defendant. Had before the rt. hon. William Downes, lord chief justice, and the hon. Judge Mayne, and a special jury of the county of Dublin, in the court of king's bench, Ireland (Dublin, 1819); (1837) 2 Jones 362.

55 *Butler v. Mountgarrett* (1855) 7 Ir. Jur. (o.s.) 149. See also (1856) 8 Ir. Jur. (o.s.) 474; and 7 H.L. 733.

56 *Jones, Lessee of Underwood v. Earl Courtown* (1794) Ridg. Lap. & Scho. 293.

57 See Anon., *The complete juryman; or, a compendium of the laws relating to jurors* (Dublin, 1774), p. 67; and T. Chitty, *Archbold's practice of the court of queen's bench*, 2 vols (London, 1845), i, p. 357.

58 E.g. *Jones, Lessee of Underwood v. Earl Courtown* (1794) Ridg. Lap. & Scho. 293; and *Seventh report on salaries*, pp 38–41. The committee noted, p. 39, that in the recent eight-day trial of Waller O'Grady at the bar of the king's bench, the clerk of the crown had charged £120 in fees. The full costs in this case were around £177. See Richard Wilson Greene, *A report on the proceedings upon an information in the nature of a quo warranto, at the suit of the king against Waller O'Grady, esq., respecting the right of appointment to the office of clerk of the peace in his majesty's court of exchequer, Ireland, tried at bar in the court of king's bench, Dublin* (Dublin, 1816).

59 *Attorney general v. Walsh* (1832) Hayes 550.

60 Huband, *Treatise*, p. 291.

61 See W. Style, *The practical register* (2nd ed., London, 1670), p. 239; (3rd ed., London, 1694), pp 288–9.

62 See W.D. Ferguson, *A treatise on the practice of the queen's bench, common pleas and exchequer of pleas in Ireland, in personal actions and ejectments* (Dublin, 1841), p. 321.

63 16 & 17 Vic., c. 113, s. 112. See the English Common Law Procedure Act, 1852 (15 & 16 Vic., c. 113).

eight special jurors being selected for each case at the assizes, the same forty-eight were to try every special jury case during the session. The twelve special jurors to try each particular case were now to be balloted for instead of allowing each party to strike off twelve.[64] This change in procedure obviously had the advantage of being less cumbersome and time-consuming – the sheriff was no longer obliged to summon and return numerous panels of special jurors. It was argued in 1855 that the rationale behind the 1853 act was to alleviate the inconvenience to jurors.[65] This was probably true insofar as fewer jurors were summoned for each assize. But it added to the discomfort of the jurors who were actually summoned, who now had to remain at the courthouse until the end of the assize, trying numerous cases. Furthermore, the parties were denied the right to object to any person on the jury list, which became a subject of grievance for many subsequent litigants.

However, the 1853 act retained the possibility of having a special jury 'struck' under the old system where a judge thought fit;[66] for example, 'cases in which, from the infirmity of human nature, men are likely, it may be unconsciously, to be swayed by political feelings'.[67] Litigants continued to seek such 'struck' juries in cases where they sought to have more control over the composition of the jury than the balloting procedure allowed. For example, they might prefer the striking procedure if they wished to reject jurors they deemed deficient in terms of experience or expertise.[68] Sometimes a struck jury was sought on the ground that the sub-sheriff could not or would not form the special jury panel honestly and impartially, either because of a connection with the parties or a material interest in the outcome of the case. For example, *Weir v. Weir*[69] involved trying the validity of a marriage settlement, and the sub-sheriff was a principal witness as to the circumstances of the marriage.[70] In *Somers v. Reilly*,[71] an action for slander, the high sheriff had been present when the alleged slanderous words had been uttered. Pigot C.B. refused the application for the special jury struck under the old system, but hinted that the array might be challenged.[72] A struck jury might be sought if the special jurors had a material interest in the outcome of the case,[73] or if one party had considerable influence over the special jurors, while the other was a stranger to the area.[74] *M'Lester v. Fegan*, *Magee v. Mark* and *Hempton v. Humphreys*

64 The juries bill, 1832 had proposed a similar measure, and the Irish judges had expressed enthusiasm, but ultimately it was dropped: *Letter regarding the jury bill 1833* (NAI, OP/1833/14).

65 *Smyly v. Hughes* (1855) 7 Ir. Jur. (o.s.) 139.

66 S. 112.

67 *Magee v. Mark* (1860) 5 Ir. Jur. (n.s.) 131.

68 *Hirsch v. Beet Sugar Co.* (1854) 6 Ir. Jur. (o.s.) 291; *Harrison v. Lynch* (1854) 3 I.C.L.R. 256.

69 (1854) 6 Ir. Jur. (o.s.) 143.

70 In *Fleming v. Taylor* (1864) 3 I.C.L.R. the returning officers to the sheriff were attorneys for the defendant. See also *Grome v. Blake* (1859) 8 I.C.L.R. app. 68.

71 (1861) 6 Ir. Jur. (n.s.) 295.

72 See pp 137–41.

73 *Belfast Water Company v. Girdwood* (1867) 1 I.L.T.R. 661.

74 E.g. *Codd v. Thompson & Cranfield* (1860) 5 Ir. Jur. (n.s.) 105; and *Barron v. West of England Insurance Co* (1854) 3 I.C.L.R. 112.

were all bribery actions taken against Conservative candidates following elections, and in all three cases the defendant sought a special jury struck under the old system because of a preponderance of liberals on the special jury book.[75] Although the mere fact that the parties were of different religious persuasions was never in itself a sufficient ground for a struck jury,[76] religion was nevertheless a factor in some cases. However, courts were generally slow to grant struck juries and the onus rested on the party applying for a special jury under the old system to prove that a fair trial could not otherwise be had.[77]

CONCLUSION

Special juries were a means of ensuring that experienced and well-to-do men tried particular cases. Such juries might be sought to ensure expertise, to ensure convictions in criminal cases connected with political agitation or simply for class reasons – some litigants did not wish their affairs to be settled by persons of relatively low social status. By the twentieth century, the expertise role of the special jury had in some ways been subsumed by the increased role played by expert witnesses in trials. Special juries were abolished in the Irish Free State in 1927,[78] but remained in existence in England and Northern Ireland until 1949.[79]

75 *M'Lester v. Fegan*: (1859) 9 I.C.L.R. app. 44; 5 Ir. Jur. (n.s.) 70. See also *M'Lester v. Quinn* (1860) 5 Ir. Jur. (n.s.) 94. *Magee v. Mark*: (1860) 5 Ir. Jur. (n.s.) 131. *Hempton v. Humphreys*: (1866) 11 Ir. Jur. (n.s.) 416.

76 E.g. *Smyly v. Hughes* (1855) 7 Ir. Jur. (o.s.) 139, which involved an alleged assault on a Church of Ireland vicar by a Catholic clergyman. See also *Hughes v. Shirley* (1866) 16 I.C.L.R. app. 6.

77 For example, *Browne v. Esmonde* (1868) I.R. 3 Eq. 81.

78 Juries Act, 1927, s. 66.

79 Juries Act, 1949.

CHAPTER FIVE

Wide-streets and valuation juries

THIS CHAPTER CONSIDERS A NUMBER of juries whose task was to conduct valuations on property. Legislation provided specifically for land and properties that were subject to compulsory purchase orders to be valued by panels of laymen. Eschewing valuations by more experienced professionals, these acts sought to use the wider community acceptance of juries and their verdicts to legitimise potentially controversial acquisitions of private property. This chapter also examines juries whose task was solely to determine damages or compensation, rather than issues of guilt or liability.[1]

WIDE-STREETS JURIES

The Dublin wide-streets commission was established by legislation in 1757 as part of a plan to improve the streetscape of Dublin.[2] The commissioners' original remit was to rebuild Essex Bridge and the street leading to Dublin Castle (Parliament Street), and their powers were subsequently extended by further legislation. They were empowered to compulsorily purchase such lands and buildings as were necessary to complete the project.[3] Where the owners of property refused to agree to the sale, or where purported owners could not demonstrate clear title, the commissioners could issue a warrant to the sheriff of the city of Dublin to empanel a jury.[4] There were no specific details in the legislation as to the jurors' qualifications, other than that they were to be 'substantial and disinterested persons'.[5] However, as will be seen, the tasks required of these juries were not straightforward; they had to examine deeds, evaluate rental incomes and so on.

1 In other contexts valuations and assessments of damages were carried out by appointed valuators (e.g. the Regulation of Cork Act, 1771–2 (11 & 12 Geo. III, c. 18), s. 1; and the Lighting Act, 1759 (33 Geo. II, c. 18), s. 27) or justices of the peace (e.g. the Timber Act, 1767 (7 Geo. III, c. 23)).

2 Dublin Wide Streets Act, 1757 (31 Geo. II, c. 19). E. Sheridan, 'Designing the capital city' in J. Brady and A. Simms (eds), *Dublin through space & time* (Dublin, 2007), p. 110, notes that the importance of the commission 'for Dublin's evolution as a capital in a European context is unique'.

3 Later, the commissioners were funded out of a coal duty: Dublin Wide Streets Act, 1781–2 (21 & 22 Geo. III, c. 17); Dublin Wide Street (Amendment) Act, 1783–4 (23 & 24 Geo. III, c. 31); and Dublin Wide Street (Amendment) Act, 1790 (30 Geo. III, c. 19). Later, a tax on clubs and card playing funded the commissioners: Dublin Wide Streets Act, 1799 (39 Geo. III, c. 53).

4 Improvement of Dublin Act, 1786 (26 Geo. III, c. 32) provided for distress and sale.

5 Dublin Wide Streets Act, 1757 (31 Geo. II, c. 19), s. 5.

Men of business and property were usually empanelled, and it is almost certain that in the early years of wide-streets juries their names were drawn from the lists of special juries. The juries usually comprised merchants, esquires and aldermen. For example, a wide-streets jury in February 1759 consisted of three aldermen, five merchants and four esquires.[6] The following month a jury was sworn consisting of ten merchants and two esquires.[7] Some men served repeatedly on these juries. From the mid-1760s onwards, professions such as goldsmith, carpenter, gunsmith[8] and even apothecary[9] began to appear, but the jury lists were still very much dominated by merchants[10] and esquires.[11] Although Dublin Corporation had little say as to the projects undertaken by the commission, the Dublin wide-streets juries were dominated by members of the corporation, indicating that the corporation had at least some influence when it came to valuations.[12]

In the early days, the Dublin wide-streets commission met at the tholsel, on Skinner's Row, near Christ Church cathedral.[13] The juries also met there, although they later convened at the custom house[14] or in the linen board room at Dublin Castle,[15] or in their own room at the royal exchange.[16]

The sheriff was to summon 'a competent number' of suitable persons. According to the legislation, between thirty-six and sixty jurors were to be returned, and some person appointed by the panel of commissioners was to draw twelve of them, with the parties allowed to challenge jurors in the usual manner. The first such precept was issued to the sheriff of the city of Dublin in December 1758, to empanel and return forty-eight jurors to appear at the tholsel on 16 January 1759.[17] The commission's clerk, Mr Howard, was 'to prepare, in the best manner he can, to be laid before the said juries a state of the grounds and houses in the possession of the executors of Primate Butler, and also of Dowager Lady Molesworth as well the inheritances, as the derivative interest thereof'. Maps were to be prepared for the benefit of the jurors by Mr Semple. This became common practice, with detailed maps frequently furnished to wide-streets juries to assist with their valuations.

As well as providing them with maps, the commissioners authorised the jurors to view the premises in question,[18] and the proceedings could be adjourned

6 *Minutes of the Dublin wide-streets commission*, 15 Feb. 1759 (DCA, WSC/Mins/1).
7 *Minutes*, 12 Mar. 1759 (DCA, WSC/Mins/1).
8 E.g. *Minutes*, 20 Nov. 1864 (DCA, WSC/Mins/1); *Minutes*, 12 Sept. 1765 (DCA, WSC/Mins/2); and *Minutes*, 21 July 1766 (DCA, WSC/Mins/2).
9 *Minutes*, 21 July 1766 (DCA, WSC/Mins/2).
10 Including, on one occasion at least, Arthur Guinness: *Minutes*, 4 Feb. 1779 (DCA, WSC/Mins/2).
11 E.g. a jury sworn in early 1865 consisted entirely of merchants: *Minutes*, 10 Jan. 1865 (DCA, WSC/Mins/1). See also *Minutes*, 7 Dec. 1771 (DCA, WSC/Mins/2); *Minutes*, 25 May 1778 (DCA, WSC/Mins/2).
12 Sheridan, 'Designing the capital', p. 121.
13 *Minutes* (DCA, WSC/Mins/1).
14 *Freeman's Journal*, 30 Jan. 1800.
15 *Minutes*, 1 Aug. 1778 (DCA, WSC/Mins/2).
16 See *Freeman's Journal*, 3 July 1814.
17 *Minutes*, 9 Dec. 1759 (DCA, WSC/Mins/1).
18 The clerk was usually ordered to attend the jurors when they viewed premises, e.g. *Minutes*, 15 Feb. 1759 (DCA, WSC/Mins/1).

repeatedly as necessary, with the jurors obliged to keep attending or risk being fined.[19] Sometimes there were repeated adjournments due to, for example, jurors being sick and unable to attend. In 1778, for instance, proceedings were adjourned seven times, primarily because of the sickness of several jurors.[20]

The jurors were sworn to 'truly and impartially enquire of the value of such houses ...',[21] and were obliged to enquire into the value of the lands and buildings, and investigate the titles, interests and rights of all interested parties.[22] Fourteen days' notice of the valuation was given to the owners or occupiers of the premises in question. The jury then assessed and determined what they considered to be an appropriate sum in compensation, and their verdict was written up on parchment, sealed, signed by the commissioners, and entered into the chancery rolls.[23] Valuations and the swearing-in of jurors were well-publicised in the press.[24] Given the nature of the work of the wide-streets commission, the juries usually valued a number of adjoining or neighbouring properties at once. For example, on 22 January 1759, a wide-streets jury delivered verdicts in relation to thirty cases, deeming the claims made either 'reasonable' or 'unreasonable'.[25] In March of that year, twenty-four different 'concerns' were 'given in charge to a jury to be viewed'.[26]

There were various difficulties associated with wide-streets juries. It was not always easy to secure sufficient jurors for the business of the commission to be conducted. The 1757 act was amended in 1759 to allow the commissioners to discharge the jurors and issue new precepts to the sheriffs of Dublin city or county from time to time to return competent juries.[27] It allowed for talesmen[28] to be used where necessary to make up juries of twelve.[29] For example, in July 1760, a juror did not appear and the persons representing various interests 'consent[ed] that George Simpson, merchant, be added to the eleven jurors who appear, in order to make the jury complete'.[30] The 1759 act also restated the sheriff's power to fine jurors who failed to appear once summoned. This was a persistent problem, common to all types of jury, as will be discussed in chapter 8. Two commissioners could sit with a jury for a trial,[31] and could charge the jury.[32] In 1800, this was altered to allow a single commissioner to sit with the jury.[33]

19 31 Geo. II, c. 19, s. 7.
20 *Minutes*, 6, 28 July; 1, 6, 10 Aug.; 9, 17 Nov. 1778 (DCA WSC/Mins/2).
21 *Minutes*, 12 Mar. 1759 (DCA, WSC/Mins/1). 22 31 Geo. II, c. 19, s. 5
23 Ibid., s. 5.
24 E.g. *Freeman's Journal*, 5 Dec. 1810. The *Dublin Gazette*, and the *Dublin Journal and Universal Advertiser* and *Saunders' Newsletter* were also used: *Minutes* (DCA, WSC/Mins/1 and 2).
25 *Minutes*, 22 Jan. 1759 (DCA, WSC/Mins/1).
26 These were categorised as inheritances, tenants of Lord and Lady Molesworth and tenants of Charles O'Hara. *Minutes*, 12 Mar. 1759 (DCA, WSC/Mins/1).
27 Dublin Wide Streets (Amendment) Act, 1759 (33 Geo. II, c. 15).
28 See pp 115–17. 29 33 Geo. II, c. 15, s. 3. 30 *Minutes*, 19 July 1760 (DCA, WSC/Mins/1).
31 33 Geo. II, c. 15, s. 2. 32 S. 4.
33 Dublin Wide Streets (Amendment) Act, 1800 (40 Geo. III, c. 61).

A member of Dublin Corporation in 1846 commented that he had never seen 'men whose consciences were more elastic' than wide-streets jurors.[34] It was not unheard of for the owners of properties being valued to attempt to influence jurors to return a high valuation. One instance of packing a wide-streets jury was brought to the attention of a parliamentary commission in 1826.[35] The parties whose properties were to be valued arranged among themselves a list of names of persons who they thought would be favourable to them, and forwarded this to the sheriff's office through their solicitor, along with a bribe. Several of the persons ended up on the jury and 'the valuations were accordingly excessive'. The same solicitor had been implicated in a similar case in 1816, and after the second incident, an alderman complained and subsequently more care was taken in returning persons to serve on wide-streets juries. John Claudius Beresford, one of the wide-streets commissioners, told the same committee of a case where the jury had been 'packed' with around five relatives and acquaintances of the person whose property was the subject of the valuation. He found out in advance that they were likely to return a valuation exceeding £10,000, but the commissioners dissolved the jury and a second jury delivered a valuation of £2,700.[36]

A builder named Michael Maley, who had frequent dealings with the wide-streets commissioners,[37] complained that from around 1810 to 1814 the sheriffs 'summoned promiscuously from the inhabitants of the city'. He said that it was difficult to ensure that there were sufficient jurors or that they were sufficiently 'respectable', leading to significant delays in valuations.[38] From about 1814 onwards, however, the remuneration for wide-streets juries was increased,[39] punctual attendance was insisted upon, and it began to be dominated by members of Dublin Corporation.[40] In Maley's view, the problem of bias was thus minimised, although the delays remained quite significant,[41] and the preponderance of corporation members meant that valuations of premises such as market houses were sometimes significantly inflated. He also observed that the respectability of

34 *Freeman's Journal*, 8 May 1846. 35 *Fifteenth report on salaries*, p. 67. 36 Ibid., p. 534.

37 E.g. see *Minutes*, 3 Oct., 12 Dec. 1810 (DCA, WSC/Mins/22); *Minutes*, 1 Sept. 1813 (DCA, WSC/Mins/25); *Minutes*, 7 Sept. 1814 (DCA, WSC/Mins/26).

38 E.g. in April 1813, 11 jurors were fined £2 10*s*. each for non-attendance, and 18 others were fined £5, *Minutes*, 28 Apr. 1813 (DCA, WSC/Mins/25). In November 1814, the commission ordered that the law agent should report every Wednesday on the progress of the various juries that were sitting. *Minutes*, 2 Nov. 1814 (DCA, WSC/Mins/27).

39 In 1814 the office of public accounts wrote to the wide-streets commissioners complaining about expenditure for jurors' refreshment appearing in their accounts. The board resolved unanimously that they had discretion to make such payments, and that they considered 'the labours of valuation juries to be very irksome', *Minutes*, 23 Feb. 1814 (DCA, WSC/Mins/26). In December they ordered that £38 2*s*. 5*d*. be paid to the master of the royal exchange coffee room to cover the cost of jury refreshments for the year. *Minutes*, 28 Dec. 1814 (DCA, WSC/Mins/27). In addition, juries around this time also tended to claim expences of 13*s*. per meeting: *Minutes*, 12 Apr., 17 May, 31 May 1815. Sometimes there were as many as 20 or 21 such meetings in relation to a particular valuation (DCA, WSC/Mins/27).

40 *Fifteenth report on salaries*, p. 535. 41 Ibid., p. 536.

wide-streets jurors was no better after 1814 because a high proportion of them were either insolvent or bankrupt.

Sometimes jury valuations and verdicts were not carried into effect – this happened, for example, after a 1790 valuation on Cutpurse Row (between Thomas Street and Cornmarket). All of the 'interests in Cutpurse Row [were] given in charge to the jury … to be valued' in November 1789.[42] The jury conducted its valuations over the subsequent months, and in September 1790 two memorials were presented to the commission on behalf of Charles White, who had built several premises on Cutpurse Row, New Row and Cornmarket. These had been jointly valued at around £450, and he was unclear as to whether all of his properties had to be demolished, or solely the houses on Cutpurse Row. It was demonstrated that White's houses on Cornmarket would not impede the development of Cutpurse Row.[43] The matter does not appear to have been satisfactorily resolved, and the buildings fell into ruin as the owners 'could neither build, let or repair' them.[44] A second jury was therefore appointed in 1801 to conduct another valuation.[45] Property owners could challenge the valuation returned by the jury – for example, in June 1813 the owners of properties on Essex Quay submitted a memorial to the commissioners complaining that the jury had undervalued the property, but ultimately there was no new valuation ordered.[46] The commissioners might also quash a jury's valuation if it was considered to be excessively high.[47]

Legislation passed in 1790 provided that wide-streets juries would not award any compensation for buildings or edifices erected after notice was given that they were going to conduct a valuation, but that they would compensate those who had discontinued building works.[48] Leases entered into after the jury had conducted its valuation and returned a verdict were void.[49] The legislation also provided that new houses built on certain Dublin streets had to conform to specified finishes, in the name of uniformity, and that the expenses incurred in so doing would also be assessed by a jury.[50] It conferred wider powers on the commissioners, who could now order the widening of any narrow streets or lanes in the city where there was waste ground or decaying buildings. Again, it was for the jury to assess the value of the properties and award compensation.

The Improvement of Dublin Act, 1786[51] empowered the commission to empanel juries to conduct valuations on properties or waste ground that were to be the subject of compulsory purchase to enable their demolition as part of the overall street-widening plan.[52] Once the purchases and demolitions had taken place, the

42 *Minutes*, 30 Nov. 1789 (DCA, WSC/Mins/9).
43 *Minutes*, 4, 24 Sept. 1790 (DCA, WSC/Mins/9).
44 Wide Streets Commission, *Extracts from the minutes of the commissioners appointed by act of parliament, for making wide and convenient ways, streets and passages in the city of Dublin* (Dublin, 1802), pp 62–3.
45 Ibid.
46 *Wide streets (Dublin) Accounts and papers; no. 1 to 8, inclusive*, HC 1828 (81) xxii, 569, p. 6.
47 *Fifteenth report on salaries*, p. 540 (Sobieski Kildahl, solicitor).
48 30 Geo. III, c. 19, ss 16, 17.
49 26 Geo. III, c. 32, s. 2.
50 30 Geo. III, c. 19, s. 21.
51 26 Geo. III, c. 32, ss 1, 5.
52 See Kenneth Milne, *The Dublin liberties, 1600–1850* (Dublin, 2009), p. 37; and Sheridan, p. 113.

commission had discretion over the design and layout of new streets.[53] A panel of wide-street jurors was prepared by sub-sheriff or clerk[54] to conduct a valuation.

Until its statutory abolition in 1849,[55] the wide-streets commission had a significant impact on the development of Dublin city,[56] and the contribution made by laypersons empanelled on its juries to conduct the valuations is often overlooked.

Dublin was not the only city to have commissioners empowered to compulsorily purchase properties in order to widen and improve streets. In the same year that the Dublin wide-streets commissioners were first appointed, a similar body was established to improve and widen Baal's Bridge in Limerick.[57] Its powers and responsibilities were similar to those of the Dublin commissioners, and it could direct the sheriff of the city of Limerick to summon juries in the same manner. The jury process was identical: jurors could be fined,[58] ordered to view premises, and obliged to attend for several days until discharged.[59] Cork also had a wide-streets commission, established in 1765.[60] The legislation named sixteen commissioners, and gave them the same powers as their Dublin counterparts,[61] meaning that they could empanel juries to conduct valuations.

In 1783, legislation established wide-streets commissioners for Waterford,[62] to be appointed by the mayor, recorder, aldermen, sheriffs and common council men. The commissioners were granted the same powers as the Dublin wide-streets commissioners. However, they could not lay out, design or widen any street without the verdict of a jury that such alterations were necessary;[63] thus the jurors had an even greater role in Waterford. On the direction of the commissioners, the sheriff of the city was to empanel between 24 and 36 jurors, from which 12 would be balloted. They had to view the streets in question and appear before the commissioners at an appointed time and place to deliver their verdict. If they deemed it necessary to widen the street, they or another jury had to ascertain the value of the lands and premises on the street.

53 Sheridan, p. 118. 54 *Fifteenth report on salaries*, HC 1826 (310) xvii, 29, p. 67.
55 Dublin Improvement Act, 1849 (12 & 13 Vic., c. 97). The commission's powers were transferred to Dublin Corporation.
56 See, for example, E. McParland, 'Strategy in the planning of Dublin, 1750–1800' in P. Butel and L.M. Cullen (eds), *Cities and merchants: French and Irish perspectives on urban development, 1500–1900* (Dublin, 1986). See Wide Streets Commission, *Extracts from minutes*, for a list of the commission's activities up to 1802. On the redesign of Dublin city generally, see Finnian Ó Cionnaith, *Mapping, measurement and metropolis: how land surveyors shaped eighteenth-century Dublin* (Dublin, 2012).
57 Baal's-Bridge Act, 1757 (31 Geo. II, c. 20). 58 31 Geo. II, c. 20, s. 13. 59 S. 6.
60 Regulation of Cork Act, 1765 (5 Geo. III, c. 24), s. 12. See E. McParland, 'The wide streets commissioners, their importance for Dublin architecture in the late eighteenth – early nineteenth century', *Bulletin Ir. Georgian Soc.*, 15:1 (1972), 1–32 at 27.
61 S. 13. Their powers were confirmed in the Regulation of Cork Act, 1777–8 (17 & 18 Geo. III, c. 38), s. 23; and the Cork Act, 1786 (26 Geo. III, c. 28), s. 50.
62 Regulation of Waterford Act, 1783–4 (23 & 24 Geo. III, c. 52), s. 25. See also E. McParland, *James Gandon: Vitruvius Hibernicus* (London, 1985), p. 146. 63 S. 27.

In 1790 powers analogous to those of the Dublin and Waterford wide-streets commissioners were vested in the mayor, community and citizens of Londonderry.[64] As in Waterford, no street could be ordered to be altered unless a specially empanelled jury gave a verdict that it was necessary.[65]

PAVING AND LIGHTING JURIES

Aside from wide-streets juries, juries were also occasionally used as part of city improvement and maintenance schemes. For example, in 1773 legislation authorised the appointment of commissioners of paving (more commonly known as the paving board) in Dublin to improve roads and pavements.[66] This followed the Westminster Paving Act, 1762,[67] which had transferred responsibility for paving and street cleaning from individuals to a public body.[68] Other acts followed for the city of London and elsewhere. The Dublin paving board came into existence in June 1774.[69] Like the Dublin wide-streets commission, 'this important municipal body played a significant role in the development of Georgian Dublin'.[70] The paving board 'applied a logical and systematic approach to improving Dublin's thoroughfares',[71] and frequently found itself in conflict with the wide-streets commission, as the two bodies operated independently.

64 Londonderry Act, 1790, s. 37. 65 S. 38.

66 Dublin Paving and Lighting Act, 1773–4 (13 & 14 Geo. III, c. 22). See Finnian Ó Cionnaith, *Exercise of authority: surveyor Thomas Owen and the paving, cleansing and lighting of Georgian Dublin* (Dublin, 2015), p. 1.

67 Westminster Paving (Amendment) Act, 1762 (3 Geo. III, c. 23). This act had been a long time in the making. White observes that '[f]rom 1709 there emerged a parliamentary obsession with the paving of Westminster's streets. Numerous paving acts in the succeeding fifteen years or so produced utterly indifferent results'. Jerry White, 'City rivalries and the modernisation of eighteenth-century London, 1720–1770', *Literatur in Wissenschaft und Unterricht*, 43:2/3 (2010), 83–102 at 93. A number of pamphlets produced in the mid-eighteenth century proposed the establishment of paving boards with centralised responsibility for paving and maintaining streets. See also Westminster Paving Act, 1761 (2 Geo. III, c. 21); Westminster Paving (Amendment) Act, 1763 (4 Geo. III, c. 39); Westminster Paving Commissioners Act, 1765 (5 Geo. III, c. 13); Westminster Paving Act, 1765 (5 Geo. III, c. 50).

68 These acts required waste 'kennels' that ran down the middles of streets to be replaced with curbside gutters. Like the Irish legislation, the English acts also provided for scavenging, cleansing and the removal of obstructions: see Roy Porter, *London: a social history* (London, 1994), p. 125. The maintenance of paving and lighting operated under different conditions in London than in Dublin, as it was less centralised. According to the *London and Westminster Review*, there were around 100 independent boards for paving and lighting around London. Many of these boards were described as 'self-appointed and irresponsible', and did not publish accounts. In the parish of St Pancras alone there were 21 such boards, with over 900 commissioners, many of whom resided elsewhere. *London and Westminster Review*, 25 (New York, July and Apr. 1836), 49. This system was, unsurprisingly, inefficient. See Lynn MacKay, *Respectability and the London poor, 1780–1870: the value of virtue* (London, 2016), pp 50–2, for a description of London streets and rubbish removal in the early nineteenth century. 69 Ó Cionnaith, *Exercise of authority*, p. 7.

70 Mary Clarke, 'Preface' in Ó Cionnaith, *Exercise of authority*, p. xi.

71 Ó Cionnaith, *Exercise of authority*, p. 121.

Part of the paving board's powers included the carrying away and disposal of gravel, sand, stones or other materials, for which the owner was to be compensated.[72] It was also empowered to purchase lands for the purpose of digging up stones, gravel and so on.[73] It appears to have purchased lands for street widening, for example around Thomas St.[74] An owner or occupier who felt aggrieved in either case could have the damages assessed by a jury at quarter sessions.[75] The act provided for the compulsory purchase of buildings or grounds within the city, with the purchase price 'ascertained upon the oaths of twelve indifferent men of the city and parishes'.[76] The procedure resembled that used for empanelling special juries: 24 jurors were to be summoned, with 12 balloted for. Their verdict was final. In 1790 the Dublin commissioners of paving and lighting were empowered to issue precepts to sheriffs to conduct valuations in the same manner as the wide-streets commissioners (that is, valuations by juries).[77] These valuations were to be carried out on land to be compulsorily purchased to facilitate the improvement of roads and streets. The extent to which such juries were actually used is unclear, although it would appear that they may have been empanelled into the nineteenth century.[78] In 1849 the paving board, considered wasteful and extravagant by some,[79] was abolished by legislation and its responsibilities passed to Dublin Corporation.[80]

Legislation in the 1780s provided that encroachments or nuisances on the streets of Waterford could be removed, and any person aggrieved by such an order could appeal to a jury empanelled especially for that purpose.[81] Similar provision was made for Londonderry in 1790.[82] In Cork, such duties tended to be carried out by market juries.[83] Some of these powers were similar to those of the Westminster annoyance juries.[84] These had been given statutory recognition in 1756,[85] and had powers in relation to annoyances, nuisances and encroachments upon public streets

72 13 & 14 Geo. III, c. 22, s. 48. 73 Ibid., s. 49.

74 *Minutes of the Dublin paving board*, 29 Nov. 1781 (DCA, PB/Mins/9).

75 Other complaints arising from the commissioners' powers were to be settled summarily by justices of the peace: 13 & 14 Geo. III, c. 22, s. 54. 76 Ibid., s. 58.

77 Dublin Paving and Lighting Act, 1790 (30 Geo. III, c. 42), s. 11.

78 E.g. *Report of the Dublin paving, cleansing, and lighting commissioners*, HC 1806 (17) viii, 473, p. 40; and *Freeman's Journal*, 30 Aug. 1808.

79 E.g. *Hansard 3*, ciii, 90–1 (2 Mar. 1849) (John Reynolds).

80 Dublin Improvement Act, 1849 (12 & 13 Vic., c. 97).

81 Regulation of Waterford Act, 1783–4 (23 & 24 Geo. III, c. 52), ss 51–3.

82 30 Geo. III, c. 31, ss 40, 43. See also s. 46 as regards trenches and reservoirs. 83 See chapter 7.

84 See Joseph Newell, *Inquest jurymen. An enquiry into the nature and duties of inquest jury-men, of the city of London, together with the by-laws of the common council, and the articles of charge. Also the law for regulating the election of constables, leet and annoyance jury for the city of Westminster, shewing the nature and duties of their office, and the general laws respecting defective weights nad measures for counties, liberties and divisions, of England and Wales* (London, 1825). Newell notes, p. 31, that what was referred to as the leet and annoyance jury in Westminster was called the inquest jury in London.

85 Westminster Juries Act, 1756 (29 Geo. II, c. 25).

and highways. Up to 48 annoyance jurors were appointed twice a year, and they perambulated in groups of 12 or more.[86] They were empowered to impose fines on persons responsible for defective pavements or street obstructions.[87] They also had powers in relation to weights and measures, similar to the powers of Irish market juries. They had the power to enter shops and warehouses, and if they found 'any weight, balance or measure, to be unlawful or defective', they could destroy it and impose a fine.[88]

OTHER VALUATION JURIES

When the wide-streets legislation provided for the carrying-out of valuations by juries, this was not an entirely novel innovation. Throughout the eighteenth century, juries were often empanelled for the purpose of conducting valuations on land or property.[89] For example, the Bog Act, 1715[90] provided for commissioners to mediate disputes over the widening of the Shannon and the draining of bogs. If a party refused to agree to such mediation, the sheriff could empanel a jury 'of able and sufficient men', legally qualified for the trial of issues, to appear before the commissioners at an appointed time and place. The jurors were then to make enquiry and assess damages for the parties. The act also provided for such jurors to take a view of the disputed lands, and for the parties to have their lawful challenges.

Similar legislation in 1717 provided that the crown could compulsorily purchase land for building barracks and lighthouses.[91] Where a dispute arose, the valuation commissioners could empanel a jury to enquire into the yearly value of the land. These jurors had to consider contracts, conveyances, leases and rents in coming to their conclusion, so it is likely that men of commerce or high standing were chosen, and that the juries resembled special juries. This act did not go into detail regarding views, challenges and the use of talesmen,[92] but since it followed only two years after the Bog Act, and the procedures were otherwise quite similar, it is likely that the practice in relation to the juries was the same.

By the late eighteenth century, juries were frequently being used to conduct valuations and settle disputes arising from compulsory purchase schemes[93] for

86 29 Geo. II, c. 25, ss 10 and 12.

87 Ibid., s. 13. This aspect of their powers was removed by 9 Geo. II, c. 25, s. 15.

88 29 Geo. II, c. 25, s. 14. In 1861 the annoyance jury was replaced by inspectors of weights and measures appointed by the court of burgesses: Annoyance Jurors (Westminster) Act, 1861 (24 & 25 Vic., c. 78).

89 This was also common practice in England, Wales and Scotland. For example, the River Trent Act, 1699 (10 & 11 Wm & M., c. 20); Improvement of Lands (Scotlant) Act, 1799 (39 Geo. III, c. 55); London Court Act, 1799 (39 Geo. III, c. 69).

90 Bog Act, 1715 (2 Geo. I, c. 12), s. 2.

91 Lighthouses Act, 1717 (4 Geo. I, c. 7), s. 1.

92 See pp 171–7, 136–49 and 115–17, respectively.

93 See generally Eamon Galligan and Michael McGrath, *Compulsory purchase and compensation in Ireland* (2nd ed., Dublin, 2013), pp 3–66.

enclosures,[94] mines,[95] road-improvement works,[96] and the building of bridges,[97] docks[98] and canals.[99] Much of this took place in the context of economic growth towards the end of the century; as Cullen observes, a 'remarkable amount of building [took] place in the second half of the century',[100] and by the end of the century, the country's 'economic prospects seemed attractive'.[101] As the economy grew rapidly, improved infrastructure was imperative, and juries seemed to be a cheap and convenient means of facilitating this.

More unusual uses of juries included the conducting of valuations of properties that were to be used for the quarantining of goods taken from ships suspected of carrying plague or other infectious diseases.[102] The purpose of the valuation was to compensate the owner of the property, who was unable to use it for the duration of the quarantine. In many cases the verdict of the valuation jury was final, and not subject to appeal,[103] suggesting a presumption of community acceptance of the

94 E.g. Merrion Square Act, 1791 (31 Geo. III, c. 45), s. 13. The Act provided that no inhabitant of the square or proprietor of any house on it could serve on a jury empanelled to award compensation to persons with an interest in the square. The juries were to be empanelled and treated like wide-streets juries.

95 Mines Act, 1723 (10 Geo. I, c. 5), s. 4; Mines Act, 1792 (32 Geo. III, c. 24); Inland Carriage Act, 1749 (25 Geo. II, c. 10), s. 5.

96 E.g. Dundalk Roads Act, 1783–4 (23 & 24 Geo. III, c. 27), s. 26; Kilkenny Turnpike Act, 1790 (30 Geo. III, c. 44), ss 31, 32; Kinnegad Turnpike Act, 1790 (30 Geo. III, c. 46), ss 32, 33; Limerick and Cork Roads Act, 1790 (30 Geo. III, c. 47), s. 12; Kilkenny Turnpike Act, 1792 (32 Geo. III, c. 39), ss 27, 28; Kilkenny Roads Act, 1793 (33 Geo. III, c. 19), s. 9; Roads Act, 1773–4 (13 & 14 Geo. III, c. 32), s. 10; Dublin Turnpike Act, 1787 (27 Geo. III, c. 59), s. 49; Cork Turnpike Act, 1799 (39 Geo. III, c. 52), s. 51.

97 Londonderry Act, 1790 (30 Geo. III, c. 31), s. 26. Jurors under this act could view premises that were to be purchased and assess their value.

98 Royal Canal Act, 1792 (32 Geo. III, c. 26), s. 7.

99 Bog Act, 1715 (2 Geo. I, c. 12), s. 2; Inland Carriage Act, 1749 (25 Geo. II, c. 10), s. 4; Inland Navigation Act, 1792 (32 Geo. III, c. 15), s. 1. The Grand Canal Act, 1771–2 (11 & 12 Geo. III, c. 31), ss 17, 18 provided that the Grand Canal Company could purchase such lands, tenements and hereditaments as necessary, and that juries were to be empanelled to assess damages payable to the owners. Lands belonging to John Hatch were valued by a jury for purchase by the Grand Canal Company in 1778: Fred Trench, 'John Hatch and the development of Harcourt Street', *Dub. Hist. Rec.*, 62:1 (2009), 70–7 at 74. See also Royal Canal Act, 1790 (30 Geo. III, c. 20). Section 6 provided that leases entered into after the serving of notice that the lands were to be valued could not be used by the jury as evidence of the land value – this suggests some earlier attempts to defraud juries by entering into inflated leases. Newry Navigation Act, 1793 (33 Geo. III, c. 10), s. 25, provided that the Newry Navigation Corporation had the same powers as other canal companies as regards the summoning and empanelling of valuation juries.

100 L.M. Cullen, *An economic history of Ireland since 1660* (London, 1972), p. 82.

101 Ibid., p. 97.

102 Quarantine Act, 1800 (40 Geo. III, c. 79), s. 5.

103 Interestingly, the Regulation of Cork Act, 1771–2 (11 & 12 Geo. III, c. 18) provided for the appointment of valuators in the city of Cork, to conduct valuations on properties within the city for the purposes of taxation. The mayors, sheriffs and common council of Cork could appoint two or more inhabitants of each parish to act as valuators. Seven or more of them acting together could make a determination as to the annual value of any house or property, and the valuations

jury's decision. This trend continued throughout the nineteenth century. For example, under the Lands Clauses Consolidation Act, 1845,[104] where land was to be compulsorily purchased, disputes over the compensation to be awarded were generally to be settled by two justices. However, where the compensation exceeded £50, a warrant could be issued to the sheriff to empanel a jury.[105] It was also open to either party to request a special jury, which was struck under the old system,[106] although the legislation provided that the panel was to be reduced to 20 rather than the usual 24.[107] This allowed the parties even greater control over the position of the jury. The first 12 who answered to their names and were not challenged were to be sworn.[108] The inquiry took place before the sheriff, who could order 6 or more jurors to view the lands in question.[109] The jury had to deliver separate verdicts if both the value of the lands to be purchased and the compensation for injury done were at issue.[110] It was noted in 1913 that these jurors were still 'struck' like special juries under the old system.[111]

This legislation was amended in 1851 in relation to railways. The Railways Act (Ireland), 1851[112] allowed a party dissatisfied with the compensation awarded by the arbitrator to have a jury sworn to assess the damages to be awarded, having regard to the value of the land, and any damage to the land as a result of the works. Further amending legislation in 1864[113] provided that such disputes could be tried by a special jury before a judge, and that the jurors could be ordered to view the lands in question.[114] Sometimes these were known as traverse juries, and occasionally less than 12 jurors could be empanelled with the consent of the parties. In the 1894 case of Teague McNamee, for example, 3 jurors were sworn.[115]

were returned to the sheriff and deposited as public records. The act made no stipulation as to the qualifications necessary; this is yet another example of the use of laypersons in the administration of law and justice during the eighteenth century. Similar provision was made for Waterford by 23 & 24 Geo. III, c. 52, s. 37, but the legislation went further and provided that valuations could be appealed, and such appeals were to be decided by juries.

104 8 & 9 Vic., c. 18. See generally Albert D. Bolton, *The Labourers (Ireland) Acts 1883 to 1906* (Dublin, 1910).

105 Ss 23, 39. 106 See pp 61–3.

107 8 & 9 Vic., c. 18, s. 54. 108 Ibid., s. 55.

109 Ibid., s. 43. 110 Ibid., s. 49.

111 *Report on juries* [C-6817] 1913, xxx, 403.

112 14 & 15 Vic., c. 70, s. 26.

113 Railways Act (Ireland), 1864 (27 & 28 Vic., c. 71), ss 2–4.

114 E.g. *Kehoe v. Great Southern and Western Rail Co.* (1886) 20 I.L.T.R. 27. A more modern example of using laypersons to determine potentially unpopular valuations of land or property related to the question of taxation in England after the Second World War. Daunton notes that '[i]n order to secure consent, and to embed the fiscal system in civil society, the amount of tax was determined by lay assessors appointed by the local commissioners, and any disputes were adjudicated by the commissioners rather than by the courts or bureaucrats'. M.J. Daunton, 'How to pay for the war: state, society and taxation in Britain, 1917–24', *Eng. Hist. Rev.*, 111:443 (1996), 882–919 at 887.

115 Traverse issue, Teague McNamee, Donegal spring assizes, 21 Mar. 1898 (NAI, 1C-49–26).

SHERIFF'S JURIES, JURIES ON WRIT OF INQUIRY AND CIVIL-BILL JURIES

A sheriff's inquisition jury was a jury of twelve empanelled to assist a sheriff in making an inquiry upon a writ.[116] The inquisition was described by Dutton as 'a manner of proceeding by way of search or examination, and is that inquiry that is made by jurors in all causes, civil or criminal, touching the matter in fact'.[117] The subject matter of the inquisition varied depending on the specific writ under which the jury was empanelled; for example, a jury might be empanelled on a writ of waste,[118] to determine whether an occupier of property had damaged or reduced its value, for example by allowing it to fall into disrepair. Sheriff's inquisition juries could be required to conduct a view,[119] so that they could better assess the nature and extent of the waste.

Where a defendant in a civil action admitted liability or allowed judgment in default, a jury could be empanelled with the sole purpose of assessing damages. These jurors were summoned on a writ of inquiry to assist the court.[120] The writ was executed by the sheriff or his deputy,[121] and both parties could make representations. It was 'the duty of the jury to observe the directions of the writ, which is diligently to enquire what damages the plaintiff hath sustained, which cannot be without evidence given to them'.[122]

Oldham points out that in some inquiries, the jury returned was a 'good jury'. The original writ of inquiry required twelve 'good and lawful men', as distinct from the twelve 'free and lawful men' for the trial of issues under the writ of *venire facias*. Tidd described the good jury as 'a better sort of common jury',[123] and they appear to have been in existence long before the special jury.[124] A good jury could be requested by the plaintiff to inquire into the damages, but it was not automatically empanelled.

In the early nineteenth century, the constitution of these juries was sometimes found to be wanting. The commissioners on duties and salaries observed in 1826 that the practice of summoning these jurors was 'very loose and dangerous to suitors', because the selection was entirely left to the bailiff. They reported that 'where the question to be decided is not litigated, no jury is sworn; in litigated cases it is frequently composed of bailiffs and other persons of a very inferior description'. In either case, where one of the parties gave notice that a jury was required, a more respectable one is chosen from the nearby householders.[125] The

116 Dutton, *Office and authority*, pp 340–1. 117 Ibid., p. 341. 118 Ibid., p. 665.
119 Ibid., p. 672. 120 Huband, *Practical treatise*, p. 75.
121 Dutton, *Office and authority*, p. 681. 122 Ibid., p. 682.
123 W. Tidd, *The practice of the courts of king's bench and common pleas, in personal actions, and ejectments*, 2 vols (9th ed., London, 1828), ii, p. 787.
124 James C. Oldham, 'The origins of the special jury', *U. Chic. L. Rev.*, 50 (1983), 137–211 at 206–7.
125 *Fifteenth report on salaries*, p. 67.

Juries (Ireland) Act, 1833 provided that jurors on inquests or writs of inquiry had to meet the same qualifications as other petty jurors.[126]

According to Duncombe, 'in writs to inquire of damages the just number of twelve is not requisite, for they may be over or under'.[127] There are examples of inquiry juries of six, sometimes referred to as master's juries[128] up to the late nineteenth century in the queen's bench and exchequer divisions.[129] By the late nineteenth century both the chancery division and the court of bankruptcy could make orders for the assessment of damages by a jury.[130] From 1891, where the amount of damages was to be determined substantially by calculation, it was no longer necessary to issue a writ of inquiry; the court or judge could direct that the amount of damages was to be ascertained by the master of the queen's bench or exchequer.[131]

Juries could also be empanelled in the context of civil bills. The civil-bill process was legislated for in the early eighteenth century[132] as a summary process for dispensing with civil cases of low monetary value. According to Greer, this was essentially a regularisation of a practice already in existence for at least a century.[133] Originally, assizes judges held this jurisdiction, but in 1796 it was 'largely transferred … to the newly created assistant barristers at quarter sessions'.[134] In 1877 the assistant barristers, when determining civil cases, became county court judges.[135] The original 1703 act had envisaged trial by a judge acting alone, although appeals were to be tried by juries at assizes.[136]

An act of 1716 stated that a jury could be used in civil-bill cases where the judge thought it proper to have a controverted fact determined by a jury 'returned immediately at the prayer of the party'.[137] Later, the assistant barristers had a similar limited power to order a jury.[138] However, seneschals in manor courts were

126 3 & 4 Will. IV, c. 91, s. 40. See also the Jurors Qualification (Ireland) Act, 1876 (39 & 40 Vic., c. 21), s. 2. Jurors on coroner's inquests were excluded from this: see p. 81.

127 Giles Duncombe, *Tryalls per pais* (London, 1655), p. 93. See also J.H. Thomas, *A systematic arrangement of Lord Coke's first institute of the laws of England*, 3 vols (Philadelphia, 1826–7), iii, p. 499 (3 Co. Inst. 155a).

128 *Report on Irish jury laws, 1881*, para. 429 (Thomas Edmondson, hon. sec. of the Dublin Jurors Association).

129 For example, *Whittaker v. Berry, Irish Times*, 12 Feb. 1894; *Scovell v. Tombe, Irish Times*, 30 Nov. 1895; *Townley v. Lyle, Irish Times*, 6 Feb. 1886; *Lowry v. Bustard, Irish Times*, 16 Apr. 1885; and *Hewitt v. Lyttle, Irish Times*, 16 Dec. 1886.

130 Chancery Amendment Act, 1858 (21 & 22 Vic., c. 57), ss 3, 4, 6 and 8; Bankruptcy (Ireland Amendment) Act, 1872 (35 & 36 Vic., c. 58).

131 Rules of the Supreme Sourt, Ireland, 1891, order 36.

132 An Act for the recovery of small debts in a summary way before the judges of assize, 1703 (2 Anne, c. 18).

133 D.S. Greer, 'The development of civil bill procedure' in John McEldowney and Paul O'Higgins (eds), *The common law tradition: essays in legal history* (Dublin, 1990), p. 28.

134 Ibid., and the Civil Bill Courts Act, 1796 (36 Geo. III, c. 25).

135 County Officers and Courts Act, 1877 (40 & 41 Vic., c. 56), s. 8.

136 Small Debts Act, 1703 (2 Anne, c. 18), ss 1, 2, 4, 6.

137 Small Debts (Amendment) Act, 1715 (2 Geo. I, c. 11), ss 1, 2.

given the power to hear civil-bill cases in 1785,[139] and were authorised 'to summon sufficient juries' to try such cases. In practice, civil-bill juries were rarely used at quarter sessions, and almost always in manor courts.[140] Under the Civil Bill Courts (Ireland) Act, 1851,[141] the chairman of the quarter sessions could sit without a jury to determine all matters of fact and law, 'but when the amount claimed exceeds twenty pounds, a jury may be summoned on the requisition of either party to the suit as a matter of right', except in ejectment or replevin.[142] The chairman could also have a jury empanelled to assist him, and the jury usually consisted of three persons,[143] although occasionally there may have been six.[144] These jurors do not appear to have been entitled to any payment.[145]

CONCLUSION

This chapter demonstrates the important role laypersons played in determining the value of land or assessing damages. The nature of the tasks to be carried out by some of these juries suggests that they probably had, or needed, a certain degree of expertise or financial nous. Coming up with a figure for damages or a valuation was not as straightforward as delivering a binary verdict in a civil or criminal trial. It is also important not to overlook the role played by laypersons in the many city and county improvement schemes mentioned here that emerged in the eighteenth century – many of which have had lasting legacies. Interference with private property rights has always been controversial, but eighteenth- and nineteenth-century legislators saw the value in having juries play a part in the process.

138 Civil Bill Courts Act, 1796 (36 Geo. III, c. 25), s. 6
139 Manor Courts Act, 1785 (25 Geo. III, c. 44).
140 Manor courts were abolished by the Manor Courts Abolition (Ireland) Act, 1859 (22 & 23 Vic., c. 14). This transferred disputes to the jurisdiction of the petty sessions courts.
141 14 & 15 Vic., c. 57.
142 T.H. Barton, *The practice of the civil bill court in Ireland* (Dublin, 1865), p. 12.
143 Ibid., p. 13.
144 E.g. *Burns v. Belfast Tramway Company*, verdict of jury. Belfast sessions, 16 June 1893 (PRONI, ANT 1/1b/1/4/33).
145 *Boyle v. Wood* (1836) 1 Cr. & Dix C.C. 522.

CHAPTER SIX

Medico-legal juries

THIS CHAPTER CONSIDERS THREE TYPES of jury broadly categorised as medico-legal: the coroner's jury, which conducted inquests to determine the cause of death; the jury of matrons, which was used to determine pregnancy; and the lunacy jury, which was empanelled to determine whether a person was of unsound mind. Jurors on all three tribunals were expected to make determinations based partially on their own skill, knowledge and experience, though as the nineteenth century progressed, expert testimony from doctors was increasingly relied upon in making their decisions. Indeed, the role of the jury of matrons was eventually taken over by qualified medical experts. The jury of matrons was abolished in 1876,[1] while the lunacy jury endured until the twentieth century and the coroner's jury is still in existence.

THE CORONER'S JURY

The history of the coroner in Ireland has been examined in depth elsewhere,[2] and it is not the intention of this chapter to provide a history of the office. By the nineteenth century, the coroner's main function related to the holding of inquests on dead bodies, and occasionally he held inquests into treasure trove[3] or wrecks.[4] Until 1898 the coroner was elected by twelve men in the county court for life,

1 Juries Procedure (Ireland) Act, 1876 (39 & 40 Vic., c. 78, s. 13).

2 Most notably, see John L. Leckey and D. Greer, *Coroners' law and practice in Northern Ireland* (Belfast, 1998); B. Farrell, *Coroners: practice and procedure* (Dublin, 2000); Michael J. Clark, 'General practice and coroners' practice: medico-legal work and the Irish medical profession, *c.*1830–1890' in Catherine Cox and Maria Luddy (eds), *Cultures of care in Irish medical history, 1750–1970* (Basingstoke, 2010); and A.J. Otway-Ruthven, *A history of medieval Ireland* (London, 1980). For the history of the English coroner, see C. Gross, *Select cases from the coroners' rolls, AD1265–1413; with a brief account of the history of the office of coroner* (London, 1896) and Roy Frank Hunnisett, *The medieval coroner* (Cambridge, 1961).

3 Treasure trove was a royal prerogative giving the crown ownership of objects made substantially of gold or silver that had been buried with the intention of recovering them, and that had no known owner. See N.E. Palmer, 'Treasure trove and the protection of antiquities', *Mod. L. Rev.*, 44:2 (1981), 178–87; Anon., 'Treasure trove', *I.L.T. & S.J.* (1894), 127; *R v. O'Toole* (1867) 11 Cox. C.C. 75; and *Attorney general v. Trustees of the British Museum* [1903] Ch. D. 598.

4 E.g. see Edward J. Bourke, 'The sinking of the Rochdale and the Prince of Wales', *Dub. Hist. Rec.*, 61:2 (2008), 129–35.

assuming good behaviour.[5] He had to reside in the county, be a lawful and fit man,[6] and be of sufficient means (and thus less likely to succumb to corruption).[7] Although originally coroners were unpaid,[8] fees were introduced in the fifteenth century amid concern over falling standards.[9] It was thought that payment might ensure the proper discharge of their functions. A similar concern underlay the introduction of minimum property requirements in the nineteenth century.[10] As with other elements of the criminal justice system, by the nineteenth century there was a growing emphasis on professionalization,[11] and by 1881 a coroner had to be a qualified doctor, surgeon, barrister, solicitor or justice of the peace.[12]

The nineteenth-century procedure for inquests was laid out in legislation. In cases of sudden or suspicious death, or the discovery of a body, the constabulary notified the district coroner. Based on the information they provided, the coroner determined whether an inquest was necessary.[13] As well as cases of suspicious deaths, the coroner had statutory obligations relating to the deaths of vulnerable persons such as prisoners, infants, hospital patients and residents of asylums and alcoholics' retreats.[14] In cases of capital punishment, the coroner had to hold an

5 Under the Election of Coroners Act, 1354 (28 Ed. III, c. 6), coroners were to be elected by the commons of the counties. The Local Government (Ireland) Act, 1898 (61 & 62 Vic., c. 37) provided that coroners were henceforth to be appointed by county councils, rather than elected. See Otway-Ruthven, *A history of medieval Ireland*, p. 179.

6 Matthew Hale, *The history of the pleas of the crown*, 2 vols (London, 1736), ii, p. 55; Election of Coroners Act, 1354 (28 Ed. III, c. 6) provided that the coroners should be 'most meet and most lawful people'.

7 The Coroners (Ireland) Act, 1846 (9 & 10 Vic., c. 37), s. 16, provided that a coroner must have an estate worth £50, or freehold life estate valued at £100 per annum.

8 W. Blackstone, *Commentaries on the laws of England*, 4 vols (15th ed., London, 1809), iv, p. 336.

9 Star Chamber Act, 1487 (3 Hen. VII, c. 1), s. 4. This extended to Ireland and remained in force until the nineteenth century. It allowed a fee of 13*s.* 4*d.* for every inquisition. For more detailed discussion of the remuneration of coroners, see Leckey and Greer, *Coroner's law*, pp 6–7.

10 Regulation of the Office of Coroner (Ireland) Act, 1822 (3 Geo. IV, c. 115), s. 1. The preamble noted that while 'anciently none were chosen coroners but persons of an estate sufficient to maintain the dignity of the office', the office had for many year 'been suffered to fall into disrepute and get into low and indigent hands'. See also the Coroners (Ireland) Act, 1846 (9 & 10 Vic., c. 37), s. 16.

11 J.S. Forsyth, *A synopsis of medical jurisprudence: anatomically, physiologically, and forsensically illustrated; for the faculty of medicine, magistrates, lawyers, coroners and jurymen* (London, 1829) is an indication of how seriously inquests came to be taken. It contained detailed chapters on dissection, recognising causes of death, storage of bodies and anatomy.

12 The Coroners (Ireland) Act, 1881 (44 & 45 Vic., c. 35), s. 2.

13 Coroners (Ireland) Act, 1846 (9 & 10 Vic., c. 37), s. 22.

14 Hale wrote that 'if a prisoner in gaol dies a natural death, yet regularly the gaoler ought to send for the coroner to inquire, because it may be possibly presumed, that the prisoner died by the ill usage of the gaoler' (*Pleas*, ii, p. 57). See also the General Prisons (Ireland) Act, 1877 (40 & 41 Vic., c. 49), s. 56; Protection of Infant Life Act, 1872 (35 & 36 Vic., c. 38), s. 8; Lunacy Commissions Act, 1853 (16 & 17 Vic., c. 96); Lunacy Acts Amendment Act, 1862 (25 & 26 Vic., c. 111); Habitual Drunkards Act, 1879 (42 & 43 Vic., c. 19), s. 27. A statement of the deceased's name and cause of death was to be drawn up and sent to the coroner, the registrar of deaths, the clerk of local authority and either the person who had been paying for the deceased's stay at the retreat, or the persons who had made a statutory declaration that the person was an habitual drunkard.

inquest within twenty-four hours of the execution to ascertain the identity of the body, and whether judgment of death had been duly executed.[15]

Where an inquest was to be held, the coroner issued a precept to the sheriff to summon an adequate number of jurors.[16] The coroner could order that the body be brought to 'the nearest convenient tavern, public house, or house licensed for the sale of spirits'.[17] The inquest and viewing frequently took place in a public house, and the coroner could fine a publican who refused to allow his premises to be used.[18] An inquest could also be held at a private house,[19] including the home of the deceased,[20] the home of a witness,[21] or the house where the body was discovered.[22] The householder, if not a relative of the deceased, could be paid up to 3*s*. 6*d*. per day.[23] Inquests might also be held in courthouses,[24] town halls,[25] industrial premises,[26] infirmaries,[27] workhouses[28] and asylums.[29] The inquest did not have to be held in the same place where the body was viewed by the jurors.[30]

15 Capital Punishment Amendment Act, 1868 (31 Vic., c. 24), s. 5. In neither of these situations would prison officers qualify as jurors.

16 Coroners (Ireland) Act, 1846 (9 & 10 Vic., c. 37), s. 22. 17 Ibid., s. 36. 18 Ibid.

19 E.g. the inquest on P. Enright of Co. Tipperary was held on 20 Mar. 1887 at the house of Edward McCormac; the inquest on the body of a man unknown was held on 23 Mar. 1887 at the house of Catherine Hughes; and the inquest on James Whelan was held on 13 May 1887 at the house of Mr Phelim in Clonmel, despite his having died in Clonmel gaol (NAI, 1C-7–127).

20 E.g. the inquest on James Gleeson of Donohill, Co. Tipperary, on 6 Aug. 1886; and the inquest on Margaret Dwyer of Moyaliffe, Tipperary, on 6 May 1887 (NAI, 1C-7–127).

21 E.g. the inquest on Edmund Mannion of Ballyfarna, Co. Tipperary on 15 Aug. 1888 was held at the house of James Cormack; and the inquest on Glen Walsh of Lisdonagh, Co. Tipperary on 25 May 1888 was held at the house of James Murphy (NAI, 1C-7–127).

22 E.g. the inquest on an unknown female child on 4 Jan. 1889 was held at the house of William Blake and his son in Tipperary, where the body was found, and where the mother, Johanna Donohoe, had been confined and given birth (NAI, 1C-7–127).

23 Coroners (Ireland) Act, 1846 (9 & 10 Vic., c. 37), sch. C.

24 E.g. the inquest on the body of an infant child found in the Liffey at Blackhall, Clane, Co. Kildare on 19 May 1890 (NAI, 1C-02–6024); the inquest on Walter Grant on 13 Nov. 1888 at the courthouse in Cloghan, Co. Tipperary; the inquest on Michael Fogerty on 16 Mar. 1888 at Carrick-on-Suir courthouse, Co. Tipperary (NAI, 1C-7–127).

25 E.g. the inquest on William Minehan on 15 Jan. 1889 at Clonmel town hall; the inquest on Patrick Kennedy on 23 Jan. 1889 at Clonmel town hall (NAI, 1C-7–127).

26 E.g. the inquest on Thomas Bewley on 29 Jan. 1889 in Dublin: see James Scannell, 'The inevitable demise of Thomas Bewley', *Dub. Hist. Rec.*, 61:2 (2008), 114–19.

27 The inquest on Patrick Nailon at Co. Clare infirmary on 17 Nov. 1879; the inquest on Patrick Barry at Co. Clare infirmary, 4 Dec. 1879 (NAI, 1D-39–112).

28 E.g. the inquest on Patrick Cormack at the Thurles workhouse in Co. Tipperary on 4 Nov. 1886 (NAI, 1C-7–127); the inquest on John Farrell, Sligo town on 23 Dec. 1895 (NAI, 1C-31–95); the inquest on John Heffernan on 20 Feb. 1887 at Cashel workhouse (NAI, 1C-7–127); and the inquest on Jane Giligan, Sligo on 9 June 1902 (NAI, 1C-31–95), which took place in the workhouse even though she was not an inmate and had not died there.

29 E.g. the inquest on Bartholemew Mannion at Sligo district lunatic asylum on 19 Mar. 1890 (NAI 1C-31–95).

30 Hawkins, *Pleas of the crown*, ii, p. 81. Bernard V. Heathcote, *Viewing the lifeless body: a coroner and his inquests held in Nottinghamshire public houses during the nineteenth century, 1828 to 1866*

The jurors had to be resident within the coroner's district and although MacNally observed in 1808 that there was no specific property requirement for a coroner's juror,[31] from 1846 the jurors had to be rated for the relief of the poor for the amount of £4 per annum.[32] Persons who were exempted by the Juries (Ireland) Act, 1833[33] from sitting on trial juries were also exempted from sitting on coroners' juries.[34] Persons who were not *probi et legalis* were disqualified,[35] and there were specific persons disqualified as jurors when it came to statutory inquests.[36] There does not appear to have been any exemption or disqualification for relatives of the deceased – in a number of inquests there were several jurors sharing the deceased person's surname, who were probably related to him or her. For example, at the inquest on Michael Crofs in Kildare in 1883, there were five other Crofs on the jury.[37] Although persons who could not read or write the English language ought to have been disqualified after 1876, there are many examples of coroner's jurors signing simply 'X' on inquests,[38] suggesting that the literacy requirement was not rigorously enforced. The £4 rateable qualification was lower than the 1830s and 1870s qualifications for trial jurors. This was to facilitate the speedy empanelling of the jury; time was of the essence when it came to inquests. The coroner could not afford to be too fussy and most inquests took place either on the same day or the day after the discovery of the body.[39]

The legislation did not specify how many jurors were to be summoned for a coroner's inquest – the 1846 act simply stated that the sheriff was directed to summon a sufficient number. However, because the agreement of twelve jurors was necessary for a valid verdict,[40] there was a common practice of summoning more

(Nottingham, 2005), p. 15, notes that in England, by the nineteenth century, the body was often left in an outhouse while the inquest took place inside the inn.

31 Leonard MacNally, *The justice of the peace for Ireland: containing the authorities and duties of that officer, as also of the various conservators of the peace*, 2 vols (Dublin, 1808), ii, p. 50.

32 Coroners (Ireland) Act, 1846 (9 & 10 Vic., c. 37), s. 23. There may not have been an equivalent property requirement for coroners' juries in England: *Report on juries* [C-6817] 1913, xxx, 403, p. 10, noted that there was 'no specific qualification'. The English Coroner's Act, 1887 (50 & 51 Vic., c. 71) simply stated that they were to be 'good and lawful men'. Evidence given to the committee indicated that the coroner usually chose men who were householders in the neighbourhood, and that there were no age restrictions.

33 3 & 4 Will. IV, c. 91, s. 2.

34 See the Juries Qualification (Ireland) Act, 1876 (39 & 40 Vic., c. 21), s. 20. Sch. 1 listed those persons absolutely freed from serving on any jury. This was broadly drafted to include coroners' juries. There was some confusion in relation to exemptions in England in the case of *Re Dutton* (1892) 1 Q.B. 486.

35 Huband, *Treatise*, p. 233.

36 For example, where death occurred in a prison, no prison officer could be a juror, and where death occurred in a mine, no person with an interest in or employed by the mine could sit on the jury.

37 Inquest on Michael Crofs, Drimfee, Co. Kildare, 3 Feb. 1883 (NAI, 1C-02-6024).

38 E.g. the inquest on Patrick Fennell of Knocknaree on 6 Jan. 1883; the inquest on John Rooney of Timahoe on 10 Jan. 1883; the inquest on Ellen Monaghan of Rickardstown on 24 Mar. 1888; and the inquest on Thomas McMahon of Longtown on 1 July 1887 (NAI, 1C-02-6024).

39 E.g. the inquest on Patrick Considine of Co. Clare on 5 Aug. 1879 (NAI, 1D-39-112).

40 Hale gives the example of *John Cobat's case* (1389), in which an inquisition was quashed because there were only eleven jurors. Hale, *Pleas*, ii, pp 160–1.

than twelve. This meant that a majority verdict would suffice, provided twelve or more jurors were in agreement. The coroner could also supplement the panel with other fit and proper persons as needed, provided they were householders and residents in the county where the inquest was to be held.[41] It was quite common to have up to fifteen jurors,[42] and in exceptional cases twenty-three or twenty-four jurors.[43] For example, at the inquest on Stephen Heffernan in 1889[44] there were twenty-three jurors. During a disturbance in Tipperary town following evictions on the Smith-Barry estate,[45] thirteen-year-old Heffernan had been shot by a pellet fired by police, despite having nothing to do with the disturbances.[46] Injured in the ankle, Heffernan later died from tetanus, and his death provoked national outrage.[47] The verdict of the coroner's jury was death 'from a gunshot wound wilfully feloniously and of malice aforethought' inflicted by constable John Toohey of the RIC. Ultimately, however, no member of the RIC was convicted of his murder.[48] Sometimes higher numbers of jurors were empanelled in cases of suspected homicide,[49] suicide[50] or infanticide.[51] Some jurors were regularly summoned for inquests.[52]

When sufficient jurors were assembled, they were sworn in. The complex system of challenges that existed in relation to trial juries[53] had no counterpart when it came to the coroner's inquest.[54] As Molloy observed, however:

41 See pp 115–17.

42 E.g. the inquest on Charles McKelleher, St John's parish, Sligo, 24 Dec. 1888 (NAI, 1C-31–95); the inquest on Michael McNamara, Co. Clare, 29 Sept. 1898; the inquest on Eliza Nolan, 23–4 July 1885, Sixmilebridge, Co. Clare; and the inquest on Patrick Reilly, Sixmilebridge, Co. Clare, 28 July 1885 (NAI, 1D-39–112).

43 Patrick Polden, 'Coroners and their courts' in John Baker, *The Oxford history of the laws of England* (Oxford, 2004–10), xi, p. 952, notes that in England it was 'uncommon' for more than fifteen jurors to be empanelled.

44 Inquest held 26 Sept. 1889 at the Tipperary workhouse (NAI, 1C-7–127). See *Freeman's Journal*, 27 Sept. 1889, and *Irish Examiner*, 26 Sept. 1889.

45 See Alvin Jackson, *Home rule: an Irish history, 1800–2000* (Oxford, 2003), pp 69–70.

46 See *Kerry Sentinel*, 11 Sept. 1889.

47 See *The Nation*, 28 Sept. 1889.

48 PRO, 30/60/12/833.

49 E.g. at the inquest on James Gleeson, Donohill, Co. Tipperary, 6 Aug. 1886 there were sixteen jurors, and a verdict of inflammation of the brain due to fractured skull 'inflicted on him on the twenty-fourth of last July wilfully and maliciously and with malice propense by some person or persons of whom there is no evidence before us'. Similarly, at the inquest on Margaret Dwyer, Moyaliffe, Tipperary, 6 May 1887, there were fifteen jurors. The verdict was death from a 'fractured windpipe' and head injuries 'wilfully and feloniously and malice propense inflicted' (NAI, 1C-7–127).

50 E.g. at the inquest on Francis Magee, found hanged at the Clonmel lunatic asylum, 20 Mar. 1888, there were fourteen jurors (NAI, 1C-7–127).

51 E.g. at the inquest on an unknown female child on 4 Jan. 1889 in Clonmel, there were fifteen jurors and the verdict was death by suffocation. At the inquest on a female child whose name was unknown on 31 Dec. 1887, there were thirteen jurors and they found that the baby had been born alive and thrown into the river Suir (NAI, 1C-7–127).

52 E.g. many of the jurors on the inquest of Eliza Nolan on 23 and 24 July 1885 were also summoned for the inquest on Patrick Reilly, four days later.

53 See pp 136–49.

54 Huband, *Treatise*, pp 238–9. See Hale, *Pleas*, ii, p. 58. However, if someone disqualified from

> strictly speaking, jurors upon a coroner's inquest are not challengeable ... but it is better to yield to any fair objection, which would in other cases be a cause of challenge than run the hazard of vitiating the inquisition by the impanelling of improper persons.[55]

Once they were sworn, the jurors viewed the body.[56] This was compulsory; as Hale pointed out, 'oftentimes much of the evidence ariseth upon the view'.[57] Huband wisely noted that '[t]he inquest should be held and the body should be viewed before the appearance of the body be altered by decomposition or otherwise'.[58] If no inquest had taken place within two days and no coroner was available, the duty devolved to the justices of the peace.[59] It was desirable, but not strictly necessary that the coroner and jury view the body at the same time.[60] Coroner's inquests were relatively informal compared with trials at the assizes or sessions. The fact that they took place in less formal surroundings, such as private houses, probably contributed to the relatively relaxed attitudes of jurors, who were known to wander off during testimony[61] – meaning not only might they miss potentially relevant testimony, but also that they left themselves open to possible interference by interested parties.

THE JURY OF MATRONS

The jury of matrons was the only nineteenth-century jury composed of women, and was used to determine pregnancy in both civil and criminal cases.[62] This jury was not regulated by statute, and its members were not required to hold freehold or comply with other typical jury qualifications or residency requirements.[63] The jury of matrons consisted of married women,[64] or widows who had experience with

serving was sworn in and took part in the finding, 'this may be the ground of a plea to the inquisition in the event of any person accused by it being arraigned upon it'. Huband, *Treatise*, p. 239.

55 Constantine Molloy, *Justice of the peace for Ireland: a treatise on the powers and duties of magistrates in Ireland in cases of summary jurisdiction in the prosecution of indictable offences and in other matters* (Dublin, 1890), p. 350.

56 S. 44 of the 1846 act provided that where the coroner did not hold an inquest within two days of death, two magistrates of the district could do so in his place.

57 Hale, *Pleas*, ii, p. 57.

58 Huband, *Treatise*, p. 241. See also Molloy, *Justice of the peace*, p. 356.

59 See 9 & 10 Vic., c. 37, s. 44, and Molloy, *Justice of the peace*, p. 346.

60 9 & 10 Vic., c. 37, c. 46. In *R v. Ingham* (1864) 9 Cox C.C. 508, the court held that the jurors did not all have to view the body together. In this case there were fifteen jurors. Fourteen of them viewed the body together and the last juror arrived late and viewed the body on his own.

61 E.g. *R v. O'Brien and Bourchier* (1882) 17 I.L.T.R. 34.

62 On the history of the custom see Blackstone, *Commentaries*, p. 395. See generally James C. Oldham, 'On pleading the belly: a history of the jury of matrons', *Crim. Jus. Hist.*, 6 (1985), 1–64, who notes that the use of women to determine whether a female litigant was pregnant dated to antiquity, 2.

63 Oldham, 'On pleading the belly', 13.

64 E.g. *R v. Wycherley* (1838) 8 Car. & P. 262: 173 E.R. 487.

childbirth; they did not have to be midwives.[65] Lord Hale wrote that in criminal cases they were to be 'discreet women'.[66] Oldham points out that while the all-female jury was used in such determinations 'for reasons of delicacy', the courts 'primarily viewed the women as experts on the subject of their inquiry'.[67] There was no list of matrons; they were summoned *de circumstantibus* from the bystanders in and around the court, and it was necessary in a number of English cases to shut the courtroom doors to prevent women in attendance from trying to avoid being empanelled.[68] The inspection of the allegedly pregnant woman by the matrons took place in a private room, and not in the courtroom.[69] In civil cases the jury of matrons was empanelled on a writ *de ventre inspiciendo*. A version of this writ from 1553 required that the woman pleading the belly be examined by twelve matrons and twelve knights, in the presence of the sheriff, but Oldham considers it unlikely that the writ was ever enforced in this manner.[70]

In criminal cases, records of women who had been sentenced to death 'pleading the belly' date to the 1220s.[71] As Oldham notes, '[a]lthough pregnancy in a female criminal defendant would not delay her trial, the court could stay her execution if she were found guilty of a capital crime in order to permit the child to be born'.[72] According to the *Complete juryman*:

> where a woman is attainted of treason or any capital crime for which she is to suffer death, and being asked what she can say for herself in stay of execution of her according to the judgment given against her? if she is with child, she may allege to that matter, and pray a jury of matrons to inspect and try whether she is with child or not; and the court will accordingly order the sheriff to return a jury of matrons, and if they find her to be with quick child, the execution shall be respited, that the child may not suffer death for the crime of the mother.[73]

Fox J. in 1808 described the plea of pregnancy as 'a plea the humanity of our law affords to persons in such a situation, not through any favour for the persons concerned, but for the innocent offspring who would be necessarily connected and involved with the fate of its unhappy parent'.[74]

After a determination that she was 'quick with child of a quick child', the defendant was allowed to continue the pregnancy to full term, and then in theory she was to be executed after she had given birth. Even as early as the twelfth century, however, there is evidence of full reprieves being granted, in cases where

65 Oldham, 'On pleading the belly', 16. 66 Hale, *Pleas*, ii, p. 413.
67 James C. Oldham, 'The origins of the special jury', *U. Chic. L. Rev.*, 50 (1983), 137–211 at 171–2.
68 E.g. *R v. Wycherley* (1838) 8 Car. & P. 262: 173 E.R. 487.
69 MacNally, *Justice of the peace*, ii, p. 51. 70 Oldham, 'On pleading the belly', 14.
71 Thomas R. Forbes, 'A jury of matrons', *Medical Hist.*, 32:1 (1988), 23–33 at 26.
72 Oldham, 'Origins', 171.
73 Anon., *The complete juryman*, p. 41. See also MacNally, *Justice of the peace*, i, p. 579.
74 *Belfast Newsletter*, 12 Apr. 1808.

further investigation was carried out after the defendant was found to be pregnant.[75] Cockburn considers that the rules governing pregnancy pleas 'were in practice manipulated to give assizes judges considerable discretion in the punishment of female felons'.[76] According to his research, the 'overwhelming majority' of those who successfully pleaded the belly were released, although Oldham is more cautious in his estimation of the number of pardons.[77] There are Irish examples of full reprieves being granted to pregnant defendants,[78] but the practice was not universal. For example, Bridget Murray was convicted in 1818, on the testimony of her twelve-year-old daughter, of aiding and abetting her paramour in the murder of her husband.[79] A jury of matrons found her to be pregnant, and she was delivered of a baby some six months later. Despite her protestations of innocence her execution was unfortunately carried out.[80] Similarly, Mary Fairfield, convicted of murder, was found pregnant by a Dublin jury of matrons in October 1783. She was brought before the court the following February and September, not yet having given birth, but eventually the court ruled that the law was to take its course.[81]

A woman who successfully pleaded the belly could not do so again if she became pregnant for a second time.[82] In March 1807 a woman named Elizabeth Gartlan pleaded the belly and was declared by a jury of matrons in Monaghan to be 'pregnant by a child quickened into life'.[83] At the following assizes, she was called into court and asked why her sentence should not be carried out, but the court again postponed the execution on being informed that sufficient time had not yet elapsed for her pregnancy to be full-term. In April 1808 she was called into court again, with Fox J. observing that 'upwards of twelve months [had] elapsed since that verdict was delivered, which is more than the ordinary course of nature requires'. He pointed out that she could not plead her belly for a second time, and she received the sentence of death.[84]

Most juries of matrons were empanelled in murder trials, but other capital felonies could also result in these juries being empanelled. For example, Mary McMahon, convicted of stealing one hundred guineas at the Limerick assizes in 1789, was found to be pregnant by a jury of matrons.[85] Sometimes a jury of

75 Ibid.

76 J.S. Cockburn, *Calendar of assize records*, xi: *Home circuit indictments: Elizabeth I and James I: introduction* (London, 1985), p. 122.

77 Ibid., pp 122–3; Oldham, 'On pleading the belly', 19–20.

78 E.g. *Freeman's Journal*, 21 Oct. 1780.

79 Ibid., 16 Mar. 1818.

80 Ibid., 15 Aug. 1818. Bridget Oakley was found not to be pregnant by a jury of matrons a year later: *Belfast Newsletter*, 10 Aug. 1819.

81 *Freeman's Journal*, 19 Aug. 1784.

82 Oldham, 'On pleading the belly', 580.

83 *Belfast Newsletter*, 12 Apr. 1808.

84 Ibid.

85 *Finn's Leinster Journal*, 4 Apr. 1789. Another eighteenth-century case was the joint trial of Rose Eustace and Elinor Rothe at the Dublin quarter sessions in 1785, neither of whom was found to be pregnant: *Belfast Newsletter*, 7 Oct. 1785. Mary Berkeley, convicted of murder, was similarly found not to be pregnant: *Freeman's Journal*, 12 July 1803.

matrons was empanelled in a criminal case in circumstances other than a convicted felon seeking to evade the capital sentence. For example, in 1793 Mary Donnel was charged with the murder of her baby, which had been found in a mill race. She claimed that she was still pregnant, and was examined by a jury of matrons, with two accoucheurs (male midwifes) present.[86] She was found to have recently given birth, and their opinion was that the birth had taken place before the discovery of the baby's body in the water. She was committed to Philipstown gaol.[87]

In civil actions, a jury of matrons might be empanelled where a widow claimed to be pregnant with the child of her recently deceased husband; or in the words of Blackstone: 'when a widow feigns herself with child, in order to exclude the next heir, and a suppositious birth is suspected to be intended'.[88] Richardson and Sayles trace the civil use of the writ of *ventre inspeciendo* back to 1220 in the records of Bracton, where they found 'discreet and law-worthy' knights and matrons jointly conducting the examination, on the application of the deceased's brother. One year later, a case was reported in which a jury of fourteen women from London was empanelled, and by 1223, the use of the writ was shown by its appearance on the plea roll.[89] Bracton described at length the writ *de ventre*, noting that the woman in question was to be:

> examined by lawful and discreet women through whom the truth may better be known ... And if the said keepers and women discover that she is pregnant, or if they are in doubt, then let them lodge her in our castle, such a one, in such a way that no maid who may be pregnant nor any other who may be suspected of contriving a deception has access to her, and let her remain in the castle until the question of her offspring may be settled.[90]

The main concern of such writs was to prevent the fraudulent substitution of someone else's baby as a male heir.[91] Another use of the jury of matrons was in cases where a wife sought a divorce or an annulment on the grounds of the impotence of her husband, and claimed that she had remained a virgin despite their cohabiting.[92] Similar bodies of women were used in witchcraft trials in Europe and America from the fifteenth century until the eighteenth century.[93]

The matrons' task was a difficult one, given the limited understanding of pregnancy before the nineteenth century. It was not enough merely to be pregnant or 'with child' – she had to be 'quick with child'.[94] Stephen noted that 'barely with

86 See Adrian Wilson, *The making of man-midwifery: childbirth in England, 1660–1770* (London, 1995).
87 *Freeman's Journal*, 21 Nov. 1793. 88 Blackstone, *Commentaries*, iii, p. 362.
89 H. Richardson & G. Sayles (eds), *Select cases of procedure without writ under Henry III* (London, 1941), pp cliii–cliv.
90 Samuel E. Thorne, *Bracton on the laws and customs of England* (Massachusetts, 1968), ii, pp 201–3, lists other writs associated with this concern.
91 See H.J. Stephen, *New commentaries on the laws of England*, 4 vols (New York, 1843), i, p. 318.
92 See Oldham, 'On pleading the belly', 4. 93 Ibid., 8–9.
94 MacNally, *Justice of the peace*, p. 580.

child, unless it alive in the womb, is not sufficient'.[95] To be quick with child generally meant that the woman (and the jurors) must have felt the child quickening, or moving in the womb – after about sixteen weeks of pregnancy.[96] Oldham notes that until the late eighteenth century, human life was not considered to have begun until this happened.[97] By the early nineteenth century this view was in decline, and the difference between a baby who had 'quickened' and one who had not was increasingly seen as arbitrary.[98] The British Medical Association described it in 1841 as 'making a distinction where there is no distinction'.[99]

The difficulties are illustrated by the 1841 case of Mary Hallinan.[100] Along with her lover, John Stanford, she was convicted at the Mayo summer assizes of murdering her husband by administering arsenic. On being convicted, she said 'she hoped they wouldn't murder her child, which she was carrying'.[101] The court directed that a jury of matrons be summoned to examine her in a private room. The sheriff returned twelve women 'after some time'.[102] They were sworn, and examined her along with a surgeon who was sworn in to assist them. A second surgeon was then sworn in, as there was some difficulty in assessing whether she was pregnant. They returned to court with a verdict that she did not 'show symptoms of quickening; that those of pregnancy are very slight at present, but that a few weeks will afford less doubtful testimony'.[103] Richards B. criticised them, saying 'that is no verdict at all. You should find whether the prisoner is pregnant or not, and if you have any reasonable doubt give her the benefit of it.' One of the matrons replied, '[w]ell, we find her pregnant'. In other words, she was pregnant, but not quick with child.[104] The judge, exasperated, told them that 'the proper form is to say whether she be quick with child or not. This is the first time I ever heard of it being refused to find a woman quick with child who was pregnant. It is not a question of nice medical science; and if you say she is pregnant it will do.' Her sentence was adjourned until the following assize.

Carlow in 1830 saw two instances of women pleading the belly having been convicted of murdering their husbands.[105] However, this was unusual: Forbes points out that 'pleading the belly' in a capital case was a relatively rare occurrence,[106] and it seems to have petered out in Ireland by the mid-nineteenth

95 J.F. Stephen, *A history of the criminal law of England*, 3 vols (London, 1883), i, p. 460.
96 See *R v. Wycherley* (1838) 8 Car. & P. 262; 173 E.R. 486.
97 Oldham, 'On pleading the belly', 18.
98 In 1829, Forsyth, *Medical jurisprudence*, p. 384, described the idea that foetal motion indicated the beginning of life as having been 'abandoned'.
99 Anon., 'Historical sketch of the British Medical Association', *British Medical J.*, 1 (1882), 847–85 at 854.
100 *Freeman's Journal*, 3 Aug. 1841.
101 *Connaught Telegraph*, 4 Aug. 1841.
102 Ibid. Their names were reported in the newspaper.
103 Ibid.
104 *Nenagh Guardian*, 7 Aug. 1841.
105 These were Catherine Hunt (*Chute's Western Herald*, 1 Apr. 1830) and Bridget Brennan (*Kerry Evening Post*, 14 Aug. 1830). The former was successful in her plea while the latter was not.
106 Forbes, 'Jury of matrons', 31.

century. The Hallinan case from 1841 appears to have been the last recorded instance of a jury of matrons being empanelled in Ireland. Forbes also notes that the use of the *ventre inspeciendo* in civil cases had probably ended in the 1830s.[107] As the century progressed, public opinion began to favour qualified physicians over amateur matrons, and doctors began to be sworn in to assist the jury in reaching their decisions. Several erroneous verdicts by juries of matrons in England led to calls for the jury's abolition during the 1870s.[108] The Juries Procedure (Ireland) Act, 1876[109] abolished the jury *de ventre inspeciendo*. In cases where pregnancy was claimed in capital-conviction cases, the prisoner was now to be examined by 'one or more medical men'. The jury of matrons was not formally abolished in England until 1931,[110] and even as late as 1913 a committee on jury law and practice noted that a jury of matrons was still 'sometimes, though very rarely empanelled'.[111]

THE LUNACY JURY

Lunacy juries were empanelled to determine whether a person was deemed to be of unsound mind. Traditionally, the crown had jurisdiction as *parens patriae* over the person and property of those deemed to be 'idiots' or 'lunatics'.[112] The power was delegated personally to the lord chancellor. This was to ensure that unscrupulous family members or outsiders did not take advantage of an insane person's circumstances. The lord chancellor's inherent jurisdiction 'over the property of lunatics was, in legal theory, unlimited and incapable of definition, but had to be exercised for the benefit of the patient'.[113] The powers became more

107 Ibid., 28.

108 See generally Jean Donninson, *Midwives and medical men: a history of inter-professional rivalries and women's rights* (New York, 1977) on the history of professional midwives and nineteenth-century knowledge of pregnancy and childbirth.

109 39 & 40 Vic., c. 78, s. 13.

110 The Sentence of Death (Expectant Mothers) Act, 1931.

111 *Report on juries* [C-6817] 1913, xxx, 403, p. 7.

112 See Clive Unsworth, 'Law and lunacy in psychiatry's "golden age"', *Ox. J. Leg. Stud.*, 13 (1993), 479–507, and Leslie Gerald Eyre Harris, *A treatise on the law and practice in lunacy in Ireland* (Dublin, 1930), p. 1. See also the Property of Idiots Act, 1323 (17 Ed. II, c. 9): the king 'shall have the custody of the lands of natural fools … and after the death of such idiots, shall render them to the right heir, so that the lands shall not be sold, nor the heir disinherited'. Additionally, the Property of Lunatics Act, 1323 (17 Ed. II, c. 10) stated: 'The king shall provide that the lands of lunaticks be safely kept without waste and they and their families … shall be maintained with the profits thereof, and that the residue be kept for their use, and be delivered unto them when they come to right mind.' For a history of the treatment of mental illness in Ireland see Catherine Cox, *Negotiating insanity in the southeast of Ireland, 1820–1900* (Manchester, 2012) and Daniel Hack Tuke, *Chapters in the history of the insane in the British Isles* (Dublin, 1882).

113 Chantel Stebbings, 'Protecting the property of the mentally ill: the judicial solution in nineteenth century lunacy law', *Camb. L. J.*, 71:2 (2012), 384–411 at 390.

wide-ranging as the nineteenth century progressed; the chancellor could 'sell or charge the corpus of the lunatic's estate, whatever his interest, in order to clear debts or to pay any expenditure for his maintenance or otherwise for his benefit'.[114] First, however, a determination had to be made as to whether the person could be deemed insane, or of unsound mind.

The chancellor could order a writ *de lunatico inquirendo*, which directed an inquiry, originally held before five escheators,[115] as to whether a named person was insane. Dutton described the writ as requiring the sheriff to call the suspected lunatic before him for examination 'and enquire by the oaths of twelve men, whether he have sufficient wit to dispose of his own lands with discretion or not, and to certify accordingly into the chancery'.[116] If the person was found to be of unsound mind, then immediate control could be exercised over his or her estate. It was open to the person to traverse this finding.[117]

The Lunacy Regulation (Ireland) Act, 1871, which was to be the primary statute governing lunacy procedures over the next century, was an attempt to further streamline and reform lunacy proceedings.[118] If the lord chancellor ordered an inquiry into a person's state of mind, that person could demand that this take place before a jury.[119] However, if the lord chancellor was of the view that the person was not of sound enough mind to make this request, he could order that the inquest take place without a jury.[120] If the jury returned a verdict that the person was of unsound mind, the person could traverse, or appeal, the finding, and the issue could be sent for trial.[121]

Lunacy commissions tended to be before special jurors, who were paid for their time and trouble.[122] Commissions of lunacy were held in public, often in very crowded courtrooms.[123] The public interest and press reporting of these

114 Ibid.

115 T.C.S. Keeley, 'One hundred years of lunacy administration', *Camb. L. J.*, 8:2 (1943), 195–200 at 196.

116 Dutton, *Office and authority*, p. 239. See also MacNally, *Justice of the peace*, ii, p. 4.

117 See the Lunacy Act, 1825 (6 Geo. IV, c. 53).

118 This act was attributable to Thomas O'Hagan. In England, the early nineteenth century had seen a number of reforms intended to streamline lunacy proceedings. The Lunatic Commissions Act, 1833 (3 & 4 Will. IV, c. 36), s. 1, provided that a commission of lunacy was to be held before one or more commissioners in lunacy. Further amendment was made by the Lunacy Commissions Act, 1842 (5 & 6 Vic., c. 84), which appointed two permanent commissioners in lunacy in England. This was confirmed by the Lunacy Commissions Regulation Act, 1853 (16 & 17 Vic., c. 70), s. 6. Many of the provisions of the 1871 act were based on the Lunacy Commissions Regulation Act, 1853 (16 & 17 Vic., c. 70), most of which had related to England and Wales only. It had abolished the compulsory jury in England and Wales, providing in s. 40 that a person who was to be the subject of a lunacy inquiry could request a jury.

119 S. 13. The inquiry had to be before a jury if the person was out of the jurisdiction: s. 18.

120 S. 16.

121 S. 97. A verdict of sanity could not, however, be traversed.

122 See p. 121. Stebbings notes, p. 392, that lunacy proceedings were prohibitively expensive for most people.

123 E.g. the commission of lunacy regarding John Gustavus Crosbie, *Irish Times*, 9, 11 and 12 Aug. 1857.

commissions[124] meant they often became 'celebrated or notorious cases in which medicine's definitions of insanity were subjected to highly public and supremely intensive investigation'.[125] Although the testimony of witnesses, including doctors, was publicly given, the person who was the subject of the lunacy commission generally testified before the commissioners and jury in private.[126]

Unsworth observes that the procedure was 'property-driven rather than person-oriented, and in practice was usually reserved for cases where control over family wealth was at issue'.[127] It was not unheard of that persons with an interest in the alleged lunatic's property would petition for them to be declared insane or of unsound mind, and the lunacy jury could be a safeguard against unscrupulous relatives. This did not always work, however. For example, the commission regarding Mary McOwen in 1872 was taken by her sister Elizabeth, a Carmelite nun. Mary was to inherit one-third of her late brother's estate, but was declared to be of unsound mind; Elizabeth was declared to be her sole heir, and therefore inherited two-thirds of the estate.[128] While earlier juries acted on their own understandings of sanity and mental disorder, there was later a greater reliance on medical evidence, which arguably diminished the role of the jury in these proceedings, although juries *de lunatico inquirendo* existed until the twenty-first century.[129]

CONCLUSION

Coroners' juries, lunacy juries and juries of matrons pushed the boundaries of lay decision-making into the realm of the medical. These juries were expected to decide not just 'ordinary' questions of fact but also complex questions involving pregnancy, mental health and causes of death. Because of the state of medical knowledge at the time, particularly up to the late nineteenth century, the gap between the jurors' knowledge and that of medical professionals was not so great as in the twenty-first century. As medical knowledge improved, however, there was a correlating increase in reliance on expert medical testimony. The rise of the expert witness has been documented elsewhere.[130] The increasing

124 E.g. the commission of lunacy regarding Margaret Watte, *Irish Examiner*, 13 July 1860.

125 Unsworth, 'Law and lunacy', 491.

126 E.g. the commission of lunacy regarding Edward Rogers, *Irish Times*, 1 Sept. 1859; the commission of lunacy regarding John Gustavus Crosbie, *Irish Times*, 9, 11 and 12 Aug. 1857; the commission of lunacy regarding Walter Coulsen, *Irish Times*, 29 Nov. 1859; and the commission of lunacy regarding John Kennedy Burke, *Irish Times*, 18 Feb. 1905.

127 Unsworth, 'Law and lunacy', 490.

128 *Irish Times*, 20 Nov. 1872.

129 See Juries Act, 1976, s. 30; and Rules of the Superior Courts, 1986 (SI 15/1986), order 64, rules 10–16. The Assisted Decision-Making (Capacity) Act, 2015 finally repealed the Lunacy Regulation (Ireland) Act, 1871.

130 E.g. Tal Golan, 'The history of scientific expert testimony in the English courtroom', *Science in Context*, 12:1 (1999), 7–32; Lloyd L. Rosenthal, 'The development of the use of expert testimony', *L. & Contemp. Problems*, 2 (1935), 403–18; Keith J.B. Rix, 'Expert evidence and the

professionalization and regulation of medicine[131] was part of a wider emphasis on professional knowledge and the rise of professional classes.[132] This went hand-in-hand with a growing recognition that a panel of untrained laypersons acting on their own experiences and knowledge may not have been best placed to make such determinations.

courts: 1. The history of expert evidence', *Advances in Psychiatric Treatment*, 5 (1999), 71–7; and Jennifer L. Mnookin, 'Idealizing science and demonizing experts: an intellectual history of expert evidence', *Villanova L. Rev.*, 52 (2007), 763–802.

131 E.g. the Apothecaries Act, 1815 (55 Geo. III, c. 194); the Medical Act, 1858 (21 & 22 Vic., c. 90); the Pharmaceutical Chemists (England) Act, 1852 (15 & 16 Vic., c. 56); the Pharmacy Act (Ireland), 1875 (38 & 39 Vic., c. 57); and the Dentists Act, 1878 (41 & 42 Vic., c. 33). See also *Report on medical education*, HC 1834 (602) xiii, 1.

132 See W.J. Reader, *Professional men: the rise of the professional classes in nineteenth-century England* (London, 1966). He notes, p. 71, that by the second half of the nineteenth century, '[t]he idea was gaining ground that if doctors and solicitors had to qualify by examination, then army officers and civil servants ought to, too'.

CHAPTER SEVEN

Mixed, market and manor-court juries

THE THREE TYPES OF JURY considered in this chapter peaked in the eighteenth century, were in decline by the early decades of the nineteenth century, and had disappeared completely by the end of that century. All three were firmly entrenched in the legal system by the eighteenth century. Mixed juries, or juries *de medietate linguae*, consisted of six locals and six aliens, and were empanelled in civil and criminal cases involving foreigners. They were infrequently used by the nineteenth century. Manor court juries operated in local courts to settle civil disputes and minor criminal offences, and were much less formal than the juries at assizes and quarter sessions. They sat very frequently and were probably the jury that people at the lower socio-economic levels were most likely to encounter. Market juries were essentially inspectors of markets, and had wide-ranging powers. Where they operated effectively, particularly around the late eighteenth century and early nineteenth century, they played an important role in regulating market practices in cities and large towns.

THE JURY *DE MEDIETATE LINGUAE*

The jury *de medietate linguae* was a variation on the petty jury that was used in cases involving foreigners.[1] Traditionally, aliens were neither obliged nor entitled to sit on regular petty juries, but could be called upon to sit on one of these mixed juries, also known as 'half-tongue' juries. The practice of using mixed juries has its roots in the history of Jews in England.[2] Separate tribunals settled disputes arising between members of the Jewish community; and from 1190, disputes between Jews and Christians were settled by tribunals comprising members from each community.[3] Similar rights were later conferred on foreign merchants, whose common-law right to mixed juries was codified in the 1353 Statute of the Staple, which stated:

1 See Matthew Dutton, *The office and authority of sheriffs, under-sheriffs, deputies, county-clerks, and coroners in Ireland* (Dublin, 1721), pp 358–9.
2 See L.H. LaRue, 'A jury of one's peers', *Washington and Lee Law Review*, 33 (1976), 841–75.
3 For a more detailed history of this type of jury see Niamh Howlin, 'Fenians, foreigners and jury trials in Ireland, 1865–69', *Ir. Jur.* (n.s.), 45 (2010), 51–81.

> if plea or debate be moved before the mayor of the staple, betwixt the merchants or ministers of the same, and thereupon to try thereof the truth, and inquest or proof is to be taken … if both parties be aliens, it shall be tried by aliens; and if both parties be denizens it shall be tried by denizens; and if the one party be denizen, and the other party alien, the one half of the inquest or of the proof shall be of denizens, and the other half of aliens.[4]

The following year the statute was confirmed and extended,[5] guaranteeing inquests *de medietate linguae*, 'in all manner of inquests and proofs',[6] including both civil and criminal actions. Pole points out that although the legislation did not alter common-law procedures, it nevertheless 'implicitly recognised that different communities had their own customs, moral perspectives and codes, which were entitled to consideration by English law'.[7] Foreign merchants' right to mixed juries was temporarily lost in the early fifteenth century,[8] but was reaffirmed in 1429.[9]

The rationale for mixed juries changed over time. While the first mixed juries had been granted to adherents of a specific religion (Judaism) rather than members of a specific ethnicity who might have a shared language, by the late sixteenth century, shared language was highlighted as the primary justification for such juries.[10] However, by the early eighteenth century the requirement that the mixed jurors be of the same nationality or speak the same language as the alien party had largely been abandoned.[11] Neither the English Juries Act, 1825[12] nor the Juries (Ireland) Act, 1833[13] made any stipulation as to the nationality of the alien jurors,[14]

4 Statute of the Staple 1353 (27 Ed. III, st. 2, c. 8).

5 Confirmation of the Statute of the Staple Act, 1354 (28 Ed. III, c. 13). See F. Pollock and F.W. Maitland, *A history of English law before the time of Edward I*, 2 vols (2nd ed., Cambridge, 1898, repr. 1911), i, p. 465.

6 Confirmation of the Statute of the Staple Act, 1354 (28 Ed. III, c. 13).

7 J.R. Pole, '"A quest of thoughts": representation and moral agency in the early Anglo-American jury' in J.W. Cairns and G. McLeod (eds), *'The dearest birth right of the people of England': the jury in the history of the common law* (Oxford, 2002), p. 109. See also M. Constable, *The law of the other: the mixed jury and changing conceptions of citizenship, law and knowledge* (Chicago, 1994).

8 As noted in chapter 3, the Qualifications of Jurors Act, 1414 (2 Hen. V, stat. 2, c. 3) provided that jurors in cases concerning homicide, disputes over land or disputes to the value of 40*s*., had to hold lands or tenements of a yearly value of 40*s*. or more. Another statute passed in the same year provided that jurors on inquests into heresy were to 'have within the realm an hundred shillings of lands, tenements, or rent by year': Inquests Act, 1414 (2 Hen. V, stat. 1, c. 7).

9 Inquests Act, 1429 (8 Hen. VI, c. 29); see James C. Oldham, 'The origins of the special jury', *U. Chic. L. Rev.*, 50 (1983), 137–211 at 211–12.

10 *R v. Dyckson* (1571) 3 Dyer 304a; 73 E.R. 683. For a detailed discussion of this case, see M. Levine, 'A more than ordinary case of "rape", 13 & 14 Elizabeth I', *Amer. J. Leg. Hist.*, 7:2 (1963), 159–64.

11 Ibid., 159; J. Lilly, *A continuation of the practical register*, 2 vols (London, 1710), ii, p. 125.

12 6 Geo. IV, c. 50. 13 3 & 4 Will. IV, c. 91.

14 See s. 47 of the 1825 act. Hawkins, writing in 1826, noted that the aliens need not have come from the same country as the accused: M. Hawkins, *Treatise of the pleas of the crown*, 2 vols (8th ed., London, 1824), ii, p. 420. Kennedy, writing in the same year, made the same point: J. Kennedy, *A treatise on the law and practice of juries* (London, 1826), p. 88.

and Purcell noted in 1848 that 'an alien, in cases of felony and misdemeanour, has a right to be tried by a jury consisting one half of alien foreigners *generally*, and not exclusively, of the prisoner's countrymen'.[15] The Naturalisation Act, 1779[16] allowed aliens to be naturalised on swearing an oath of allegiance, before the chief magistrate of any town or city. They would then be 'deemed, adjudged and reputed liege, free, and natural subject or subjects of this kingdom in every respect, condition and degree to all intents, constructions and purposes'. Such naturalised aliens could serve on petty and grand juries,[17] and probably lost their entitlement to a jury *de medietate linguae*.

Despite the changes to their functions and purpose, mixed juries endured until the early nineteenth century,[18] although from 1833 they were restricted to criminal cases.[19] There were a number of high-profile trials involving juries *de medietate linguae* in England,[20] but few reported instances of them being used in Ireland. There certainly does not appear to be any evidence of their use in cases involving native Irish speakers, as such cases generally involved the use of interpreters, and native Irish speakers could not be considered aliens.[21] The most high-profile case of a mixed jury in Ireland was the 1865 trial of Captain John McCafferty for treason-felony. McCafferty[22] was a US-born citizen[23] who was prosecuted for his part in Fenian activities in 1865. He was tried at the subsequent Cork special commission,[24] and the sheriff was able to return a panel of twelve foreigners within

15 Purcell, *Criminal law*, p. 166. 16 Naturalisation Act, 1779 (19 & 20 Geo. III, c. 29), s. 2.

17 In *R v. Henry and John Sheares* (1798) 27 How. St. Tr. 255, a grand juror, John Decluzeau, was objected to on the ground that he was an alien, having been born in France. However, Decluzeau had sworn the oath of allegiance and was deemed to be qualified to serve as a grand juror.

18 See Lilly, *Practical register*, ii, p. 157 and G. Duncombe, *Tryalls per pais: or, the law of England concerning juries by nisi prius*, 2 vols (8th ed., London, 1766), ii, p. 240.

19 The Juries Act (Ireland), 1833 (3 & 4 Will. IV, c. 91), s. 38. See also the English Juries Act, 1825 (6 Geo. IV, c. 50), s. 47.

20 E.g. *Giuseppe Sidoli's Case* (1832) 1 Lew. 244; 168 E.R. 1027; *R v. Giorgetti* (1865) 4 F. & F. 546; 176 E.R. 684; *R v. Ayes* (1825) R. & R. 166; 168 E.R. 741; *R v. Bernard* (1858) 1 F. & F. 239; 175 E.R. 709, 8 St. Tr. (n.s.) 887; *Levinger v. The queen* (1870) 7 Moo. P.C. (n.s.); 17 E.R. 26; and the notorious *R v. Manning and Manning* (1849) 1 Den. 468; 169 E.R. 330, 2 Car. & K. 387; 175 E.R. 372.

21 There are records of court interpreters being used in Meath until at least 1826: J. Brady, 'Irish interpreters at Meath assizes', *Ríocht na Midhe*, 2:1 (1959), 62–3. See also Lesa Ní Mhunghaile, 'The legal system in Ireland and the Irish language 1700–*c*.1843' in M. Brown and S. Donlan (eds), *The laws and other legalities of Ireland, 1689–1850* (Surrey, 2011), pp 331–6. E.g. interpreters were used in the Maamtrasna trials: see T. Harrington, *The Maamtrasna massacre* (Dublin, 1884); J. Waldron, *Maamtrasna: the murders and the mystery* (Dublin, 1992); Mary Phelan, 'Irish language court interpreting, 1801–1922' (PhD, Dublin City University, 2013); and M. Dungan, *Conspiracy: Irish political trials* (Dublin, 2009), pp 129–70. Controversially, a police officer interpreted for the prisoners during the trial, because there was no salaried court interpreter available in Dublin, where the trials took place: Phelan, p. 95. Interestingly, Phelan, p. 87, notes that at the Maamtrasna inquest, a coroner's juror acted as interpreter. All of this indicates that the *medietate* jury had more to do with nationality than language.

22 Various reports of the case refer to the prisoner as McRafferty, McAfferty and McCafferty.

23 *Cork Constitution*, 16 Dec. 1865.

24 J. Savage, *Fenian heroes and martyrs* (Boston, 1868), p. 178, and *Freeman's Journal*, 16, 18 Dec. 1865.

an hour of Fitzgerald J. making the order for the jury *de medietate*.[25] McCafferty was ultimately acquitted on the direction of the court.[26] Two years later, Captain John Warren, a naturalised American citizen, also sought to be tried by a mixed jury for his involvement in the Fenian rebellion.[27] At his trial for treason-felony at the Dublin special commission in 1867, Pigott C.B. refused the application for the jury *de medietate linguae*, emphasising that the person claiming such a jury 'must *be* an alien'. He pointed out that 'he who is once under the allegiance of the English sovereign remains so for ever'.[28] At the same commission, Irish-born U.S. citizen Augustine Costello was also denied a jury *de medietate*.[29]

Following these cases, and criticism by the 1868 royal commission[30] and in the houses of parliament,[31] in 1870 juries *de medietate linguae* were abolished in both England and Ireland.[32] In the same year, the English Juries Act, 1870[33] allowed aliens to sit on regular juries for the first time, provided they satisfied the other qualifications.[34] However, a legislative oversight meant that there was no equivalent measure passed in relation to Irish juries, and aliens continued to be excluded. Interestingly, mixed tribunals continued to be considered a viable option in other jurisdictions. For example, mixed courts were established in Egypt in 1875 to deal with disputes involving foreigners. These mixed courts 'had especially drafted codes, based on a civil law format but with significant Islamic and local principles'.[35]

25 *Cork Examiner*, 15 Dec. 1865. The shorthand writer's transcript of the trial listed the alien jurors as Raymond de Venicom, Scipic Chalrel, Felicier Venille, Charles Sivel, Alphonse de Pautem, George Pistoli, Pasquali Tomassini, Nicholas George Yarrdi, Auge Mollard, Paolo Stefano Minich, John Firmo and Frederick Antonio Klein. Anon., *Cork special commission, December 1865, Queen v. John McCafferty (shorthand-writer's report of the proceedings upon the application on the part of the prisoner for a jury de medietate linguae)* (Cork, 1866), p. 3.
26 *Cork Examiner*, 16 Dec. 1865.
27 *Freeman's Journal*, 31 Oct. 1867 and W.G. Chamney, *Report of the trial of John Warren for treason-felony* (Dublin, 1867), pp 6–7.
28 When this was refused, Warren then directed his counsel to retire, and conducted his own defence. *Freeman's Journal*, 31 Oct. 1867. See A.M. Sullivan, *The dock and the scaffold* (Dublin, 1868), p. 74.
29 *Freeman's Journal*, 7 Nov. 1867. The comments of T.M. Healy some years later in the house of commons suggest that there may have been others who successfully claimed the right to a mixed jury. Referring to cases tried in Dublin, he mentioned 'a time when we had American prisoners brought up for trial, in which case one-half of the jurors were aliens, thereat being picked out from the common jury class'. He also added: 'I cannot remember that there was any difficulty in conducting those trials. The government obtained convictions, and the common jurors proved to be perfectly capable of understanding the technical charges of the judges.' *Hansard 3*, cccxv, 1246 (7 June 1887). It is possible, however, that Healy was confusing the Dublin and Cork trials.
30 *Report on naturalization*, HC 1868–9 (4109) xxv, 607, p. xi.
31 See *Hansard 3*, cxcix, 1131, and ibid., 1129–32 (3 Mar. 1870) (HL).
32 33 & 34 Vic., c. 14.
33 33 & 34 Vic., c. 77.
34 The Juries (Ireland) Act, 1871 (34 & 35 Vic., c. 65) contained no such provision.
35 Mark S.W. Hoyle, 'The mixed courts of Egypt: an anniversary assessment', *Arab Law Quarterly*, 1:1 (1995), 60–8 at 60.

THE MARKET JURY

Unlike the other categories of jury outlined above, market juries did not operate within the confines of a trial or inquest. These were men empowered to inspect markets, bake-houses and other places where food was prepared or held out for sale, to ensure that all relevant regulations were being followed. Some market juries had medieval origins. For example, in 1333 it was ordered in Kilkenny that 'six lawful men' be appointed to examine all weights and measures in the town and question bakers about the price of their bread.[36] When Cavan was granted its first charter in 1610, it declared that the corporation was to have weekly markets and two fairs per year 'with all the usual trappings – a court of piepowder, a market jury, constables, appraisers and petty constables'.[37]

Other market juries were created by statute in the eighteenth century. For example, an act of 1765 observed that the rapid growth of Cork city meant that the mayor could not 'so strictly attend the inspection of the markets of the said city as usual'.[38] It allowed justices of the peace to issue a precept to the sheriff to return twenty-four 'citizens of the same city', twelve of whom could be sworn as a market jury for the city. They remained the market jury until the next quarter sessions, and could be fined for failing to carry out their duty.[39] Any three or more of these jurors could, 'at reasonable hours' visit the 'markets, store houses, working houses, cellars and shops in the said city, where provisions and victuals are sold or made up or making up for sale in the said city, and to inspect the quality of the said provisions and victuals'. They had the power to seize any food or ingredients 'fraudulently or illegally made up', or found in the hands of traders or manufacturers not in compliance with the various rules and regulations governing markets. The jurors could bring the food and its owner or seller before the mayor, to be dealt with in accordance with the law. Three years later an amending act was passed because 'many of the abuses, intended to be reformed by the said market jury, escaped punishment by reason of the difficulties in getting three of the said market jury to attend together'.[40] This allowed the market jurors to act individually, with the same effect.[41] Three Cork market jurors could also seize 'any stand, table,

36 Patrick Logan, *Fair day: the story of Irish fairs and markets* (Belfast, 1986), pp 18–19.

37 Ibid., pp 46–7. A court of piepowder or *piepoudre* determined cases arising during fairs and markets. See Charles Gross, 'The court of piepowder', *Quarterly J. of Economics*, 20:2 (1906), 231–49. Holton notes that the term evolved from the French word for pedlar, *pied pouldre* and was also translated as 'dusty foot'. Karina Holton, 'From charters to carters: aspects of fairs and markets in medieval Leinster' in Denis A. Cronin, Jim Gilligan and Karina Holton (eds), *Irish fairs and markets: studies in local history* (Dublin, 2001), p. 32.

38 Regulation of Cork Act, 1765 (5 Geo. III, c. 24), s. 15.

39 Ó Drisceoil notes that in Cork, the market jury was 'empowered to enforce regulations and prevent practices "injurious to their fellow citizens", such as the blocking of streets and bridges by "fruit women and chairmen"'. Diarmuid Ó Drisceoil and Donal Ó Drisceoil, *Serving a city, the story of Cork's English market* (Cork, 2011), p. 43.

40 Regulation of Cork Act, 1771–2 (11 & 12 Geo. III, c. 18), s. 33.

41 See also the Cork Bread Act, 1814 (54 Geo. III, c. 197), s. 21.

basket, roots, fruit, blocks, timber, planks, benches, sticks, casks, anchor, or other obstruction or annoyance' from the streets.[42]

Legislation couched in similar language was enacted with respect to Dublin in 1773.[43] Forty-eight of the 'most respectable citizens' of Dublin were to be summoned, and twenty-four sworn as a market jury at the quarter sessions. No qualifications were specified, but an act of 1775 exempted barristers, practising attorneys, physicians and surgeons because it would be 'inconvenient to the publick' if they were obliged to serve.[44] In the same year, further legislation extended the market jury to several cities.[45] The method of summoning and swearing-in market jurors was the same as under the Cork act, as was the rule that they could act singly as well as collectively. They had the same powers of inspection and seizure[46] and could also specifically examine and seize bread that was not in compliance with the assize of bread,[47] and weights and measures that were less than the standard weight or measure.[48] It was an offence to accost or molest market jurors carrying out their duties.[49] These provisions were repeated in an act of 1787,[50] although in the Dublin liberties of Saint Sepulchres and Thomas Court and Donore,[51] a minimum of four market jurors had to act together. These jurors had to be 'principal inhabitants' of the liberty, and could bring seized foodstuffs or responsible persons before the seneschal, to be distributed to the poor or to prisons.[52] Bye-laws governed market juries in some towns.[53] These sometimes gave additional powers to market juries, such as the power to pass presentments for the lighting, cleaning and general upkeep of towns, or regulating the town corporation's property.[54] The market jury of Belturbet, Co. Cavan, had a particularly wide remit: it was a court of arbitration; it was empowered to 'divide the bogs' in cases of disagreement; it could determine cases of trespass on

42 Regulation of Cork Act, 1777–8 (17 & 18 Geo. III, c. 38), s. 23.

43 Dublin Paving and Lighting Act, 1773–4 (13 & 14 Geo. III, c. 22), s. 73.

44 Dublin Paving (Amendment) Act, 1775–6 (15 & 16 Geo. III, c. 20), s. 43.

45 Market Juries Act, 1773 (13 & 14 Geo. III, c. 20). A market jury had been established in Ennis in 1752. These were 'self-appointed custodians', as there was no legal provision for such a body. Despite their lack of legal standing, the market jury endured for some fifty years: Sean Spellissy, *A history of County Clare* (Dublin, 2003), p. 43. 46 S. 9.

47 S. 10. Section 12 obligated the chief magistrate in each city to publish the assize of bread at least once a month in a local newspaper.

48 S. 11. On the confusion surrounding weights and measures in England, see Julian Hoppit, 'Reforming Britain's weights and measures, 1660–1824', *Eng. Hist. Rev.*, 108:426 (1993), 82–104.

49 E.g. in *R v. Brady* (1801) in Richard Rowe, *Reports of interesting cases, argued and determined in the king's law courts of England and Ireland, the houses of parliament, and military courts* (Dublin, 1824), p. 534, the defendant was convicted for verbally abusing a market juror.

50 An Act for establishing market juries in cities, 1787 (27 Geo. III, c. 46).

51 See Milne, pp 39–41.

52 *Report on prisons in Ireland*, HC 1809 (265) vii, 577, p. 29.

53 E.g. Monaghan: *First report on municipal corporations in Ireland*, I [C-23–28] HC 1835 xxvii, xxviii, 51, 79, 199, p. 953.

54 E.g. Kells, Co. Meath: *First report on municipal corporations*, p. 386.

commonage or private property. It could also inspect fences and count cattle on the commons, and it was consulted in the free granting of common lands to poor persons to build upon.[55] Similarly, in the town of Cavan, the market jury could appoint constables and appraisers, impose and levy fines and fees, and generally regulate the government of the town.[56] The composition of the market jury could be of considerable local political interest.[57]

While there were usually 12 market jurors appointed, the number could be as low as 2 or 3[58] or as high as 23[59] or 24.[60] A foreman was appointed in some places.[61] Originally market juries tended to be appointed at each session; later they were appointed annually, and the market jury of Belturbet, Co. Cavan, acted for at least seven years.[62]

Market juries went into decline in many places in the 1820s,[63] sometimes as a result of a lack of local support.[64] Serving on such juries was considered 'most troublesome',[65] 'rather heavy'[66] and generally very inconvenient.[67] In 1835 the commission on municipal corporations heard that many towns and cities no longer had market juries, including Athlone, Carlow, Kildare, Naas, Trim, Dingle, and Enniskillen, where the inhabitants formed their own associations 'to prevent or detect fraud, by forming a market jury'.[68] The lack of market juries was 'felt to be an inconvenience'.[69] While cities such as Waterford, Dublin and Limerick continued to have active and efficient market juries,[70] some towns had market juries in name only – for example, the leet court jury of Dungarvan appointed a market jury each year, but only as a matter of custom – the persons named on the jury neither served nor were called on to serve.[71] In Castlebar, market juries were

55 Ibid., pp 963–4.
56 Ibid., p. 549. The commissioners considered many of the market jury's activities to be illegal.
57 E.g. *Letter from John James Burgoyne, Strabane, to the earl of Abercorn*, 8 Aug. 1810 (PRONI, D623/A/124/31); 22 Aug. 1810 (PRONI, D623/A/124/35); 13 Sept. 1810 (PRONI, D623/A/124/39); and 1 Oct. 1810 (PRONI, D623/A/124/43).
58 E.g. Antrim: *First report on municipal corporations*, p. 646.
59 Ibid., p. 386 (Kells) and p. 400 (Kildare). In Dublin in 1859 there were twenty jurors empanelled, *Irish Times*, 5 May 1859. Twenty-four were sworn the following year, mostly the same men. *Irish Times*, 11 Jan. 1860.
60 E.g. Coleraine. *Municipal corporations (Ireland), appendix*, I [C-26, 29] HC 1836 xxiv, 297, p. 1029.
61 E.g. Belturbet, ibid., p. 963. 62 Ibid.
63 E.g. Naas in 1823: *First report on municipal corporations*, p. 421; Trim in 1829: ibid., p. 470.
64 Ibid.
65 *Fifteenth report on salaries*, HC 1826 (310) xvii, 29, p. 503 (Walter Golding, a bailiff of Dublin).
66 *Report on manor courts*, HC 1837 (494) xv, 1, p. 28 (T.F. Kelly, a seneschal of Dublin).
67 *Report on fairs and markets*, I [C-1910] HC 1854–5 xix, p. 395.
68 Athlone: ibid., p. 330; Carlow: ibid., p. 369; Kildare: ibid., p. 400; Naas: ibid., p. 421; Trim: ibid., p. 470; Dingle: ibid., p. 499; Enniskillen: *Municipal corporations appendix*, p. 1068.
69 *First report on municipal corporations*, pp 291 and 470.
70 Waterford: ibid., p. 147; Dublin: *Municipal corporations appendix*, p. 435; Limerick: *First report on municipal corporations*, p. 559; others included Athy (p. 334), Dundalk (p. 903), Drogheda (p. 825) and Belturbet (p. 961).
71 *First report on municipal corporations*, p. 265.

occasionally sworn but did not carry out their functions properly, and in Ennis, market juries were retained 'principally … for convivial purposes'.[72] By the 1850s the decline was even more evident, as testimony given before the fairs and markets commission demonstrates.[73]

Many of the duties traditionally carried out by market juries came to be taken over by police or corporations[74] and the market jury eventually became redundant. The Summary Jurisdiction (Ireland) Act, 1851, for example, empowered head constables in petty sessions districts to be the inspectors of weights and measures, and provided for the summary fining of persons in breach of market regulations.[75] In 1874, the Dublin clerk of the peace described the market jury as a farce, and observed that 48 men were summoned and 24 were chosen, who 'never [did] anything'.[76] Both the Statistical Society of Ireland[77] and the parliamentary committee on Irish juries[78] recommended the abolition of market juries, which was effected by the Juries (Procedure) Ireland Act, 1876.[79]

JURIES IN LOCAL COURTS

As well as the assizes, quarter sessions and petty sessions, justice was also administered in a 'confusing conglomeration'[80] of borough courts (sometimes called tholsel courts) and manor courts. Mainly originating in the seventeenth century, by the nineteenth century local courts were in decline, but there were still some 200 manor courts in existence in the 1830s.[81] They were abolished in 1859.[82] Manor courts operated as courts leet, generally meeting twice a year for criminal offences and some civil transactions,[83] and courts baron. These courts were probably the most commonly encountered in the eighteenth and early nineteenth centuries, as they were held monthly or every three weeks and dealt with petty actions. McMahon points out that 'the difference between the courts leet and baron was often blurred'.[84] In some manor courts, proceedings operated wholly or

72 Ibid., pp 496, 511.
73 *Report on fairs and markets*, regarding Dundalk (p. 2), Tuam (p. 69), Galway (p. 77), Ennis (p. 152) and New Ross (p. 252).
74 *Report on the Irish jury system*, HC 1874 (244) ix, 557, para. 2739 (Charles Kernan, Dublin clerk of the peace).
75 14 & 15 Vic., c. 92, ss 17 and 18. 76 *Report on Irish jury system*, 1874, paras 2739–42.
77 Anon., 'Report of committee on suggestions for diminishing the excessive summoning of jurors in the county and city of Dublin 1874', *J.S.S.I.S.I.*, 6 (1870–9), 378–84 at 380.
78 *Report on Irish jury system*, 1874, p. iv. 79 S. 22.
80 R.B. McDowell, *The Irish administration, 1801–1914* (1st ed., London, 1964), p. 115.
81 T.C. Barnard, 'Local courts in later seventeenth and eighteenth-century Ireland' in Brown and Donlan (eds), *The laws and other legalities*, p. 33.
82 Manor Courts Abolition (Ireland) Act, 1859 (22 & 23 Vic., c. 14).
83 Richard McMahon, 'Manor courts in the west of Ireland before the Famine' in D.S. Greer and N.M. Dawson (eds), *Mysteries and solutions in Irish legal history* (Dublin, 2001), pp 115–16.
84 McMahon, 'Manor courts', p. 116.

partially through the Irish language, with claimants, jurors and witnesses speaking the language, and some seneschals or officials understanding it.[85]

Although they dealt with minor cases, the importance of manor courts should not be overlooked in any examination of lay participation in the justice system. These were the juries that people of the labouring classes were most likely to encounter and serve upon. The jurors in these courts were selected and summoned from the estate by the seneschal,[86] and in the west at least, 'the majority of jurors appear to have been drawn from the ranks of the shopkeepers and the small farmers'.[87] In one court the jurors were selected by seneschal from the 'most respectable part of the crowd' in attendance, the seneschal having given up issuing printed summonses because of the risk of interference with jurors.[88] Duncombe wrote in the seventeenth century that jurors at the court leet or sheriff's turn only had to have freehold worth 20*s*., or copyhold of 20*s*. 8*d*. per annum,[89] but it is unclear whether this qualification was ever enforced in practice in nineteenth-century Ireland. MacNally was of the view that any person could be empanelled on a jury in a court leet, regardless of whether they lived locally.[90] Males aged between 12 and 60 were liable to serve.[91] The parties were entitled to object to any jurors who they did not consider to be disinterested. Once selected, the jurors swore an oath to give a 'true verdict'. Although there were supposed to be 12 jurors, there were often juries generally made up of either 5, 7 or 9 jurors.[92] Some jurors served quite frequently. One juror told the committee that the persons frequently sitting on manor juries in Galway were 'idle people about the streets, who had nothing else to do'.[93] McMahon points out that 'opinion was divided on the quality of the persons concerned'.[94]

Leet juries carried out various adjudicative and presentment functions – for example, they could 'limit, ascertain and appoint the number of watch houses' in their liberties, and determine their locations and who ought to maintain them.[95] There were variations in the duties of jurors in local courts around the country. In Dungarvan, Co. Waterford, for example, it was said that the leet jury performed 'important duties', including presenting the sums to be paid for quayage and anchorage on all vessels loading and unloading or anchoring in the harbour, and appointing a harbour master.[96] Leet juries resembled grand juries in this regard, and the leet jury in Mallow was made up of 23 or 24 'respectable inhabitants'. It

85 Phelan, 'Irish language court reporting', pp 116–18. 86 Ibid., p. 118. 87 Ibid., p. 147.
88 *Report on manor courts*, 1837, p. 268 (Joseph Raughan, seneschal of a number of manors in Co. Clare).
89 An Act for returning of sufficient jurors, 1483–4 (1 Rich. III, c. 4).
90 Leonard MacNally, *The justice of the peace for Ireland: containing the authorities and duties of that officer, as also of the various conservators of the peace*, 2 vols (Dublin, 1808), ii, p. 50.
91 Ibid., p. 109. 92 McMahon, 'Manor courts', p. 147.
93 *Report on manor courts*, 1837, p. 114 (Timothy Fitzpatrick).
94 McMahon, *Manor courts*, p. 147.
95 Parish Watches Act, 1719 (6 Geo. I, c. 10), s. 1; *First report on municipal corporations*, p. 291.
96 Ibid., p. 265.

presented a high constable who collected the county cess within the manor.[97] In the Dublin liberties, three members of the leet jury could, with the seneschal, 'cause, order and direct the levelling, new paving, raising, and mending the publick pavements', in order to remove and prevent public nuisances. They could give written notice to the tenants of properties to mend the pavements outside their properties within fifteen days.[98] If the property owners failed to do as they were requested within forty days,[99] the seneschal and leet jurors could employ pavers to carry out the work, and the payment was to be levied on the property owners by distress. The seneschal and three leet jurors could also order the removal of encroachments or nuisances such as stairs and cellar doors from streets, and if the inhabitant or owner refused, workmen could be employed and paid for in the same manner. Leet grand juries in the Dublin liberties and in other cities and towns could seek funding for scavengers to remove 'filth and rubbish' from the streets.[100]

CONCLUSION

With so many categories of jury, particularly in the late eighteenth and early nineteenth centuries, one might imagine that a significant proportion of the population would have had experience of jury service. However, the reality was that, with the exception of some manor-court juries, the jury of matrons, and men called upon *de circumstantibus* to fill spaces on incomplete juries, jury service remained the exclusive right and responsibility of men of property. In Dublin, the same men, largely connected with the corporation, were summoned to sit on grand juries, special juries and wide-streets juries and in many ways could be said to have exercised a monopoly on justice in the capital.

Chapters 3–7 illustrate the official encouragement of lay participation in the administration of justice in the eighteenth and nineteenth centuries. Notwithstanding the disappearance of several categories of jury, Irish society and the legal profession remained wedded to the idea of lay participation, even as complaints were frequently levelled against the standard of person being empanelled for the various juries. Because the burden of jury service fell repeatedly on a small pool of men, it was generally difficult to compel these men to attend and serve on the various types of jury.

97 Ibid., p. 291.
98 Dublin Paving Act, 1717 (4 Geo. I, c. 11), s. 2. Amended and extended by the Paving Act, 1719 (6 Geo. I, c. 15). Outside of the liberties this was undertaken by the lord mayor, sheriffs and aldermen. See also Kenneth Milne, *The Dublin liberties, 1600–1850* (Dublin, 2009), p. 25.
99 Reduced to fourteen days in 1719, s. 1.
100 Paving Act, 1719 (6 Geo. I, c. 15), s. 5.

CHAPTER EIGHT

Securing jurors' attendance

OFFICIALS FREQUENTLY EXPERIENCED difficulties in securing the attendance of sufficient numbers of qualified jurors to try civil and criminal cases, to carry out the functions of market juries and to conduct valuations. A number of factors contributed to this difficulty: the relatively small pool of qualified jurors for most of the eighteenth and nineteenth centuries;[1] the problem of juror intimidation during periods of unrest;[2] the unwillingness of men to submit to the discomfort and inconvenience of many forms of jury service; and inefficiencies and corrupt practices in the drawing-up of jurors' lists.[3]

SUMMONING JURORS

Traditionally, jurors for trials, inquests and valuations were summoned under the writ of *venire facias*,[4] which commanded the sheriff to summon 'twelve free and lawful men'[5] of the area. As noted in chapter 2, in practice more than twelve were summoned, in order to ensure that a complete jury could be empanelled. In civil cases, between thirty-six and sixty were usually returned, depending on the legislation, while in criminal trials, much greater numbers were summoned so that defendants could exercise their rights to challenge jurors peremptorily and for cause.[6] Writing about assizes on the English home circuit, Cockburn notes that the demand for jurors fluctuated depending on how many prisoners were awaiting trial.[7]

In the eighteenth century and early nineteenth century, all jury summonses in Ireland were hand-delivered by the sheriff, or, more typically, his deputy, six days before their attendance was required.[8] Generally, the sheriff or sub-sheriff brought the summons to the prospective juror's home and showed it to him;[9] if the juror

1 See p. 51. 2 See pp 158–61. 3 See pp 21, 34.

4 See J.S. Cockburn, *Calendar of assize records*, xi: *Home circuit indictments: Elizabeth I and James I: introduction* (London, 1985), pp 26–7. The *venire facias* was abolished in Ireland by the Common Law Procedure (Ireland) Act, 1853 (16 & 17 Vic., c. 113), s. 109.

5 By contrast, the original writ of inquiry required twelve 'good and lawful men': James C. Oldham, 'The origins of the special jury', *U. Chic. L. Rev.*, 50 (1983), 137–211 at 206–7.

6 The crown could also exercise its right to order potential jurors to stand aside: see pp 148–9.

7 Cockburn, *Calendar of assize records*, xi, p. 56.

8 See, e.g., the Regulation of Juries Act, 1755 (29 Geo. II, c. 6), s. 2; and the Juries (Ireland) Act, 1833 (3 & 4 Will. IV, c. 91), s. 18. The English Juries Act, 1825 (6 Geo. IV, c. 50), s. 25 was identical.

9 One commentator in 1873 considered that this imposed an 'immense expense' on sheriffs: *Report on juries (Ireland)*, HC 1873 (283) xv, 389, para. 925 (Thomas de Moleyns).

was absent, a written note containing the substance of the summons was usually left with some other person residing with him.[10] This was not always successful; it is evident that sometimes servants intercepted summonses, falsely claiming that their employers were not at home.[11] The Juries (Ireland) Act, 1871[12] allowed jury summonses to be delivered by post in Dublin city,[13] but other parts of the country were considered to have less reliable postal services so this innovation was restricted to the capital.[14] When any summons was delivered by post, two days were allowed for its delivery, in addition to the four days' notice required by statute.[15] This was extended to county Dublin in 1872.[16]

The 1873 parliamentary committee considered the possibility of extending the postal summons to other parts of the country.[17] It was clear from witnesses, however, that the postal arrangements in rural areas were not of an adequate standard: in many areas there was no delivery service; post offices were thin on the ground; and it was often left to local residents to arrange for the collection of their own post. It was suggested to the committee that the postal summons could be introduced in the counties close to Dublin,[18] but that it was unrealistic to propose such measures in remote counties such as Donegal, Clare, Kerry, Monaghan and Cavan.[19] There were no postmen in rural areas; letters were collected by individuals from local post offices.[20] Besides, one witness bluntly observed that a man who was 'so obscure as to be beyond the reach of postal communication' was obviously 'some very low and coarse sort of personage', and thus unfit for jury service in the first place.[21] Chief

10 (3 & 4 Will. IV, c. 91), s. 18.

11 Ibid., para. 774 (Serjeant Armstrong). In an English case *Ex Parte Sir Thomas Clarges, Bart* (1827) 1 Y. & J. 399; 148 E.R. 726, it was deemed to be the duty of the person receiving the letter either to appraise his principal of it, or to inform the court why his principal could not attend.

12 34 & 35 Vic., c. 65, s. 22.

13 In England, the Juries Act, 1862 (25 & 26 Vic., c. 107) provided for the summoning of jurors by post.

14 This was despite the fact that the number of post towns had increased by 60% in the first decades of the nineteenth century: R.B. McDowell, *The Irish administration*, p. 86. See also Anthony Trollope, 'History of the post office in Ireland' in *Third report on the post office*, HC 1857 (2195) iv, 293, app. J, p. 57. On the Dublin postal system, see J. Stafford Johnson, 'The Dublin penny post: 1773–1840', *Dub. Hist. Rec.*, 42:3 (1942), 81–95. In 1829 a commission of enquiry had highlighted the need for reform of the Irish postal system: *Nineteenth report of the commissioners of inquiry into the collection and management of the revenue arising in Ireland and Great Britain. Post-office revenue, United Kingdom: part II. Ireland*, HC 1829 (353) xii, 1.

15 The Juries Procedure (Ireland) Act, 1876 (39 & 40 Vic., c. 78), s. 6.

16 The Juries (Ireland) Amendment Act, 1872 (36 & 37 Vic., c. 25), s. 8.

17 *Reports on juries (Ireland)*, HC 1873 (283) xv, 389.

18 Ibid., paras 4555–6, 4701–9 (William Ormsby, sub-sheriff of the city and county of Dublin), and paras 3962–3 (Thomas Wilkinson, sub-sheriff of Co. Wexford).

19 Clare and Kerry: ibid., para. 3720 (Alexander Morphy, crown solicitor for Clare and Kerry); Monaghan: ibid., paras 4553–4 (John Reilly, a Monaghan attorney); Cavan: ibid., paras 3808–13, 3821 (James Robinson, chairman of Co. Cavan).

20 Ibid., para. 4702 (John Reilly).

21 Ibid., paras 772–95 (Richard Armstrong, first serjeant at law); and paras 1202–3 (James Hamilton, chairman of Co. Sligo).

Justice Monahan suggested that in Ireland, if a man received a jury summons in the post, 'He would put it in his pocket, or on the dresser; he would never hear of it again. We are not such particular people at all'.[22] However, there were some areas outside Dublin – including several towns in Cork – where there was a letter-delivery service,[23] meaning that the postal summons would run smoothly in those areas, and several witnesses foresaw few difficulties in extending the postal summons.[24] Nevertheless, the postal summons was not extended at that time, and the issue arose once more before the 1874 parliamentary committee.[25] While some witnesses again expounded the benefits of summoning jurors by post,[26] at least in urban areas,[27] others preferred the use of civil-bill process servers[28] or summons servers,[29] who would operate under the immediate control of the magistrates.

The idea of utilising the police force in the delivery of jury summonses had received short shrift the previous year, but those witnesses advocating the use of the Royal Irish Constabulary proved most persuasive in 1874.[30] George Bolton, the Tipperary crown solicitor, gave two reasons why the constabulary should 'unquestionably' adopt this role: first, they were certain to reach all of the jurors; and second, they could report to the crown solicitor if any 'improper' persons were summoned.[31] Others pointed out that in most parts of the country there was 'almost total freedom from crime',[32] leaving the RIC ample time for serving jury summonses. The committee recommended that jury summonses 'should be served by the constabulary, but with power to the judge of assize, by order, to substitute service by post in any particular venue'.[33] Thus the Juries Procedure (Ireland) Act, 1876 provided that summonses were to be made 'four clear days' in advance of an assizes, by a constable or sub-constable of the RIC.[34] The summons was to be delivered 'to the person to be summoned, or in case he shall be absent from his usual place of abode, by leaving such summons with some person therein inhabiting'. As an alternative it would be lawful for any judge to 'direct that the summonses for the attendance of jurors in such county … shall for such period as may be specified in such order be served by post'.[35] In addition to the specific

22 Ibid., paras 2725–30, 2743–4.

23 Ibid., paras 3592–7 (Joseph B. Johnson, sub-sheriff of Co. Cork).

24 Ibid., paras 772–95 (Armstrong); see also, e.g., paras 1485, 1524–5 (George Battersby, crown prosecutor for Kildare and Westmeath).

25 *Report on the Irish jury system*, HC 1874 (244) ix, 557.

26 Ibid., para. 92 (Hamilton); and para. 486 (William Ormsby, sub-sheriff of Dublin).

27 Ibid., paras 2077–80 (Armstrong).

28 Ibid., paras 2452–5 (Charles Burke, master of the court of common pleas).

29 Ibid., paras 313–17 (Robert Fergusson, chairman of the west riding of Co. Cork); para. 1310 (John Leahy, chairman of Co. Limerick); and para. 2726 (Charles Kernan, Dublin clerk of the peace).

30 In fact, the RIC were encouraged to have a good relationship with their local communities: B. Griffin, 'Prevention and detection of crime in nineteenth-century Ireland' in N.M. Dawson (ed.), *Reflections on law and history* (Dublin, 2006), p. 99.

31 *Report on Irish jury system*, 1874, para. 1512. 32 Ibid., para. 1311 (Leahy).

33 A bill was presented to the house of commons: *Hansard 3*, ccxviii, 967 (22 Apr. 1874).

34 S. 6. 35 S. 8.

duties laid down in the act, section 7 went on to state that the RIC were to 'afford assistance to sheriffs and other officers in the execution of this act',[36] as long as this did not interfere with their permanent duties.

SMALL POOLS AND POOR ATTENDANCE

The fact that the 1833 act applied the same qualifications in all parts of the country led to an unequal supply of jurors in the various counties.[37] In counties of towns, the proportion of jurors to population was generally quite high – on average there was one juror to every forty-eight inhabitants, as can be seen in table 8.1.

Table 8.1 Ratio of jurors to general population in counties of towns[38]

County	Ratio	County	Ratio
Carrickfergus	1:30	Galway town	1:68
Cork city	1:56	Kilkenny city	1:65
Drogheda town	1:57	Limerick city	1:85
Dublin city	1:59	Waterford city	1:46

There was relatively little variation in the ratio of jurors to population in most towns and cities, with Carrickfergus and Limerick representing two extremes. There was significant variation when it came to rural counties, however – as can be seen from table 8.2.

Looking at the country as a whole, the average ratio of jurors to general population in rural counties was one for every 138 persons. This indicates that the burden of jury duty was not evenly spread throughout Ireland; the frequency with which one was likely to be summoned as a juror may to some extent have depended on whether one lived in a town or not.

In the 1830s, the Irish judges wrote to clerks of the crown and peace in each county asking for details of the number of jurors not attending, or failing to answer to their names.[39] Although the information returned was incomplete,[40] it is possible to summarise the incidence of non-attendance in a number of counties; see tables 8.3 and 8.4. On average, attendance stood at around 54 per cent.

36 For example, in 1873 RIC officers were instructed to help in the revision of jury lists. Circular of 1 Oct. 1873, *Revision of jurors' lists 1881* (NAI, CCS/1881/682).

37 John McEldowney, 'Lord O'Hagan and the Irish Jury Act 1871' (PhD, Cambridge University, 1981), p. 149.

38 *Judicial statistics (Ireland)* [C-8563] HC 1864 (52) lii, 657, p. xxx.

39 *Jury panels* (NAI, OP/1832/549).

40 In some counties, returns were made of the number of grand jurors summoned and appearing; in others, the number of jurors summoned was given, but not the number attending.

Table 8.2 Ratio of jurors to general population in counties

County	Ratio	County	Ratio
Carlow	1:61	Antrim	1:82
Kilkenny	1:73	Armagh	1:220
Kildare	1:60	Donegal	1:222
King's	1:193	Fermanagh	1:77
Meath	1:62	Londonderry	1:108
Queen's	1:74	Monaghan	1:106
Westmeath	1:92	Tyrone	1:165
Wexford	1:91		*Ulster Average: 1:140*
Wicklow	1:102		
	Leinster Average: 1:90		
Clare	1:188	Galway	1:202
Cork (E.R.)	1:97	Leitrim	1:140
Cork (W.R.)	1:165	Mayo	1:220
Kerry	1:91	Roscommon	1:225
Limerick	1:88	Sligo	1:191
Tipperary (N.R.)	1:214		*Connacht Average: 1:190*
Tipperary (S.R.)	1:111		
Waterford	1:113		
	Munster Average: 1:133		

Table 8.3 Attendance at the 1832 spring assizes

County	Number summoned	Number serving	% serving
Carlow	162	120	74
Clare	192	133	69
Cork city	244	96	39
Donegal	183	53	54
Galway city	259	55	21
Kerry	140	109	78
King's	156	60	39
Limerick	180	162	90
Longford	175	106	61
Queen's	365	99	27
Tipperary	223	144	65
Westmeath	260	75	29

Table 8.4 Attendance at the 1832 summer assizes

County	Number summoned	Number serving	% serving
Carlow	196	71	36
Clare	181	130	86
Cork city	302	103	34
Donegal	101	81	80
Galway city	250	29	13
Kerry	113	75	66
King's	168	68	41
Limerick	180	167	93
Longford	156	126	81
Queen's	288	100	35
Tipperary	384	177	46
Westmeath	217	60	28

There are, however, significant variations, with attendance as high as 93 per cent in Co. Limerick, and as low as 13 per cent in Galway city. The high number of persons summoned in the latter suggests that low attendance may have been anticipated, and, to some extent, tolerated. On the whole, it appears that the lowest attendance levels appeared to be in urban areas – the cities of Cork and Galway, for example. It is possible that the smaller pool of qualified jurors in cities and towns led to the frequent summoning of some individuals, who may have become frustrated and consequently begun to ignore summonses. Ineffective or inefficient summoning practices may also have contributed, as well as failure to enforce attendance through the use of fines, as will be explored further below.

The extent of the problem of non-attendance in the late 1870s can be illustrated by again comparing the number of jurors summoned with the numbers actually attending in each county, as in table 8.5.

As with the earlier figures, the percentage of those summoned who actually appeared varies greatly from county to county, with a high of over 100 per cent and a low of 26 per cent. This is not an exact indication of the number of people who ignored jury summonses, as there would have been various other factors involved, such as illness, death and out-of-date or incorrect information.[41] Table 8.5 does indicate, however, those counties where there may have been difficulties in obtaining a complete jury panel. Excluding those counties for which complete information is not available, it seems that on average about half (53.6 per cent) of all jurors summoned actually served, which is consistent with the earlier figure.

Clearly, low attendance by jurors was a recurring problem around the country. In one case in 1813 a sheriff even went so far as to send a coach around to jurors'

41 Note also, that some jurors may have been counted twice, through serving on multiple juries.

Table 8.5 Attendance at the 1879 spring assizes[42]

County	Total jurors	Number summoned	Number serving	% serving
Antrim	7,048	282	192*	
Armagh	2,056	355	68*	
Carlow	696	148	48	32
Cavan	868	173	50	29
Clare	1,158	209	72	34
Cork	4808	273	95*	
Donegal	1,008	158	108	68
Down	4,169	225	96*	
Dublin	—	—	—	—
Dublin city	—	—	—	—
Fermanagh	845	160	96	60
Galway	939	273	288	105
Kerry	1,055	155	132*	
Kildare	1,063	168	87*	
Kilkenny	1,442	174	72	41
King's	764	210	60	29
Leitrim	330	107	72	67
Limerick City	477	99	24*	
Londonderry	2,013	161	149	93
Longford	433	53	0	0
Louth	976	104	12*	
Mayo	649	218	180*	
Meath	1,701	119	108	90
Monaghan	680	248	84	34
Queen's	821	148	48	32
Roscommon	817	203	48	24
Sligo	557	104	110	106
Tipperary	2,675	470	164*	
Tyrone	201	168	132	79
Waterford	1,288	168	132	79
Westmeath	879	188	48	26
Wexford	1,942	108	38*	
Wicklow	977	154	48	31

42 *Return of the number of jurors summoned at the spring assizes, 1879*, HC 1878–9 (249) lix, 351. In Dublin, there were no spring assizes, but a commission court was held four times a year. In Galway and Sligo, more jurors served at the assizes than were actually summoned. Perhaps talesmen were used. Alternatively, one might speculate that perhaps jury service was a hugely popular pastime in the west. A '*'indicates that the number represents only the numbers of jurors serving in criminal cases; no information is available in some counties as to the number of jurors sitting on civil cases, so overall percentages are not given.

residences on the day of a high-profile trial in the king's bench, but still few came.[43] Although representation in the jury box became a hot political issue at various stages during the period, the reality was that many persons sought to avoid jury service if at all possible. In 1825 it was said that in Limerick, grand juries of eighteen or nineteen were often empanelled, with some of them taken from the petty jurors' book.[44]

Poor attendance was attributable to several factors. At certain periods, potential jurors feared for their safety[45] – for example, in 1881 it was observed that 'the juror who is known either to have taken part in a conviction, or to have resisted an acquittal … occupies a position of great unpleasantness'.[46] Even during the controversies surrounding Catholic representation on Armagh juries in the early 1860s,[47] it transpired that one Catholic, Charles McGee, 'returned thanks to Mr. Hardy [the sub-sheriff] for not summoning me in times when riots etc were going on, and I did not want to be brought into trouble'.[48] According to the Armagh Protestant Association, this had been a 'universal feeling' among Catholics until the 1861 agitation.[49]

Sometimes the reasons for non-attendance were rather more prosaic; a common excuse was the bad state of the roads.[50] One juror in March 1888 explained that it was 'as much as a man's life is worth' to travel forty miles in bad weather.[51] Economic reasons also prevented jurors from attending, as Patrick Durkan, 'victualler to the lord lieutenant' could testify. He wrote to the Mayo clerk of the peace:

> I take the liberty to ask a favour of you. I got a summons to attend as a juror at Castlebar on Saturday the 31st and as it is our Easter market here and having no help to attend, I hope you will get me off this time.[52]

In the same year, a man simply wrote, 'Could you get me knocked off being an engineer'.[53] Others were unwilling to put up with the cramped and uncomfortable conditions in courthouses and jury accommodation in particular. Service on market juries was laborious and time-consuming, and sitting on a jury of matrons was deemed unpleasant. Valuation juries were required to grapple with complex

43 Anon., *The trial of Mr. John Magee for a libel on the duke of Richmond, which took place in the court of king's bench, Dublin* (London, 1813), p. 7.
44 *Report on the state of Ireland 1825*, HC 1825 (129) viii, 1, p. 328 (Maj. Gen. Richard Bourke).
45 See pp 29–33.
46 *Report on Irish jury laws*, HL 1881 (430) xi, 1, para. 2287 (John George Gibson, QC).
47 See pp 29–33.
48 Anon., *The plot discovered: digest of the action for libel, Hardy v. Sullivan, tried before the lord chief justice of the queen's bench, Dublin, in Nov., 1861* (Armagh, 1862), pp 8–9.
49 Ibid., p. 9.
50 This also partly justified the introduction of the Winter Assizes Act. See p. 140.
51 *Office of the clerk of the crown and peace, Mayo 1877–96* (NAI, 1C/76/102).
52 Ibid. 53 Ibid.

questions and had the added burden of having to travel to view the lands or premises that they were to value. Juries summoned for coroners' inquests or criminal trials were not paid for their time, and those with the lowest property ratings often struggled with the expense of having to travel away from their businesses and farms for jury service.

Wealthier men were particularly averse to jury service after O'Hagan's 1871 reforms[54] forced them to share the jury box with men of lesser social standing. The marquess of Lansdowne, for example, noted that such men were 'not very anxious to do their duty as jurors, or to be shut up for hours in the box with small farmers and tradesmen for their colleagues'.[55] It was said that 'aldermen would pay a fine of a hundred pounds cheerfully to avoid being called upon a jury'.[56] It was partially with this in mind that the Dublin Jurors Association had been established in 1875.[57] Several prominent members of the Dublin mercantile community objected to mixing with 'queer people of all sorts'[58] and 'the scum of the city'.[59] Some individuals took the drastic step of registering their property in their wives' names. Members of both the Dublin and Waterford jurors associations brought this to the attention of the 1881 parliamentary committee.[60] Men who did this could also, by implication, lose their parliamentary franchise, which perhaps illustrates the great lengths to which Dublin's merchant class were prepared to go in order to avoid jury service.

The declining proportion of jurors from the higher social groups was noticeable in the years following O'Hagan's reforms. In 1876 O'Hagan himself described as 'a great public evil' the general shirking by upper-class jurors, claiming that they had 'too much abandoned to their humbler colleagues' the duties imposed on them by the legislation.[61] An *Irish Times* article of 1877 referred to 'the usual difficulty ... in obtaining the attendance of a sufficient number of gentlemen'.[62] Particularly in the wake of the criticisms of the 'new' jurors in the 1870s, O'Hagan and others were of the view that it was desirable to have wealthy men on juries, partly because jurors should be 'to some extent ... removed beyond the probable rank of the usual classes of offenders',[63] and partly because they were expected to exercise a certain

54 The Juries (Ireland) Act, 1871.

55 *Hansard 3*, cclxi, 1039 (23 May 1881) (HL). Benjamin Whitney, clerk of the peace and clerk of the crown for Co. Mayo, indicated that, in general, the upper-class jurors considered it to be beneath them to serve on common juries: *Report on Irish jury laws*, 1881, para. 2593.

56 *Report on Irish jury laws*, 1881, para. 784 (John Byrne, Dublin rate collector). In 1826, Laurence McDonnell, a paper manufacturer, told a parliamentary commission that he gave the sheriff £1 or a guinea each Christmas to avoid being summoned as a juror, and said that this was a common practice: *Fifteenth report on salaries*, p. 473.

57 See pp 12–13. 58 *Freeman's Journal*, 30 Jan. 1875 (McComas). 59 Ibid., 30 Apr. 1878.

60 *Report on Irish jury laws*, 1881, para. 823 (T. Newenham Harvey, secretary of the Waterford Jurors Association). Thomas Edmonson, the honorary secretary of the DJA, para. 442, cited a Dublin employer that told some of its employees to 'enter your premises in the names of your wives, and then you will not be summoned as jurors'. He also cited one instance of a man taking out a lease in his wife's name 'on purpose to evade service on a jury', para. 475.

61 *Hansard 3*, ccxxxi, 498 (4 Aug. 1876) (HL). 62 *Irish Times*, 3 Oct. 1877.

63 *Report on Irish juries*, 1873, para. 348 (Thomas de Moleyns, chairman of Co. Kilkenny and crown

level of authority over other, less experienced jurors[64] and would be more likely to favour convictions in criminal cases.[65] They were also deemed to be 'better qualified for the sifting of evidence and arriving at a proper conclusion', as a result of their superior education.[66]

THE IMPOSITION OF FINES

When an assize, session, valuation, inquest or commission began, the names on the jury panel were called, and fines could be imposed on jurors who failed to appear. Most legislation that provided for trials, valuations or inquests by juries also allowed fines to be imposed on jurors who failed to attend.[67] For example, the Bog Act, 1715[68] allowed for fines of 40*s*. to be imposed on defaulting jurors. Similarly, the general reluctance to sit on market juries[69] necessitated the use of fines to compel market jurors to do their duty. Non-attendance by jurors was also a persistent problem in the early years of the wide-streets commission. In March 1759, for example, eight wide-streets jurors did not appear when called and were fined £10 each.[70] A few days later, those who had been fined made representations as to why their fines ought to be remitted: these included such excuses as 'bad state of health', 'out of town' and 'thought he was on the former jury'.[71] In November 1759 a precept was issued to return 60 'persons qualified' for a wide-streets jury.[72] When the jurors' names were called in December, 23 were fined £5 for not appearing.[73] The following week, the jurors were called once more, and again 16 did not appear and were fined £5; and 12 of these 16 were repeat offenders from the previous week.[74] By the 1770s the fines for wide-streets juries appear to have been reduced to 40*s*.,[75] but throughout their existence the amounts of fines varied.[76]

prosecutor for Limerick). Whiteside C.J. said, para. 4231, that there was a convict on one of the recent juries in Clonmel, Co. Tipperary.

64 Barry J., *Report on Irish jury laws*, 1881, para. 1407, thought that if there were even one educated man on the jury, the others would listen to him. Charles Kelly, chairman of Co. Clare, said, para. 3032, that some gentlemen had informed him that 'when they have been on a jury, some of the humbler class of jurors have asked them how they must vote, saying, "I will vote as your honour wishes", "whichever way your honour tells me".'

65 Ibid., paras 152–3 (Jeremiah Blake, crown solicitor for Cork).

66 Ibid., paras 2601–2 (Whitney).

67 E.g. Dublin Wide Streets Act, 1757 (31 Geo. II, c. 19), s. 7; the Dublin Wide Streets Act, 1759 (33 Geo. II, c. 15), s. 2.

68 Bog Act, 1715 (2 Geo. I, c. 12), s. 2. 69 *First report on municipal corporations*, p. 369.

70 *Minutes*, 12 Mar. 1759 (DCA, WSC/Mins/1). 71 *Minutes*, 15 Mar. 1759 (DCA, WSC/Mins/1). 72 *Minutes*, 12 Nov. 1759 (DCA, WSC/Mins/1).

73 *Minutes*, 14 Dec. 1759 (DCA, WSC/Mins/1). The fact that they had been served with summonses was proven by Thomas Jones and John Neiler, sheriff's bailiffs.

74 *Minutes*, 17 Dec. 1759 (DCA, WSC/Mins/1). 75 *Minutes*, 6 July 1778 (DCA, WSC/Mins/2).

76 For example, in 1814 jurors were fined £3 each: *Minutes*, 9 November 1814 (DCA, WSC/Mins/27).

Nineteenth-century legislation provided that fines would be imposed on those who failed to answer to their names after the jurors' list was called out three times.[77] In some instances the jurors were present in court but simply did not answer in the hope that the list would not be called again and they would not have to serve.[78] Sometimes if there were insufficient jurors, they were called and threatened with heavy fines; this usually resulted in sufficient jurors appearing.[79]

There was a perception that fines for non-attendance were not to be taken seriously; for example, in 1832, 22 men had been fined £5 for non-attendance at the Kildare quarter sessions, but 10 later had their fines remitted.[80] In the 1870s it was said that so many £10 fines were imposed in Cork one year that 'they would have amounted in all to thousands of pounds' had they been enforced, but that in reality, only £9 had been levied.[81] This was part of a wider problem of non-enforcement of fines: for example, at the Dublin quarter sessions in 1839, warrants were issued for £801 1*s*., but only £4 6*s*. was levied.[82] Difficulties relating to the levying, collection and lodging of fines were addressed in various pieces of legislation,[83] but the problem remained.

At Tim Kelly's high-profile second trial for the Phoenix Park murders[84] the special jurors were called on fines of £100 and the attorney general was at pains to dispel any rumours that fines would not actually be enforced, emphasising that the crown would insist upon the payment of any fines imposed.[85] An examination of the warrants for non-attendance fines issued in Mayo between 1880 and 1883 show that there were a number of repeat offenders,[86] suggesting that the fines were either

77 Juries (Ireland) Act, 1833 (3 & 4 Will. IV, c. 91), ss 32 and 41; Juries (Ireland) Act, 1871 (34 & 35 Vic., c. 65), s. 48; and 39 & 40 Vic., c. 78, s. 4(1). For comparison, see the English Juries Act, 1825 (6 Geo. IV, c. 50), s. 52.

78 William G. Chamney, *Report of the trial of the queen a. Thomas Beckham, before the right honourable Mr. Justice Fitzgerald and the right hon. Baron Deasy, at the special commission for the County Limerick opened at Limerick on the 16th of June, 1862* (Dublin, 1862).

79 E.g. Richard Wilson Greene, *A report of the trial of James Forbes, William Graham, George Graham, Matthew Handwich, Henry Handwich and William Brownlow, for a conspiracy to create a riot, and to insult and assault his excellency the lord lieutenant, in the theatre royal, and also for a riot* (Dublin, 1823); and Anon., *A full and accurate report of the arraignment and subsequent extraordinary and highly interesting trial of Roger O'Connor, esq, of Dangan castle, County Meath and Martin McKeon, his gate-keeper on a charge for feloniously conspiring, aiding, and abetting in the robbery of his majesty's mail from Dublin to Galway, at Cappagh Hill in the county of Kildare on the second day of Oct. 1812, and for the robbery of Bartholemew St Leger at the same time and place* (Dublin, 1817). In both cases, absent jurors were first called on £20 fines and then on £50 fines.

80 *Return of Kildare jurors*, HC 1833 (602), (724) xxxv, 501, 503.

81 *Report on the Irish jury system*, 1874, paras 967–8 (John Buller Johnson, sub-sheriff of Co. Cork).

82 NAI, OP-1844–122.

83 E.g. the Fines (Ireland) Act, 1838 (1 & 2 Vic., c. 99); and the Fines (Ireland) Amendment Act, 1839 (2 & 3 Vic., c. 92); the Fines (Ireland) Act, 1843 (6 & 7 Vic., c. 56), s. 32 and the Fines Act (Ireland), 1851 (14 & 15 Vic., c. 90), s. 2.

84 See pp 151–3, 159. 85 *Freeman's Journal*, 24 Apr. 1883.

86 *Office of the clerk of the crown and peace, Co. Mayo, 1881–1899* (NAI, CCP 1c/76/100a).

an ineffective deterrent, or were simply not enforced. Some men were fined at least once a year for failure to appear upon being summoned as a juror.[87] It was generally agreed that judges tended to be 'very soft-hearted',[88] and would 'generally remit the fines on all who do not attend'.[89] Of the few judges who claimed to impose fines frequently,[90] not many could confirm that the fines were eventually levied.[91] They were supposed to be imposed unless some 'reasonable excuse' was proved by oath or affidavit. Evidence of illiteracy,[92] for example, or a medical certificate,[93] would suffice.[94] Many fines could not be enforced because the person had either left the county, or their residence was unknown.[95] After 1875, some jurors enlisted the help of the Dublin Jurors Association,[96] while others went so far as to petition the lord lieutenant for remittance of their fines.[97] As one commentator noted in 1874, '[y]es, a great number are fined, and then they get time to appeal, to make excuses; and they come before the judges at the next after sittings, and they generally get off somehow'.[98] Witnesses before the 1876 committee were critical of the system, saying that they considered the apparatus for fining jurors to be ineffective.[99]

It is clear from some of the foregoing examples that the value of the fine varied, and there was inconsistency in the value of fines permissible under legislation. Two

87 Robert Carson, for example, ignored jury summonses almost every year for two decades. Ibid.

88 *Report on Irish jury system*, 1874, para. 225 (de Moleyns). Leahy, para. 1423, claimed that he tended not to impose the fines, 'but the fear of it has a very good effect, particularly with regard to trying to compel gentlemen of position to attend on the grand jury'.

89 Ibid., para. 1303. A controversy arose in 1877 as to whether the master of the court of exchequer had the power to impose and enforce jury fines: see *In re levying of jurors' fines by master of court of exchequer. Brief on behalf of the crown* (NAI, CCS/1877/448).

90 For example, Lefroy J. claimed (ibid., para. 2124) to act 'very strictly' in such matters, and Deasy B. claimed (para. 2499) that he 'always inflicted fines'.

91 Ibid. (Deasy B.), para. 2499.

92 E.g. in 1888 John Garvey, a solicitor, wrote on behalf of John Carroll to the Mayo clerk of the crown and peace to state that his client was illiterate, and could not serve. *Crown and peace, Mayo, 1881–99* (NAI, 1C/76/102).

93 Jurors at the 1866 Fenian trials in Dublin were called over on fines of £50, and it was reported that 'a considerable number of jurors answered'. However, the report also states that '[s]everal of them gave in medical certificates that they were in ill-health'. Anon., *Report of the proceedings at the first sitting of the special commission for the county of the city of Dublin held at Green-Street Dublin for the trial of Thomas Clarke Luby and others* (Dublin, 1866), pp 66, 317.

94 However, some judges refused to accept medical certificates to exempt jurors from service: Fitzgerald J. in *R v. Beckham* (1862) stated that it was his policy to 'pay no attention' to such certificates.

95 NAI, OP-1844–122.

96 E.g. *Irish Times*, 1 Mar. 1889. A Mr Carnegie appeared in the court of queen's bench along with the secretary of the DJA, Mr Carter, before justices Johnson, O'Brien and Holmes, and had his fine remitted.

97 E.g. *Memorial addressed to the lord lieutenant from Peter Tierney, Tuam, Co. Galway, 27 Oct. 1819* (NAI, CSORP/1819/914). The petitioner was a Galway shopkeeper and the £10 fine formed 'the principal of his stock in trade'.

98 Ibid., para. 489.

99 *Report on Irish jury system*, 1874, para. 558 (Ormsby). He also stated, para. 490, that in 1873 the entire amount of fines paid amounted to £28.

separate acts of 1790 provided for fines of 40*s*.,[100] a typical amount, and £10,[101] which was very high.[102] In the early nineteenth century, the sum of the fine imposed was left to the court's discretion.[103] The Juries (Ireland) Act, 1833[104] and the Lands Clauses Consolidation Act, 1845[105] both provided that judges could impose fines of at least £10, while the 1871 act allowed judges to fine up to £100, and sheriffs, coroners and commissioners could fine up to £5.[106] It was suggested that a smaller, more realistic fine would be a better deterrent, especially if it could not be remitted,[107] except on affidavits obtained by the juror.[108] Following these discussions, the 1876 act[109] provided that the fine for non-attendance was to be at least 40*s*., 'or such larger sum as the court shall under the circumstances think fit'. There are examples of fines of £2 and £4 in the late nineteenth century, which suggests that the amount of the fine may have crept up somewhat.[110]

The Fines Act (Ireland), 1851[111] gave jurors thirty days in which to pay, or else face 'distress' (seizure of their property) or imprisonment. Such fines could be appealed, and the party in question could apply to the relevant court for a reduction or a remittance.[112] Jurors who were fined would often appeal, and entered into recognizances to appear at the next assizes or quarter session. An examination of the warrants issued in Mayo between 1880 and 1883 shows that this practice was common.[113] In 1888, there appear to have been a number of warrants issued on persons who did not have sufficient property or goods within the county to meet the fine;[114] of 14 fines levied, 7 were remitted for this reason: 2 had emigrated to America; 3 had their fines remitted by the lord lieutenant; one had not received a jury summons; and in one case no reason was given for the remittance. A Belfast juror who was fined £2 submitted a memorial that he had been in Liverpool selling horses to the Liverpool tramway company at the time of the quarter sessions, and was at pains to emphasise that his absence 'was entirely due to the foregoing cause and the nature of his contract as aforesaid, and not from want of any respect to the honourable court nor any desire to evade the discharge of his duties as a juror'.[115]

100 Londonderry Act, 1790 (30 Geo. III, c. 31), s. 27.
101 Royal Canal Act, 1790 (30 Geo. III, c. 20), s. 2. 102 8 & 9 Vic., c. 18, s. 41.
103 In *R (Richmond) v. Magee* (1813), p. 7, the attorney general sought to have jurors called on fines of £100, but the chief justice said that £50 was as high as the court ever went.
104 3 & 4 Will. IV, c. 91, s. 32. 105 8 & 9 Vic., c. 18, s. 44.
106 Juries (Ireland) Act, 1871 (34 & 35 Vic., c. 65), s. 48.
107 This was the suggestion of Kernan, the first commissioner of valuation in Ireland, paras 2681, 2715.
108 Ibid., para. 2123 (Lefroy). 109 39 & 40 Vic., c. 78, s. 4.
110 E.g. *Re John K. Wilson*, Belfast quarter sessions, 13 Jan. 1898 (PRONI, Ant 1/1b/9/9) and *The queen v. James Kelly. Juror's Appeal*, Belfast quarter sessions, 10 Jan. 1898 (PRONI, Any 1/1b/1/9/1).
111 14 & 15 Vic., c. 90, s. 2. 112 14 & 15 Vic., c. 90, s. 9.
113 *Crown and peace, Mayo, 1881–99.* 114 Ibid.
115 *The queen against James Delaney. Notice of appeal against jurors' fines* (PRONI, ARM 1/10/4/17).

Some legislation specified what the money collected in jurors' fines was to be used for. For example, the act establishing a wide-streets commission for Waterford[116] provided that fines imposed on jurors and witnesses for non-attendance were to be used 'for the sole purposes of widening and keeping in repair the streets, lanes and avenues' of the city.[117]

THE USE OF TALESMEN

If, despite the authorities' best efforts to summon an adequate number of jurors, on threats of heavy fines, an insufficient number of jurors appeared in court, a number of bystanders would be requested to fill in for absent jurors. This was known as seeking a *tales de circumstantibus*,[118] and the men so empanelled were known as the tales or talesmen.[119] Described as 'an expeditious administrative convenience',[120] it was a procedure long used[121] in civil and criminal cases, as well as in relation to valuation and inquest juries. In Ireland, the tales procedure or something resembling it was used in relation to all types of jury, as difficulties in securing enough jurors were a constant problem. A tales could be granted in special-jury cases as well as common-jury cases.[122] When it came to special juries, although the legislation allowed for the substitution of talesmen in situations where a 'full jury' did not appear, judges were unwilling to accept a verdict by a jury entirely composed of such persons. The general consensus seems to have been that

116 Regulation of Waterford Act, 1783–4 (23 & 24 Geo. III, c. 52), s. 25. 117 Ibid., s. 13.

118 J.H. Thomas, *A systematic arrangement of Lord Coke's first institute of the laws of England*, 3 vols (Philadelphia, 1826–7), iii, p. 499 (3 Co. Inst. 155a).

119 English cases included *Harvey v. Chelmsford* (1791) Cro. Jac. 678; 79 E.R. 587 (2 talesmen); *Denbaugh v. Woodly* (1780) Cro. Jac. 316; 79 E.R. 271 (11 talesmen); *Stevens v. Aldridge* (1818) 5 Price 334; 146 E.R. 625 (9 talesmen); *Snook v. Southwood* (1826) R. & M. 429; 171 E.R. 1073 (5 talesmen); and *R v. Hill* (1825) 1 C. & P. 667; 171 E.R. 1360 (4 talesmen).

120 J.B. Post, 'Jury lists and juries in the late fourteenth century' in J.S. Cockburn and Thomas A. Green (eds), *'Twelve good men and true': the criminal trial jury in England, 1200–1800* (Princeton, 1988), p. 68.

121 Legislation on the use of talesmen dated from the sixteenth century. The Juries in Wales Act, 1543 (34 & 35 Hen. VIII, c. 26), s. 10, provided that in Wales, if 9 jurors were sworn in, a *tales de circumstantibus* could be used to fill the remaining 3 spaces. This provision was continued by an act of 1545 (37 Hen. VIII, c. 22), and was made perpetual in 1549 (2 & 3 Ed. VI, c. 32). The Juries (Circumstantibus) Act, 1557 (4 & 5 P. & M., c. 7) did not require that there be nine of the original jurors sworn in. In 1562, another act was passed regarding Welsh juries: the Juries (Circumstantibus) Act, 1562 (5 Eliz. I, c. 25). This also did away with the requirement of nine jurors in Wales. An act from 1572 (14 Eliz. I, c. 9) provided that both plaintiffs and defendants could also pray a *tales de circumstantibus*. The purpose of this was '[f]or the avoiding of great and chargeable delays oftentimes happening unto tenants and defendants'. The Nisi Prius (Middlesex) Act, 1576 (18 Eliz. I, c. 12) extended the tales to further remedy delays in trials. In 1696, the Regulation of Juries Act (7 & 8 Will. III, c. 32), s. 3, provided for the tales.

122 See *Lewis v. Gibbons* (1846) Bl. D. & O. 62. This case related to Samuel Lewis' *Topographical dictionary of Ireland* (Dublin, 1837).

there ought to be at least one juror among them who qualified as 'special'. In *Drumgoold v. Home*,[123] for example, a verdict delivered by twelve talesmen was later set aside.

There were also difficulties experienced in securing the attendance of sufficient numbers of valuation jurors, and various pieces of legislation allowed for the use of talesmen. For example, the Bog Act, 1715[124] provided that if enough qualified jurors could not be found, the sheriff was to return 'other honest and indifferent men of the standers by, or that can be speedily procured to attend that service'. Under an act of 1790, jurors were to be summoned to value lands in Londonderry,[125] and bystanders could serve as talesmen if necessary. It was not specifically stated that the jurors or talesmen had to be duly qualified. The Lands Clauses Consolidation Act, 1845[126] allowed indifferent bystanders to be sworn as talesmen if necessary. If a special jury was empanelled, the talesmen had to be qualified as either special or common jurors.[127] While the original wide-streets legislation made no mention of talesmen, the 1859 act provided that a tales could be used where there were not enough jurors in attendance, suggesting that difficulties had been encountered in ensuring that sufficient jurors turned up to serve on wide-streets juries. The talesmen could be 'other persons of the said county of city of Dublin then present' – there was no mention of such talesmen having to hold jurors' qualifications.[128]

There was Irish legislation dealing with talesmen in the seventeenth and eighteenth centuries,[129] and the Juries (Ireland) Act, 1833[130] outlined the procedure for criminal and civil trials. Where there were insufficient jurors either as a result of non-attendance or the use of challenges, either party in a civil or criminal action could request a tales. A judge could 'command the sheriff … to name and appoint, as often as the need shall require, twelve other able men of the county, city or town then present'. Where a special jury was struck for the trial of any issue, the talesmen 'shall be such as shall be impanelled upon the common jury panel to serve at the same court, if a sufficient number of such men can be found'. The names and addresses of the talesmen were to be written on cards, and selected at random from a box.[131] The 1871 act[132] did not alter the law in relation to the tales – the drafters' focus was elsewhere – and the procedures continued as laid down in 1833.

123 (1837) 1 Hud. & Br. 412. 124 Bog Act, 1715 (2 Geo. I, c. 12), s. 2.
125 Londonderry Act, 1790 (30 Geo. III, c. 31), s. 26. 126 8 & 9 Vic., c. 18, s. 41.
127 8 & 9 Vic., c. 18, s. 55.
128 Dublin Wide Streets (Amendment) Act, 1759 (33 Geo. II, c. 15), s. 3.
129 Tales (Tipperary) Act, 1695 (7 Will. III, c. 19); and Special Juries Act, 1777–8 (17 & 18 Geo. III, c. 45), ss 9–10. Section 9 provided that if an issue was likely to remain untried for default of jurors, then the judge could order the sheriff to 'name and appoint, as often as need be, twelve such other able persons of the said county then present, to whom no cause of challenge doth lie'.
130 3 & 4 Will. IV, c. 91, s. 28.
131 This resembles the procedures used in calling a jury in a civil case.
132 The Juries (Ireland) Act, 1871 (34 & 35 Vic., c. 65), s. 42.

The talesmen were generally selected from persons who happened to be present in the courtroom or around the courthouse, and the term '*de circumstantibus*' refers to people 'standing about'. In 1862, a Catholic from Armagh described how he was 'caught up off the street and carried into the courthouse for want of a juryman'.[133] In *Hodgens v. Reed*[134] a plaintiff sought to have the talesmen returned from the other jury panels,[135] because he considered that the persons present in the courthouse were likely to be prejudiced against him. The chief justice, however, ruled that the usual practice in Irish courts was that the tales should be *de circumstantibus*. Because the procedure was quite vague as to who could be asked to serve, there were on occasion doubts as to the sheriff's impartiality in selecting the bystanders. The array of a tales called when there were insufficient jurors could be challenged on the ground of the partiality of the sheriff.[136]

Some contemporaries were critical of the frequent use of talesmen. One anecdote was that:

> [i]n a case that was tried not long ago, not being able to get a petit jury from the panel, some persons were named from the people in court, and amongst them was one person who put himself rather forward on the occasion, and was sworn in; it appeared afterwards, that he had purposely thrown himself in the way, in order to procure the acquittal of a friend who was then to be tried for assault and battery; he kept the jury out for several hours, and they were obliged to be discharged without finding a verdict.[137]

Many commentators were uncomfortable at the thought of complicated or important cases falling into the hands of unqualified jurors, partly because such men were seen as likely to be unintelligent and uneducated. Clinton further explains that the property qualification had been seen by many as a means of ensuring that jurors were above bribery: '[t]he presence of large numbers of tales on the jury was therefore thought to increase the likelihood of corruption'.[138]

CALLING OVER THE JURORS

When jurors appeared in court their names were 'called over' in accordance with a prescribed procedure, which originally differed depending on whether the case was civil or criminal. Under the 1833 act,[139] which echoed legislation from a century

133 *Hardy v. Sullivan* (1862), p. 9. 134 (1831) 4 Law Rec. (o.s.) 88.

135 This was frequently the practice in England: W. Tidd, *The practice of the courts of king's bench and common pleas in personal actions and ejectment* (9th ed., London, 1828), p. 858; and *R v. Dolby* (1823) 2 B. & C. 104.

136 This was successfully done in the English case of *R v. Dolby* (1823) 2 B. & C. 104.

137 *Report on the state of Ireland*, 1825, p. 329 (Bourke).

138 F.W. Clinton, 'Structure of judicial administration and the development of contract law in seventeenth-century England', *Colum. L. Rev.*, 83:1 (1983) 35–137 at 65, 67.

139 3 & 4 Will. IV, c. 91, s. 19.

earlier,[140] in civil cases, the name, place of abode and 'addition'[141] of every juror was written on a separate piece of parchment or card. These were delivered to the judge's clerk or registrar, who saw that they were put into a box. Whenever any issue was brought on to be tried, the registrar shook the box in open court, and drew out twelve cards. When each card was taken from the box, the name of the juror was called out in court, and if any of the men whose names were then called did not appear, or did not answer, further cards were drawn as necessary. The twelve jurors were sworn in. After delivering a verdict, the names were returned to the box, 'there to be kept with the other names remaining at that time undrawn, and so *toties quoties* as long as any issue remains to be tried'. With the consent of the parties, the twelve jurors could also try any subsequent issue, without having their names returned to the box and re-drawn. This was known as the ballot procedure.[142]

The procedure differed somewhat in criminal cases. Generally there was no ballot, and names were called in the order in which the sheriff had listed them on the panel – this was either in order of social rank or, later, in alphabetical order. A mandatory ballot was not introduced for criminal cases until the Juries Procedure (Ireland) Act, 1876.[143] Before this, however, it was open to a criminal defendant to seek the crown's consent to have the jurors balloted for. The reasons for requiring a ballot varied from case to case, but usually rested on the suspicion or possibility of unfairness. In some instances, for example, the jurors' names were set out alphabetically on the list, meaning that members of the same family could end up sitting on the same jury.[144] In *R v. Frost*,[145] an indictment for high treason, the clerk of the crown began to call over the names of the jurors who had appeared in alphabetical order, but counsel for the prisoner requested that they be taken by ballot. The attorney general had no objection, so the court acquiesced. A year later, in *R v. Carroll*,[146] an indictment for robbery, the prisoner similarly requested that the crown consent to having the names called by ballot. The crown here refused, claiming that they had no authority from the attorney general to accede to such a novel application, and without such consent there could be no ballot. In *R v.*

140 Regulation of Juries Act, 1735 (9 Geo. II, c. 3), s. 7. An Act for continuing and amending the several acts for the better regulation of juries, 1745 (19 Geo. II, c. 10), ss 2, 3 had also provided for a ballot procedure, albeit slightly different because the initial balloting was carried out by judges of the superior courts in Dublin. This was to create the grand panel for the county, from which the sheriff could then draw twelve jurors, by ballot, as necessary.

141 An addition of estate or quality was whatever was 'added' to a man's name to indicate his status, such as 'esquire' or 'gentleman'. See the case *Nash v. Battersby* (1790) 2 Lord Ray. 986; 92 E.R. 157. An addition of mystery would be a man's profession, such as 'painter' or 'manufacturer'. An addition of place would be a description of where the man was from, such as 'of Merrion Street'.

142 See also the Juries (Ireland) Act, 1871 (34 & 35 Vic., c. 65), s. 41. Wide-streets juries were also balloted for: *Fifteenth report on salaries*, p. 536.

143 39 & 40 Vic., c. 78, s. 19.

144 At the 1836 Belfast quarter sessions there were six Johnsons on the jury: *Ulster Times*, 7 July 1836.

145 (1839) 9 Car. & P. 129.

146 (1840) 1 Cr. & Dix C.C. 337.

Colgan, Doherty and Kelly,[147] Hayes, representing Doherty, applied to have the names taken by ballot, referring to *Frost*. Bushe C.J. pointed out that unlike in *Frost*, here there was no alphabetical arrangement of jurors' names on the panel. Hayes insisted that this only served to make his case stronger:

> for if there were an alphabetical arrangement it could not be reasonably alleged that the placing of the jurors in the panel was regulated by anything save the initial letters of their names; but in Ireland the usage is to place the better or more respectable class higher on the panel, the jurors of an humbler class being placed lower down.

The solicitor general opposed the motion because it 'implied an imputation on the sheriff', and because there was a risk of setting a precedent for a cumbersome and unnecessary practice. Bushe C.J. refused the application. In an 1862 case there was a disagreement between counsel and judges about the order in which to call over the jurors, with Fitzgerald J. insisting that the names should be read in the order in which they appeared on the panel.[148]

These struggles over the use of the ballot procedure should be viewed in the broader context of the battle to control the composition of the jury. The calling-over and swearing of the jurors could take hours if attendance was poor and the list had to be called several times. For example, in *R v. O'Connor and McKeon* it took two and a half hours.[149]

PAYMENT IN CIVIL CASES

One reason outlined above for people's reluctance to serve on juries was the potential cost involved, in terms of both time and money. Attendance at assizes or quarter sessions could necessitate travel and accommodation expenses,[150] and took jurors away from their farms and businesses. This was particularly problematic in larger counties and in winter assizes counties. The Winter Assizes Acts provided for the joining of several counties as one 'winter assizes county', with the result that the judges on circuit did not have to travel to every county to deal with criminal matters in wintertime.[151] However, it also meant that some jurors had to travel longer distances, as the assizes town might be located in a different county. An 1854 article in the *Irish Jurist*, for example, referred to a recent case in which a five-day trial had ended up costing a special juror an estimated £2 10*s*.[152]

147 (1841) 2 Cr. & Dix C.C. 80. 148 *R v. Beckham* (1862), p. 11.

149 *R v. O'Connor and McKeon* (1817).

150 The *Irish Jurist* noted in 1854 that it was 'a well known fact that assizes time is the harvest of the inn-keepers and owners of lodgings in the town, and jurors have no special immunity from these extra charges'. Anon., editorial, *Ir. Jur.* (o.s.), 6 (1854) 221.

151 The Winter Assizes Act, 1876 (39 & 40 Vic., c. 57) and the Winter Assizes Act, 1877 (40 & 41 Vic., c. 46). 152 Ibid.

However, only some categories of juror received any payment for their time. Traditionally, jurors with a higher social ranking were returned on the civil panel,[153] and unlike jurors on criminal trials, they were entitled to some reimbursement of their expenses. The precise origin of the custom of paying the expenses of common jurors is 'difficult to ascertain'.[154] Jurors traditionally could not accept bribes or payment for their verdicts, but were entitled to some sort of reimbursement. Fourteenth-century legislation provided that if jurors in any case took a reward for their verdict, they were liable to be imprisoned for one year and fined, with half of the fine going to the injured party.[155] The fine was to be ten times the amount of the bribe.[156] So a distinction was drawn between taking a bribe or a payment for a verdict on the one hand, and receiving a fee after delivering the verdict on the other. This distinction was still relevant in the eighteenth century: the author of *The complete juryman* wrote in 1752 that '[i]n civil causes jurors are to be paid for their trouble and attendance. But if they take any thing for giving their verdict, at common law they are punishable by fine and imprisonment.'[157]

Bacon wrote that 'jurors in all civil causes are to be paid for their trouble and attendance, and the quantum is to be proportioned according to the distance of place, badness of the weather &c'.[158] The sums payable to civil jurors varied over time. Oldham notes that common jurors at *nisi prius* in England during the seventeenth and eighteenth centuries earned between 8*d.* and 1*s.* apiece.[159] Talesmen received between 4*d.* and 8*d.*[160] *The complete juryman* stated in 1752 that jurors in civil cases tried within the same county were entitled to 8*d.*, and when they tried cases at bar in a foreign county, they were entitled to £5.[161] The sums payable to wide-streets juries could be quite high, given that they had to meet repeatedly. For example, a wide-streets jury that was sworn in February 1790 gave their inquisition in September 1790 in relation to properties around College Green. The minutes of the commission state that the jury 'demanded compensation for their trouble and attendance at nineteen meetings on said valuation'. It was ordered that £12 7*d.* be paid to the foreman, James Williams, 'for

153 See p. 27.
154 *Vickery v. London, Brighton and South Coast Railway Co.* (1870) L.R. 5 C.P. 165 (Bovill C.J.). According to the *Mirror of justices*, before 1100, it was common practice for plaintiffs to award 4*d.* to each common juror after the delivery of the verdict. Then, during the reign of Henry I, it was ordained that jurors on inquests and at assizes 'should not take fees', because they acted *ex officio.* W. Whittaker (ed., tr.), *The mirror of justices* (London, 1895), pp 46–7.
155 Penalties for Juror Act, 1360 (34 Ed. III, c. 8).
156 Punishment of Act, 1364 (38 Ed. III, st. 1, c. 12).
157 Anon., *The complete juryman*, p. 182.
158 M. Bacon, *A new abridgement of the law*, 5 vols (London, 1768), iii, p. 277.
159 James C. Oldham, *Trial by jury: the seventh amendment and Anglo-American special juries* (New York, 2006), p. 275. Provision was made in the seventeenth century for covering the costs of jurors 'lying out' – in other words for their bed and board, as well as for the bailiffs and tipstaffs attending them: Anon., *The complete juryman*, p. 182.
160 See the English case *Vickery v. London, Brighton and South Coast Railway* (1870) L.R. 5 C.P. 165; E. Powell, *The attorney's academy* (London, 1647), pp 141–2; and Duncombe, p. 216.
161 Anon., *The complete juryman*, p. 182

the trouble and attendance of said jury on said valuation'.[162] In January of the same year, a wide-streets jury had been paid £5 4*s*., 'being the compensation ... for their trouble and attendance at eight meetings on the valuation of interests in Park Gate Street'.[163] The commissioners on duties and salaries reported in 1826 that jurors on writs of inquiry or inquisition received 1*s*. each.[164]

Special jurors received higher fees than common jurors. In England, they were entitled to one guinea during the eighteenth and nineteenth centuries.[165] However, in Ireland, the Juries Regulation Act, 1800[166] provided that every special juror was to be paid £1 2*s*. 9*d*. by the party that had applied for said jury. Later, the Juries (Ireland) Act, 1833[167] specified no fixed sum to be paid to special jurors, leaving it to the courts' discretion. This was because the judges, when asked their opinion on the bill of 1832, had considered the proposed limitation of special jurors' fees to £5 as being inadequate.[168] In 1868 a select committee[169] recommended that special jurors in England be paid one guinea per day, rather than per cause, and the English Juries Act, 1870[170] accordingly provided that a special juror was entitled to £1 1*s*. per day.[171] This was repealed in 1871 however,[172] and the Irish act of the same year[173] made no provision for the payment of jurors. When one witness gave evidence in 1881 that before O'Hagan's Act there had existed in Dublin a class of persons who continually served on juries, and that 'in fact, some of them followed it as a profession',[174] the earl of Derby was somewhat aghast: '[d]o you mean that jurors serve on common juries for the sake of 1*s*. 9*d*.?'[175]

Special jurors acting in other contexts were also usually paid; for example, if they acted on lunacy commissions. At one such commission in 1859,[176] the jurors refused to give their verdict until they were informed as to who would pay them, given that the person who was the subject of the inquiry was indigent. An editorial in the *Irish Times* following this case remarked that 'a commission *de lunatico inquirendo* is the most extravagant process known to the law'; as well as the jurors and lawyers, the two commissioners received ten guineas per day. The paper described this as 'nothing less than to waste an alleged lunatic's property in law, in order to determine whether he is, or is not, likely to waste it himself'.[177]

162 *Minutes*, 24 Sept. 1790 (DCA, WSC/Mins/9).
163 *Minutes*, 8 Jan. 1790 (DCA, WSC/Mins/9). 164 *Fifteenth report on salaries*, p. 81.
165 The English Jury Act, 1751 (24 Geo. II, c. 18) and the English Juries Act, 1825 (6 Geo. IV, c. 50), s. 35. However, account must be taken of the differences between the English and Irish pounds.
166 40 Geo. III, c. 72, s. 7. 167 3 & 4 Will. IV, c. 91.
168 *Letter regarding the jury bill 1833* (NAI, OP/1833/14).
169 *Report on special and common juries*, HC 1867–8 (401) xii, 677, p. 49.
170 (33 & 34 Vic., c. 77), s. 22. 171 The same act allowed 10*s*. per day to common jurors.
172 Juries (Amendment) Act, 1871 (34 Vic., c. 2). 173 Juries (Ireland) Act, 1871 (34 & 35 Vic., c. 65).
174 *Report on Irish jury laws*, 1881, para. 490 (Constantine Molloy, crown prosecutor for King's County).
175 The drafters of O'Hagan's Act were also aware of this practice: McEldowney, 'Lord O'Hagan', pp 155–6.
176 Commission of lunacy regarding John Gustavus Crosbie, *Irish Times*, 12 Aug. 1857.
177 *Irish Times*, 12 Aug. 1859.

Like lunacy juries, wide-streets juries added to the significant overall costs of proceedings.[178] John Claudius Beresford explained that in the early nineteenth century the wide-streets commissioners had struggled to return juries to conduct valuations because of the tediousness of their task. In 1816 they increased the remuneration for such jurors from 1*s*. per valuation to one guinea per day.[179] The expense associated with such juries was consequently quite high, as they often sat for several days.[180] For example, there were thirty-eight valuation inquests held in Dublin between 1820 and 1830, and in many instances juries sat a dozen times on the same valuation. The highest number of days claimed for a valuation was twenty-eight,[181] although one of the commissioners pointed out that a 'day' in this regard meant from 11 a.m. until 2 p.m.[182] Michael Maley, a builder and developer, claimed that there were wide-streets juries paid between £800 and £900 around 1823 and 1824.[183] As Sheridan points out, the juries 'often spent many months establishing title and value, interviewing the owners and inhabitants of every house'.[184] Wide-streets jurors tended to serve repeatedly; for example, jurors who were paid over £11 each for valuing properties on Skinner Row in 1820 also valued houses around Francis Street a few months later, earning over £7 each.[185] By the mid-nineteenth century wide-streets juries were perceived as something of a racket; a commentator in 1846 noted that some jurors 'were appointed on no less than twenty valuations, and some of them spent several days on one valuation'.[186] It was also observed that the sheriff of Dublin continually returned members of the corporation for such juries, so that they would benefit from the high fees, thus strengthening his relationship with them.[187]

It was also customary in some places for the parties to treat the jurors to a meal after the delivery of the verdict. Usually this was paid for by the successful party. As Forsyth observed in 1852 in relation to English juries:

> The party with whom they have given their sentence giveth the inquest their dinner that day most commonly; and this is all they have for their labour notwithstanding that they come some twenty, some thirty or forty miles or more to the place where they gave their verdict. All the rest is their own charge.[188]

178 In both cases, the sheriff charged £3 3*s*. to empanel such a jury: *Fifteenth report on salaries*, p. 81. By comparison, for returning an ordinary *venire* with a panel attached they charged 2*s*. 4*d*.

179 *Fifteenth report on salaries*, pp 505 (Golding) and 534 (Beresford). This was not grounded in statute.

180 E. Sheridan, 'Designing the capital city' in J. Brady and A. Simms (eds), *Dublin through space & time* (Dublin, 2007), p. 121

181 *Wide streets (Dublin). Returns of the number of inquests held*, HC 1830 (149) xxvi, 293.

182 *Fifteenth report on salaries*, p. 538 (Leland Crosthwaite). 183 Ibid., p. 535.

184 Sheridan, *Designing the capital*, p. 122.

185 The commissioners estimated their overall spend at around £25,000 per annum: Wide Streets Commission, *Extracts from minutes*, p. 19.

186 *Freeman's Journal*, 8 May 1846. 187 *Fifteenth report on salaries*, p. 536 (Maley).

188 T.W. Forsyth, *History of trial by jury* (London, 1852), ch. 18.

This appears to have been grounded in custom, rather than in law. Similarly, manor-court juries were often paid for their service, either with money or whiskey, by the successful party in a civil action.[189] It was suggested by some commentators before the 1837 commission on manor courts that it was the possibility of free drink that incentivised many to sit on such juries.[190]

Sometimes jurors who attended did not ultimately serve because the case did not proceed. If this was the fault of the parties, the jurors might be paid,[191] but if it was because of insufficient jurors attending, they were not. The rationales for these rules are inconsistent. In the latter instance, as Bacon wrote, the jurors were 'not to be paid, for nobody has received any benefit from their attendance, and consequently not obliged to make them any recompense'.[192] However in the former instance, there was similarly no verdict but the jurors were paid by the parties. It is unclear whether the money was thus intended as compensation for a loss, or payment for a service. Johnson observed that common jurors in civil cases were paid 'a guinea for a verdict'.[193]

Because most jurors received little or no compensation for their service, the practice of bribing or attempting to bribe jurors was not uncommon. The effects of receiving a bribe seem to have varied from case to case: if found guilty of embracery,[194] a juror could be subject to a fine or imprisonment,[195] but in the nineteenth century this was quite rare. The verdict might be declared void,[196] or the jury might be discharged if the bribe was discovered at an early stage.[197] More typical, however, was the imposition of a fine on the juror – in theory up to ten times the amount received, though the extent to which such fines were actually paid is difficult to ascertain. It was not always the parties who approached the jurors with the bribe – sometimes the jurors themselves demanded payment in advance from one or other of the parties.[198]

189 R. McMahon, 'Manor courts in the west of Ireland before the Famine' in D.S. Greer and N.M. Dawson (eds), *Mysteries and solutions in Irish legal history* (Dublin, 2001), p. 148. See also R. McMahon, 'The courts of petty sessions and the law in pre-Famine Galway' (MA, NUI Galway, 1999), pp 33–4.

190 *Report from the select committee on manor courts, Ireland; together with the minutes of evidence, appendix and index*, HC 1837 (494) xv, 1, pp 43 (John Jagoe) and 115 (Timothy Fitzpatrick).

191 E.g. the English case *Hunt v. Hollis* (1658) 2 Sid. 77; 82 E.R. 1267.

192 Bacon, *Abridgement*, iii, p. 277. See also J. Lilly, *The practical register*, 2 vols (2nd ed., London, 1745), ii, p. 157.

193 *Report on Irish jury system*, para. 999.

194 Embracery was a common-law misdeameanour: See J. Stephen, *A digest of the criminal law* (London, 1877), pp 77–8 and W. Hawkins, *Treatise of the pleas of the crown*, 2 vols (4th ed., London, 1762), i, p. 259.

195 The Juries (Ireland) Act, 1833 (3 & 4 Will. IV, c. 91), s. 48.

196 E.g. the English case *Sir John Smith and Peaze* (1687) 1 Leo. 17; 74 E.R. 16.

197 E.g. the English case *Richard Noble* (1713) How. St. Tr. 731. A juror was offered £20 to bring in a verdict of not guilty against a defendant who was charged with murder and treason. This offer was made by the defendant's attorney, who pledged £1,000 for the whole jury in exchange for an acquittal. The jury was set aside, and a new jury was called over, with each new juror being closely questioned about any similar offers or threats.

198 E.g. *Byrne v. Chester & Holyhead Railway Co.* (1856) 8 Ir. Jur. (o.s.) 511.

PAYMENT IN CRIMINAL CASES

Those who participated in the criminal justice system as jurors generally received no payment. For example, legislation dealing with coroners' inquests specified fees for coroners, witnesses, and persons who allowed viewings or inquests to take place in their homes, but it made no provision for the payment of jurors' expenses.[199] Coroners' juries tended to be from the immediate locality of where the body was discovered or where the inquest took place, however, and were unlikely to incur serious expenses. Juries of matrons were summoned *de circumstantibus* and their examination probably did not take long, and so they too were unlikely to be at a loss. However, at the trial of Mary Hallinan in 1841, after delivering their verdict the forematron asked the court, 'Aren't we to be paid?', to which the clerk of the crown replied, 'Oh, Mr. Bourke the sub-sheriff will settle with you' – suggesting that they might have received some payment for their time.[200]

Criminal trial jurors who might be summoned from the opposite end of the county, to attend for several days, usually received nothing. Exceptions to this were situations involving changes of venue (if the jury had to travel),[201] and cases involving the view of a location or premises.[202] The Juries Procedure (Ireland) Act, 1876[203] provided that a judge could order that the costs and expenses incurred by having a view in criminal cases were to be paid by the crown. Special jurors in trials at bar were also paid in proportion to the distance they had travelled and the duration of time spent away from their homes.[204]

One reason for the distinction between civil and criminal jurors was probably that in civil actions, the jurors' fees would be borne by the parties, which would be unworkable in a criminal context: defendants would often be too poor to pay, and it was undesirable that the crown should have to pay. Another reason for the distinction was that civil cases were considered to be more complicated, involving more technical and documentary evidence. The demands on jurors' time were considered to be 'proportionately greater' in civil, rather than criminal cases.[205] This is further evidenced by the fact that certain types of civil cases called for special jurors, deemed to be better equipped to deal with complex issues.

In the second half of the nineteenth century calls were made for better remuneration for jurors.[206] Criminal jurors, in particular, tended to be the least well-off, and consequently the least equipped to bear the expenses of jury service. Houston referred in 1861 to 'the shamefully inadequate remuneration … which is made to jurors, even those on the special jury list'.[207] Dodd observed in 1881 that

199 The Coroners (Ireland) Act, 1846 (9 & 10 Vic., c. 37).

200 *Connaught Telegraph*, 4 Aug. 1841. 201 See chapter 12.

202 E.g. in *McGhee d. Bishop of Derry v. Harvey* (1827) 1 Hud. & Br. 106 the defendant claimed £20 to cover the expenses of the jurors who conducted the view.

203 (39 & 40 Vic., c. 78), s. 11.

204 Huband, *Practical treatise*, p. 959; and *Attorney general v. The primate* (1837), 2 Jones 362.

205 (1854) 6 Ir. Jur. (o.s.) 221. 206 E.g. (1854) 6 Ir. Jur. (o.s.) 221.

207 Houston, 'Observations', p. 108.

'in the administration of the law … the only persons now who are not remunerated for their services are the high sheriffs, justices of the peace and jurors'.[208] The first two of these, he argued, were positions of dignity, honour and respect, and were self-rewarding in that regard. Jurors, however, received neither 'honours or social dignity from their position'. Jurors themselves sometimes actively sought better compensation before delivering a verdict, both in civil actions[209] and on lunacy inquiries.[210] The problem was exacerbated when the Juries (Ireland) Act, 1871[211] lowered the property qualification for jury service and brought men of more modest means into the jury pool: we saw in chapter 3 that some of the new jurors who appeared in court were dressed in rags, and some could not afford the travel and accommodation costs.

T. Newenham Harvey, a printer and self-professed expert on Irish jury laws,[212] who was the honorary secretary of the Waterford Jurors Association, pointed out that in Waterford, '[a] man who owns land of the value of forty pounds or occupies a ten pound house, is often exceedingly poor', and that unpaid jury service 'is a great tax indeed on him'. He felt that county jurors who were 'of a low class', ought to be paid such a sum 'as might seem reasonable in the circumstances; that I think would only be fair'. To illustrate the poverty of some jurors, Harvey told the committee of an incident that had occurred in Co. Waterford. A number of jurors were summoned to the far end of the county, but failed to attend. They were fined, and upon their failure to pay, the sheriff was instructed to seize their goods in lieu. Arriving at their respective homes, he found them to be 'in so poor a condition that they had no goods to seize'. The judge ordered that they be imprisoned, but in fact, 'there was such an outcry raised in the county that the idea was given up'.[213]

Although some were of the view that criminal jurors should continue to be unpaid,[214] the general feeling was that more substantial remuneration was essential if the jury system was to continue in operation. Different rates of remuneration were suggested.[215] In 1874, William Ormsby, the sub-sheriff of Dublin, said that he heard repeated complaints about the payment of jurors.[216] He suggested paying

208 Dodd, 'Grievances', p. 224. Similarly, Thomas de Moleyns QC, chairman of Co. Kilkenny, described jury duty as a thankless and unpaid service: *Report on Irish jury laws*, 1881, para. 1660, and George Bolton, Tipperary crown solicitor, para. 3957, said that those who carried out this duty were 'men of humble means, and men who cannot afford it'.

209 E.g. *Byrne v. Chester & Holyhead Railway Co* (1856) 8 Ir. Jur. (o.s.) 511; *Lindsay v. Keatinge, cited in Fifteenth report on salaries* (1826), p. 429.

210 E.g. commission of lunacy regarding John Gustavus Crosbie, *Irish Times*, 12 Aug. 1857.

211 34 & 35 Vic., c. 65.

212 He told the 1881 committee, para. 813, 'I have been on the jury lists for a number of years, and as a juror who is harassed with incessant service, I gave great study to the law.'

213 Ibid.

214 *Report on Irish jury system*, 1874, paras 1000 (Johnson) and 1039 (Henry West, chairman of Co. Wexford).

215 E.g. Joseph Buller Johnson suggested £3 for a verdict, to be divided among the jurors: ibid., para. 999.

216 *Report on the Irish jury system*, HC 1874 (244) ix, 557, paras 495–6.

special jurors £1 a day and common jurors 5*s*. for attending, whether or not they tried a case.[217]

AGITATION FOR BETTER REMUNERATION

Towards the end of the century there was a concerted effort to secure better remuneration for jurors. The drafters of the 1871 act did not recommend the introduction of payment for all jurors, as had been done in England under the 1870 act.[218] It was feared that this would give rise to a class of professional 'guinea jurors', as had previously been seen to happen with special juries. Still, the Dublin Jurors Association sought to increase the remuneration for special jurors to a guinea per day, and for common jurors to either half a guinea or 5*s*.[219] Commentators continued to highlight the poverty experienced by jurors who had to travel for assizes or quarter sessions, and urged that such jurors ought not to be left out of pocket. For example, James Gilhooloey, a Cork MP, pointed out to Chief Secretary Balfour in 1899 that men summoned to the recent Bantry quarter sessions, rated at £6, had to make a ninety-mile round trip.[220] Many attempts were made at the turn of the twentieth century to provide for adequate remuneration for jurors in both England and Ireland,[221] and resolutions were passed by several

217 Ibid., paras 496–7. 218 McEldowney, 'Lord O'Hagan', pp 155–6.

219 *Report on Irish jury laws*, 1881, para. 423 (Edmondson).

220 *Hansard 4*, lxvi, 1451 (20 Feb. 1899) (HC). Balfour, in response, noted that only two of the jurors had undertaken a journey of that length, and that they were all rated for £11.

221 E.g. Jurymen's expenses (Ireland) bill, 1892, *Hansard 4*, i, 171 (10 Feb. 1892) (bill 118); *Jury bill*, HC 1894 (120) iv, 667; Jurors' payment bill, 1895, *Hansard 4*, xxx, 567 (12 Feb. 1895) (HC) (bill 98); *Payment of jurors (Ireland) bill*, HC 1895 (85) v, 393; *Payment of jurors (Ireland) bill*, HC 1896 (75) v, 535; Payment of jurors (Ireland) bill, 1896, *Hansard 4*, xxxvii, 536 (17 Feb. 1896) (HC) (bill 75); *Jurors' payment bill*, HC 1896 (98) iii, 497; *Payment of jurors bill*, HC 1896 (83) v, 531; Payment of jurors bill, 1896, *Hansard 4*, xxxvii, 569 (18 Feb. 1896) (HC) (bill 83); *Jurors' expenses bill*, HC 1897 (217) iv, 77; Jurors' expenses bill, 1897, *Hansard 4*, xlviii, 1531 (4 May 1897) (HC) (bill 217); *Jurors' expenses bill*, HC 1898 (164) iv, 579; Jurors' expenses bill, 1898, *Hansard 4*, lv, 1438 (30 Mar. 1898) (HC) (bill 164); *Jurors' payment bill*, HC 1900 (251) ii, 539; Jurors' expenses bill, 1900, *Hansard 4*, lxxxiii, 376 (16 May 1900) (HC) (bill 217); *Legal procedure (Ireland) bill*, HC 1901 (10) ii, 637; *Jurors' expenses bill*, HC 1901 (31) ii, 563; Jurors' expenses bill, 1901, *Hansard 4*, lxxxix, 458 (19 Feb. 1901) (HC) (bill 31); *Jurors (Ireland) bill*, HC 1901 (49) ii, 567; *Jurors' expenses bill*, HC 1904 (77) ii, 405; Jurors' expenses bill, 1904, *Hansard 4*, cxxx, 261 (18 Feb. 1904) (HC) (bill 77); *Jurors' expenses (Ireland) bill*, HC 1905 (49) ii, 697; Jurors' expenses (Ireland) bill, 1905, *Hansard 4*, cxli (21 Feb. 1905) (HC) (bill 49); *Jurors' expenses bill*, HC 1906 (43) ii, 735; Jurors' expenses bill, 1906, *Hansard 4*, clii 699 (23 Feb. 1906) (HC) (bill 43); *Jurors' expenses bill*, HC 1907 (44) ii, 543; Jurors (expenses) bill, 1907, *Hansard 4*, clxix 566 (18 Feb. 1907) (HC) (bill 44); *Payment of jurors bill*, HC 1908 (68) iv, 71; Payment of jurors bill, 1908, *Hansard 4*, clxxxiii, 1432 (10 Feb. 1908) (HC) (bill 68); *Payment of jurors bill*, HC 1909 (98) iv, 345; *Jurors' payment (Ireland) bill*, HC 1910 (120) ii, 339; Payment of Jurors (Ireland) bill, 1910, *Hansard 5*, xvi, 1246 (13 April 1910) (HC); *Payment of jurors bill*, HC 1911 (84) iv, 599; Payment of jurors bill, 1911, *Hansard 5*, xxii, 217 (28 Feb. 1911) (HC); *Payment of jurors bill*, HC 1912–13 (36) iv, 229; Payment of jurors bill, 1912, *Hansard 5*, xxxiv, 627 (21 Feb. 1912) (HC) (bill 36).

county poor-law guardians advocating the payment of jurors' expenses.[222] The practice of paying one guinea (or 21*s.*) to a common jury in a civil case endured into the twentieth century,[223] until section 62 of the Juries Act, 1927 provided that they were to be paid 5*s.* each by the successful party.

CONCLUSION

Clearly, empanelling a complete jury to try a case or conduct a valuation was not always a straightforward matter, due to people's natural reluctance to undertake a duty that was, for the most part, thankless and either unpaid or underpaid. This reluctance contrasts with perceptions of jury service as a privilege jealously guarded by landed proprietors. Throughout the eighteenth and nineteenth centuries, compelling the attendance of jurors was a constant battle and a source of frustration for officials. Fines were often threatened but rarely enforced, and even at that, wealthier men were sometimes happy to pay to evade jury service. Tales procedures were frequently used, meaning that the extensive legislatively prescribed juror qualifications were often left by the wayside. Because some legislation dealing with talesmen did not specify that they had to hold property, in theory then this resort to the tales extended jury participation to include men otherwise unqualified. When considered alongside the various types of jury discussed in previous chapters, this could mean that lay participation may have been slightly wider than previously thought.

Considering the emphasis placed on the constitutional importance of trial by jury throughout the eighteenth and nineteenth centuries, and the pro-jury rhetoric of the period, it is somewhat surprising that there was no similar emphasis on adequate remuneration for those involved. The distinction drawn between civil and criminal jurors is anomalous to the modern jurist; given that the stakes were so much higher in criminal cases, shouldn't those jurors have been treated at least as well? But the nineteenth-century mindset was different. Criminal jurors were at the lower end of the socio-economic scale and could therefore be compelled to undertake these duties, which were not considered to be too difficult. Men on civil juries, however, were likely to be better educated and conversant with commercial practices. Their time had monetary value and the cases they dealt with were longer and more complicated. So, remuneration operated on the basis of the complexity of the service rendered, and not on the jurors' financial need or the seriousness of the potential consequences of their verdict.

222 E.g. *Hansard 4*, xlvii, 201 (8 Mar. 1897) (HC) (Balfour). It was later noted in the house of commons that over nine English county councils 'and a great many minor bodies' had petitioned the home office for juror payment: *Hansard 4*, clxvi, 1527 (10 Dec. 1906) (HC). In 1911, Lloyd George said that he had no means of estimating the overall costs involved in paying jurors' expenses: *Hansard 4*, xxix, 1899 (16 Aug. 1911).

223 W. Huband, *A practical treatise on the law relating to the grand jury in criminal cases, the petty jury and the coroner's jury* (rev. ed., Dublin, 1911), p. 957: 'The right of the jury to this payment is grounded, not upon any statute, but on long established usage.'

CHAPTER NINE

Jurors' oaths

THE OATH WAS A CENTRAL PART of the jury process. All jurors, whether their role was to adjudicate, present or value, acted on their oaths, or later, on affirmations. Shapiro notes that:

> [f]or most if not all of its history, Anglo-American law has included oaths as part of its fact determination process ... Oaths were required of most participants in the legal process: judges, lawyers, sheriffs and undersheriffs, grand jurors, trial jurors and witnesses.[1]

The manner in which oaths were administered and recited sometimes lacked solemnity, and during periods of unrest there were frequent allegations that jurors disregarded their oaths. Often, separate oaths were administered to the foreperson and to the rest of the jurors. Sometimes jurors were sworn severally, instead of individually, which may have lessened the oath's perceived seriousness. Superstitions around oaths, some of which may have been unique to Ireland, led to practices such as 'kissing the thumb', discussed further below.

THE VARIOUS JURORS' OATHS

Different oaths were administered to different types of jury, but most made reference to the jurors' 'skill and knowledge' or 'skill and understanding'. The grand juror's oath evolved over time, and Shapiro points out that only later versions emphasised the necessity of a truthful verdict.[2] At the beginning of the assizes the foreman of the grand jury was sworn first, and then the others. In the mid-nineteenth century, Gabbett gave the form of the foreman's oath as follows:

> as foreman of this grand jury you shall diligently enquire as well on behalf of our sovereign lady the queen as of the body of the county of ___ and true presentment make of all such persons matters and things as shall be lawfully given you in charge: her majesty's counsel, your fellow jurors or your own you shall not disclose: you shall not present any person matter or thing through malice hatred or evil will; nor shall you leave any person matter or

1 Barbara J. Shapiro, 'Oaths, credibility and the legal process in early modern England: part one', *L. & Humanities*, 6:2 (2012), 145–78 at 145, 148. 2 Ibid., p. 159.

> thing presentable unpresented through fear favour or affection; but in all things you shall present the truth, the whole truth and nothing but the truth according to the best of your skill and knowledge: so help you God.[3]

Some judges emphasised the importance of the grand jurors' oath in their charge.[4]

Other juries of inquiry had similar oaths. For example, the wide-streets jury's oath was 'truly and diligently to enquire into all such matters, as shall be given to them in charge, and true verdict to give according to their evidence'.[5] The coroner's jury's oath was couched in similar language:

> You shall diligently inquire and true presentment make of all such matters and things as shall be given you in charge on behalf of our sovereign lady the queen touching the death of _____ now lying dead whose body you have the view: you shall present no man from hatred malice or ill-will, nor spare any through fear favour or affection: but a true verdict give according to the evidence and the best of your skill and knowledge. So help you God.[6]

The market juror's oath was somewhat vaguer; they swore to 'well, truly and diligently execute the office of a market juror of the said city without favour or affection, malice or ill-will to any person or persons whatsoever'.[7] The forematron of the jury of matrons swore as follows:

> You as forematron of this jury shall well and truly try whether the prisoner at the bar, be with child of a quick child, and thereof a true verdict shall return according to the best of your skill and understanding; so help you God.[8]

After the forematron, the remaining jurors were then similarly sworn.

The oath of the petty juror evolved over time. While in earlier versions they swore to speak the truth, 'in the later versions, they were to decide on the basis of the evidence they heard in court',[9] which is indicative of jurors' evolving role.

Although in the seventeenth and eighteenth centuries, petty juries might have been severally sworn,[10] by the nineteenth century they swore individually. In nineteenth-century criminal trials, the oath was administered as follows:

3 J. Gabbett, *A treatise on the criminal law: comprehending all crimes and misdemeanours punishable by indictment*, 2 vols (Dublin, 1843), ii, p. 269.

4 E.g. Christopher Robinson, *A charge given to the grand juries of the county of the city of Dublin and county of Dublin: at a sitting of the his majesty's commissions of oyer and terminer, and general gaol delivery, for the said counties, on Monday the 15th day of Dec. 1760* (Dublin, 1760).

5 Dublin Wide Streets Act, 1759 (33 Geo. II, c. 15), s. 4.

6 Gabbett, *Criminal law*, ii, p. 58.

7 Dublin Paving and Lighting Act, 1773–4 (13 & 14 Geo. III, c. 22), s. 73.

8 *Report of the oaths commission, 1867* [C-3885] 1867 xxxi, 1, pp 20–1.

9 Shapiro, 'Oaths, credibility: part one', p. 166.

10 Ibid. According to Bacon, if there was no challenge then the twelve jurors could be sworn together. M. Bacon, *A new abridgement of the law*, 5 vols (London, 1736), iii, p. 268.

> The clerk of the crown orders the crier to call the juryman who stands highest on the panel, and having directed the latter to look upon the prisoner, and to take the book in his right hand, he administers to him the following oath: 'You shall well and truly try, and true deliverance make, between our sovereign lady the queen and the prisoner at the bar, and all such other prisoners and traversers as shall be given you in charge, and a true verdict give according to the evidence.'[11]

The juror then swore on the Bible and kissed it.[12] In civil cases, the jurors swore 'to try this suit of *nisi prius* between party and party, according to the evidence as shall be given you in court'.[13]

ADMINISTERING OATHS

The manner in which oaths were administered was different in Ireland than in England. When each juror's name was called he came forward to the bar of the court to be sworn on a Bible. After each juror was sworn, he was set apart in the jury box, and when twelve men had been appropriately sworn in, the clerk directed the crier to 'count them'. Having counted the jurors, the crier asked the jurors if they were all sworn, then said 'twelve good men and true, stand together and hear your evidence'.[14] At this point the judge might tell the remaining potential jurors that they were discharged, unless they were required to remain for other pending cases. After the jurors were sworn in, the crier in felony cases made the following proclamation:

> If any one can inform my lords the king's justices, the king's attorney general, or the king's sergeant, on this inquest now to be taken between our sovereign lady the queen and the prisoner at the bar, of any felonies or misdemeanours done or committed by the prisoner at the bar, let him come forth, and he shall be heard; for the prisoner now stands at the bar upon his deliverance.[15]

The oath was administered and the juror placed his hand on the Bible and kissed it.[16] In Ireland, the oath was not considered to have commenced until after the

11 T. Purcell, *A summary of the criminal law of Ireland* (Dublin, 1848), p. 188.

12 Bacon noted in 1736 that in capital cases, the prisoners were told that 'these good men now called, and appearing, are to pass on their lives, and death; therefore, if they will challenge any of them, they are to do it before they are sworn': Bacon, *New abridgement*, iii, p. 268.

13 Anon., *The book of oaths, and the severall forms thereof, both antient and modern* (London, 1715), p. 113.

14 Sometimes the word '*countez*' would be used. Gabbett, *Criminal law*, ii, p. 396.

15 Ibid., pp 396–7.

16 In *R v. Luby* (1866), pp 69–70, a juror was reluctant to be sworn, apparently on grounds of ill-health, and repeatedly refused to kiss the book, despite being repeatedly told to do so by counsel for the prisoner and Keogh J.

clerk had said 'juror, look upon the prisoner; prisoner, look upon the juror',[17] whereas in England the oath was considered to have commenced as soon as the juror took the book in his hand. In fact, it appears from Gabbett's *Treatise* that the prefix 'jurors look on the prisoner – prisoner look on the juror' was an almost exclusively Irish practice.[18] These seemingly minor differences could have a significant impact when it came to challenges because a juror could not be challenged after the swearing-in had begun. At the trial of Fenian Thomas Luby, as soon as a particular juror told Isaac Butt, counsel for the defendant, where he lived, the registrar said 'prisoner, look on the juror ...'. Butt interrupted, wishing to challenge, but Keogh J. told him that he was too late; the swearing-in had begun. Butt accepted this, but asked that the registrar go a little slower.[19]

Hickey describes the 'superstitious legalism which pervaded Irish peasant culture during the eighteenth and nineteenth centuries'[20] and points out that:

> Rural Irish Christianity of that time reflected a popular belief that supernatural punishment was largely connected to specific external actions, rather than to internal thoughts and motivations. A superficial, act-centred concept of sin which was more redolent of magic and sorcery than of theological Christianity prevailed. This rural Irish attitude implies a significant residue of pagan belief underlying peasant Catholicism of the eighteenth and nineteenth centuries.[21]

A manifestation of this was the practice by some jurors of kissing their thumb instead of the Bible, 'to avoid the supernatural sanction of the oath'.[22] Joy C.B. in *R v. Campbell*, for example, noted that 'every species of shift was resorted to, in order to avoid the taking of an oath, such as kissing the thumb instead of the book'.[23] While some commentators were of the view that thumb-kissing demonstrated a lack of reverence for the oath, Hickey argues that '[i]f the consequences of perjury were not feared, there would be no reason to attempt such evasive measures'.[24]

ACCOMMODATING DIFFERENT BELIEFS

The history of accommodating different religious minorities on juries is inextricably bound up with those persons' ability to testify in court. In the

17 *R v. Hughes* (1843) 2 Cr. & Dix C.C. 396. 18 Gabbett, *Criminal law*, ii, p. 396.
19 Anon., *Report of the proceedings at the first sitting of the special commission for the county of the city of Dublin held at Green-Street Dublin for the trial of Thomas Clarke Luby and others* (Dublin, 1866), pp 322–3. The calling of the jury in this case took over three hours.
20 É. Hickey, *Irish law and lawyers in modern folk tradition* (Dublin, 1999), p. 166. 21 Ibid.
22 Ibid., p. 115. See also *Report on Irish jury laws*, HL 1881 (430) xi, 1, para. 4280 (Fitzgerald J.).
23 *Ulster Times*, 16 July 1836. A juror kissed the thumb in *R v. Timlin*: Anon., *Trial of priest Timlin for riot and assault* (Dublin, 1847), p. 4. 24 Hickey, *Irish law and lawyers*, p. 117.

eighteenth century, despite Coke's remonstrations that all 'infidels' should be excluded from giving evidence,[25] it was nevertheless customary to allow Jewish persons to testify,[26] having sworn on the Old Testament.[27] It was not until 1744, however, that this competence was extended to other non-Christians. In *Omichund v. Barker*,[28] the English court of chancery held that any person who believed in a god and in the solemn obligation of an oath was competent to testify once he had been sworn in whatever manner his conscience and religious convictions would find binding. Although the form of oath might vary, 'still the substance is the same, which is that God in all of them is called upon as a witness to the truth of what we say'.

Certain religious groups objected outright to taking oaths. Quakers emerged after the English civil war in the mid-seventeenth century as dissenters from the established church, and were opposed to swearing oaths. This placed them at a distinct disadvantage in legal proceedings. Late seventeenth-century legislation granted them the right to give evidence on affirmation in civil cases in England.[29] An Irish act of 1723[30] allowed Quakers to make an affirmation instead of an oath on 'any lawful occasion'. It specifically referred to issues relating to trade, small debts arrears, ejectments, elections and proving wills. It made no explicit reference to a general right to affirm when testifying in court. By 1828, Quakers could give evidence on affirmation in criminal proceedings.[31]

Some minorities had no objection to swearing but would not do so on a Bible – instead they preferred to swear with an uplifted hand. In a number of Irish cases in the 1830s witnesses and jurors were refused leave to swear in this manner.[32] In 1833, legislation was passed establishing the right of Quakers, Moravians and Separatists to make affirmations in all proceedings requiring an oath.[33] This

25 Coke defined the oath in exclusively Christian terms, reflecting his view that all 'infidels are in law perpetui inimici, perpetual enemies … for between them, as with the devils, whose subjects they be, and the Christian, there is perpetual hostility, and can be no peace': *Calvin's Case* (1609) 7 Co. Rep. 1; 77 E.R. 377.

26 M. Hawkins, *Treatise of the pleas of the crown*, 4 vols (7th ed., London, 1795), iv, p. 153.

27 *Robeley v. Langston* (1685) 2 Keb. 314; 84 E.R. 196.

28 (1744) Willes 538; 125 E.R. 1310.

29 Quaker Affirmations Act, 1696 (7 & 8 Will. III, c. 34).

30 Quaker Affirmations Act, 1723 (10 Geo. I, c. 8). Continued by Quaker Affirmations Act, 1727 (1 Geo. II, c. 5); and Quaker Affirmations Act, 1735 (9 Geo. II, c. 16). The right to affirm was extended to Moravians in England in 1748: Settlement of Moravians in America Act, 1748 (22 Geo. II, c. 30).

31 Law of Evidence Amendment Act, 1828 (9 Geo. IV, c. 32).

32 *R v. Logan* (1837) 1 Cr. & Dix C.C. 188n concerned a witness who was a Scottish Covenanter; *R v. McCarron* (1832) 1 Cr. & Dix C.C. 186 concerned a juror who was a seceder at the Monaghan summer assizes. Bushe C.B. noted that McClelland B. had uniformly refused to allow swearing with uplifted hand. *R v. Campbell* (1833) 1 Cr. & Dix C.C. 187n involved Dr Henry Cooke, the president of the Presbyterian synod of Ulster, who considered swearing on the Bible to be 'unscriptural' and 'superstitious'.

33 The Affirmations (Quakers and Moravians) Act, 1833 (3 & 4 Will. IV, c. 49) and the Affirmations (Separatists) Act, 1833 (3 & 4 Will. IV, c. 81). Daniel O'Connell expressed his approval for such a move, describing a recent case where an insurance office had lost a considerable sum of money for

included both testifying in court and taking a juror's oath.[34] Similar provision was made for former Quakers and Moravians in 1838.[35] Legislation to facilitate Presbyterians swearing by uplifted hand was proposed in 1837.[36] While there was some concern that jurors and witnesses would consider an affirmation to be less solemn and binding than an oath, and would be more likely to violate its terms,[37] the legislation was nevertheless passed. Unlike some earlier legislation, it applied to jurors and witnesses in all proceedings and provided that oaths should be 'administered in such a form and with such ceremonies as such person may declare to be binding'.[38] In *R v. Woods*[39] this declaration was held not to be essential.

The Common Law Procedure Amendment Act (Ireland), 1856[40] confirmed that witnesses in all cases who were opposed to taking an oath on religious grounds could instead make a solemn affirmation or declaration. Legislation went further in the 1860s. The Juries Act (Ireland), 1868[41] provided that an affirmation could be administered if the court or relevant officer was satisfied as to the sincerity of the juror's objection to being sworn. The affirmation had the same effect as an oath, and its form was:

> I [A.B.] do solemnly, sincerely and truly affirm and declare that the taking of any oath is, according to my religious belief, unlawful; and I do solemnly, sincerely and truly affirm and declare …

Atheists presented a different problem. At common law, a legal oath in court required 'nothing but the belief of a God, and that he will reward and punish us according to our deserts'.[42] Affirmations were similarly understood. A witness' own notions of honour were not considered a valid substitute for the fear of divine wrath. A critical limitation on the decision in *Omichund v. Barker*[43] was that persons who 'do not think [God] will either award or punish them in this world or

want of the testimony of a man who could not take an oath. *Hansard 3*, xv, 1293 (27 Feb. 1833). During the debate over this legislation, reservations were expressed over having Quakers sitting on juries 'because they had scruples of conscience about inflicting punishment'. *Hansard 3*, xviii, 1015 (HL) (Lord Wynford) (20 June 1833).

34 In 1833 a select committee of the house of commons examined the issue of Quakers' affirmations in the context of a Quaker MP who refused to be sworn. *Select committee on Quakers report*, HC 1833 [6] xii, 137.

35 Affirmations Act, 1838 (1 & 2 Vic., c. 77).

36 *Hansard 3*, xxxix, 610 (5 Dec. 1837) (James Gibson).

37 The duke of Wellington told the house of lords that he feared that 'unless great circumspection were used', this reform could 'have the effect of encouraging a species of inferior evidence in judicial cases'. *Hansard 3*, xliv, 145 (12 July 1838). Others such as the earl of Wicklow feared that the act would have the effect of abolishing oaths altogether, and were opposed to such a sweeping move.

38 Validity of Oaths Act, 1838 (1 & 2 Vic., c. 105).

39 (1841) 2 Cr. & Dix C.C. 268; 1 Jebb & B, app. vii.

40 19 & 20 Vic., c. 102, s. 23. 41 31 & 32 Vic., c. 75, s. 3.

42 W. Huband, *A practical treatise on the law relating to the grand jury in criminal cases, the petty jury and the coroner's jury* (rev. ed., Dublin, 1911), p. 584.

43 (1744) Willes 538; 125 E.R. 1310.

the next, cannot be witnesses in any case or under any circumstances, for this plain reason, because an oath cannot possibly be any tie or obligation upon them'. In an 1881 case in England a juror claimed to have no religious belief, and because he could neither swear nor affirm (because affirmations were derogations granted on religious grounds) he was set aside.[44] Such instances continued throughout the 1880s, and finally in 1888 the Oaths Act[45] provided that anyone who objected to being sworn, either on the ground that it was against his religious belief, or because he had no religious belief, could make a solemn affirmation instead of an oath 'in all places and for all purposes where an oath is or shall be required by law'. The affirmation was to have the same force and effect as an oath, and was as follows: 'I, AB, do solemnly sincerely and truly declare and affirm …'

CONCLUSION

Procedures for swearing in jurors could be quite prescriptive and detailed and were often the subject of dispute or challenge. Errors or irregularities in the swearing-in of jurors could affect the validity of a verdict.[46] For example, in *Adair v. Malone*,[47] John Welsh of Rogerson's Quay was summoned instead of John Welsh of King St. He was sworn in without objection, and the mistake was not discovered until some time after the trial. The judge refused to quash the verdict, pointing out that there was 'no contrivance, but a mistake which reasonable precaution might have prevented, and it is not alleged that any injustice has been done by it'.[48] Conversely, in *R v. Delaney*,[49] when the jurors returned to court after deliberating their names were called out as usual. When the name Bernard Flynn was called, it transpired that there was no such person on the jury, and that a man called Bernard Fagan had answered to the name of Flynn and been sworn in under that name. This was deemed to be a mistrial and the conviction was quashed. Following this the Criminal Law (Ireland) Act, 1828[50] provided that a judgment could not be stayed or reversed on the grounds of misnomer or misdescription of a juror.[51] If a person who was not on the jurors' book was sworn in, the verdict could not be impeached unless he was challenged at the appropriate time.[52]

44 (1881) 15 *I.L.T. & S.J.*, 459. 45 51 & 52 Vic., c. 46, s. 1.

46 See the English cases of *R v. Inhabitants of St. Michael, Southampton* (1770) 2 Wm. Bl. 718; 20 E.R. 20; *Muirhead v. Evans* (1851) 2 L.M. & P. 294; and *Mansell v. The queen* (1857) D. & B. 375.

47 (1826) Batty 557. 48 See pp 19–21. 49 (1828) Jebb C.C.R. 88; 169 E.R. 1048.

50 9 Geo. IV, c. 54, s. 32.

51 Mistakes continued to be made, however: at Daniel O'Connell's 1844 trial, a John Jason Rigby was sworn as John Rigby. *State trial (Ireland). Return to an address of the honourable the house of commons, dated 21 May 1844; for, copies of all affidavits and pleadings filed in the cause of The queen v. Daniel O'Connell and others, in the queen's bench, in Ireland, from the 10th day of Oct. to the 1st day of Dec. 1843; and also, from the 1st day of Apr. 1844 to the time when this return shall be complied with; together with copies of all indorsements (if any) made thereon*, HC 1844 (395) xliv, 225, p. 54.

52 Juries (Ireland) Act, 1871 (34 & 35 Vic., c. 65), s. 17.

Anything to do with religious beliefs or practices could prove problematic in Ireland. As Hickey observes, 'Ireland presents a confusing image when it comes to the importance and sacredness of oaths among ordinary people. Dire warnings as to the evil consequences of perjury clash with statements that lying under oath was "as common as grass".'[53] From time to time complaints were made about how Irish jurors regarded their oath.[54] Other complaints related to the manner in which oaths were administered: in 1825, for example, it was said that the hurry and 'extraordinary confusion'[55] with which the civil business was carried out in the lower courts tended to make jurors disregard the sanctity of their oaths. The oath was often 'administered in a very irregular and improper way; very often it is administered, not by the officer of the court, but by attornies'.[56] In the 1830s, Carleton similarly criticised the 'indifferent, business-like manner in which the oaths are put, the sing-song tone of voice, the rapid utterance of words'.[57] Witnesses before the 1881 parliamentary committee complained that the oath was 'very antiquated', and 'not at all understood by the people who take it',[58] and members of the committee remarked that it was 'all Hebrew to the jury'.[59] One witness said that although jurors were as a rule inclined to respect the oath as such, the particular form of the oath did not convey a clear idea of their duty.[60] However, despite legal changes allowing affirmations instead of oaths, the form of the jurors' oath remained largely unchanged for several hundred years.

53 Hickey, *Irish law and lawyers*, p. 107.

54 In 1737 Hope had criticized Irish jurors for tending to disregard their oaths in criminal cases: 'in most men passion and interest are superior to principle, and govern without disguise. In many they conceal themselves under a show of reason, and so impose upon conscience': J. Hope, *Dissertation on the constitution and effects of a petty jury* (Dublin, 1737), p. 10.

55 *Report on the state of Ireland 1825*, HC 1825 (129) viii 1, p. 329. Such complaints seem to have been somewhat common around this time: Hickey, *Irish law and lawyers.*

56 Ibid.

57 W. Carleton, *Traits and stories of the Irish peasantry*, 2 vols (2nd ser., Dublin, 1832), i, p. 276.

58 *Report on Irish jury laws*, 1881, para. 2527 (Thomas Boyd, Tipperary crown solicitor).

59 Ibid., para. 3393 (Lord Emly).

60 Fitzgerald J., para. 4278, however, argued that jurors 'perfectly understand what they are about'.

CHAPTER TEN

Challenges and jury packing

THE RELIGIOUS AND POLITICAL composition of juries was controversial because it was seen as having the potential to affect the outcome of all types of civil and criminal cases,[1] especially those of a political hue. High-profile political cases where jury composition appeared to have been a crucial factor included the 1844 trial of Daniel O'Connell;[2] the 1848 state trials;[3] and various high-profile trials during the Land War in the 1880s.[4] These prominent cases generated fierce debate and fuelled perceptions that the composition of a criminal trial jury was a matter of utmost importance. Different policies and practices in relation to jury composition developed in different parts of the country. For example, it was said in the 1820s that in Tipperary, Catholics and Protestants were mixed indiscriminately on civil juries, but that 'in cases which are either political or conceived to be so, or which have any connection with the disturbances of the county, Roman Catholics are studiously excluded'.[5]

One means of altering the composition of a jury at a particular trial was through the use of jury challenges. Criminal cases in Ireland tended to be prosecuted by crown counsel,[6] selected by crown solicitors, who were in turn appointed by the

1 The impact of jury composition on outcomes is a frequent theme in discussions about lay participation systems: see, e.g., J.B. Post, 'Jury lists' in J.S. Cockburn and Thomas A. Green (eds), *'Twelve good men and true': the criminal jury in England, 1200–1800* (Princeton, 1988), which notes, p. 68, that 'the composition of a jury inevitably has some bearing on the exercise of its functions'. See also P.G. Lawson, 'Lawless juries? The composition and behaviour of Hertfordshire juries, 1573–1624' in Cockburn and Green, ibid. and James C. Oldham, *Trial by jury: the seventh amendment and Anglo-American special juries* (New York, 2006).

2 See pp 22–4, *R v. O'Connell* (1844) 7 Ir. L.R. 261 and *O'Connell v. R* (1844) 11 Cl. & F. 155; 8 E.R. 1061.

3 See J.G. Hodges, *Report of the trial of John Mitchel for felony, before the right hon. baron Lefroy, and the right honourable Justice Moore, at the commission court, Dublin, May, 1848* (Dublin, 1848); J.G. Hodges, *Report of the proceedings under the Treason Felony Act, 11 Vic., c. 12, at the commission court, Green-Street, Dublin, Aug. and Oct. 1848* (Dublin, 1848); *Freeman's Journal*, 25 May 1848; *Juries: petition against exclusion of Roman Catholics* (NAI, OP/1848/110); and Sean McConville, *Irish political prisoners, 1848–1922: theatres of war* (London, 2003), pp 40–4.

4 E.g. the 'Sligo trials': see further below and chapter 11.

5 *Report on the state of Ireland*, HC 1825 (129) viii 1, p. 87 (Richard Sheill). Similar statements were made in relation to Westmeath in the 1830s: *Report on the state of Ireland*, HC 1831–2 (677) xvi 1, para. 3694 (Rev. John Burke, a Roman Catholic clergyman).

6 For a comparative analysis, see W.H. Dodd, 'The preliminary proceedings in criminal cases in England, Ireland, and Scotland, compared', *J.S.S.I.S.I.* (1878), 201–9. See also W.N. Hancock, 'The

attorney general.[7] Both crown counsel and defence counsel were entitled to challenge jurors both 'for cause' and without cause.[8] The right to challenge was a safeguard against biased or otherwise unsuitable jurors, and was traditionally seen as a vital aspect of jury trial.[9] The rules were fairly complex, and the volume of case law generated by disputes over challenges[10] is some indication of the perceived importance of the practice in Ireland. By contrast, challenges do not appear to have been used as much in English trials.[11] The challenge procedure was an important mechanism for determining who sat upon a jury, especially in the eighteenth and early nineteenth century before the extensive statutory regulation of juror qualifications. Stephen observed in 1883 that given the early role of jurors as witnesses, the right to challenge jurors was 'in very ancient times equivalent to the choice of the witnesses by whom matters of fact were to be determined'.[12]

HOW WERE CHALLENGES DECIDED?

There were two types of challenge: challenges to the polls and challenges to the array.[13] A challenge to the array was an objection to the way in which the jury panel had been compiled – in other words the entire jury was objectionable, usually because of bias or partiality on the part of the sheriff or his deputy.[14] Challenges to the array came in two guises: principal challenges and challenges for favour. A

cost of adopting a complete system of public prosecution in England, as illustrated by the results of the working of the Scotch and Irish systems of public prosecution', *J.S.S.I.S.I.* (1878), 271–4.

7 See John McEldowney, 'Crown prosecutions in nineteenth-century Ireland' in Douglas Hay and Francis Snyder (eds), *Policing and prosecution in Britain, 1750–1850* (Oxford, 1989).

8 See R. Browne Blake, '"A delusion, a mockery, and a snare": array challenges and jury selection in England and Ireland, 1800–1850', *Canadian J. Hist.*, 39:1 (2004), 2–26.

9 See John McEldowney, 'Stand by for the crown: an historical analysis', *Crim. L. Rev.* (1979), 272–83 at 273. According to Coke, the term 'challenge' was 'derived of the old word caloir or chaloir', which in one signification is to care for, or foresee. 'And for that to challenge jurors is the meane to care or foresee that an indifferent trial be had, it is called calumnaire, to challenge, that is to except against them that are returned to be jurors.' J.H. Thomas, *A systematic arrangement of Lord Coke's first institute of the laws of England*, 3 vols (Philadelphia, 1826–7), iii, p. 509 (3 Co. Inst. 155b). See also M. Bacon, *A new abridgement of the law* (London, 1736), p. 251.

10 E.g. *R v. Fitzpatrick* (1838) Cr. & Dix Abr. 513; *R v. Conrahy and Lalor* (1839) 1 Cr. & Dix C.C. 56; *Patrick Wood's case* (1841) Ir. Circ. Ca. 276 (1832) 1 Cr. & Dix 189n; *Lavin and Healy's case* (1843) Ir. Circ. Ca. 813; *O'Brien v. The queen* (1848) 1 Ir. Jur. (o.s.) 169; 2 Cl. & F. 465; *R v. Burke* (1867) 10 Cox C.C. 519; and see M. O'Callaghan, *British high politics and a nationalist Ireland: criminality, land and the law under Foster and Balfour* (Cork, 1994), pp 61–70.

11 A.M. Sullivan, writing about the trial of Roger Casement in London in 1916, observed that 'no one who had practiced in an English court had ever seen a jury challenged. No one in an Irish court had ever seen a jury sworn without challenge.' A.M. Sullivan, *The last serjeant* (London, 1952), p. 272. See N. Howlin, 'Who tried Roger Casement?', *History Ireland*, 25 (2017) (forthcoming).

12 James Stephen, *A history of the criminal law of England*, 3 vols (London, 1883), i, p. 301.

13 3 Co. Inst. 155b.

14 E.g. W. Ridgeway, *Report of the trial of Thos. Kirwan merchant, for a misdemeanour, charged to be committed in violation of the Convention Act* (Dublin, 1812); Anon., *The trial of Mr John Magee for*

principal challenge, according to Coke, was 'so called because if it be found true, it standeth sufficient of itself, without leaving anything to the conscience or discretion of the triors'.[15] Principal challenges appear to have been a rarity by the nineteenth century,[16] and were eventually abolished by the Juries (Procedure) Ireland Act, 1876.[17] The principal challenge to the array was distinguishable from the challenge for favour, which was left to the court's discretion. To use one of Coke's examples, 'if the plaintiff or defendant be tenant to the sheriff, this is no principal challenge; for the lord is in no danger of his tenant; but *è converso* it is a principal challenge; but in the other he may challenge for favour and leave it to trial'.[18] In other words, these were situations where there was no presumption of influence or favour, but where influence or favour might be shown to exist.

When the array was challenged, two triers were appointed to determine whether the challenge ought to stand.[19] Evidence had to be produced to convince them that, for example, the panel had been prejudicially formed. Depending on whether a challenge was to the array of the principal panel, to the array of the tales,[20] or to the polls, the trier of the challenge varied. For example, Coke said that if the array was challenged, it was to be tried by 'two of them that be empanelled to be appointed by the court'. This would appear to have been the usual practice. In the Derrymacash affair, discussed in chapter 2, had a challenge to the array been taken it would have been tried by the first to jurors sworn. Because they happened to be Catholics, the challenge was not made. Another example is *R v. Hughes*,[21] in which Crampton J. appointed a grand juror and a petty juror as triers of a challenge, but counsel for the defendant objected to the former, who had been on the grand jury that had found the bills of indictment against his client. Crampton J. allowed the objection, and ordered the man to stand aside until another juror could be sworn in. The issue was then tried by two sworn petty jurors. According to Hale, however, the mode of trying a challenge to the array was at the court's discretion.[22]

a libel on the duke of Richmond, which took place in the court of king's bench, Dublin (London, 1813); and J.G. Hodges, *Proceedings under the Treason Felony Act* (trial of Kevin O'Doherty).

15 3 Co. Inst. 158a. In *Bruce v. Grady*, for example, at the Limerick summer assizes in 1816, the plaintiff stated that the sheriff owed him several large sums of money, and thus was 'not indifferent between the parties, and unfit to return a jury in the present action'. G.E. Bruce, *An authentic report of the interesting trial for a libel contained in the celebrated poem, called 'The nosegay'* (Limerick, 1816), p. 2.

16 Abbott C.J. noted in 1821 that in England at least, the jury was almost never challenged on this ground: *R v. Edmonds* (1821) 4 B. & Ald. 471; 106 E.R. 1009. See also *O'Connell v. The queen* (1844) 11 Cl. & F. 155; 8 E.R. 1061.

17 39 & 40 Vic., c. 78, s. 17.

18 Co. Litt. 155b.

19 See John McEldowney, 'Lord O'Hagan and the Irish Jury Act 1871' (PhD, Cambridge University, 1981), pp 108–9.

20 See pp 115–16.

21 (1842) 2 Cr. & Dix C.C. 396.

22 'Sometimes it is done by two attorneys, sometimes by the two coroners, and sometimes by two of the jury, with this difference, that if the challenge be for kindred in the sheriff, it is most fit to be tried by two of the jurors returned; if the challenge found in favour of partiality, then by any other two assigned thereunto by the court.' Hale, *Pleas*, ii, p. 275.

Before the reforms introduced by O'Hagan's Act in 1871,[23] judges frequently dealt with allegations of irregularities in the preparation of jurors' lists or jurors' books.[24] Generally such challenges to the array were disallowed. For example, in *R v. Fitzpatrick*[25] the prisoner alleged that the justices at revision sessions had 'wilfully struck out' 355 of the 750 names on the jurors' book, without giving the required notice to the persons. The sheriff had also inserted names of unqualified persons, and thus the lists were 'unlawfully altered'. The challenge was disallowed, however, 'because it did not state any valid objection to the persons whose names appeared in the panel, nor did it aver, that the "jurors' book" contained an insufficient number of names'. In *R v. Conrahy and Lalor*[26] Torrens J. considered such a challenge to be 'radically bad', and ruled that the relevant legislative provisions were merely 'directory', as opposed to mandatory, and that failure to comply with them could not mean that 'the whole fabric of justice would fall to the ground'.[27] The fact that no specific juror was objected to seems to have carried weight in this and other similar cases.[28] Similarly, in *R v. Burke*[29] the court, relying on *R v. O'Connell*,[30] ruled that a challenge to the array could only succeed where the sheriff had been guilty of some wilful default. Array challenges were quite common in cases where there was a perception of religious bias, with lawyers in the high-profile state trials of Kevin O'Doherty[31] and William Smith O'Brien[32] alleging that irregularities in the compiling of jury lists had led to a skewed representation of Catholics and Protestants. At the latter trial, the questioning of the clerk of the crown, sub-sheriff and jurors lasted for five days. At neither trial was the challenge to the array upheld.

There was a rare successful challenge to an array in Tyrone in 1862. The prisoner in *R v. Donnelly* claimed that the sub-sheriff, Samuel Wensley Blackall, had placed on the panel jurors whose names had not been returned by the clerk of the peace for that year, and who were not lawfully qualified. He also omitted the names of other, qualified men who were on the list.[33] It was alleged that the jurors returned were more likely to convict the prisoner. Crown counsel demurred to the challenge – in other words, admitted to the facts but denying that these were good grounds for a challenge.[34] However, Christian J. held that the facts amounted to a

23 34 & 35 Vic., c. 65. 24 See pp 22–4. 25 (1838) Cr. & Dix Abr. 513.
26 (1839) 1 Cr. & Dix C.C. 56. 27 Hodges, *Proceedings under the Treason Felony Act*, p. 525.
28 See, e.g., *Browne v. Esmonde* (1868) I.R. 3 Eq. 81; *The queen v. O'Connell* (1844) 7 Ir. L.R. 261; and *R (Little) v. Rea* (1864) 16 I.C.L.R. 428. 29 (1867) 10 Cox C.C. 519. 30 (1844) 7 Ir. L.R. 261.
31 Reported in Hodges, *Proceedings under the Treason Felony Act*.
32 J.G. Hodges, *Report of the trial of William Smith O'Brien for high treason, at the special commission for the Co. Tipperary held at Clonmel, Sept. and Oct. 1848* (Dublin, 1849), pp 59–106. Smith O'Brien was one of the leaders of Young Ireland, a nationalist group that led a failed rebellion in 1848–9. All three leaders of Young Ireland were prosecuted for sedition: Thomas Francis Meagher and William Smith O'Brien for inflammatory speeches, and John Mitchel for seditious articles published in his newspaper, the *United Irishman*. See Robert Sloan, *William Smith O'Brien and the Young Ireland rebellion of 1848: the road to Ballingarry* (Dublin, 2000).
33 *Tyrone assizes (jury panel)*, HC 1862 (232) xliv, 251, p. 1.
34 *Hansard 3*, clxvi, 760 (10 Apr. 1862) (HC) (Robert Peel).

sufficient challenge, and that the panel was quashed as regards this particular case. Another high-profile challenge to an array was seen in the case of *R v. McKenna*.[35]

The question of whether a failure to properly summon jurors amounted to a good ground on which to challenge the array arose in numerous cases.[36] One case that attracted considerable attention was *R v. Sheridan and Kirwan*.[37] Thomas Kirwan, a Catholic, was charged with a misdemeanour under the Convention Act, 1793,[38] and challenged the array on the ground that the crown had assisted the sheriff in choosing a panel largely consisting of Orangemen. His lawyers were 'surreptitiously informed' of several procedural irregularities, and attempted to demonstrate that the crown had played a significant role in determining the jury panel's composition.[39] The crown solicitors, William and Thomas Kemmis (father and son), were questioned about their role in shaping the jury list.[40] It emerged that on the Friday before the trial, the Kemmises had been provided with a copy of the panel while the defendant was denied a copy. Over the weekend they had marked the panel to indicate the order in which jurors should be listed, and the revised list was published on Monday. An examination of the list indicated that fourteen names on the original list had not subsequently been summoned for the panel. Despite the strong evidence that the panel had been tampered with by the crown solicitors, the triers found against the challenge to the array. The jury thus composed convicted Kirwan. As Browne points out, this case demonstrated the

35 See John McEldowney, 'The case of *The queen v. McKenna* and jury packing in Ireland', *Ir. Jur.* (n.s.), 12 (1977), 339–54.

36 E.g. in *Gillespie v. Cumming* (1839) 1 Cr. & Dix C.C. 294, the array was quashed after it was submitted that the *distringas* had not been lodged with the sheriff six days in advance. See also *Dundalk Western Railway Co v. Gray* (1840) 1 Cr. & Dix C.C. 332 and *Walters v. Hughes* (1840) 2 Ir. L.R. 362. However, in *Doe d. Johnson and others v. Henry* (1841) 2 Cr. & Dix C.C. 247, Doherty C.J. considered the first day of the assizes to count as one of the six days. This may have been indicative of the courts' growing reluctance to allow such challenges. In *Fogarty v. The queen* (1846) 10 Ir. L.R. 53, the prisoner claimed that the jurors had not been 'duly or at all summoned as by law they ought', and that the entire panel had not been summoned six days in advance. However, all of the jurors on the panel were present, so Ball J. refused to allow the challenge. See also *R v. Rea* (1864) 16 I.C.L.R. 428; *Ronayne v. Elliott* (1841) Ir. Circ. Ca. 215; *Executors of Brown v. Fitzgerald* (1842) Ir. Circ. Ca. 483; *Lessee Kingston v. Dwyer* (1842) Ir. Circ. Ca. 517; *Lessee of Taylor v. Gibney* (1846) Bl. D. & O. 85; *Moore v. O'Reilly* (1853) 6 Ir. Jur. (o.s.) 60; and *Dunne v. Ryan* (1853) Ir. Jur. (o.s.) 62.

37 (1811) 31 How. St. Tr. 543 and W. Ridgeway, *Trial of Kirwan and Sheridan, M.D., for misdemeanours charged to be committed in violation of the Convention Act* (Dublin, 1811). See *Freeman's Journal*, 7, 8, 13, 21 Nov. 1811. Also tried were Henry Edward Taafe, John Joseph Burke and John Breen, known as the 'Catholic delegates'.

38 Convention Act, 1793 (33 Geo. III, c. 29).

39 Browne, 'A delusion', 11.

40 This was the same William Kemmis who later observed that he had heard many men objecting to serving on juries, because they were not freeholders in the county: *Report on the state of Ireland*, HC 1839 (486) xi, 1; xii, 2, para. 1922. He added, para. 6956, that he did not consider this practice as jury packing; 'packing a jury is a different thing; it is putting a jury to acquit or convict'. If the sheriff 'returns four or five hundred names upon the jury it can scarcely be called packing a jury'. He termed this 'selection', para. 6963, and thought it unlikely that 400 men summoned for an assizes could all be of a similar opinion or colour, para. 6967.

difficulty of getting triers to accept the proof establishing a challenge to the array, even when courts permitted defence lawyers to question officials extensively.[41] The 1871 act[42] did away with such challenges, and provided that there could be no challenge to a panel of jurors on the ground that any or all of them had not been duly summoned.

CHALLENGES TO THE POLLS

In addition to challenging the array, parties could also challenge the polls.[43] This was an objection to a specific juror.[44] Sometimes the parties saw the jury panel in advance and were able to mark their preferences if they knew anything of the jurors' reputations.[45] In other instances, challenges were based more on jurors' appearances at trial. Challenges to the polls could also be either 'for favour' (denoting partiality or bias) or 'principal'. A principal challenge to the polls was so called 'because, if it be found true, it standeth sufficient of itself without leaving any thing to the conscience or discretion of the triors'.[46]

When there was a challenge to the polls, two triers were appointed by the court.[47] In *R v. O'Coigly, O'Connor and others*,[48] Buller J. appointed two men who were not on the jury to try a challenge of a juror who had referred to the defendants as 'damned rascals'.[49] At the trial of Thomas Luby in 1866, Isaac Butt challenged a juror for being too old, and proposed to examine him as to his non-residence. Because the grand jurors had already left the court, two clerks of the crown were sworn instead.[50]

At common law, challenges to the polls came under four heads:[51] *propter honoris respectum* (in respect of honour);[52] *propter defectum* (for want or default);[53] *propter*

41 Browne, 'A delusion', 11–15. 42 34 & 35 Vic., c. 65, s. 23. 43 Co. Litt. 156b.
44 Giles Duncombe, *Tryalls per pais* (London, 1655), p. 30, wrote that it was 'a challenge to the particular persons, and these be of four kinds, that is to say, peremptory, principal, which induce favour, and for default of hundredors'. By the nineteenth century, only the first two were relevant.
45 E.g. in *R v. D'Arcy, Walsh and others*, John d'Arcy marked his preferred jurors, five of whom were ultimately sworn on the jury – he was found not guilty (NLI, MS 44,529/8).
46 Duncombe, *Tryalls*, p. 131.
47 3 Co. Inst. 158a. 48 (1798) 26 How. St. Tr. 1191.
49 Similarly, in *Gillespie v. Cumming* (1839) 1 Cr. & Dix C.C. 294, two bystanders in court were appointed as triers, with the parties' consent. 50 *Report of Dublin special commission*, 1866, p. 318.
51 See also H.H. Joy, *The admissibility of confessions and challenge of jurors in criminal cases in England and Ireland* (Philadelphia, 1843), p. 95.
52 Duncombe, *Tryalls*, pp 132–3.
53 Ibid., p. 132. See further pp 133–7. This consisted of three sub-categories: the first was *patriæ*, meaning 'as aliens born' (aliens were disqualified by the common law, and also later by the Jurors Qualification (Ireland) Act, 1876; see p. 95); the second was *libertatis* (jurors had to be freemen); and the third was *annui census or liberi tenementi* (a challenge for want of freehold). Another sub-category, according to W. Huband, *A practical treatise on the law relating to the grand jury in criminal cases, the petty jury and the coroner's jury* (rev. ed., Dublin, 1911), p. 253, was default of a juror due to infancy or mental or physical incapacity.

affectum (for bias or partiality); or *hundredorum* (for want of hundredors).[54] The challenge *propter affectum* could either be a principal challenge, or a challenge for favour.[55] An example of a case where jurors were challenged *propter affectum* was *R v. Hughes*.[56] At Hughes' second trial for murder,[57] Crampton J. allowed counsel to ask some of the jurors whether they had expressed any opinion as to the guilt or innocence of the prisoner. One juror stated that at the last trial he had expressed such an opinion, and was successfully challenged *propter affectum*. Another stated that he might have expressed an opinion regarding the evidence at the former trial, but not as to the prisoner's guilt or innocence. Yet another claimed to have formed an opinion on reading about the previous trial in newspapers. Both of these jurors were sworn in.[58] There was no limit to the number of challenges to the polls for cause in civil and criminal trials,[59] and if a challenge to the polls for cause failed, a prisoner might still succeed with a peremptory challenge of the particular juror.[60]

Something as trivial as the misspelling of a juror's name could be a good ground for challenge. For example, Richard Barker de Burgh was summoned as Richard De Burgh at the trial of Daniel O'Connell in 1844, and later at the trial of John O'Leary in 1866. On both occasions he was successfully challenged.[61] In *R v. Delaney* a juror named Bernard Flynn was called, and a man named Bernard Fagan answered and was duly sworn in under that name.[62] There was no person called Flynn on the panel, but the sheriff had transcribed the name Fagan incorrectly. Counsel for the prisoner objected unsuccessfully to this before the guilty verdict was delivered, and the conviction was subsequently quashed.

54 Advancement of Justice Act, 1707 (6 Anne, c. 10), s. 6, noted that 'great delays do frequently happen in trials by reason of challenges to the arrays of panels of jurors, and to the polls, for default of hundredors'. It provided that there could be no challenge for want of hundredors. A hundredor was a person who lived in a 'hundred', a small geographical subdivision (of supposedly 100 people) of a county.

55 Duncombe, *Tryalls*, p. 137. 56 (1841) Ir. Circ. Rep. 274.

57 Reported as *R v. Hughes* (1842) 2 Cr. & Dix C.C. 396.

58 At *R v. Gray*, tried at the Monaghan Lent assizes in 1842, counsel for the prisoner similarly asked a juror whether he had formed an opinion of guilt or innocence. This was after counsel for the crown had objected to the juror being challenged peremptorily. See below, and David Johnson, 'The trials of Sam Gray: Monaghan politics and nineteenth century Irish criminal procedure', *Ir. Jur.* (n.s.), 20 (1985), 109–34.

59 See 3 Co. Inst. 158a. As discussed below, in some cases there were very high numbers of challenges.

60 See, e.g., J. Levy, *Home circuit. Meath summer assizes. Trim, Wednesday July 30, 1834. The king versus Jas. Slevin, Michl. Devine and Pat M'Kenna (before Mr Justice Burton)* (Dublin, 1836); George Joseph Browne, *A report of the whole of the proceedings previous to, with a note on the evidence on, the trial of Robert Keon, gent. for the murder of George Nugent Reynolds, esq.* (Dublin, 1788); and Ridgeway, *A report of the trial of Roger O'Connor, esq., and Martin McKeon, at the Trim assizes, 1817* (Dublin, 1817).

61 Anon., *Report of the argument and judgment on the case reserved from the special commission for the county of the city of Dublin, 1866* (Dublin, 1866), p. 328. Another juror at O'Leary's trial was challenged, p. 330, 'on the ground that an initial letter is given in place of his name: '"H." is no name'. The attorney general objected to this ground of challenge, and the juror was directed to stand aside. 62 (1828) Jebb C.C.R. 88; 169 E.R. 1048.

The Juries Act (Ireland), 1871[63] introduced limited reforms in relation to challenging jurors.[64] It provided that if any person was returned as a juror whose name was on the general jurors' book, want of qualification was no longer a good ground of challenge. There was a presumption of due execution of the jurors' book. However, it was a good cause of challenge if it could be shown that the name of the juror did not appear on the relevant jurors' book, with the onus of proof resting on the challenging party.[65] It was also a good cause of challenge if a juror was not returned in accordance with the provisions regarding the rotation of jurors contained in section 19 of the act.

PEREMPTORY CHALLENGES BY CRIMINAL DEFENDANTS

As well as the various challenges for cause discussed above, which were allowed in both civil and criminal cases, defendants in criminal cases were entitled to challenge a certain number of jurors peremptorily, or without stating any reason.[66] Blackstone outlined the rationale for this:

> how necessary it is that a prisoner when put to defend his life should have a good opinion of his jury, the want of which might totally disconcert him: the law wills not that he shall be tried by any one man against whom he has conceived a prejudice, even without being able to assign a reason for such his dislike. Because upon challenges for cause shown if the reason assigned prove insufficient to set aside the juror, perhaps the bare questioning of his indifference may sometimes provoke a resentment; to prevent all ill consequences from which, the prisoner is still at liberty, if he pleases, peremptorily to set him aside.[67]

There were mixed views as to the peremptory challenge's value. Joy, for example, described it in 1844 as 'eminently characteristic of the humanity of our system of criminal jurisprudence'.[68] However, later commentators were deeply sceptical of the right.[69] Blackstone was also somewhat caustic when he wrote about prisoners being allowed 'an arbitrary and capricious species of challenge to a certain number of jurors, without showing any cause at all: which is called a peremptory challenge: a provision full of that tenderness and humanity for which our English laws are justly famous'.[70] Criticisms generally focused on the number of challenges allowed.

63 34 & 35 Vic., c. 65.
64 The drafters of the legislation made no significant recommendations as regards jury challenges. McEldowney, 'Lord O'Hagan', p. 156.
65 Juries Act (Ireland), 1871, s. 23. 66 Duncombe, *Tryalls*, p. 130. See also 3 Co. Litt. 156b.
67 W. Blackstone, *Commentaries upon the laws of England*, 4 vols (London, 1822), iv, pp 346–7.
68 Henry Holmes Joy, *On peremptory challenges of jurors, with the judgment of the queen's bench in The queen v. Gray* (Dublin, 1844), p. 1.
69 J. Stephen, *A digest of the criminal law* (London, 1887), i, pp 301–2; E.P.S. Counsel, *Jury packing in Ireland* (Dublin, 1887), p. 11. 70 Blackstone, *Commentaries*, iv, p. 346.

In misdemeanours involving multiple defendants, each was entitled to his full number of challenges unless the prisoners consented to join their challenges.[71] In cases where defendants refused to join their challenges, they would often then be tried separately.[72] Where two or more persons were jointly indicted, by contrast, their total number of peremptory challenges did not exceed six.[73] This proved controversial in a number of high-profile cases in the 1880s.[74]

At common law a prisoner charged with a felony was allowed to challenge thirty-five jurors without showing cause.[75] However, between 1500 and 1800 the position with regard to capital felonies was complicated by the gradual extension of the defendant's right to plead benefit of clergy.[76] By 1820, the position was as follows:

71 Hale, *Pleas*, ii p. 268, commented that '[i]f twenty men were indicted for the same offence, though by one indictment, yet every prisoner should be allowed his peremptory challenge of thirty-five persons'. E.g., the *Ulster Times* reported on an 1836 murder trial where the prisoners 'agreed to join in their challenges, and the full number was challenged on the part of the prisoners'. This was the trial of Doughney, Judge and Egan for the murder of William Carter in Queen's County. Notably, not a single individual was objected to by the crown. All but three Protestants were challenged by the prisoners. *Ulster Times*, 31 Mar. 1836.

72 Huband, *Treatise*, p. 651. See, e.g., *R v. Dunne* (1832) 1 Cr. & Dix C.C. 190n; W. Ridgeway, *A report of the proceedings in cases of high treason at a special commission of oyer and terminer, held for the county and city of Dublin, in the month of July, 1798* (Dublin, 1798) (trials of John and Henry Sheares); Anon., *A report of the trials of James Dunn and Patrick Carty for conspiring to murder the earl of Carhampton, with a dedication to that noble lord* (Dublin, 1797); W. Ridgeway, *A report of the trial of Felix Rourke upon an indictment for high treason* (Dublin, 1803); and *R v. Hanly* (1832) 1 Cr. & Dix C.C. 188.

73 *R v. McGinley and Burns* (1877) 11 I.L.T.R. 58.

74 John Crilly, who was jointly tried with four others for conspiracy in 1887, complained that '[w]hile the crown has practically the power of selecting the jury by excluding, without cause shown, all jurors, till those upon whom they can rely are reached, the five persons on trial *had between them the right of peremptory challenge to six jurors only* [emphasis in original]'. Daniel Crilly, *Jury packing in Ireland* (Dublin, 1887), p. 11. Counsel, *Jury packing*, p. 9, similarly remarked that at the controversial Sligo trials of the same year, 'peasants from a neighbouring county were tried in batches from four to nine on a charge of opposing their own eviction, and aiding in obstructing the eviction of others, their kin or neighbours. This being a misdemeanour, each batch of prisoners could only challenge six jurors.' See further chapter 11.

75 According to Duncombe, *Tryalls*, p. 130, the reason for this number was that it was just 'under the number of three juries'. A similar statement was made by Hale, *Pleas*, ii, pp 259–60. See also G. Gilbert, *The history and practice of civil actions, particularly in the court of common pleas* (2nd ed., London, 1761), p. 99.

76 Johnson, 'Sam Gray', 129. See also A. Lyon Cross, 'The English criminal law and benefit of clergy during the eighteenth and early nineteenth century', *Amer. Hist. Rev.*, 22:3 (1917), 544–65; and L. MacNally, *The justice of the peace for Ireland*, 2 vols (Dublin, 1808), i, pp 364–72. Originally, benefit of clergy was a privilege enjoyed by clergymen that allowed them to be tried in ecclesiastical courts rather than the common law courts. The former were considered to be more lenient. At first, in order to plead benefit of clergy, defendents had to appear before the court tonsured and in clerical garb. Over time this was replaced by a test of literacy, with the result that the privilege was extended to all defendents who could read. Because the Biblical passage defendents were required to read was almost always Psalm 51, simply being able to recite the psalm was sufficient. Reforms

> All felonies except petty larceny and mayhem were theoretically punishable with death, but clergyable felonies were never punished with death nor were persons convicted of such felonies sentenced to death ... A great number of felonies had been excluded from benefit of clergy in the course of the eighteenth century and when a person was convicted of such an offence he had to be sentenced to death, but the judge might order him to be transported instead, and such an order had all the effects of a conditional pardon.[77]

Johnson points out that 'in this world of legal fantasy, peremptory challenges were still allowed in all felonies'.[78] In 1828 benefit of clergy was abolished in Ireland,[79] and few felonies remained capital. The same act reduced to twenty the number of peremptory challenges allowed in felonies.[80] Between 1829 and 1843 Irish courts took the view that the right to challenge peremptorily could only be exercised by a person indicted for a felony punishable by death, as opposed to one punishable by transportation.[81] They emphasised that the distinction was not between felonies and misdemeanours, but between capital and non-capital felonies.[82] In 1832 Daniel O'Connell pointed out that the distinction between felonies punishable by death and those punishable by transportation was not founded in law, and the attorney general conceded that there was no such distinction in English law.[83]

Such was the Irish courts' stance until 1843, when *R v. Gray* was decided.[84] This, according to Johnson, was a 'test case' that secured judicial recognition of the principle that a prisoner was entitled to peremptory challenges in non-capital felonies.[85] Sam Gray was a prominent Monaghan Orangeman, unpopular with Catholics,[86] who was tried five times in relation to an incident involving a fatal

in the Tudor period meant that benefit of clergy could only be invoked once by an individual; they were branded on the thumb to prevent them from relying on the privilege in the future. Some offences were 'unclergyable', meaning that an accused person was precluded from claiming benefit of clergy. By the eighteenth century, benefit of clergy was available to all first-time offenders for lesser felonies.

77 Stephen, *Digest*, pp 471–2. 78 Johnson, 'Sam Gray', 109.

79 Criminal Law (Ireland) Act, 1828 (9 Geo. IV, c. 54), s. 12. It had been abolished in England by the Criminal Statutes (Repeal) (England) Act, 1827 (7 & 8 Geo. IV, c. 27), s 6.

80 9 Geo. IV, c. 54, s. 9. See the English Juries Act, 1825 (6 Geo. IV, c. 50), s. 29.

81 For example, *R v. Phelan* (1832) 1 Cr. & Dix 189n (reported as *Anonymous*, see 6 Ir. L.R. 266) and *R v. Whelan* (1832) 1 Cr. & Dix 189n, both decided at the 1832 Queen's County spring assizes.

82 *R v. Adams and Langton* (1832) Jebb C.C.R. 135.

83 Both Peel and Crampton, the solicitor general for Ireland, objected to the question being raised. It was stressed that the chief justice and 'another eminent judge' in Ireland had recently argued that the distinction was grounded on authority. This would appear to have been *R v. Adams and Langton* (1832) Jebb C.C.R. 135 and James Mongan, *Report of trials at a special commission at Maryborough, 1832* (Dublin, 1832), pp 241, 257. Bushe C.J. and Smith J. refused to receive Adams' peremptory challenge, as the case was not a capital felony. O'Connell later referred to them as 'rascally Irish judges'. O'Connell to P.V. Fitzpatrick in M. O'Connell, *The correspondence of Daniel O'Connell*, 8 vols (vols i–ii Shannon, 1972; vols iii–viii Dublin, 1974–80), letter 1999.

84 (1843) 6 Ir. L.R. 259. 85 Johnson, 'Sam Gray', 109. 86 Ibid., 113.

shooting. At his first trial he was acquitted, despite the crown having ordered eleven jurors to stand-by. He was immediately charged with two further offences, and the case was brought from the quarter sessions to the assizes because of his considerable local influence.[87] Torrens J. refused to try the case, threatening to send it back to the quarter sessions, and Gray was admitted to bail, to the dismay of the Catholic community and the authorities. In fact, such was the strength of the reaction to this case, that it was difficult for the crown simply to let the case drop.[88] A year later, Gray was again charged with having 'wilfully, feloniously and maliciously' fired a loaded pistol with intent to kill, but this trial was called to a halt when, on the third day, a juror was seized with 'an attack of rigor and trembling'.[89] At the third trial, in July 1842, the jurors were unable to agree on a verdict.[90] An application was made successfully to the court of queen's bench for a change of venue.[91] At the fourth trial at the spring assizes in March 1843,[92] twenty-two jurors were set aside by the crown, while Gray peremptorily challenged one.[93] He was acquitted, but the crown refused to release Gray from custody, and he was tried again at the summer assizes for suborning to commit perjury. This time he was tried before Perrin J. and a special jury.[94] He challenged six jurors, but the crown did not set any aside, presumably because special jurors were considered more likely to convict – as they did. Gray was sentenced to transportation for life.[95] However, the execution of this was delayed. The matter was referred to the queen's bench, where it was held that Gray ought not to have been allowed to challenge jurors peremptorily in a non-capital case.

Perrin J. had realised that the practice of restricting peremptory challenges to capital cases was something of an Irish oddity, but was content to adhere to it. A majority in the court of queen's bench upheld the rule restricting peremptory challenges.[96] They were aware that in England, prisoners were allowed peremptory challenges in such cases, but were mindful of the fact that this had never been judicially determined; in Ireland, on the other hand, the *Phelan* and *Whelan* cases had expressly forbidden it. Gray's case was then successfully appealed to the house of lords, where Lord Campbell and the majority of the common-law judges held that the right to peremptory challenge could only be abolished by statute. Campbell also pointed out that the crown had an unlimited right to peremptory challenge, and that it would be 'inconsistent with all the rules of justice' if the prisoner did not have some comparable right, even if not exercisable to the same

87 Johnson, 'Sam Gray', 125, comments that this procedure was 'highly irregular and illustrates the legal quagmire into which the crown had waded in its determination to put Sam behind bars'.

88 Ibid., 126. 89 *Northern Whig*, 19 and 22 Mar. 1842.

90 *R v. Gray* (1843) 3 Cr. & Dix C.C. 238.

91 See *R v. Conway* (1858) 7 I.C.L.R. 507, p. 514. See also chapter 12.

92 (1843) 3 Cr. & Dix C.C. 238. 93 *Freeman's Journal*, 17 Mar. 1843.

94 *Belfast Newsletter*, 21 July 1843.

95 Ibid. The jury recommended mercy. Johnson, 'Sam Gray', 128.

96 *R v. Gray* (1846) Cr. L.R. 259. It is interesting that the dissenting judge here was Perrin J., who appears to have reversed his opinion in the intervening period.

extent. The conviction was set aside, and a *venire de novo* was issued, allowing Gray to be tried a sixth time, but he was released a month later, after a personal intervention by Pennefather C.J.[97] The result of this case was that defendants in non-capital cases were henceforth allowed to challenge up to twenty jurors peremptorily.[98]

After the ruling in *Gray*, the discrepancy between the English and Irish rules grew even further.[99] For example, in England, there was no right to peremptory challenge in cases of misdemeanours or in civil actions,[100] while in Ireland a defendant could challenge peremptorily in misdemeanours, although the Juries Procedure (Ireland) Act, 1876[101] restricted the number of such challenges to six.[102] Joy pointed out that the authorities were very much scattered, and that 'many important and authentic sources of information have been hitherto unnoticed'.[103] Although this was an issue in almost all criminal cases, there were not 'two consecutive pages in any law book upon this right of peremptory challenge'.[104] It was not until after the introduction of legislative reforms in 1871 that the serious problems occasioned by the extension of the peremptory challenges to non-capital cases were fully appreciated. It will be seen that this problem was very much to the fore after 1881.

THE STAND-ASIDE POWER

Related to the defendant's right to peremptorily challenge jurors was the crown's discretionary right to order jurors to 'stand aside'. It meant that the crown could exclude certain jurors without showing cause. The origin of the right can be traced to a statute of 1305 that stated that 'if they that sue for the king will challenge any of those jurors, they shall assign of their challenge a cause certain, and the truth of the same shall be inquired of'.[105] The courts interpreted this as meaning that the crown did not have to state the cause of the challenge until the whole panel was gone through,[106] and McEldowney notes that in practice, the crown could 'direct that jurors stand-by, postponing the giving of cause until the entire panel was gone through. In fact the crown seldom gave cause for standing such jurors aside.'[107] A juror who was asked to stand aside was only being asked to do so temporarily, but in reality, a second calling-over of the panel was rarely resorted to,[108] and so those

97 Johnson, 'Sam Gray', 132. 98 Ibid., 110. 99 See Joy, *Confessions*, p. vi.

100 See *R v. Blakeman and others* (1850) 3 Car. & K. 97; 175 E.R. 479, *Marsh v. Coppock* (1840) 9 Car. & P. 480; 173 E.R. 920, and *Creed v. Fisher* (1854) 9 Exch. 472; 15 E.R. 202.

101 39 & 40 Vic., c. 78, s. 10.

102 See *R (Bridge) v. Casey* (1877) 13 Cox C.C. 646 and *R v. Parnell and others* (1881–2) 8 L.R. Ir. 17.

103 Joy, *Confessions*. 104 Ibid., p. vii. 105 Challenge of Jurors Act, 1305 (33 Ed. I, stat. 4).

106 McEldowney, 'Stand by', 275. He notes that the power was questioned during the 1794 state trials of Horne Tooke, John Thelwall and Thomas Hardy, but that it was 'generally upheld'. Ibid., p. 276. 107 Ibid.

108 Cases where the panel was called over twice were *R (O'Connor) v. Waring* (R.W. Greene, *A report*

men did not make it onto the jury. It thus appeared that the crown had considerably greater powers of challenge than the accused.

The power was controversial because it was unlimited. In the early decades of the nineteenth century, opinions differed as to whether the power was abused.[109] William Kemmis, for example, admitted that while he often set aside numerous jurors, this was never on religious or political grounds.[110] Kemmis, it might be remembered, was implicated in jury packing allegations at several high-profile political trials including the trials of Kirwan in 1816,[111] Blanchfield and Byrne in 1831,[112] Daniel O'Connell in 1844[113] and William Mitchel in 1848.[114] Even if the procedure was used sparingly, it rankled with those who were asked to stand aside; some interpreted it as an affront to their integrity.[115]

In 1812 Hugh Fitzpatrick, a Catholic, was tried for publishing a pamphlet on the penal laws that criticised the duke of Richmond for allowing the execution of Phillip Barry, believed to be innocent, in 1810.[116] Fitzpatrick was tried at bar by a special jury from which 'every Catholic was excluded'. It was said that '[t]he Catholics may talk of estates purchased with their hard-earned wealth – but they are far surpassed by old Kemmis, the crown prosecutor and conductor of the government prosecutions for the last twenty-one years'.[117] Following this, Denys Scully wrote that 'to pack a jury [was] a phrase perfectly intelligible and familiar in Ireland',[118] and said that crown solicitors 'uniformly set aside and reject Roman Catholic jurors'.[119] In his view, being asked to stand aside was 'a disparagement of [a man's] character as a citizen'.[120] Local police often advised crown solicitors as to which jurors to set aside, and there were frequent allegations that the largely

of the trial of Daniel Waring upon the prosecution of Roger O'Connor, esq., at an adjournment of the commission for the county of the city of Dublin, before the Hon St George Daly and the Hon Edward Mayne, for Perjury (Dublin, 1817)) and the second trial of Kevin Izod O'Doherty (Hodges, *Proceedings under the Treason Felony Act*). At the trial of John McClure at the Cork special commission in 1867, initially 189 jurors answered when called. When the names were called a second time, more men answered, apparently because some trains had arrived into Cork: Anon., *Reports of proceedings at the special commissions (1867) for the county and city of Cork, and the county and city of Limerick, in cases of high-treason and treason-felony, at the summer assizes of the same year, for the counties of Clare and Kerry* (Dublin, 1871), p. 28.

109 *Report on the state of Ireland*, 1839, para. 4551 (William Samuel Tracy, a Limerick R.M.).

110 Ibid., paras 7041–2 (Kemmis), 7838 (Edward Tierney, crown solicitor on the northwest circuit) and 8419 (Edward S. Hickman, crown solicitor for the Connacht circuit).

111 William Ridgeway, *Report of the trial of Thos. Kirwan Merchant, for a misdemeanour, charged to be committed in violation of the Convention Act* (Dublin, 1812).

112 A case arising out of tithe agitation: *Hansard 3*, vi, 91 (16 Aug. 1831). 113 See pp 22–4.

114 Hodges, *Report of the trial of John Mitchel.*

115 E.g. see a letter from John Hughes, who was asked to stand aside at the 1844 Monaghan assize: *The Nation*, 11 May 1844.

116 *R v. Fitzpatrick* (1813) 31 How. St. Tr. 1170.

117 *Hugh Fitzpatrick* (NLI, MS 11,421(1)d), attributed to Denys Scully.

118 Denys Scully, *A statement of the penal laws which aggrieve the Catholics of Ireland: with commentaries* (2nd ed., Dublin, 1812), p. 223.

119 Ibid., p. 230. 120 Ibid., p. 231.

Protestant police tried to keep Catholics off juries, particularly in political cases. For example, Daniel O'Connell told the 1825 parliamentary committee that magistrates in Cork had attended prosecutions and set aside Catholic jurors until he complained of it.[121] Similarly, in 1831, another committee heard that at the recent assizes in Maryborough (Portlaoise), every Catholic was set aside by the crown, on the direction of the police constable.[122] The sub-inspector of Queen's County, Hugh Boyd Wray, admitted that he advised the crown solicitor as to who were 'bad' jurors.[123] At Castlepollard, the constable was also said to object to Catholics.[124]

From 1835 onwards, attorneys general occasionally issued instructions to crown solicitors, '[p]artly to provide a uniform policy of challenging jurors and also to indicate situations where the power should not be exercised'.[125] Johnson notes that the guidelines laid down by successive attorneys general were quite restrictive.[126] The first instructions were issued verbally by Louis Perrin, stating that jurors should not be ordered to stand by because of their religion or politics.[127] There had to be a 'good substantive objection'.[128] John Richards adopted the same approach. Michael O'Loghlin issued instructions in 1836 that jurors should only be set aside where they were 'connected with the parties in the case'.[129] The instructions proved quite unpopular with lawyers.[130] In 1839 Maziere Brady echoed the prohibition against objecting to jurors on grounds of religion or politics, and exhorted crown solicitors to state the grounds on which they ordered jurors to stand by. That same year, W.S. Tracey observed that the crown never set aside jurors any more, but considered that this defeated the ends of justice.[131] However, William Kemmis, crown solicitor, observed that 'the lower class of people have greater confidence in the juries, because they see the crown never set any body aside'.[132] Brady observed in 1841 that his instructions had been misconstrued as meaning that the crown's right to order jurors to stand aside had been abolished completely.[133] He acknowledged that there were cases where it was 'expedient, for the due administration of justice, that persons should be set aside on being first called',[134] and allowed the power to be used against members of secret societies, persons from the immediate locality of the case if much excitement had been generated,

121 *Report on the state of Ireland*, 1825, p. 118.

122 *Report from the select committee on the state of Ireland; with the minutes of evidence, appendix and index*, HC 1831–2 (677) xvi, 1, para. 3580 (John Bray, a Roman Catholic juror).

123 Ibid., paras 3950–5. 124 Ibid., paras 3736–7 (Burke).

125 McEldowney, 'Stand by', 277. See also David Johnson, 'Trial by jury in Ireland 1860–1914' *J. Leg. Hist.*,17:3 (1996) 270–91 at 283; *Jurors (Ireland). Instructions given to crown solicitors respecting challenge of jurors*, HC 1842 (171) xxxviii, 339; and *Guidance of crown solicitors in relation to the impannelling of jurors*, HC 1894 (33) lxxii, 29.

126 Johnson, 'Trial by jury', 283. 127 *Instructions to crown solicitors*, 1842, p. 1.

128 *Report on the state of Ireland*, 1839, para. 9122 (Maxwell Hamilton, crown solicitor for the north-east circuit).

129 See ibid., para. 7028 (Kemmis). 130 Johnson, 'Trial by jury', 283.

131 *Report on the state of Ireland*, 1839, paras 4543–5. 132 Ibid., para. 7230.

133 *Instructions to crown solicitors*, 1842, p. 1. 134 Ibid., p. 2.

publicans and non-English speakers (except on juries *de medietate linguae*).[135] However, in all such instances, the crown solicitor was to 'state the grounds on which he thought to exercise it'.[136] What Johnson terms the 'definitive' guidelines were issued in 1867 by Robert Richard Warren. According to these, the crown solicitor was to be given a list of the jurors who were to be summoned four days before the assizes, which he could then scrutinise to determine those he would require to stand by.[137] Whether any of these instructions had any great effect on the use of the power is unclear, and Johnson notes that the crown used the power 'with great vigour, on occasions to the point where it laid itself open to the charge of jury packing'.[138] Further guidance was provided by a rule of 1894 that demonstrates how the grounds for ordering jurors to stand aside had broadened over the course of the century.[139] This allowed a juror to be stood aside on grounds of affinity, partiality, bodily or mental infirmity, or because they were from the same town or locality where the case arose. In addition, the crown could stand-aside those who were 'likely to be hindered from giving an impartial verdict, by favour towards the accused, or fear of the consequences to their persons, their property or trade, although same may not admit of legal proof.[140]

The stand-aside power was probably something of an Irish solution to an Irish problem, and was seldom exercised in England,[141] where charges of jury packing were less frequent. Johnson opines that the overuse of the stand-by power did not come about until after the appearance of the 'new' jurors under the Juries Act (Ireland), 1871.[142] However, the high-water mark of the controversy was not reached until the 1880s, when several high-profile criminal cases saw the crown seeking to exclude Catholics and nationalist sympathisers from juries altogether.[143] The next section will consider claims of jury packing in more detail.

UNPACKING JURY PACKING

The term 'jury packing' can, in a general sense, be understood as including all attempts to 'pack' a jury with sympathisers for a particular side. This could encompass the actions of officials such as the cess collectors, clerks of the crown, magistrates and sub-sheriffs involved in the drawing up and revising of county jurors' books. By the second half of the nineteenth century, however, it came to

135 *Report on juries (Ireland)*, HC 1873 (283) xv, 389, para. 1746.
136 See McEldowney, 'Stand by', 276.
137 *Rule for impannelling of jurors*. The instructions remained largely unchanged until a clause was added in 1894 to the effect that no juror was to be challenged 'on account of his religious or political beliefs or his calling'. Johnson, 'Trial by jury', 283, adds that this was 'clearly added by the liberals to placate Irish nationalists'. McEldowney, 'Stand by', 280, has pointed out that there does not appear to have been any similar guidelines laid down for English crown solicitors.
138 Johnson, 'Trial by jury', 282. 139 *Rule for guidance.* 140 Ibid., p. 1.
141 Johnson, 'Trial by jury', 277, 282–3. 142 Ibid., 283.
143 E.g. the 'Sligo trials', see p. 160.

1. The jury at the trial of Robert Emmet ('The trial of Robert Emmet, September 19th, 1803', *The Shamrock*, Christmas 1892). Image courtesy of the National Library of Ireland.

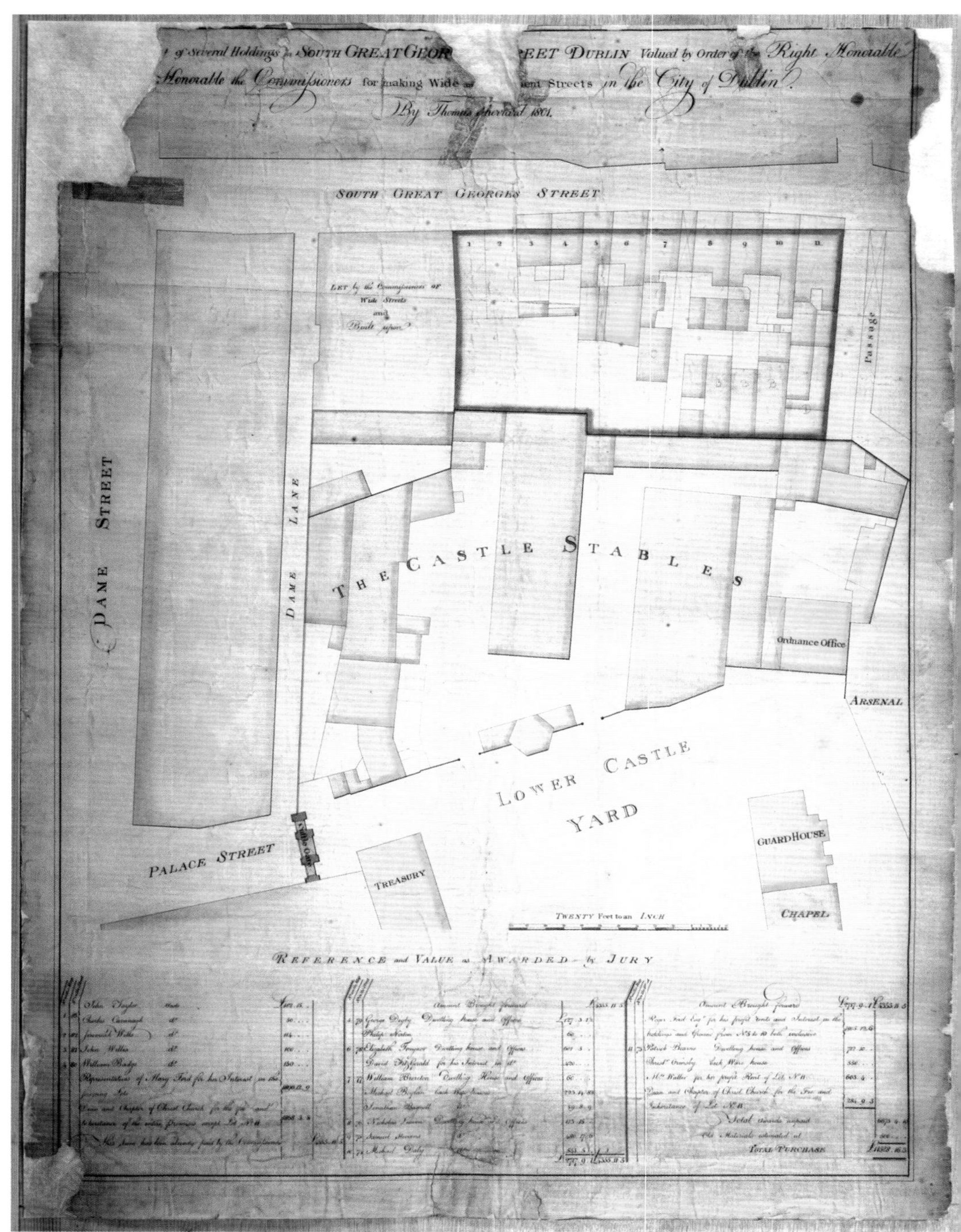

2. A wide-streets commission map of Dame Street, showing a jury's valuations. Image courtesy of Dublin City Library and Archive.

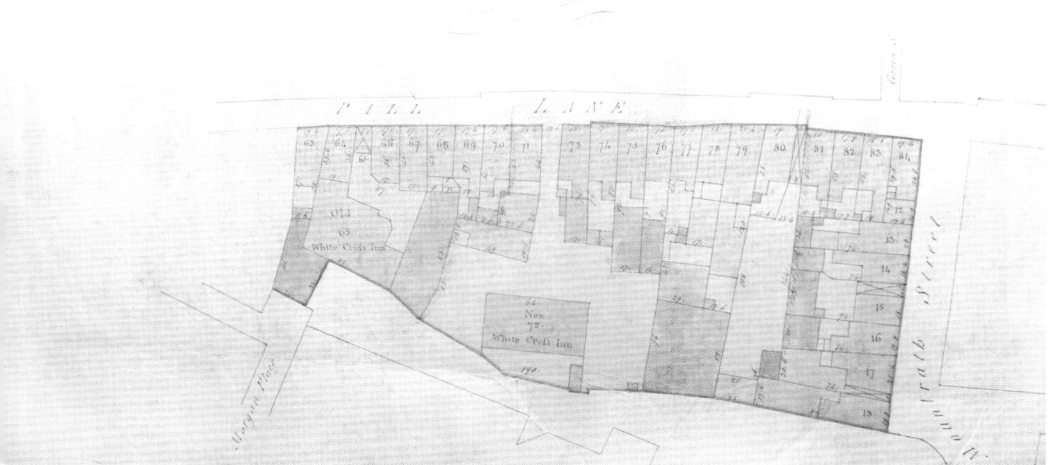

3. A wide-streets commission map of premises to be valued by a jury. Image courtesy of Dublin City Library and Archive.

4. The Dublin tholsel, where wide-streets jurors met ('Picture of tholsel, Dublin' by James Malton, London). Image courtesy of the National Library of Ireland.

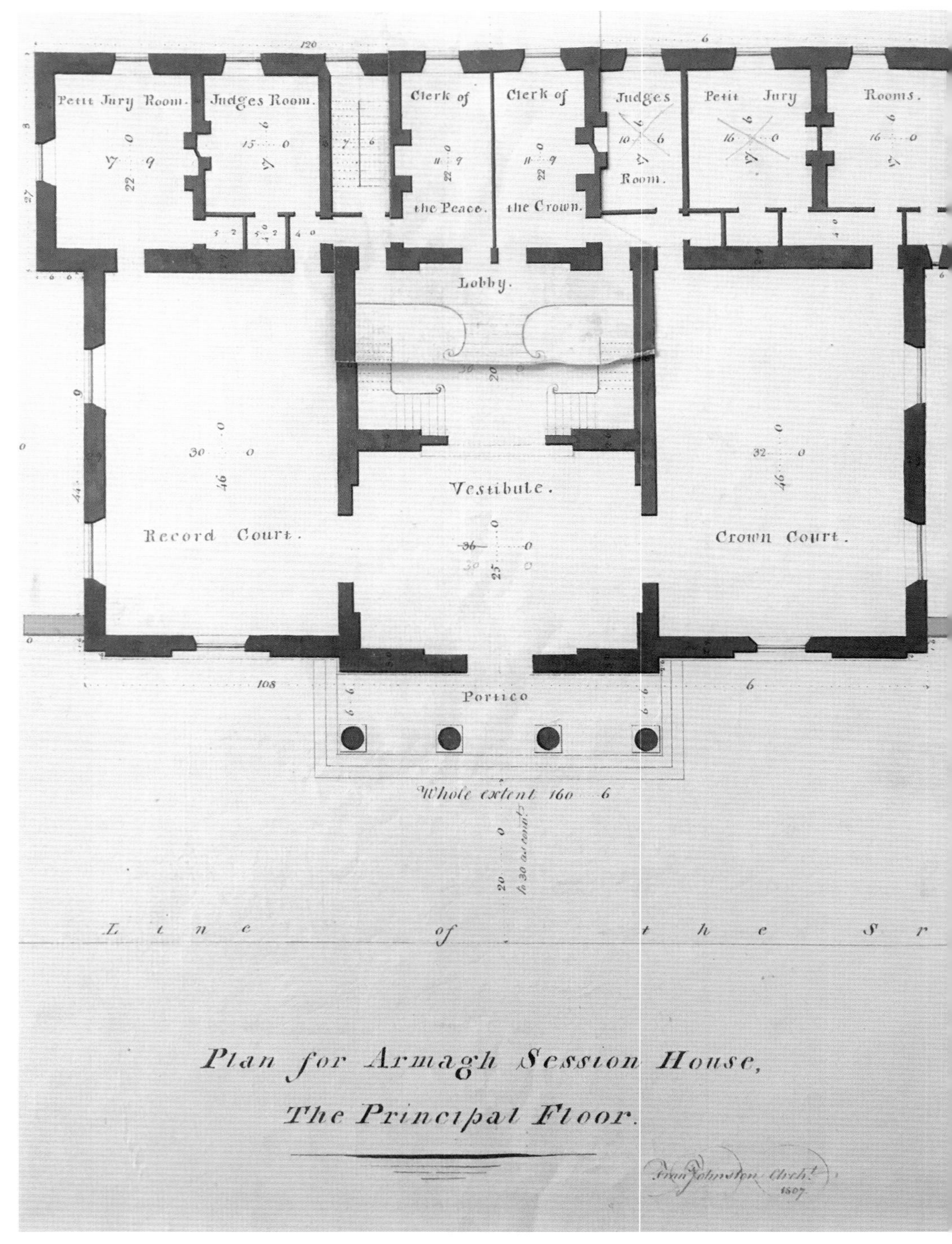

5. A plan of the Armagh sessions house by Francis Johnston, showing facilities for jurors. Image courtesy of the Irish Architectural Archive.

6. The Gresham Hotel, Dublin, where jurors spent the night on occasion ('Gresham Hotel' by Robert French). Image courtesy of the National Library of Ireland.

7. Revision of jury lists at the recorder's court in Dublin, for the Dublin state trials (*Illustrated London News*, 17 Feb. 1844). Image courtesy of the National Library of Ireland.

8. Packing the jury for Daniel O'Connell's trial ('Justice to Ireland – or Saxon law', William Tell, *Hints & Hits* no. 12). Image courtesy of the National Library of Ireland.

9. The four judges at Daniel O'Connell's trial at bar (*Illustrated London News*, 25 Nov. 1843). Image courtesy of the National Library of Ireland.

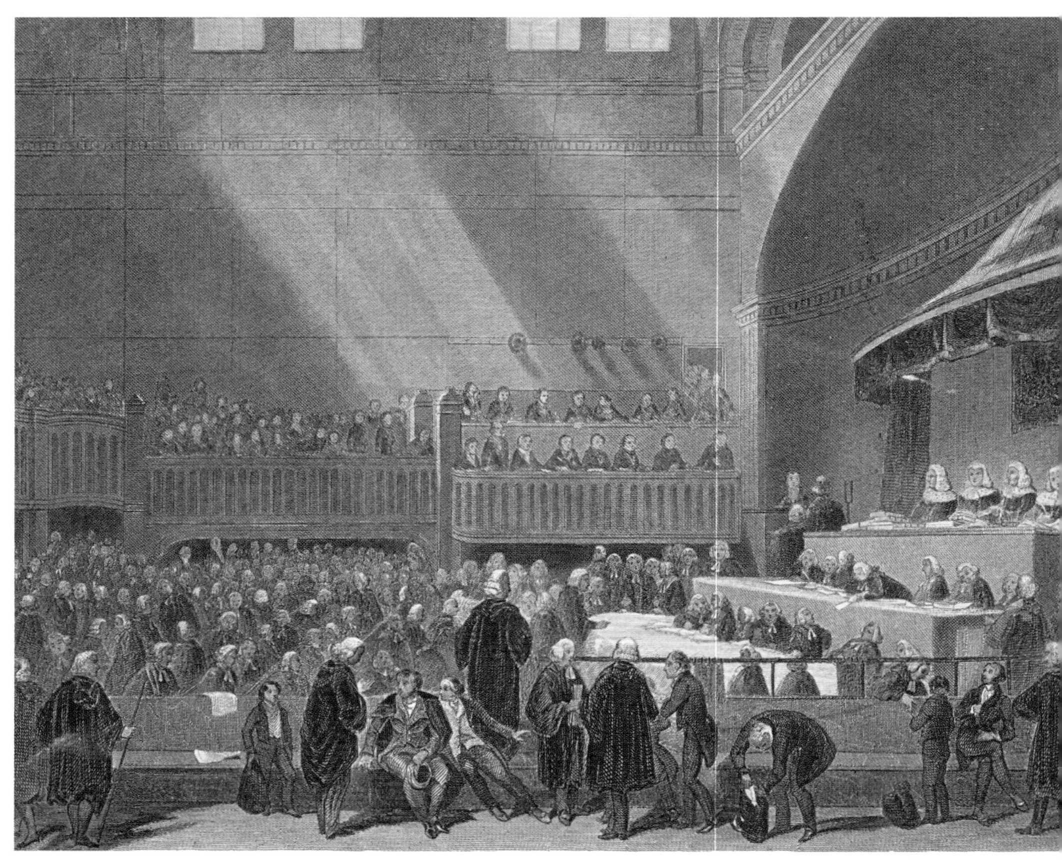

10. The trial of Daniel O'Connell (John Rogers, London, 1844). Image courtesy of the National Library of Ireland.

11. At the Clonmel special commission in 1848, jurors were obliged to spend the night together in a room described as 'cheerless' (*Illustrated London News*, 7 Oct. 1848). Image courtesy of the National Library of Ireland.

12. Jurors in the box at one of the Fenian trials in the 1860s (*Le Journal Illustré*). Image courtesy of the National Library of Ireland.

13. Fenian John McCafferty, who sought to be tried by a jury *de medietate linguae*. Image courtesy of the National Library of Ireland.

14. Thomas O'Hagan, 1st Baron O'Hagan by W & D Downey, 1860s (© National Portrait Gallery, London).

15. Statue of James Whiteside, Four Courts, Dublin. Image courtesy of the Irish Architectural Archive.

COURT HOUSE
JUDGES PROTEST
ALL ROUND COERCION.
GL—DST—NE (to Irish Judges.) "You have been continually complaining that Irish juries will not convict prisoners; and when I make you Judges, Juries, Hangmen, and all, you won't have that. Now, I will have you to do as I wish, whether it brings the judicial office into contempt or not. As for evidence, the police *shall* supply that. So, ghee-hup! Get on there!"

16. Judicial protest at the proposed introduction of juryless trials in 1882 (*Weekly Freeman*, 10 June 1882). Image courtesy of the National Library of Ireland.

HIGH COURT of JUDICATURE
BENCH AND JURY BOX
PETTY SESSIONS BENCH
SUMMARY JURISDICTION
NO APPEAL
CRIME ACT
RECKONING WITHOUT HIS HOST.
GL—DS—TONE.—Juries be dashed ! I know how we'll get the Verdicts we want, and plenty of them too."
IRISH JUDGES.—" We will not sit on this Bench with those words on it, and we protest against this attempt to injure the administration of the Law in Ireland and to impair the respect entertained for the Bench."
VOICES FROM PETTY SESSIONS BENCH.—" Give us as much power as you like, and we wont be too squeamish in using it."

17. Further judicial protest at the proposed introduction of juryless trials in 1882 (*Weekly Freeman*, 27 May 1882). Image courtesy of the National Library of Ireland.

PETHER THE PACKER
Packing the Jury in the Court House, Maryborough.
"All Catholics—stand aside. Papists are perjurers, not to be trusted on their oaths."

18. Peter O'Brien, commonly referred to as 'Peter the Packer' for allegedly packing juries using the 'stand-aside' procedure (*United Ireland*, 26 Oct. 1889). Image courtesy of the National Library of Ireland.

19. Cartoon depicting the exclusion of Catholics from juries in 1889 (*Weekly Freeman*, 26 Oct. 1889). Image courtesy of the National Library of Ireland.

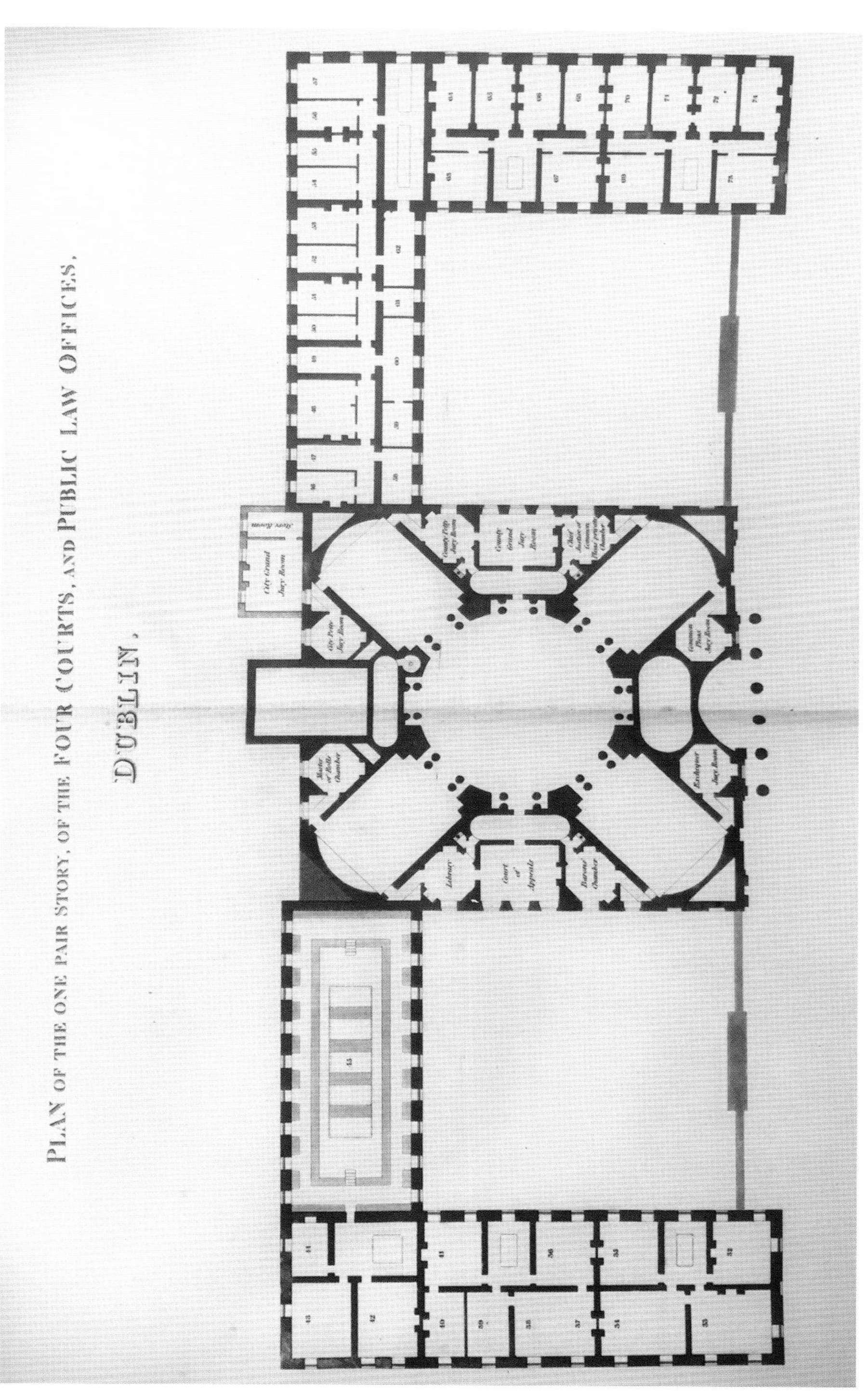

20. Plan of the Four Courts, Dublin, 1813, detailing jurors' facilities, by James Basire, from *Reports from the commissioners respecting the public records of Ireland, 1810–1815*. Courtesy of the Irish Architectural Archive.

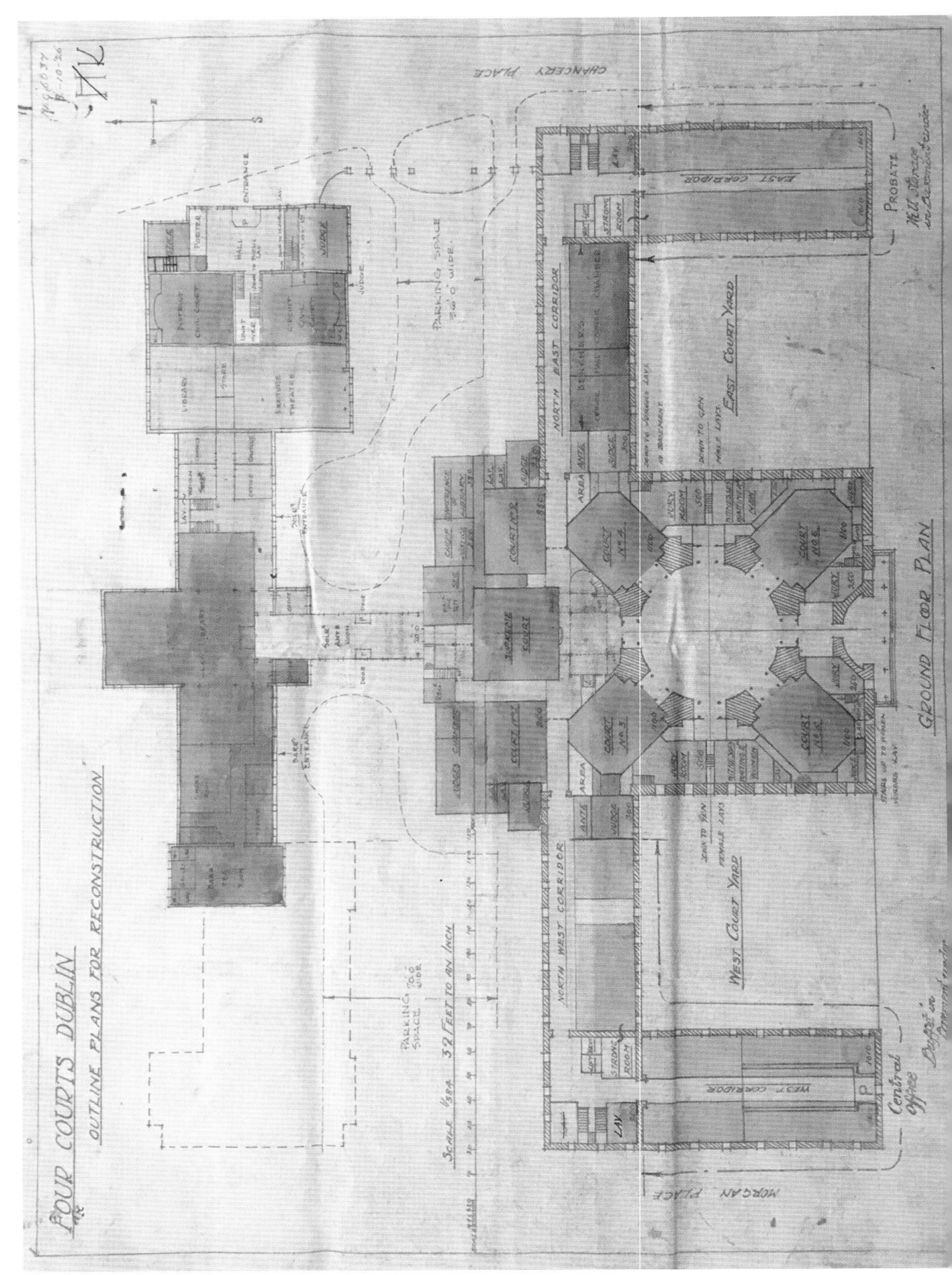

21. Plan of the refurbished Four Courts, Dublin, detailing jurors' facilities, by William Murray. King's Inns Collection, Irish Architectural Archive.

refer more specifically to the overuse of the crown's stand-aside power. Speaking in the house of lords in 1887, Baron Fitzgerald said that '[b]y jury-packing was popularly meant the exclusion of Roman Catholics who were returned on the panel from taking part in trials'.[144] When taken to the extreme, this could effectively result in hand-picking the jurors to try a particular case, helping to secure convictions in even the most extremely divisive political trials. Nationalist writers were critical of what they considered to be the widespread practice of jury packing:

> it is notorious that, in every political or party case in Ireland, the crown solicitor brings into court a printed panel, marked so as to show the jurors likely to convict – the local police and others having furnished information as to the leanings or bias, creed or party of every juror on the panel ... is not all this a ghastly mockery of trial by jury?[145]

At the 1865 Fenian trials,[146] the crown exercised this power to a degree that piqued many observers, although as Kostel points out, defence counsel were not slow to use their own peremptory challenges and challenges for cause, and 'the weight of numbers alone made jury-packing, at least in its most blatant forms, difficult for the crown to achieve'.[147] At O'Leary's trial, when the guilty verdict was returned, the prisoner commented that 'the government which had so safely packed the bench, could not fail to make sure of its juries'.[148] At the Cork commission in 1867, similar tactics were employed, with hours spent arguing over challenges.[149] Many of the prisoners' challenges for cause were disallowed, and they were obliged to use their peremptory challenges.

During and after the Land War of 1879–82, prosecutions in political and agrarian cases became increasingly difficult, due in a large part to the intimidation of witnesses and jurors.[150] As a result, Corfe writes that it 'became customary ... to pack the juries with men of conservative and unionist sympathies, which usually meant members of the respectable Protestant middle class'.[151] Increasing use was made of change-of-venue procedures, discussed in the next chapter, with political or agrarian cases being transferred from the south and west to Dublin. The Prevention of Crime (Ireland) Act, 1882[152] was passed in the aftermath of the gruesome murders of Lord Frederick Cavendish, the chief secretary, and his

144 *Hansard 3*, cccxi, 1287 (4 Mar. 1887) (HL). 145 Counsel, *Jury packing*, p. 10.

146 The offices of the Fenian newspaper, the *Irish People*, were raided in September 1865, resulting in the prosecutions of leaders O'Donovan Rossa, Luby and O'Leary.

147 R.W. Kostel, 'Rebels in the dock: the prosecution of the Dublin Fenians, 1865–6', *Éire-Ireland*, 34 (1999), 79–80. Once Butt had used up his 20 peremptory challenges, he began to challenge for non-residence, asking unwanted jurors to prove a Dublin address.

148 *Report of the Dublin special commission*, 1866, p. 628.

149 *Reports of proceedings at the special commissions (1867) for the county and city of Cork and the county and city of Limerick* (Dublin, 1871).

150 T. Corfe, *The Phoenix Park murders: conflict, compromise and tragedy in Ireland, 1879–1882* (London, 1968), p. 150. 151 Ibid. 152 45 & 46 Vic., c. 25.

undersecretary, T.H. Burke.[153] This coercive legislation abrogated the right to trial by jury and allowed cases of treason, murder and assault to be tried by special commissions of three judges. It also provided for special juries to be used instead of common juries in certain criminal cases. This met with fierce opposition, with the *Freeman's Journal* describing it as 'a tremendous instrument ... perhaps the fiercest coercion act ever proposed for Ireland'.[154] The Irish bench was of the view that the proposed measures 'would seriously impair the public confidence in the administration of justice in Ireland'.[155]

The controversy reached a fever pitch during the Gray affair, which stemmed from the *Freeman's Journal* reporting on several cases tried under the provisions of the act.[156] One such case was the trial of Francis Hynes for murder before Lawson J. and a special jury. The crown ordered twenty-six men to stand aside, most of whom were Catholics, and the defendant challenged eleven peremptorily. Hynes was convicted by a jury entirely composed of Protestants, and was subsequently executed.[157] During the trial, the *Freeman's Journal* published allegations of drunken misconduct by the jurors.[158] The *Journal* had also recently published a number of articles alleging jury packing. Edmund Dwyer Gray – a nationalist MP, high sheriff of Dublin, former lord mayor and editor of the *Journal* – was fined £500 by Lawson J., and sentenced to three months' imprisonment for contempt of court, which caused a furore.[159] A parliamentary committee examined the circumstances of his imprisonment,[160] and Gray testified in relation to a number of alleged 'jury packing' cases he had written about in the *Journal*. He told the committee that the Dublin jury panel consisted of 193 names, of whom 112 were Catholic, 80 were Protestant and one was Jewish. Of the cases brought up to Dublin for trial under the 1882 act, all were tried by juries entirely composed of Protestants, except for one jury on which the Jewish man was empanelled.[161]

153 See p. 58; F.S.L. Lyons, *Ireland since the Famine* (London, 1971), pp 168–9; and Felix M. Larkin, 'Lord Frederick Cavendish and the Phoenix Park murders of 1882', *Hist. Ire.*, 22:3 (2014), 28–31. See also *Hansard 3*, cclxix, 315–20 (8 May 1882) (HL) and ibid., 320–6 (8 May 1882) (HC).

154 *Freeman's Journal*, 12 May 1882.

155 Anon., 'The administration of justice in Ireland', *I.L.T. & S.J.*, 16 (1882), 232, reporting on a meeting of the judges. For further discussion of the operation and effects of the act, see H. Humphreys, *The Prevention of Crime (Ireland) Act 1882, 45 & 46 Vict., cap. 25, with a review on the policy, bearing, and scope of the Act* (Dublin, 1882). He noted, p. vi, that trial by jury had 'failed by reason of a large portion of the community having, through fear or a corrupt motive, lost its sense of horror at the commission of certain crimes'.

156 E.g. *R v. O'Connor and others*, *Freeman's Journal*, 11 Aug. 1882; *R v. Bryan, Kinsella and Duggan*, *Freeman's Journal*, 15 Aug. 1882; *R v. Kenny*, *Freeman's Journal*, 15 Aug. 1882; and *R v. Walsh*, *Freeman's Journal*, 4 May 1881.

157 *Dublin commission court (Francis Hynes)*, HC 1882 (408) lv, 167, p. 16.

158 See p. 191.

159 See the *Pall Mall Gazette*, 8 Mar. 1882 and Corfe, *The Phoenix Park murders*, p. 233.

160 *Report from the committee on privilege (Mr. Gray)*, HC 1882 (406) xii, 503.

161 *Dublin commission court (Francis Hynes)*, p. 28.

A few months later, another high-profile prosecution saw the crown once more making quite extensive use of the 'stand-aside' procedure. These were the trials arising from the murders of members of the Joyce family in Maamtrasna, County Galway, on 17 August 1882.[162] Two days after the discovery of the murders, ten men were arrested and charged. Patrick Joyce was the first to be tried before Barry J. and a special jury in Dublin in November 1882. Peter O'Brien QC, known as 'Peter the packer', was the crown prosecutor,[163] and a commentator remarked that the juries in the Maamtrasna trials 'were packed after the manner of all political and agrarian trials in Ireland'.[164] Two special jury panels, consisting of 200 names, were called over by the deputy clerk of the peace, though only 117 men answered;[165] 19 men were challenged by the prisoner, and George Bolton, the crown solicitor, ordered 36 men to 'stand by'.[166] At the trial of Myles Joyce, the crown ordered 27 men to stand aside, and the prisoner challenged 15 without cause and unsuccessfully challenged one juror for cause.[167] Both men, along with Patrick Casey, were found guilty, and were executed on 15 December, and it later became clear that Myles Joyce had in fact been innocent. Both Patrick Joyce and Patrick Casey made dying declarations that Myles was innocent, and admitted their guilt.[168] Myles made a dying declaration of innocence, and, the following summer, Thomas Casey claimed responsibility for the murder and for perjury.[169]

Allegations of jury packing arose once again in 1883 at the trial of the Invincibles for the Phoenix Park murders.[170] At Timothy Kelly's first trial, twenty-nine special jurors were ordered to stand-by.[171] The jury was unable to reach a verdict,[172] and Kelly was tried again a few days later.[173] At the second trial forty jurors were asked to stand by,[174] and Kelly was acquitted.[175] At least forty-two jurors were ordered to stand by at the trial of Michael Fagan, who was convicted.[176]

It was not just in political trials that juries were thought to be packed. At the trial of a blind man named Smith for murder in Cavan in 1873, despite involving no

162 Tim Harrington, *The Maamtrasna massacre: impeachment of the trials* (Dublin, 1884), p. i.

163 See generally N. McAree, *Murderous justice: a study in depth of the infamous Connemara murders* (Limerick, 1990).

164 Harrington, *The Maamtrasna massacre*, p. iv.

165 J. Waldron, *Maamtrasna: the murders and the mystery* (Dublin, 1992), p. 62.

166 Harrington, *The Maamtrasna massacre*, p. 3.

167 Ibid., pp 32–3.

168 Ibid., p. v.

169 Ibid., pp vi–vii.

170 See E.P. de Blaghd, 'Tim Kelly, guilty or not guilty?', *Dub. Hist. Rec.*, 25:1 (1971), 12–24. See also *Leeds Mercury*, 15 Jan. 1883 and *Manchester Times*, 27 Jan. 1883.

171 *Freeman's Journal*, 20 Apr. 1883.

172 See *Aberdeen Weekly Journal*, 20 Apr. 1883 and *Freeman's Journal*, 21 Apr. 1883.

173 See *Freeman's Journal*, 24 Apr. 1883. It was reported that the jurors in this case were cheered whenever they left the courthouse: *Bristol Mercury*, 23 Apr. 1883.

174 At the second trial, the jurors were sent back to their room five times, yet two of them held out in favour of an acquittal.

175 He was finally convicted at a third trial, and sentenced to death.

176 The *Leeds Mercury*, 26 Apr. 1883, reported that there were 42 jurors ordered to stand-by, but it was reported in the house of commons that there were 54 jurors ordered to stand by: *Hansard 3*, cclvxiii, 1134–5 (26 Apr. 1883) (HC).

agrarian or political feeling, 'in the presence of the attorney general, the crown solicitor set aside fifty-six jurors out of the panel'.[177] Johnson lists numerous other examples of the overuse of the power, including the high-profile trial of Montgomery, an RIC sub-inspector, for the murder of a bank clerk in County Tyrone at the 1873 spring assizes.[178] Although not involving political, religious or agrarian considerations, it was estimated that over 200 jurors were summoned, and 120 were set aside by the crown.[179] The 1871 act had just come into effect, and this was an attempt to exclude many of the new jurors, who were considered unfit and unable to carry out their duties. Allegations of packing were also made in relation to civil cases and wide-streets juries.[180]

Despite the extreme cases in the 1880s, claims that jury packing was endemic must be taken with a pinch of salt. While there were certainly high-profile cases in which the crown ordered a large number of jurors to stand aside, it must be acknowledged that defendants also made robust use of their right to challenge jurors peremptorily. From the 1830s to the 1870s the stand-aside power was used rather sparingly and there are many examples of cases in which the crown's use of the stand-aside power was matched (or very nearly matched) by a defendant's use of peremptory challenges. There are also numerous instances in which the defendant's peremptory challenges outnumbered the crown's stand-asides. Claims of jury packing were often exaggerated. For example, jury packing was alleged to have occurred at the trial of Thadeus Derrig and seven other Catholics for Whiteboy-related offences in Mayo in 1851. The crown solicitor, Isidore Burke (who, incidentally, was a Catholic himself), was alleged to have ordered every Catholic juror to stand aside.[181] The jury empanelled was entirely composed of Protestants. In fact, out of a panel of 159, there were 9 jurors ordered to stand by and they were Catholics.[182]

To assess the extent to which the stand-aside power was matched by the defendant's use of peremptory challenges, a number of reported trials dating from 1777 to 1890 have been examined (see table 10.1). Many of these were high-profile political cases such as the Phoenix Park and Maamtrasna prosecutions, the 1798 and 1803 treason prosecutions, and cases arising out of the tithe agitation in the 1830s and the Young Ireland prosecutions in the 1840s – cases in which the crown had a strong interest in securing a verdict. Of the 50 cases considered, the stand-asides outnumbered the peremptory challenges in 24 instances (about 48 per cent). In one case, the crown and defendant made equal use of their challenges, and in 25 instances the defendant made greater use of his peremptory challenges. Based on this, it would seem that the crown and the defendant made more or less equal use of their respective rights.

177 *Report on jury system (Ireland)*, HC 1874 (244) ix, 557, para. 3.

178 See *Lloyd's Weekly Newspaper*, 9 Mar. 1873; *The Graphic*, 15 Mar. 1873; and *Belfast Newsletter*, 22 July 1873, 31 July 1873. See also the *Report on Irish jury system*, 1874, paras 1–6 (James Hamilton, chairman of Co. Sligo) and para. 2555 (Baron Deasy).

179 *Report on Irish jury system*, 1874, para. 3.

180 See p. 67.

181 *Freeman's Journal*, 18 Mar. 1851.

182 *Jury panel (Mayo)*, HC 1851 (235) l, 655.

Table 10.1 Stand-asides and peremptory challenges compared[183]

Case	Date	Stand-asides	Peremptory challenges	Verdict
R v. Keon	1777	13	19	Guilty
R v. Fitzgerald	1786	15	16	Guilty
R v. Vance	1790	27	9	Not guilty
R v. Carty	1797	3	17	Guilty
R v. Dunn	1797	8	20	Guilty
R v. Finerty	1797	2	0	Guilty
R v. Bond	1798	4	20	Guilty
R v. McCann	1798	22	19	Guilty
R v. Sheares	1798	11	13	Guilty
R v. Byrne	1803	3	5	Guilty
R v. Clare	1803	1	15	Guilty
R v. Donnelly	1803	2	3	Guilty
R v. Doran	1803	3	2	Not guilty
R v. Emmet	1803	12	19	Guilty
R v. Howley	1803	14	12	Guilty
R v. Kearny	1803	5	8	Guilty
R v. MacIntosh	1803	6	18	Guilty
R v. Roche	1803	5	12	Guilty
R v. Rourke	1803	14	19	Guilty
R v. Sheridan	1811	22	0	Not guilty
R v. Kirwan	1812	6	0	Guilty
R v. O'Connor	1812	39	38, but 4 withdrawn	Not guilty
R v. Fitzpatrick	1813	5	0	Guilty
R (O'Connor) v. Waring	1817	6	0	Not guilty
R v. Forbes	1823	16	0	Jury discharged
R v. St. Leger	1829	5	13	Not guilty
R v. [St.] Leger 2	1829	7	20	Not guilty
R v. Pearce	1829	37	20	Not guilty
R v. St Leger	1829	5	13	Not guilty
R v. Hodgens	1830	4	7	Not guilty
R v. Delany	1832	1	20	Guilty
R v. Kennedy	1832	1	0	Not guilty
R v. Ryan	1832	1	0	Jury discharged
R v. Byrne	1842	1	15	Not guilty
R v. Martin	1848	1	1	Guilty
R v. O'Doherty (2)	1848	14	23	Jury discharged
R v. Petcherine	1856	7	0	Not guilty
R v. Beckham	1862	4	11	Guilty
R v. Warren	1867	4	20	Guilty
R v. Pigott	1868	3	0	Guilty
R v. Sullivan	1868	1	0	Guilty
R v. Hynes	1882	26	11	Guilty
R v. O'Connor	1882	20	6	Guilty
R v. Bryan	1882	10	3	Guilty
R v. Kenny	1882	6	3	Guilty
R v. Kelly	1883	40	20	Not guilty
R v. Fagan	1883	42/54	20	Guilty
R v. Joyce (Myles)	1884	27	13	Guilty
R v. Joyce (Patrick)	1884	37	19	Guilty
R v. Redmond	1890	29	5	Not guilty

183 Citations for all of these cases can be found in the bibliography.

Certain types of cases attracted more peremptory challenges, and it can be seen from table 10.1 that there were many instances where the number of peremptory challenges far outweighed the number of stand-asides. For example, at the 1797 trials of Carty and Dunn for conspiring to murder Henry Lawes, the earl of Carhampton (and commander-in-chief of her majesty's forces in Ireland), the defendants refused to join their challenges and were tried separately. Carty challenged 17 jurors peremptorily, compared with just 3 stand-asides; Dunn challenged the full 20, compared with 8 stand-asides.[184] In the 1798 trial of Oliver Bond for treason, the defendant challenged 20 while the crown ordered 4 men to stand aside.[185] At the trial of Walter Clare for treason in 1803, the defendant peremptorily challenged 15, while the crown only set aside a single man.[186] By the second half of the nineteenth century, however, there were fewer cases where the defendant's challenges outweighed the crown's.

Based on this small sample of cases and a consideration of the literature, it is suggested that it was not until after 1882 that jury packing became a live issue. Undoubtedly a number of the cases tried under the 1882 act referred to by Gray did involve overuse or abuse of the stand-aside power, and allegations of packing were fairly made. The 1880s were a difficult period for law enforcement in Ireland. However, the paucity of trial records means that it is difficult to systematically assess challenge and stand-aside procedures in order to determine the veracity of claims about jury packing. Those cases that were extensively reported in pamphlets and newspapers tended to be exceptional – cases in which the public had a keen interest, often on political grounds – and it is possible that the reports may over-represent the true incidence of jury packing.

CONCLUSION

As outlined in chapter 2, cess collectors, clerks of the peace and crown and local justices were tasked with creating and maintaining lists of jurors for each county, and could exclude otherwise qualified men and include those who were not legally qualified, leading to an imbalance or a non-representative jurors' book. As this chapter demonstrates, it was sheriffs, and, in criminal cases, crown solicitors, who were best placed to pack juries for individual trials. While allegations of jury packing may have been rife in nineteenth-century Ireland and in later discussions of the period, most serious jury packing was limited to high-profile cases such as state trials. Juries in ordinary civil and criminal cases did not tend to be packed, although the juror-qualification laws in the first half of the century meant that religious and political representation on such juries was never ideal.

184 *R v. Dunn and Carty* (1797).
185 *R v. Bond* (1798) 27 How. St. Tr. 523.
186 W. Ridgeway, *A report on the trial of Walter Clare upon an indictment for high treason* (Dublin, 1803).

CHAPTER ELEVEN

Juror intimidation and the venue for trial

ALTHOUGH THE COMMON LAW favoured the trial of criminal offences and civil actions in the neighbourhood where the alleged offence took place or where the cause of action arose, there were some circumstances that required a change of venue.[1] These could be fairly benign, such as the facilitation of a view, convenience to witnesses and so on. A venue might also be changed as a result of the intimidation of jurors and witnesses. All jurors faced the possibility of intimidation, either from parties interested in ensuring that they delivered the 'right' verdict or valuation, or afterwards, from those unhappy with the verdict that had been delivered. This was, and arguably still is, one of the problems inherent in the jury system. In 1737, James Hope entreated the lord lieutenant to reform the Irish jury system to avoid the use of 'disputing, teezing, sollicitation, fear or favour' to secure verdicts.[2] During periods of unrest, bribes, threats and even physical violence could affect jurors' verdicts in both civil and criminal cases.[3] Coroners' juries could equally be subject to intimidation: for example, at the controversial inquest into the death of a man named Walsh in Carlow in the 1830s, the coroner was alarmed when the venue for the inquest was surrounded by persons who wanted a verdict of wilful murder to be returned.[4] Wide-streets juries could come under pressure from property owners to return inflated valuations.[5] Although intimidation could present itself as an issue in relation to all types of jury, the main focus of this chapter will be the intimidation of criminal trial juries.

1 It is not intended to examine in detail the procedures relating to changing the venue in civil cases; this chapter will focus only on the change of venue as it related to juries. For a more detailed discussion of the various aspects of the venue, see generally William Huband, *A practical treatise on the law relating to the grand jury in criminal cases, the petty jury and the coroner's jury* (rev. ed., Dublin, 1911), pp 79–96. See also Anon., 'Change of venue and transfer of actions commenced in the chancery division', *I.L.T. & S.J.*, 17 (1883), 93.

2 J. Hope, *Dissertation on the constitution and effects of a petty jury* (Dublin, 1737), p. 29.

3 During the 1830s tithe agitation, Irish judges remarked that 'the duty of jurors is often discharged at the peril of property and life'. *Letter regarding the Jury Bill 1833* (NAI, OP/1833/14).

4 *Report on the state of Ireland*, HC 1839 (486) xi, xii 1, paras 8187–92 (Thomas Harris Carroll). The case was generally referred to as *Slye's case*.

5 E.g. see *Fifteenth report on salaries*, HC 1826 (310) xvii, 29, p. 67, and discussion in chapter 5.

INTIMIDATION

Sometimes jurors experienced threats in advance of serving – these could be generalised, or else, if the jury panel became public, specifically targeted at an individual. This could be quite serious, especially where secret societies were involved. In a memorandum on juror intimidation compiled in the 1830s, an R.M. from Roscommon claimed that '[s]everal persons who are in the habit of serving as jurors' had told him that for certain agrarian offences, 'if they dared to find the prisoners guilty, they, their families and property might be injured'.[6] The 1830s and 1850s saw representations made before parliamentary committees highlighting the dangers facing jurors who delivered politically unpopular verdicts.[7] Intimidation could take the form of signed or anonymous letters; public notices; verbal threats;[8] damage to property, including livestock; or physical altercations.

The trial of John Mitchel, one of the leaders of Young Ireland,[9] for example, attracted a considerable amount of attention and nationalist newspapers such as the *Freeman's Journal* reproduced some of the threatening notices and placards posted around Dublin at the time of the trial. A placard that appeared in Dublin just before Mitchel's trial warned prospective jurors that if they convicted him, 'the blood of that innocent man of truth [will] be on you and yours to all eternity!'[10] The authorities could not do much to prevent this sort of thing, other than removing such notices when they were brought to their attention.[11] Instead, the authorities focused their attention on ensuring jurors' attendance in spite of such threats, for example by levying fines or changing the venue of trials.[12]

Despite the alleged secrecy of the jury room, a juror who held out against the popular vote sometimes found that his name became public.[13] For example, a resident magistrate from Tipperary reported in 1833 that notices had been posted

6 *Memorandum on juror intimidation*, 1833 (NAI, OP/1833/579).

7 E.g. *Report from the select committee of the house of lords, appointed to enquire into the state of Ireland in respect of crime, and to report thereon to the house*, HC 1839 (486) xi, 1; xii, 2, para. 1882 (Hill Wilson Rowan, a Co. Down R.M.); paras 1060–6 (Maj. George Warburton of the Royal Constabulary) and paras 10,528–9 (Patrick Finn); and *Report from the select committee on outrages (Ireland)*, HC 1852 (438) xiv, 1. See in particular the testimony of Brabazon, para. 4214; Bartholomew Warburton, a magistrate, paras 78–82; and Golding, para. 803. It should be noted however, that several witnesses before the 1831 committee were of the view that jurors' verdicts were generally accepted, and that there were rarely negative consequences for jurors who delivered unpopular verdicts: *Report on the state of Ireland*, HC 1831–2 (677) xvi, 1, para. 1198 (Col. John S. Rochford, a Queen's County magistrate).

8 E.g. *R v. Fay* (1872) I.R. 6 C.L. 436. See the *Anglo Celt*, 22 June 1872.

9 See pp 136, 138, 158.

10 Reproduced in the *Freeman's Journal*, 25 May 1848. Mitchel was convicted and transported to Van Diemen's Land, and in 1853 he escaped and made his way to the United States, where he worked a journalist: see F.S.L. Lyons, *Ireland since the Famine* (London, 1971), p. 98.

11 See p. 159.

12 See pp 161–9.

13 In other cases, it was merely known how many jurors favoured an acquittal. For example, at the Smith O'Brien trial there were reputedly 10 jurors in favour of a conviction, and 2 who held out, with the result that there was no verdict. See Anon., 'Our jury system', *Dub. U.J.*, 32 (1848), 717.

around the town of Fethard, 'threatening Mr William O'Leary, one of the jurors who brought in a verdict of guilty against the anti-tithe composition'.[14] Another example was the trial of Peter Barrett at a special commission in Galway in 1869.[15] He was discharged after a three-day trial when the jurors were unable to reach a verdict.[16] It was later alleged that 'several of the jurors were threatened, and thereby intimidated and prevented from attending the assizes'.[17] An R.M. swore that there had been 'a system of terrorism and intimidation ... studiously and effectually practiced and exercised upon the jurors'.[18] A rumour circulated that eleven of the jurors had been in favour of an acquittal.[19] The name of the wayward juror (Jackson) became known, and the prosecution claimed that he had been 'hunted, stoned and ill-treated by the mob, and was with much difficulty rescued by a Roman Catholic clergyman and a number of the constabulary'.[20] Accounts of the attack on Jackson differed, with some claiming that his assailants were merely women and children, representing a low level of threat.[21]

The best-known attack on a juror was that on Denis Field by the Invincibles in 1883.[22] Field had been a member of the jury that convicted Michael Walsh for the murder of police constable Kavenagh at Letterfrack.[23] During the trial, the foreman and Field had been seen passing what were in fact perfectly innocuous messages to and from the crown solicitor and were 'assumed to be asking his advice on their verdict'.[24] The names of jurors in this and seventeen other cases tried under the Prevention of Crime Act were published, along with their occupations, religions, home addresses and the details of the cases on which they had acted.[25] Soon after the trial, Field was attacked while walking home,[26] on the same night that an attempt was made on the life of Lawson J.

14 *Memorandum on juror intimidation*, 1833 (NAI, OP/1833/579).
15 (1870) Ir. Rep. 4 C.L. 285. 16 *Galway Express*, 2 Oct. 1869.
17 *R v. Barrett* (1870) Ir. Rep. 4 C.L. 285, p. 286.
18 *Affidavit of John B. Greene, 20 Nov. 1869* (NAI, CCS/1870/197).
19 *Galway Express*, 2 Oct. 1869.
20 *R v. Barrett* (1870) Ir. Rep. 4 C.L. 285, p. 286. See also the *Galway Express*, 2 Oct. 1869, where it was reported that the mob had attempted 'the summary execution of a refractory juryman'. Jackson was 'hooted and groaned', and 'attacked with bricks and stones, and one old woman seemed so bitter that she brought out a sod of turf and rolled it in the mud before throwing it at him'. The attorney general believed that such happenings had 'no precedent in the history of Irish trials'. *Freeman's Journal*, 17 Jan. 1870. See also *Affidavit of Rev John Dooley, 29 Nov. 1869* (NAI, CCS 1870/197).
21 *Affidavit of Edward Rochford, 3 Oct. 1869* (NAI, CCS/1870/197). It was also claimed that around the time when Jackson was being assailed, a rock or large stone was thrown at the carriage in which the judges were proceeding from the courthouse: *R v. Barrett* (1870) Ir. Rep. 4 C.L. 285, p. 286. See *Freeman's Journal*, 17 Jan. 1870.
22 See E.P. de Blaghd, 'Tim Kelly, guilty or not guilty?', *Dub. Hist. Rec.*, 25:1 (1971), 12–24 at 13.
23 Walsh was sentenced to death, but this was commuted to life imprisonment by the lord lieutenant: *Western Mail*, 28 Nov. 1882.
24 T. Corfe, *The Phoenix Park murders: conflict, compromise and tragedy in Ireland, 1879–1882* (London, 1968), p. 234.
25 *Analysis of the juries on the Phoenix Park murder and Field attempted murder trial* (PRO 30/60/12).
26 *Western Mail*, 28 Nov. 1882; *The Times*, 10 Feb. 1883.

As the 1880s continued and the agrarian agitation gained further momentum, juror intimidation became an even greater problem. There was a general feeling that in most, if not all, political and agrarian cases, 'a certain number of the jury are influenced by terror or sympathy',[27] thus rendering it virtually impossible to secure a fair trial in such cases. As one witness before the 1881 select committee pointed out, the 'power and organisation of the Land League at present in the south and west is such as to influence all juries to such a degree that you cannot regard them as fit to try a case involving a question of an agrarian or political character'.[28] A memorandum from the constabulary office in 1887 stated that juror intimidation was being 'carried out to a considerable extent both privately and in the press';[29] it detailed a number of instances of juror intimidation in 1886. At the Cork winter assizes, there were fifty prisoners tried for moonlighting, and a crowd that gathered at the train station to be addressed by John O'Connor MP shouted 'down with Cork juries' several times. In advance of the Sligo trials, a rally was organised for 28 November. Seventy defendants were awaiting trial in relation to recent events on the Woodford estate in Galway, and William O'Brien, John Dillon and others said they would be in attendance 'to appeal to Sligo jurors to express their condemnation of efforts of government to assassinate liberty of press and victimise the gallant defenders of Saunder's Fort'. The county inspector of the RIC reported that 'two gentlemen as a deputation of the jurors called on the county inspector and asked that the meeting should be prohibited as calculated to intimidate them'. The meeting was deemed to be 'clearly calculated to intimidate jurors' so it was prohibited by the magistrates.[30]

Similarly, papers from the chief secretary's office around the same period detail numerous instances of 'failures of justice' from all over the country, where juries failed to convict in the face of apparently clear evidence. In many cases this was attributed to juror intimidation, although juror sympathies were probably also a factor. For example, at Galway, the crown solicitor reported that 'it was nearly impossible to get a conviction at any agrarian or party case at these assizes. The respectable jurors on the panel were conspicuous by their absence while the farming classes attended in good force.' In Fermanagh, in the case of *R v. Bowes*, it was reported that a Protestant was charged with having stabbed two Roman Catholics, one of whom admitted he had shouted 'Home rule!' The report noted that '[t]here was no ground for the pretence that Bowes acted in self-defence. The jury disagreed.' In *R v. Horgan* in Kerry, a prosecution for setting fire to a hayrick, 'the evidence for the prosecution was as strong as circumstantial evidence could well be. The judge's charge was almost peremptory for a conviction. The agrarian element however presented itself and there was an immediate verdict of acquittal.'

27 Ibid., para. 2144 (Serjeant John O'Hagan).
28 Ibid., para. 4019 (Cecil Moore, solicitor and registrar of the common pleas).
29 *Memorandum as to state of Ireland*, 1887 (PRO, 30/60/12).
30 See Daniel Crilly, *Jury packing in Ireland* (Dublin, 1887) and E.P.S. Counsel, *Jury packing in Ireland* (Dublin, 1887).

William Ryan, the Tipperary crown solicitor, wrote that 'in Tipperary in cases of an agrarian character it is impossible to get a jury to convict, no matter how clear the evidence may be'. He also added that the 'better class' of jurors frequently asked to be stood aside, 'and, when I stated I would not be justified in doing so, but suggested if they did not answer, I would try not to have them fined, their reply invariably was, that would not do, they had been canvassed and should answer'.[31] It is, however, important to emphasise that such occurrences were generally confined to cases that were in some way connected to political agitation, and were not typical of nineteenth-century jury trials. Despite the types of problems outlined here, the crown persisted with jury trials throughout the 1880s.

CHANGING THE VENUE OF CRIMINAL TRIALS

One way of dealing with the problem of juror intimidation and sympathy with the accused was for the crown to use the stand-by power, as discussed in chapter 10. Another option was to seek to have the venue for the trial changed. At common law, as noted, the general rule was that the trial of any crime should take place in the county where the alleged crime had been committed.[32] In certain circumstances, however, an indictment could be moved from an inferior court up to the court of queen's bench by a writ of *certiorari*,[33] which could order that the issue be tried at bar, by *nisi prius* in another county, or by *nisi prius* in the original county. Until the 1880s, the procedures for securing a change of venue were cumbersome and costly; an accused had no automatic right to apply for such a writ,[34] security for costs had to be given,[35] and certain time limits had to be observed.[36] Unless it was necessary

31 *Balfour papers* (PRO, 30/60/7).

32 See, for example, W. Hawkins, *Treatise of the pleas of the crown*, 2 vols (8th ed., London, 1824), ii, p. 403. Inevitably, numerous exceptions to this rule were developed, and many were put on a statutory footing. See M. O'Shaughnessy, 'The venue for trials, civil and criminal', *J.S.S.I.S.I.*, 4:30 (1865), 193–203 at 195 and Glanville Williams, 'Venue and the ambit of criminal law', *L.Q. Rev.*, 81 (1965), 276–88, 395–421, 518–38.

33 The writ of *certiorari* was issued either out of the court of chancery, the crown side of the court of queen's bench, or the court of common pleas. It was addressed to judges or officers in inferior courts, commanding them to certify or return the records of a case pending before them, to the end that justice might be done. See also A. Fitzherbert, *The new natura brevium* (London, 1677), p. 245. The writ of *certiorari* to remove an indictment from an inferior court rendered all subsequent proceedings in that court void. See Hawkins, *Pleas*, ii, p. 292.

34 A writ of *certiorari* could, however, be obtained as a matter of course by the attorney general on behalf of the crown: Hawkins, *Pleas*, ii, p. 287. A defendant, on the other hand, could not obtain an order for such a writ as a matter of course – he had to state some ground for the application. See rule 28 of the Crown Office (Ireland) Rules, 1891.

35 A party seeking to remove an indictment by *certiorari* had to enter into a recognizance with condition to proceed with the trial, and to pay the costs of the other party in the event that he was unsuccessful. The exceptions to this rule were the attorney general or the prosecutor of a corporate body. See rules 29, 30 and 31 of the Crown Office (Ireland) Rules, 1891.

36 Once the jury had been sworn in, this was considered too late, according to the English case of *R v. North* (1795) 1 Salk 144; 91 E.R. 433.

for the jurors to view the location of the alleged crime,[37] or for the case to be tried by a special jury, an application by a defendant had to be based either on the ground that a fair trial could otherwise not be secured, or on the ground that difficult questions of law were likely to be raised at the trial.

Applications to change the venue of criminal trials were, unsurprisingly, most frequent during times of political turmoil. In response to the rural agitation of the 1830s the Trial of Offences (Ireland) Act, 1833[38] was passed, allowing for the trial of violent offences relating to the tithe agitation by a jury in any adjoining county, or in Dublin. This rested on an assumption that a fair trial was not possible in the agitated counties. In the 1870s, activities of the ribbon movement in the midlands were examined by a parliamentary committee, and several witnesses spoke of changing the venue in order to avoid the ribbon society's influence.[39] Procedures under the Peace Preservation (Ireland) (Amendment) Act, 1870[40] were cumbersome, and consequently the power to have the venue changed was underused.[41] An indictment had to be found at the assizes in a proclaimed county, and then the trial postponed while an application was made to the queen's bench.

It was not only in political or agrarian cases that a change of venue might be sought. High-profile murders arising out of lovers' quarrels or testamentary disputes, for example, aroused considerable local interest, and were fodder for the regional press.[42] Libel cases also saw applications for changes of venue, usually as a result of the high-profile nature of such cases when public figures were involved.[43] Another interesting category of case where changes of venue were deemed necessary were those concerning clerical influence at elections.[44]

The parliamentary committee appointed during the agrarian upheavals of the 1880s to examine Irish jury laws[45] devoted considerable attention to the laws and

37 Before 1871, there could be no view in a criminal case at the assizes without the consent of the prosecutor. The Juries (Ireland) Act, 1871 (34 & 35 Vic., c. 65), s. 11, stated that on the trial of any indictment or information, the court could, at any time after the jurors were sworn and before they gave their verdict, order that they conduct a viewing. The procedures for views in criminal cases were quite distinct from the procedures in civil actions.

38 3 & 4 Will. IV, c. 79. Also known as the Change of Venue Act, this temporary measure expired in 1834.

39 *Report on Westmeath*, HC 1871 (147) xiii, 547, paras 1652–3 (George Augustus Rochford Boyd, a Westmeath grand juror); paras 453–4 (George Talbot, a Westmeath R.M.); and para. 1038 (William Morris Reade, a Westmeath R.M.).

40 33 Vic., c. 9, s. 29.

41 *Report on Westmeath*, 1871, paras 2485–7 (Robert Julian, crown solicitor for Westmeath and King's County).

42 E.g. *R v. Fay* (1872) I.R. 6 C.L. 436, which concerned Fay's alleged murder of his pregnant lover; *R v. McEneany* (1878) 14 Cox C.C. 87; 2 L.R. Ir. 236, concerning the prisoner's alleged murder of his own brother; see *Northern Standard*, 25 Aug., 15 Sept. 1877, *Meath Herald*, 15, 22 Sept. 1877, 15 June 1878; and the *Belfast Newsletter*, 20 Dec. 1877.

43 E.g. *R (Lord Lucan) v. Cavendish* (1847) 2 Cox C.C. 175; 10 Ir. L.R. 536, and *R (Bridge) v. Casey* (1877) 13 Cox C.C. 614.

44 E.g. *R v. Conway* (1858) 7 Ir. C.L.R. 507 and *R v. Duggan* (1873) I.R. 7 C.L. 94.

45 *Hansard 3*, cclxi, 1033 (23 May 1881) (HL) (marquess of Lansdowne).

procedures relating to changing the venue in criminal cases. Some witnesses who testified before the committee felt that there ought to be a simpler mechanism for having the venue changed in cases of 'local excitement'.[46] It was generally felt that existing procedures were insufficient,[47] and that some sort of alternative would have to be introduced. Justices Lawson and Fitzgerald were both highly critical of the procedures associated with securing a change of venue[48] with the latter noting that 'the defendant in a criminal case is not very likely to be a monied man',[49] that 'the expense of what we call change of venue is very great',[50] and that controversial trials ought to be moved as far away from the original county as possible.[51] While some went so far as to suggest trying controversial agrarian trials in England,[52] others considered it sufficient to move such cases from the south and west to Ulster,[53] away from the influence of the Land League, 'because in the north of Ireland … you find in the jury box men of every shade and opinion'.[54] Others argued against what they perceived to be the folly and inherent unfairness of such an extreme step, pointing out that this would 'cause a great amount of dissatisfaction'.[55] An R.M. from Munster saw the procedure as essentially pointless:

> The revolution in Ireland is pretty well general now, except in those counties which we may call the Protestant counties, where Orangism has a considerable footing; it would certainly look like an unfair thing to take a so-called nationalist, and put him up to be tried by a jury of Protestants, many of whom, no doubt, would be Orangemen; unless you did that, I do not see where you would take him to.[56]

It was suggested by two members of the Irish bench that temporary suspension of trial by jury would be preferable to some of the more extreme suggestions put to the committee,[57] whose eventual recommendation was that 'in all crimes of a political or agrarian complexion it is desirable to offer every facility for the removal of the trials whenever the circumstances of the locality appear to call for such a step …'[58] In the house of lords, the marquess of Lansdowne later highlighted the need for drastic measures and observed that:

46 For example, *Report on Irish jury laws*, 1881, paras 3387, 3396 (Robert Ferguson, QC, chairman of the west riding of Co. Cork).
47 George Bolton, Tipperary crown solicitor, ibid., para. 3899, said the current system entailed 'great expense and waste of time'.
48 Ibid., paras 4059, 1456, 1350, 4199. 49 Ibid., para. 4205.
50 Ibid., para. 4207. The additional expense related mainly to witnesses.
51 Ibid., para. 3446 (John Chute Neligan, QC, chairman of Meath, Westmeath, King's County and Longford).
52 Ibid., para. 926 (Stephen Huggard, clerk of the peace for Kerry), and para. 265 (Henry Arthur Blake, a Galway R.M.).
53 Ibid., para. 2146 (O'Hagan), and para. 4019 (Moore). 54 Ibid., para. 167 (Blake).
55 Ibid., para. 3664 (William O'Connor Morris, Kerry quarter sessions chairman and county court judge). 56 Ibid., para. 3197 (Clifford Lloyd, a Cork and Limerick R.M.).
57 Ibid., para. 3665 (Morris), and para. 4212 (Fitzgerald). 58 Ibid., p. ix.

> as miscarriages of justice were often owing to local and social influences, these influences might be avoided by transferring the trial, in all cases where such influences might be expected to operate, to places beyond the reach of such influences.[59]

The Prevention of Crime (Ireland) Act, 1882,[60] discussed earlier, provided, inter alia, for the trial of certain offences by special juries and the removal of trials to Dublin. The first of these cases, sent from Kerry,[61] Cork,[62] Westmeath[63] and Galway,[64] were tried in August 1882 before Lawson J. at a crowded Green Street courthouse.[65] He began with the trial of five men from Kerry, charged with unlawful assembly,[66] and the attorney general observed that '[u]nhappily the condition of Ireland for some time past had been such that, whether from terrorism or sympathy, local juries had not been equal to the strain put upon them of deciding impartially between the crown and prisoners charged with offences'.[67] When it came to sentencing, Lawson J. was clear about his view of the change of venue. Noting the difficulty with securing convictions for similar cases in Kerry, he added that 'there never was a case in which a public officer exercised a sounder discretion than the attorney-general did in bringing you for trial before a jury who neither sympathise with you nor have any fear of the miserable combination in which you embarked'.[68] The defendants were found guilty.[69]

The National League replaced the Land League in October 1882 and agrarian agitation escalated during the late 1880s, with the launch of the Plan of Campaign in 1886.[70] The plan involved tenants offering to pay landlords reduced rents, and, if landlords did not cooperate, refusing to pay any rent at all. This led to widespread evictions. In a speech near Rosslea in January 1887, John Dillon referred to this as 'a policy which no Irish jury will convict us for adopting'.[71] While the plan was successful on a number of estates, some landlords held out against the rent reductions, famously the marquess of Clanricarde in Co. Galway. Opposition to evictions on his Woodford estate in Galway led to a number of controversial trials under the 1887 act, the venue of which was moved to Sligo.[72]

59 *Hansard 3*, cclxviii, 435–8 (31 Mar. 1882) (HL). 60 45 & 46 Vic., c. 25, s. 6(2).
61 *R v. O'Connor and others, Freeman's Journal*, 11 Aug. 1882.
62 *R v. Bryan, Kinsella and Duggan, Freeman's Journal*, 15 Aug. 1882.
63 *R v. Kenny, Freeman's Journal*, 15 Aug. 1882.
64 *R v. Walsh, Freeman's Journal*, 4 May 1881. Referred to as the Letterfrack murder case.
65 *Freeman's Journal*, 11 Aug. 1882. 66 *R v. O'Connor and others, Freeman's Journal*, 11 Aug. 1882.
67 Ibid. 68 *Freeman's Journal*, 15 Aug. 1882. 69 See p. 152.
70 See p. 60, L.M. Geary, *The Plan of Campaign, 1886–1891* (Cork, 1986) and F.S.L. Lyons, *Ireland since the Famine* (Dublin, 1985), pp 181–7. 71 *The Times*, 12 Jan. 1887.
72 These were the Sligo trials referred to on p. 160. See E.C. Hamilton, *The Woodford evictions: report submitted to the committee of the Property Defence Association at their meeting on Thursday, the 21st Oct., 1886* (Dublin, 1886); E.P.S. Counsel, *Jury packing* (2nd ed., Dublin, 1887), p. 9; R.B. O'Brien, *Dublin Castle and the Irish people* (2nd ed., London, 1912), pp 131–2; and 'Observations made by the lord chief baron, previous to sentencing the prisoners found guilty of willfully obstructing the sheriff in the execution of his duty' in Anon., *Judgments of the superior courts in*

Tenants who took over farms where evictions had taken place were known as land-grabbers and were ostracised by the community. This system of boycotting was criminalised by the Criminal Law and Procedure (Ireland) Act, 1887.[73] This also provided for summary trials[74] for certain offences relating to boycotting, or 'taking part in criminal conspiracy to compel or induce others not to fulfil their legal obligations, or not to let, hire, use or occupy any land, or not to hire any person or persons in the ordinary course of trade'.[75] Defendants could also be summarily tried for participating in riots or unlawful assemblies. Under section 3, defendants in proclaimed districts could be tried by special juries. The propertied men who sat on such juries were considered less likely to sympathise with the National League's cause. The attorney general could also seek a change of venue if it appeared to him that a fair and impartial trial could not be had in the proclaimed county where the indictment was found.[76]

CHANGE OF VENUE IN CIVIL ACTIONS

What made change of venue in civil cases[77] distinctive was that there existed until 1877 a difference between local and transitory actions.[78] The two can broadly be categorised as real and personal actions.[79] In local actions, the venue had to be laid

Ireland in cases under the Criminal Law and Procedure (Ireland) Act 1887, and others (Dublin, 1889), pp 23–30. See also *Hansard 3*, cccx, 387–9 (1 Feb. 1887) (HC); ibid., 896–7 (8 Feb. 1887) (HC); ibid., 1389–90 (14 Feb. 1887) (HC); and Anon., 'Directing jurors to standby in criminal prosecutions', *I.L.T. & S.J.*, 21 (1887), 72.

73 50 & 51 Vic., c. 20. Also known as the Crimes Act, 1887. *Hansard 3*, cccxiii, 88–182 (31 Mar. 1887) (HC); ibid., 245–345 (1 Apr. 1887) (HC).

74 S. 11 provided that in Dublin, the trial was to take place before a divisional justice; elsewhere, before two R.M.s.

75 S. 2(1). Prosecutions under this legislation were widely reported in the press. E.g. *Freeman's Journal*, 8 Sept. 1887; *Kerry Evening Post*, 13, 14 Sept. 1887; *Freeman's Journal*, 28 Oct. 1887; *The Nation*, 29 Oct. 1887; *Kerry Sentinel*, 4 Nov. 1887; *Irish Examiner*, 5 Nov. 1887; *Dundalk Democrat*, 12 Nov. 1887; and *Irish Examiner*, 17 Dec. 1887.

76 S. 4. See *O'Brien v. The queen* (1890) 26 L.R. Ir. 451.

77 There were rules as to the time at which a motion to change the venue could be made (see Huband, *Treatise*, pp 425–31), costs (ibid., pp 449–51), and as to the form of the supporting affidavit (ibid., pp 431–4). Judges and attorneys enjoyed the privilege of laying and retaining the venue: see *Bishop of Kilmore v. Lord Plunket* (1829) 2 Law Rec. (o.s.) 256. The conduct of the parties could be taken into account in deciding whether to grant a change of venue: *Wilson v. Thompson* (1856) 1 Ir. Jur. (n.s.) 187. There were rules about changing the venue to a more limited jurisdiction (see *Reid v. Mangan* (1856) 1 Ir. Jur. (n.s.) 132), and rules about changing to an adjoining county: see *McDermott v. Lord Mayor of Dublin* (1830) 3 Law Rec. (o.s.) 315. There were also rules governing who could apply for a change of venue: see Huband, *Treatise*, pp 440–6.

78 See O'Shaughnessy, *The venue for trials*, pp 194–5. After 1877 the distinction between local and transitory actions was relevant only in cases where the cause of action arose abroad. Where a cause of action arising in another jurisdiction was local in nature, it could not be tried in Ireland: Supreme Court of Judicature Act, 1877 (40 & 41 Vic., c. 57), s. 33.

79 Gilbert noted that '[o]riginally every fact was laid in the place where it was really done: and

in the place where the cause of action arose, while in transitory actions, the plaintiff was free to choose his own venue. Until the fourteenth century, this system was subject to extensive abuse; for example, a plaintiff in a transitory action would lay his venue at a considerable distance from the place where the action arose, thus forcing the defendant to travel, with his witnesses, across the country. Legislation in 1382 put a stop to such practices,[80] and was intended to 'compel the suing out of all writs arising upon contract in the very county where the contract arose, by ordaining that if the writ was of one county and the plaintiff of another, the writ should be quashed'.[81] However, this statute did not expressly forbid the writ to be sued in a foreign county, and to remedy this, the Regulation of Attornies Act, 1404 compelled all attorneys to swear against doing so.[82] Until the mid-nineteenth century, a plaintiff in a civil action could lay the venue in the county of his choice, but the defendant retained the right to have the venue changed to the county where the cause of action occurred.

By the mid-seventeenth century[83] this was secured by means of motion and affidavit.[84] Even in local actions, the court could order a change of venue if it were shown that a fair trial could not be had in the place where the cause of action arose. This remained the practice until an English rule of 1853 provided that to effect a change of venue, either a special order of the court or the consent of the parties was necessary.[85]

The Common Law Procedure Amendment Act (Ireland), 1853[86] allowed the venue in civil actions to be laid 'in any county which the plaintiff thinks proper',[87] and provided that the court would permit a change of venue 'on special grounds

therefore the written contracts bore date at a certain place, and the trespasses on land were in their nature local': G. Gilbert, *The history and practice of civil actions, particularly in the court of common pleas* (2nd ed., London, 1761), pp 83–93. Gilbert also describes how the demise of the system of frankpledge brought about the distinction between local and transitory actions.

80 The Trial of Writs of Debt Act, 1382 (6 Rich. II, stat. 1, c. 2).

81 *Santler v. Heard* (1828) 2 Black. W. 1031; 96 E.R. 605.

82 (1402) 4 Hen. IV, c. 18. Repealed by the Statute Law (Ireland) Revision Act, 1872 (35 & 36 Vic., c. 98).

83 The Arrests of Judgment Prevention Act, 1665 (17 & 18 Cha. II, c. 12), s. 1. The English equivalent was the Statute of Jeofails 1665 (16 & 17 Cha. II, c. 8).

84 This was considerably more straightforward than the writ of *certiorari*. After this act, a judgment would not be reversed on the ground that the venue was incorrect. The Special Juries and Trials (Ireland) Act, 1825 (6 Geo. IV, c. 51), s. 2, enabled the court to change the venue in local actions to an adjoining county. The Advancement of Justice (Ireland) Act, 1840 (3 & 4 Vic., c. 105), s. 47, provided that local actions in the superior courts could, on the application of either party, be ordered to be tried in a different county. This corresponded with the Civil Procedure Act, 1833(3 & 4 Will. IV, c. 42), s. 22.

85 Rule 18 of 1853 made under the authority of the Common Law Procedure Act, 1852. Barry L.J. noted in *Hegarty v. Mackay* (1891) 28 L.R. Ir. 338 that the question as to which practice ought to be adopted in consequence of this rule was referred to a committee of judges.

86 16 & 17 Vic., c. 113, s. 62.

87 S. 196 related to actions of ejectment, and stated: 'The venue shall be laid in the county in which the lands are situated, but the court or a judge may, on the application of either party, order that the trial shall take place in any county or place other than that in which the venue is laid'.

only, and not merely because the cause of action accrued in any particular place or county'.[88] This provision also allowed the court or a judge to order that the venue be changed on grounds of convenience. The defendant no longer enjoyed the privilege of having the venue changed to the place where the cause of action arose. The changes wrought by the 1853 act were not without their detractors.[89] Although their purpose was to 'simplify and amend' superior court procedure, to render it 'less dilatory and expensive', and to rid it of technicalities that could get in the way of substantive justice,[90] in reality they conferred an unfair advantage on plaintiffs, particularly where there was an imbalance of wealth between the parties.[91]

The ills of the 1853 act were remedied by the Supreme Court of Judicature Act (Ireland), 1877.[92] This provided that the plaintiff could name 'the county or place in which he proposes that the cause shall be tried', but that a judge could 'direct the same to be tried in any other county or place'. The provision went on to state that 'so far as shall be reasonably consistent with the convenient and speedy discharge of business,[93] every issue and question of fact to be submitted to a jury shall be tried in the county or place where the cause of action shall have arisen'. This was a popular move amongst the judiciary. The unambiguous terms of the provision meant that the plaintiff no longer enjoyed an arbitrary right to change the venue and 'restore[d], in a considerable degree, the old common-law right of the defendant to have certain actions tried in the same place where the cause of action arose, and thus to abolish the mischief caused by the act of 1853'.[94] This brought Irish practice into line with that in England, and Fitzgerald J. in the queen's bench commented that it had effectively done away with the rules regulating venue.[95] The court could now order that an action be tried before a jury in the county where it arose, unless the interests of justice demanded that it be tried elsewhere. All actions, including real actions, were now treated as though they were transitory.[96]

88 See *Morrissey v. Connell* (1856) 1 Ir. Jur. (n.s.) 174, where Monahan J. discussed the precise meaning of the new legislation.

89 E.g. *Tute v. Matthew* (1866) 1 I.L.T. & S.J., 646; *Hegarty v. Mackay* (1891) 28 L.R. Ir. 338, n. 2. Apparently, however, the bill had been supported by both the bench and the bar. *Hansard 3*, cxxix, 796 (26 July 1853) (HL) (Lord Brougham).

90 *Hansard 3*, cxxiii, 257 (19 Nov. 1852).

91 O'Shaughnessy, *The venue for trials*, p. 197.

92 40 & 41 Vic., c. 57, s. 33.

93 Barry J. in *Lynch v. Burke* (1878) 12 I.L.T. & S.J., 202, interpreted this as, 'I do not think that by the "speedy discharge of business" is meant the particular case, but the general business of the country.' See also *Mooney v. Smith* (1883) 17 I.L.T.R. 110, *Bell v. Alexander* (1890) 24 I.L.T.R. 77, and *Brady v. Royal Insurance Co.* (1879) 13 I.L.T. & S.J., 372.

94 *Hegarty v. Mackay* (1891) 28 L.R. Ir. 338. Barry L.J.'s interpretation of s. 33 was subsequently relied upon: see *McConchy v. Madden* (1890) 28 L.R. Ir. 338.

95 *Cussen v. Moloney* (1878) 2 L.R. Ir. 188.

96 See in this regard *McIlwee v. Money* (1878) 12 I.L.T. & S.J., 89, *Lynch v. Burke* (1878) 12 I.L.T. & S.J., 202, *Fox v. Fenton* (1878) 12 I.L.T.R. 64, *Brady v. Royal Insurance Co.* (1879) 13 I.L.T. & S.J., 372 and *Chambers v. Crawford* (1887) 21 I.L.T.R. 14.

There were several circumstances under which the venue of a civil case could be changed. The first was the 'speedy discharge of business',[97] which was expressly recognised in section 33 of the 1877 act.[98] Matters for consideration included the residence of witnesses,[99] as well as whether a witness was poor,[100] dying or about to travel abroad.[101] Other factors included the poverty of the party or parties,[102] the necessity of conducting a view, and the inconvenience of bringing public officers from their place of work.[103] Jellet noted in 1860 that the motion must show 'the existence of a preponderance of convenience'.[104] As with criminal trials, a common reason for seeking a change of venue for a civil trial was the existence of local prejudice. Albeit not limited to religious or political differences, these were key factors in determining whether a fair trial could be had in the neighbourhood where the dispute arose. Palles C.B. declared in *O'Connell v. Arnott*[105] that there was 'no hard and fast line' in determining whether to grant a change of venue, and the main question was where, under the circumstances, the fairest trial could be had. Disputes over property often generated a considerable amount of local agitation, and litigation could be protracted and bitter. Such disputes were exacerbated when one of the parties was thought to exercise considerable or undue influence amongst the local jurors.[106] Influence with local jurors could result from

97 For example, see *Jennings v. Lindsey* (1853) 6 Ir. Jur. (o.s.) 81, *Guardians of the Youghal Union v. Atkinson* (1859) 9 I.C.L.R., app. xvii, and *Frazer v. Edwards* (1856) 5 I.C.L.R. 540.

98 The 'speedy discharge of business' was relied upon as a ground for having the venue changed before the Supreme Court of Judicature (Ireland) Act, 1877 (40 & 41 Vic., c. 57), in cases where convenience demanded it. See, for example, *Jennings v. Lindsey* (1853) 6 Ir. Jur. (o.s.) 81, *Guardians of the Youghal Union v. Atkinson* (1859) 9 I.C.L.R. app xvii, and *Frazer v. Edwards* (1856) 5 I.C.L.R. 540. Cases where a change of venue was granted on this ground after the Judicature Act were *Brady v. Royal Insurance Co.* (1879) 13 I.L.T. & S.J., 372; *Mooney v. Smith* (1883) 17 I.L.T.R. 110; and *Bell v. Alexander* (1890) 24 I.L.T.R. 77.

99 See *Geary v. Warren* (1843) 5 Ir. L.R. 425; *Shegog v. Murphy* (1844) 7 Ir. L.R. 550; *Watson v. Keneally* (1841) 3 Ir. L.R. 214; *Lorimer v. McElrath* (1843) 5 Ir. L.R. 588; *Chambers v. Crawford* (1887) 21 I.L.T.R. 14; *McLoughlin v. Royal Exchange Assurance Co.* (1844) 9 Ir. L.R. 510; *Blest v. Neil* (1848) 12 Ir. L.R. 518; *Doyle v. Hammond* (1854) 6 Ir. Jur. (o.s.) 306; *Morrissey v. Connell* (1856) 1 Ir. Jur. (n.s.) 174; *Fleming v. Fleming, In the goods of Thring* (1878) I.R. 7 Eq. 409, and *Fox v. Fenton* (1878) 12 I.L.T.R. 64.

100 See *Reid v. Mangan* (1856) 1 Ir. Jur. (n.s.) 132.

101 See the English cases of *Ross v. Napier* (1860) 30 L.J. Exch. 2 and *Channon v. Parkhouse* (1860) 13 C.B. (n.s.) 341; 143 E.R. 136.

102 E.g. *McKeown v. Stewart* (1856) 1 Ir. Jur. (n.s.) 127; *Bumfort v. Grueler* (1861) 6 Ir. Jur. (n.s.) 392; *McDermott v. Jameson* (1855) 1 Ir. Jur. (n.s.) 51; and *Banks v. O'Sullivan* (1856) 2 Ir. Jur. (n.s.) 99.

103 See *Allen v. Cork and Bandon Railway Co.* (1856) 1 Ir. Jur. (n.s.) 139; *Cronin v. Purcell* (1855) 1 Ir. Jur. (n.s.) 10; *Wilson v. Thompson* (1856) 1 Ir. Jur. (n.s.) 187; and *Walsh v. Hopkins* (1867) 1 I.L.T.R. 26.

104 H.P. Jellett, *An outline of the practice of the superior courts of common law in Ireland in personal actions and ejectment* (Dublin, 1865), pp 32–3. In *Rutledge v. Irwin* (1848) Bl. D. & O. 229, an application was made to change the venue to Sligo, where the cause of action arose, and where most of the witnesses resided.

105 (1881) 15 I.L.T. & S.J., 311.

106 E.g. *Lessee of the commissioners of the town of Enniskillen v. Earl of Enniskillen* (1847) 12 Ir. L.R. 36; *Boyse v. Smith* (1840) 12 Ir. L.R. 366; *Lessee Smith v. Casual Ejector and Lessee Smith v.*

one party's standing within the community,[107] political allegiances,[108] or the fact that while one party was well-known locally, the other was a stranger.[109] Other civil cases where changes of venue were sought because of local prejudice were testamentary disputes, actions for unjust imprisonment, cases concerning local elections, cases concerning city markets and disputes over the payment of tithes.[110] Where religious or political sentiment ran high, the courts tended to allow the venue to be changed.[111] Libel actions against newspapers also frequently saw change-of-venue applications because of the influence of local and regional papers in their areas of circulation. If newspapers continued to publish details of the case, this strengthened the application for the change of venue. In other cases, the very fact of the libellous article could be considered sufficient evidence that the jurors of the county would be partisan.[112] High-profile examples of such libel actions were *Ryder v. Burke*,[113] an action taken by an Anglican clergyman against the proprietor of the *Galway Mercury*, and *Gallagher v. Cavendish*,[114] an action taken by a Roman Catholic clergyman against the proprietor of the *Mayo Telegraph*. The former concerned allegations that a Catholic priest had impregnated his young housekeeper, while the latter concerned a highly contested election of the guardians of the Castlebar Union in 1841.

CONCLUSION

We saw in previous chapters that jury service could be time-consuming, irritating, thankless and unpaid; as this chapter demonstrates, it could also be dangerous.

Nangle (1841) 1 Leg. Rep. 302; and *Shaughnessy v. Lambert* (1839) 2 Jebb & S. 421.

107 E.g. *Lessee of the commissioners of the town of Enniskillen v. Earl of Enniskillen* (1847) 12 Ir. L.R. 36 and *Kelly v. Londonderry & Enniskillen Railway Co.* (1856) 3 Ir. Jur. (n.s.) 392.

108 E.g. *Lessee of Dowdall v. Dowdall* (1827–28) 1 Ir. Law Rec. 355 KB.

109 E.g. *Lessee of Jackson v. Lodge* (1839) 1 Ir. L.R. 161. Other real actions where a change of venue was sought were *Cussen v. Moloney* (1878) 2 L.R. Ir. 188 and *Kilkenny Gas Co. v. Somerville* (1878) 2 L.R. Ir. 192.

110 For testamentary disputes see, e.g., *Chambers v. Crawford* (1887) 21 I.L.T.R. 14 and *Fleming v. Fleming, In the goods of Thring* (1873) I.R. 7 Eq. 409. The judge in the latter case intimated that it would be advantageous for the witnesses to be known by the jurors. For unjust imprisonment see, e.g., *Kelly v. Londonderry & Enniskillen Railway Co.* (1856) 3 Ir. Jur. (n.s.) 392 and *Londonderry Standard*, 7 May, 16 July 1857 and *Stewart v. Lynar* (1838) 1 Ir. L.R. 199; for local elections see, e.g., *Dowling v. Sadlier* (1854) 3 I.C.L.R. 603; for city markets see, e.g., *Shea v. Adams* (1867) 1 I.C.L.R. 450 and *McDermott v. Lord Mayor, etc., of Dublin* (1830) 3 Law Rec. (o.s.) 315; for disputes concerning payment of tithes see, e.g., *Meara v. Blake* (1835) 4 Law Rec. (o.s.) 62. This was reported anonymously, but Huband, *Treatise*, p. 415, gives the parties' names.

111 E.g. *Meara v. Blake* (1835) 4 Law Rec. (o.s.) 62 and *Stewart v. Lynar* (1838) 1 Ir. L.R. 199. The 1874 committee found that there was a strong likelihood of jurors being unable to reach agreement where a case had a religious or political slant: *Report on the Irish jury system*, HC 1874 (244) ix, 557, para. 2396.

112 E.g. *Kelly v. Colhoun and others* (1899) 33 I.L.T.R. 43.

113 (1847) 10 Ir. L.R. 474.

114 (1841) 3 Ir. L.R. 375.

Jurors faced the possibility of physical violence, damage to their property, intimidation and boycotting. However, such extremes were generally limited to specific periods of rural unrest in particular parts of the country, and were not generally representative of jury trials in the nineteenth century. While the political intimidation of jurors could be a serious problem for the effective and fair trial of civil actions and criminal offences, it is clear that this was not the only factor that led to motions for changes of venue. Typical small-town squabbles and rivalries, and, of course, the frailty of human nature, were all factors that led to cases being tried in different locations.

CHAPTER TWELVE

Jurors as active participants

WHILE THE JURY IN THE COMMON-LAW world has generally come to be associated with passivity,[1] this chapter considers the relatively active role played by many juries in late-eighteenth- and nineteenth-century trials.[2] In many cases they did more than simply sit silently in the jury box listening to testimony. The market jury, of course, played a very active role in inspecting and patrolling marketplaces, seizing suspect or sub-standard foodstuffs and apprehending those responsible. Wide-streets juries had to visit premises that were to be the subject of purchase orders, examine title deeds and complex, esoteric documentation, interview relevant people and come up with valuations for the properties. Juries *de ventre inspeciendo* had to physically examine and question women who claimed to be pregnant. Coroners' juries did not simply hear testimony from witnesses as to probable causes of death; they actually had to be present when the body was being examined and witness its state for themselves. Trial juries could also play an active role. This varied from travelling to the location of an alleged offence in advance of a criminal trial in order to better understand the evidence, to asking questions of lawyers and cross-examining witnesses during trial. It is argued that Irish juries did not evolve into passive recipients of testimony until later than writers such as Langbein have suggested in relation to English jurors.

THE VIEW

The first example of jurors taking active part in proceedings is 'the view'. From the twelfth century, juries in all real actions were ordered to view lands that were the subject of dispute prior to their appearing in court. The procedure appears to have had its roots in the medieval 'perambulation', which was a mechanism to determine

1 Note, however, the 'active jury reform movements' evident in the United States from the 1990s on. See, e.g., Albert Dzur, *Punishment, participatory democracy and the jury* (Oxford, 2012), pp 126–8; J.S. Berkowitz, 'Breaking the silence: should jurors be allowed to question witnesses during trial?', *Vanderbilt L. Rev.*, 44 (1991), 117–48; B.M. Dann, '"Learning lessons" and "speaking rights": creating educated and democratic juries', *Indiana L.J.*, 68 (1993), 1229–79; and Akhil Reed Amar, 'Reinventing juries: ten suggested reforms', *University College Davis L. Rev.*, 28 (1995), 1169–94.

2 For further discussion of the active role of jurors, see Niamh Howlin, 'Irish jurors: passive observers or active participants?', *J. Leg. Hist.*, 35:2 (2014), 143–71.

the boundaries of an estate by walking around its perimeter.[3] The view was an integral part of the writ of *novel disseisin*,[4] and could also be deemed necessary in actions of trespass and nuisance.[5] By the early thirteenth century, jurors were required to 'have a view' in actions of waste.[6] It was not necessary in every case to have the jury view the disputed lands in their entirety; it depended on whether the action was one of waste, *novel disseisin* or nuisance. Viner pointed out that every acre need not be shown; the person entrusted with the task of showing the land to the jurors, known as the shower, could 'shew the field and that he claims so many acres in that field, and another field and so on'.[7]

3 It was used as 'a technique to fix the exact dimensions of an estate on the occasion of a donation, a foundation or a litigation' or to determine disputed boundaries: C. Flower (ed.), *Introduction to the curia regis rolls, AD 1199–1230* (London, 1943), p. 428. See also R.C. Van Caenegem, *Royal writs in England from the conquest to Glanvill* (London, 1958–9), p. 77. Van Caenegem comments that while this was obviously a 'very concrete and visual' method for determining boundaries, it also appears that the perambulators themselves could be summoned to settle any subsequent disputes, if still alive. He further observes that 'the technique of the perambulation appeared in name from the late eleventh century onwards', and appears to have been a common, everyday practice, well rooted in popular tradition. Towards the middle of the twelfth century, the procedures in many respects came to resemble – albeit loosely – the viewing by a jury. For example, in many cases the number of perambulators grew from two or three individuals in early years, to twelve. Further, there is evidence of a case from 1127 cited in R.C. Van Caenegem, *English lawsuits from William I to Richard I* (London, 1990–1), i, p. 249, where the perambulation was expressly linked to a sworn verdict 'of honest men of the hundred'. He also cites a case some sixty years later where parties agreed to accept the outcome of a perambulation, because it would be on oath.

4 Seisin was 'the obvious, peaceful and presumably lawful enjoyment of a thing, an office or a status and, among other things, of land … Seisin was the central point of land law. It was the basis of economic life': Van Caenegem, *Royal writs*, p. 262. To lose one's land was to be disseised of the tenement, and the action of *novel disseisin* was a quick and efficient means of judicial redress offered by the king's justices. See Flower, *Curia regis*, p. 165.

5 J. Impey, *The new instructor clericalis* (4th ed., London, 1788), p. 201. It is clear that in nuisance cases, considerable importance attached to the view, and jurors were obliged to thoroughly inspect the entire holding: F.M. Nichols, *Britton: an English translation and notes* (Washington, D.C., 1901), p. 118.

6 Waste was an action available to be taken against a life tenant, for causing damage to the land that reduced its value; see A. Lyall, *Land law in Ireland* (3rd ed., Dublin, 2010), pp 268–70. The Statute of Gloucester 1278 (6 Ed. I, c. 5) enacted that 'he which shall be attainted of wast[e] … shall recompense thrice so much as the wast[e] shall be taxed at'. Under this act, a remedy for an action of waste included forfeiture of the land in question. W. Huband, *A practical treatise on the law relating to the grand jury in criminal cases, the petty jury and the coroner's jury* (rev. ed., Dublin, 1911), p. 101, considered it likely that, had it not previously existed, the necessity of a view in these cases would have been created by this statute. W. Blackstone, *Commentaries on the laws of England*, 4 vols (17th ed., London, 1830), iii, p. 227, noted that in such cases, the sheriff was to take a jury of twelve men, and 'go in person to the place alleged to be wasted, and there inquire of the waste done, and the damages; and make a return or report of the same to the court, upon which the judgement is founded'.

7 C. Viner, *A general abridgement of law and equity*, 24 vols (2nd ed., London, 1791), xxi, p. 566. If a man were in fear of his life, it sufficed to bring the jurors to some place from which they could view the land, without actually stepping foot on it. One proviso was that 'if the jurors come near to the land, but there is a hill between them and the land, so that they cannot see it, yet the law adjudges

By the eighteenth century views were generally carried out with one object in mind: if the jurors viewed lands that were the subject of dispute before reaching their verdict, they were more likely to reach an informed and just verdict. Furthermore, in cases of complex or technical evidence, a view could provide the jurors with a better understanding of the facts in issue. Wide-streets juries always had to view properties that were the subject of valuation, and were often provided with detailed maps and plans.[8] Although originally views were granted in cases involving disputes over the ownership of land,[9] in the nineteenth century they were also sought in cases involving disputes over boundaries, cases involving construction or repairs, and insurance claims.[10] The 1833 act explicitly stated that a judge could order a view in any civil or criminal case where it was 'proper and necessary' to ensure jurors' 'better understanding the evidence'.[11] Although less commonly used in criminal cases than in civil actions, it was not unheard of for a prosecutor or defendant in a criminal case to request a view of the locality where an alleged crime was committed.[12] The Juries Act (Ireland), 1871[13] stated that the court in a criminal trial could, at any time after the jurors were sworn and before they gave their verdict, order that they have a view.

this a sufficient view'. This appears to defeat the purpose of ordering the view, and indicates that by the late eighteenth century, the view had been somewhat alienated from the function for which it was conceived.

8 See pp 65–6.

9 A 1285 statute provided 'that from henceforth view shall not be granted but in case when view of land is necessary'. Waste Act, 1285 (13 Ed. I, c. 14). See Van Caenegem, *English lawsuits*, i, pp 278, 630, 672. Viner, *General abridgement*, xxi, pp 552–4, lists thirty-five writs and actions where a view was considered necessary. See also Anon., *The complete juryman: or, a compendium of the laws relating to jurors* (Dublin, 1774), pp 76–8.

10 Boundary disputes: see, e.g., *Loughnan v. Dempsey* (1860) 6 Ir. Jur. (n.s.) 86, which concerned a question as to the title of certain premises abutting one another, and Hughes B. considered a view necessary for the jurors. See also *Barbour v. McCleery* (1845) 3 Cr. & Dix C.C. 390 and *R v. Magill* (1859) 8 I.C.L.R. app. 62. Construction disputes: see, e.g., *Walsh v. Murray* (1827) 1 Hud. & Br. 10. Insurance claims: see, e.g., *McDonnell v. Carr* (1832) Hayes 375, an action on a fire-insurance policy. An application was made to have the venue changed from Limerick to Cork, the scene of the fire, in order that a view might be facilitated. Counsel for the plaintiff objected, asking, '[i]f the premises have been burnt, what is there for the jurors to view?' Joy C.B. commented that a view was 'essential' in such a case, and Foster J. pointed out that 'notwithstanding the destruction of the premises, there may still be enough remaining, to shew that the fire broke out in two or three places at once; and thus lead to the proof of the premises having been maliciously burnt by the plaintiff himself'.

11 3 & 4 Will. IV, c. 91 , s. 16. E.g. in *R v. Magill* (1858) 8 I.C.L.R., app., p. lxii, a prosecution for the obstruction of certain paths near Belfast's Cave Hill. Lefroy C.J. was of the opinion that a view of the hill was necessary.

12 E.g. *R v. McNamara* (1878) 4 L.R. Ir. 185 and the English case *R v. Martin and Webb* (1872) L.R. 1 C.C.R. 378. A view was sought by the defendants in the Maamtrasna trials, discussed in chapter 10, but this was refused: Tim Harrington, *The Maamtrasna massacre: impeachment of the trials* (Dublin, 1884), p. iv.

13 34 & 35 Vic., c. 65, s. 11.

Occasionally a change of venue was ordered to facilitate a view,[14] because a judge had no power to order a sheriff to bring jurors out of their own county for the purpose of a view.[15] Under the Winter Assizes Act, 1876,[16] counties Clare and Kerry, and the cities and counties of Limerick and Cork, were to be joined in 1878 as one winter assizes county, and the assizes were to be held in Cork city. As a result of this rule, the assizes county stretched over a hundred miles from east to west and over two hundred from north to south. *R v. McNamara*[17] illustrates the effect this had on the rules relating to view juries. At his third trial for murder at the Cork winter assize, the defendant sought an order of *certiorari* to remove the indictment to the court of queen's bench, on the ground, inter alia, that it was imperative in the interests of a fair trial, that the jury examine the place and neighbourhood of the alleged murder. Fitzgerald J. pointed out the inconvenience of having the jurors travel over a hundred miles from Cork city to Clare: 'I can well imagine the necessary cloud of Royal Constabulary skirmishers at Mallow, Charleville, Limerick, Ennis and Crisheen, to keep off the outer world.' The expedition would likely be fraught with difficulties: the jury would not be allowed to separate; the journey itself would take two full days; the December weather posed a peril to the jurors' health; the best men in Cork would be likely to evade such an onerous duty; and the tour had to be 'personally conducted', 'under the guidance of the sheriff and accompanied by a number of sworn bailiffs'. In light of these considerations, the view was not granted.

In 1707, legislation had provided that in cases where it seemed 'proper and necessary' that the jurors should have a view, the court could order special writs of *distringas* or *habeas corpus*, which commanded that the sheriff 'have six out of the first twelve of the jurors … at the place in question, some convenient time before the trial, who then and there shall have the matters in question shown to them by two persons'.[18] Literal interpretation of this led to ludicrous situations, such as causes being put off because the viewers were not 6 of the first 12 jurors – despite the fact that 9 or 10 of the jurors may have had the view.[19]

Further legislation throughout the eighteenth century regulated the practice of views.[20] Under the 1735 act, the six jurors who had the view were subject to the

14 E.g. *Loughnan v. Dempsey* (1860) 6 Ir. Jur. (n.s.) 86 (Dublin to Belfast); *Atkinson v. Mills* (1863) 8 Ir. Jur. (n.s.) 153 (Dublin to Kildare). See also the English case of *Hodinott v. Cox* (1807) 8 East. 263; 103 E.R. 344.

15 See the English cases *Stoke v. Robinson* (1889) 6 T.L.R. 31 and *Malins v. Lord Dunraven* (1845) 9 Jur. 690.

16 39 & 40 Vic., c. 57. This act was extended to Ireland by the Supreme Court of Judicature (Ireland) Act, 1877 (40 & 41 Vic., c. 57), s. 63. See p. 40.

17 (1878) 4 L.R. Ir. 185.

18 The Advancement of Justice (Ireland) Act, 1707 (6 Anne, c. 10), s. 8. An identical provision was contained in an English act of the same name (4 Anne, c. 16), s. 8. The sheriff was to certify to the court that the view had been had in the approved manner. See also J. Lilly, *A continuation of the practical register*, 2 vols (London, 1710), ii, pp 400–1.

19 See B.J. Sellon, *The practice of the courts of king's bench and common pleas*, 2 vols (London, 1792), ii, p. 451.

20 Regulation of Juries Act, 1735 (9 Geo. II, c. 3), s. 10.

parties' mutual consent, and were the first men to be sworn on the jury. In the event that the parties could not agree, then either the proper officer of the respective court or the judge before whom the case was to be tried would name the six.[21] Although earlier legislation had provided for the challenge of view jurors,[22] the Juries (Ireland) Act, 1833 provided that where there had been a view, the viewers should not be challenged, because the case could not proceed without the six viewers.[23]

Outside of the carefully prescribed procedures outlined in legislation, jurors occasionally took it upon themselves to view premises that were the subject of dispute. For example, in *Cavendish v. Hope Assurance Company*,[24] involving insurance cover for a fire at the plaintiff's home, a number of jurors made an unannounced visit to the house, believing it to be their 'duty to investigate every circumstance with the most scrupulous attention, and to acquire every possible information'.[25] They threatened Cavendish's gatekeeper until he granted them admittance,[26] and during their inspection of the house, one juror went so far as to use a saw to remove a piece of board from the floor of the library.[27] In *Tyrrell v. Bristow*,[28] two or three jurors called to the plaintiff's house on a Sunday in the middle of the trial. With the plaintiff, they examined the premises that were the subject of the dispute, and chatted with him about the case. The plaintiff admitted that they had called, but denied having spoken about the dispute. Serjeant O'Loghlen argued that 'it would be rather a harsh measure to visit the misconduct of the jury, if such it be, upon an innocent plaintiff, who held no communication with the jury, whose conduct he could not control'. The court struck out the verdict for the plaintiff, describing him, however, as 'blameless'. In both cases, the judges were extremely critical of the jurors' actions: in *Tyrell* they were described as 'improper', while in *Cavendish* they were deemed 'extraordinary' and 'unprecedented'.[29]

21 Regulation of Juries Act, 1755 (29 Geo. II, c. 6), s. 7.
22 Regulation of Juries Act, 1739 (13 Geo. II, c. 5), s. 2.
23 3 & 4 Will. IV, s. 17. This provision was identical to the English Jury Act, 1730 (3 Geo. II, c. 25), s. 4. This statute also provided that in any civil or criminal case, where it appeared necessary and proper that a view be had, the party seeking the view was to deposit a sum with the under-sheriff, which was intended to cover the expenses incurred in taking the view. For an example of a view taken by six jurors, see, e.g., *Draft order for a view jury in Clair v. Cochrane*, Belfast sessions, 16 June 1893 (PRONI, Ant/1/1b/1/4/34).
24 John Henry Doyle, *A full report, with notes, of the trial of an action, wherein the hon Frederick Cavendish was plaintiff, and the Hope Assurance Company of London were defendants; held before the right hon John Lord Norbury, chief justice of the common pleas in Ireland, and a special jury* (Dublin, 1813). 25 Ibid., p. 236.
26 Anon., *The judgment pronounced by Mr justice Fletcher, &c., &c., in Cavendish v. Hope Assurance* (1813), p. 13.
27 Letter from Cavendish to Needham (one of the jurors), 4 Nov. 1813, repr. in *Hibernian Journal*, 10 Jan. 1814.
28 (1833) 1 Law Rec. (n.s.) 91.
29 Anon., *The judgment by Fletcher*, p. 13.

The common law commissioners recommended in 1852 that either party to a civil action should be at liberty to apply to a court or judge for an order 'for the inspection by the jury, or by himself or his witnesses, of any premises or chattels the inspection of which may be material to determine the question in dispute'.[30] They also noted that the English Juries Act, 1825[31] – and, by implication, the Juries (Ireland) Act, 1833[32] – confined the view to 'the place in question'. They noted that this was construed so that it applied only to cases of a local nature, and it was suggested that 'numerous other cases might be adduced in which an inspection would be of great advantage, as when the quality or construction of machinery, or the condition or value or identity of goods, is in dispute'.[33] The Juries (Ireland) Act, 1871[34] also referred only to the view of a 'place', but under the rules of the supreme court (Ireland) 1891,[35] a court was empowered to order a view of chattels.[36]

Sometimes a view was deemed unnecessary, and a map or a model sufficed.[37] In *R v. Wright*, for example, one of the trials arising out the Derrymacash affray,[38] the jury was given a map of the locale where the riot and assaults took place.[39] At the trial of Sam Gray, a model of his house was used in addition to a map of the area.[40] In *Cavendish v. Hope Assurance*, a model of the insured house was given to the jury for inspection,[41] and in *R v. Spollen*, a 'very complete and elegant set of models' of Dublin's Broadstone terminus and other buildings were used to assist the jury in determining how a murder had been perpetrated.[42] In *Delany v. United Dublin Tramways Co.*,[43] a model of one of the defendant's horse-drawn tramcars was

30 *Second report on pleading* [C-1626] HC 1852–3, xl, 701, p. 739.
31 6 Geo. IV, c. 50, s. 23. 32 3 & 4 Will. IV, c. 90, s. 17. 33 Ibid.
34 34 & 35 Vic., c. 65, s. 38. 35 Order L, rules 3–5.
36 Rule 4 held that it was lawful for a court, upon the application of any party, to make, upon just terms, 'any order for the detention, preservation or inspection of any property or thing being the subject of such cause or matter or as to which any question may arise therein'. The order could also authorise any persons to 'enter upon or into any land or building in the possession of any party … to authorise any samples to be taken or any observation to be made or experiment to be tried which may be necessary or expedient for the purpose of obtaining full information or evidence'. Rule 5 stated that a court could 'inspect any property or thing' regarding which a question arose in the course of any trial, with or without a jury.
37 In 1881 it was pointed out that an action for the obstruction of light to a building could be tried in the court of chancery by a single judge, guided by a map or a model. However, if a similar action was tried in one of the courts of common law, the jury were obliged to view the building, imposing an unnecessary strain on them: W.H. Dodd, 'Some grievances of jurors', *J.S.S.I.S.I.*, 8 (1879–85), 223–7.
38 See pp 30–3. 39 *Shorthand writers' notes*, HC 1861 (315) lii, 315, p. 75
40 *Freeman's Journal*, 17 Mar. 1843.
41 *Cavendish v. Hope Assurance* (1813). The report also contains a diagram of the house plans, p. 41.
42 *R v. Spollen* (1857), p. 1. See also the English cases of *Attorney general v. Green* (1814) 1 Price 130; 145 E.R. 1375 and *Hodinett v. Cox* (1807) 8 East. 263; 103 E.R. 344.
43 (1891) 30 L.R. Ir. 725. This was an action for damages for injuries sustained by the plaintiff on attempting to mount a moving tram-car while intoxicated. The conductor of the tram had allegedly pushed him from the vehicle, with the result that he was caught up in the machinery and dragged along the ground for some distance.

produced in evidence. This was an exact replica of the machine in question, made to one-twelfth the size of the original, under the supervision of an engineer. The use of maps, models and other visual aids increasingly replaced the view procedure in the late nineteenth and early twentieth century.

ACTIVE PARTICIPATION DURING THE TRIAL

Aside from views, there were other ways in which jurors played a relatively active role in trials, often speaking out and asking questions, for example. There appears to have been a relatively high incidence of such interaction: an examination of 213 nineteenth-century trial reports indicates that jurors spoke out in at least half of the cases.[44] It is likely that juror interaction was under-reported, as some authors may not have deemed such information worth recording.[45] Whether a jury interacted in a particular case appears to have been linked to whether it was a common or a special jury (see table 12.1). Approximately one-third of the cases considered were decided by special juries, while almost two-thirds were decided by common juries. Common jurors appear to have interacted more and asked more questions.

Table 12.1 Breakdown of special and common jury cases

	Special jury	Common jury	Unknown	Total
Number of cases	69	126	18	213
Cases with interaction	34 (49.28 %)	81 (64.28 %)	5	120

This is somewhat surprising, given that one might expect special jurors to be more confident as a result of their higher social standing, and less likely to be in awe of the judge and the proceedings. It is also possible to break down the cases in terms of whether they dealt with civil or criminal matters. Approximately two-thirds of the cases considered were criminal trials, and 58.57 per cent of these had some juror interaction, as illustrated by table 12.2. This is slightly higher than the incidence of jury interaction in civil cases, which stood at around 52 per cent.

44 See appendix one for the list of cases considered here. Full references are given in the bibliography. Juror interaction was identified in 120 or 56.33% of the cases considered. This may, however, be an underestimation of the extent of juror interaction. For example, of the 213 jury trials, 11 gave no details about the jury at all, and it is possible that there might have been jury interaction in these cases. If these are discounted, the percentage of cases with juror interaction is raised to almost 60% (59.41%).

45 Some reporters, such as William Ridgeway, were particularly assiduous in detailing everything said at trial, including questions from jurors.

Table 12.2 Breakdown of civil and criminal cases

	Civil	Criminal	Total
Number of cases	73	140	213
Cases with interaction	38 (52.05 %)	82 (58.57 %)	120

It would appear from this that jurors were slightly more likely to ask questions in criminal trials than in civil actions. The reasons for this are not immediately clear. The traditional rhetoric, as discussed, was that civil cases involved much more complicated fact patterns and more technical evidence than criminal cases, and thus the jury's job in such cases was a harder one. This was, for example, part of the rationale for not paying criminal jurors.[46] However, the serious consequences arising from a criminal conviction may have prompted jurors to probe more deeply in such cases. Before delivering a verdict that could result in a sentence of imprisonment, transportation or death, jurors had to assure themselves of the guilt of the accused, beyond reasonable doubt. Chitty's reference to 'that caution which always prevails when life is in question, and the anxiety of judges to look on every circumstance with the most favourable eye for the defendant'[47] could just as easily be applied to criminal juries.

A final distinction may be drawn between cases where there was just one instance of interaction (such as a single question posed by a juror) and cases where there was more extensive interaction. In the cases where there was juror interaction recorded, this took the form of frequent or sustained questioning in 74 per cent of the civil cases[48] and 80 per cent of the criminal trials.[49] So it is clear that in most instances jurors did more than ask a single question; they were quite engaged with the trial and asked multiple questions or made multiple interjections.

Asking witnesses questions was the most common type of juror interaction reported.[50] In most instances, it was done during a witness's cross-examination.

46 See pp 124–6.

47 J. Chitty, *A practical treatise on the criminal law: comprising the practice, pleadings, and evidence which occur in the course of criminal prosecutions*, 4 vols (London, 1816), i, p. 556.

48 In approximately 10 of the 38 civil cases where there was juror interaction, this took the form of a single question or comment; in the remaining 28 there was more sustained questioning. E.g. in *Gallagher v. Cavendish* (1841) the common jurors asked 33 questions, and had a witness recalled for further questioning: John Henry Doyle, *An ample report of the important libel record tried before Baron Richards, at the Galway assizes, on the fifth and sixth of Aug., the Rev Michael Gallagher, Islandeady, being plaintiff, and the honorable Frederick Cavendish, proprietor of the Mayo Telegraph newspaper, defendant* (Castlebar, 1841). In *Cavendish v. Hope* (1813) there were some 81 questions asked: *Cavendish v. Hope Assurance* (1813).

49 In 16 out of 82 cases there was only a single instance of interaction, while in 66 of the cases there was extensive questioning.

50 E.g. M. Browne, *Irish gallantry! Fairburn's edition of the unprecedented trial between Mark Browne*

Hayes wrote in 1842 that '[n]o question should be asked of any witness by a juror until the examination and cross-examination of that witness have closed'.[51] However, this may have been somewhat aspirational; until the mid-nineteenth century at least, jurors often simply interjected and interrupted examination or cross-examination to pose a question directly to the witness,[52] though they may in some cases have raised their hands.[53] Their questions were almost never screened or filtered by the court or counsel,[54] though a judge might direct a witness not to answer a specific question, as will be discussed later. After their retirement, the jury could request that a witness be recalled so that they could hear the testimony again, or pose additional questions of their own.[55] This would be done in open court (except on lunacy commissions),[56] and it seems that both parties' consent was necessary. In *R v. Leary and Cooke*,[57] for example, an indictment for murder, having deliberated for thirty minutes, the jury returned to court and the foreman stated that one of the jurors wanted to ask a question of a crown witness. Counsel for the prisoner refused to consent to this, fearing that it would amount to a reopening of the case, and Ball J. refused to allow the question to be asked in the absence of such consent, and ordered that the jurors reach a conclusion on the evidence currently before them. The jurors in this case gave a verdict of guilty in relation to one of the defendants, but were unable to reach agreement with regard to the other, and were discharged.[58]

Where jurors directly questioned witnesses, there often tended to be more than one question asked. A question to a witness could lead to several follow-up questions, though it is not always clear from the reports whether several jurors joined in the questioning, or whether it originated from one particularly

and Joseph Blake for adultery (4th ed., Dublin, 1817). The jury in that case retired for a mere 8 minutes.

51 Edmund Hayes, *Crimes and punishments, or a digest of the criminal statute law of Ireland*, 2 vols (2nd ed., Dublin, 1842), ii, p. 448.

52 Writing about eighteenth-century England, Beattie similarly observes that procedure was rather chaotic, and that jurors could ask questions and often did so simply by 'blurting them out'. J.M. Beattie, 'Scales of justice: defence counsel and the English criminal trial in the eighteenth and nineteenth centuries', *L. & Hist. Rev.*, 9:2 (1991), 221–61 at 222.

53 E.g. Anon., *Trial of James Spollen for the murder of Mr George Samuel Little at the Broadstone terminus of the Midland Great Western Railway, Ireland, Aug. 7th, 8th, 10th & 11th, 1857* (Dublin, 1857). During the cross-examination of the defendant's son, Monahan C.J. said 'a juror wished to ask a question', and the juror said 'the question has been asked, my lord' (p. 56). This conjures an image of a juror perhaps raising his hand and waiting patiently for his opportunity to ask a question.

54 An exception to this appears to be the trial of James Spollen, when some of the jurors' questions were asked by the attorney general: *R v. Spollen* (1857), p. 44.

55 Hale, *Pleas*, ii, p. 296; Leonard MacNally, *The justice of the peace for Ireland: containing the authorities and duties of that officer, as also of the various conservators of the peace*, 2 vols (Dublin, 1808), ii, p. 68; J. Bingham, *A new practical digest of the law of evidence, inc. the juryman's complete guide* (London, 1796), p. 80.

56 See pp 88–90.

57 (1844) 3 Cr. & Dix C.C. 212, *Freeman's Journal*, 26 Mar. 1844 and *Nenagh Guardian*, 27 Mar. 1844.

58 See pp 210–13.

enthusiastic juror. Some of the reports indicate particularly talkative juries,[59] with numerous witnesses subjected to questioning.

As well as questioning witnesses, there were other ways in which jurors made their voices heard at trial.[60] Sometimes they argued for better compensation and accommodation;[61] for example, the special jurors in *Gabbett v. Clancy and Dwyer* secured for themselves better lodgings and a hot meal while deliberating.[62] This was a five-day trial over fishery rights in Limerick, and it was proposed to accommodate the jurors in the grand-jury room. This was deemed unsuitable because of the many doors and passages leading to it, so instead, members of the bar vacated their room, where the jurors ate their dinner and spent the night.[63] The jurors' confidence in demanding better conditions may in part have stemmed from the fact that they were special jurors, and were possibly less intimidated by the courtroom, the lawyers and the judge.

Jurors also made their voices heard by questioning the judge during his charge,[64] interrupting counsel during their opening or closing statements,[65] scolding witnesses for prevaricating,[66] joking[67] and making sarcastic comments

59 E.g. Anon., *Trial of Thomas Donnelly, Nicholas Farrell (alias Nicholas Tyrell), Laurence Begley (alias Laurence Bayly) and Michael Kelly, for high treason; before the court holden under a special commission at Dublin* (Dublin, 1803), in which there were some 17 questions asked by jurors; and *R v. Doran* (1803) 28 How. St. Tr. 1041, in which there were 26 questions.

60 Similarly, John H. Langbein, *The origins of adversary criminal trial* (Oxford, 2005), describes, p. 319, how jurors could question witnesses, ask for them to be summoned, and 'volunteer information about persons, places and commercial practices.'

61 E.g. J.S. Armstrong, *Report of the trial of William Burke Kirwan for the murder of Maria Louisa Kirwan, his wife, at the island of Ireland's Eye, in the county of Dublin* (Dublin, 1853), p. 82; *Byrne v. Chester & Holyhead Railway Co.* (1856) 8 Ir. Jur. (o.s.) 511; Richard Adams, *Special report of the trial in the high court of justice in Ireland, exchequer division, on 15th to 20th June, 1887, before Mr Justice O'Brien … on the case of the Corporation of Dublin versus Tedcastle* (Dublin, 1887). See also the reports of the proceedings in *Freeman's Journal*, 16, 17, 18, 20, 21 June 1887.

62 William O'Brien, *The fishery case. A report of the case Poole Gabbett, esq., a. Thomas Clancy and Thomas Dwyer, tried before Mr justice Ball, and a special jury, at Limerick summer assizes, 1841, and which occupied the court for over five days* (Limerick, 1841). See *Freeman's Journal*, 2 Aug. 1841 and Anon., 'Illegality of crown grants of public fisheries in Ireland', *Dub. Rev.*, 11 (1841), 356.

63 *Gabbett v. Clancy and Dwyer* (1841), p. 99. The special jurors in *Dublin Corporation v. Tedcastle* (1887) were less successful in securing a better deal for themselves. See pp 188–91.

64 E.g. *R v. Calwell Spear, Irish Times*, 1 Nov. 1862; A.H. Rowan, *The trial of James Vance, esquire, one of the high sheriffs of the city of Dublin, on Thursday the 25th day of Feb., 1790* (Dublin, 1790), p. 50; and A.B. Mosse, *Report of the trial of an action, wherein John Birch, an Englishman, was plaintiff, and Joshua Paul Meredith, esq of the city of Dublin, was defendant, for seduction by the defendant of the plaintiff's daughter, Sarah Birch, before the right hon John, Lord Norbury, chief justice of his majesty's court of common pleas in Ireland, and a special jury of the city of Dublin, on Thursday the 22nd day of April, 1819* (Dublin, 1819), p. 29.

65 E.g. W.R. Furlong, *Action for libel. Report of the case of Angeli v. Galbraith, as tried before the lord chief justice at the Kildare summer assizes, 1856; and before the lord chief baron in the court of exchequer, at the after-sittings, Michaelmas term, 1856* (Dublin, 1857), p. 350.

66 E.g. Anon., *Persecution of Protestants in the year 1845, as detailed in a full and correct report of the trial at Tralee, on Thurs., Mar. 20, 1845, for a libel on the Rev. Charles Gayer* (Dublin, 1845), p. 45.

67 Anon., *A full report of the trial of the issues directed by the court of exchequer in Ireland in the case of Edward Dowling v. Edward Lawler* (Dublin, 1854), p. 89.

about witnesses' testimony.[68] They might also ask for particular evidence[69] or copies of the indictment,[70] make observations about the evidence[71] or ask for witnesses to be recalled.[72] In one case a juror had information about the case and so was sworn as a witness.[73] In another, the jurors were having difficulty reaching what they considered to be a just verdict, and asked the judge if they could give a verdict for the plaintiff, conditional on him entering a bond to refrain from doing certain things.[74] In *Gayer v. Byrne*, a witness was being difficult and evasive and breaking into Irish from time to time, and the court and the jury 'beckoned him off the table'.[75]

A rather unique form of juror participation was seen in the case of *Cavendish v. Hope Assurance Company*,[76] discussed earlier. This was the case where a group a jurors decided to visit a house that was the subject of a potentially fraudulent insurance claim. The case went on for several days before Lord Norbury, with numerous witnesses for both sides closely questioned by the special jurors. When it emerged that that some of the jurors had conducted an unauthorised view of Cavendish's house,[77] counsel proposed that these jurors could be sworn as witnesses to testify as to what they had observed. The jurors refused, and their fellow jurors also wished to view the house. It was then proposed that if all the jurors were to have a view of the premises, they should be accompanied by two sworn witnesses,[78] instead of the usual showers.[79] Allowing witnesses to accompany the view was highly unusual.[80] The jurors expressed a strong preference as to which witnesses they wished to accompany them to the house – both of them were architects. The judge suggested a different witness, but the jurors were adamant, and ultimately got their own way.[81]

68 E.g. *Angeli v. Galbraith* (1857), p. 468. 69 E.g. *R v. Calwell Spear, Irish Times*, 1 Nov. 1862.

70 E.g. W. Ridgeway, *A report of the trial of George Lidwell and Thomas Prior. Upon an information, filed ex officio, by his majesty's attorney general, for sending and delivering a challenge to Cholmeley Dering, esq., colonel of the Romney Fencibles* (Dublin, 1800), p. 50.

71 E.g. Anon., *A full and complete report of the trial, the king at the prosecution of the marquis of Westmeath, against Anne Connell, John Monaghan, Bernard Maguire, Patrick Farley, and William Mckenzie at Green-Street, Dublin, at the commission of oyer and terminer, Jan., 3rd and two succeeding days* (Dublin, 1825), p. 38.

72 E.g. Anon., *A report of the trial of Michael Keenan, for administering an unlawful oath* (Dublin, 1822), p. 49 and J.G. Hodges, *Report of the trial of William Smith O'Brien for high treason, at the special commission for the county Tipperary held at Clonmel, Sept. and Oct. 1848* (Dublin, 1849), p. 844.

73 Anon., *The trial of Mary Heath, upon an indictment for perjury, before the Lord Chief Justice Marley, and the justices of the court of king's bench in Ireland* (Dublin, 1745).

74 *Gabbett v. Clancy and Dwyer* (1841).

75 *Gayer v. Byrne* (1845), p. 55. Witnesses usually sat on a chair placed on a table when testifying in the early nineteenth century. Witness boxes were not common features in courtrooms at that time.

76 *Cavendish v. Hope Assurance* (1813).

77 Ibid., p. 236. 78 Ibid., pp 236–7.

79 However, communication often took place and courts were sometimes inclined to take a lenient position on this: see the English case of *Goodtitle d. Symons v. Clark* (1746) Barnes 457; 94 E.R. 1002. 80 *R v. Martin and Webb* (1872) L.R. 1 C.C.R. 378.

81 *Cavendish v. Hope* (1813), pp 237–8.

The view duly took place and court was reconvened the following day – the fifth day of the trial. When the jurors returned to court, the foreman insisted on reading out a paper they had prepared.[82] This was essentially a piece of over-the-top rhetoric to the effect that they had viewed the premises and reached a conclusion of which they were certain. They then informed the judge that as they had already made up their minds, they had no desire to listen to closing statements from counsel or to a charge from the judge himself.[83] The jurors found the fire to have been deliberately started by Cavendish.

There were several possible reasons for jurors to question witnesses. The first, and probably the most obvious, was the pursuit of truth. Jurors cross-examined witnesses to test their stories, to acquire more detailed accounts, or to satisfy themselves that the witness was being truthful. This is evidenced by the probing nature of the questions asked in many cases. The fact that jurors tended to ask more questions in criminal trials suggests that they were conscientious about their role.

Another possible reason for juror questioning was a desire to be a part of the 'show' that was the Irish trial. Courtrooms presented witnesses, lawyers and judges with a willing audience, a gripping narrative and a dramatic setting. Trials were opportunities for entertainment, and their goings-on were reported at length in local newspapers. Certain cases attracted large crowds,[84] and sometimes ticketing was used to control numbers.[85] Counsel took the opportunity to flex their oratorical and dramatic muscles, making lengthy speeches and generally playing to the gallery.[86] Witnesses too were known to 'play up' to the audience, by making jokes, being obtuse and showing as much disrespect as they dared. The cheeky

82 Ibid., pp 239–40.

83 Ibid., p. 241.

84 E.g. J. Hatchell, *Report of the trial of an action wherein Nicholas Higgins, gent. was plaintiff and Thomas Higgins, gent. attorney, defendant. Before the right hon John Lord Norbury, lord chief justice; and a special jury of the city of Dublin, in the court of common pleas, Ireland* (Dublin, 1813) (forgery); Anon., *Action for libel against Saunders' News-Letter. Hugh Brabazon versus Joseph T. Potts esq. tried before the honourable Baron Hughes and a special jury of the county of Galway* (Dublin, 1862); J.P. Hatchell, *A report of the trial of Edward Sheridan, MD upon an indictment for a misdemenour at the bar of the king's bench, on Thursday and Friday, the 21st and 22nd days of November 1811* (Dublin, 1811) (the Four Courts was so crowded that the persons on the jury list could not make their way into the courtroom); P. M'Loskey, *The trial and conviction of a Franciscan monk, at Mayo spring assizes, 1852, for burning and blaspheming the holy scriptures: with observations on the fact and the defence made for it* (Mayo, 1852) (*R v. Bridgeman*); and James Doyle, *A special report of the trial of the Rev Vladimir Petcherine (one of the Redemptorist Fathers) in the court house, Green-Street, Dublin, December 1855, on an indictment charging him with burning the Protestant Bible at Kingstown* (Dublin, 1856).

85 E.g. admission to court was by ticket in *R v. Spollen* (1857) and in 'an important breach of promise case' in Sligo in 1890, for which admission was charged at between 6*d*. and 1*s*.: *Sligo Chronicle*, 8 Mar. 1890.

86 R.B. McDowell observes that the Irish bar was 'distinguished for forensic skill and "rhetorical elegance" rather than for profound learning and an interest in jurisprudence' in T.W. Moody and W.E. Vaughan (eds), *A new history of Ireland, iv: eighteenth-century Ireland, 1691–1800* (Oxford, 1986), p. 707.

irreverence of witnesses is a common feature of the trial reports considered. It is possible that jurors too wished to play a part in the entertainment, and one way of doing this was to make their voices heard. For example, in *Dowling v. Lawler*, a special juror provoked laughter in the courtroom when he commented on counsel's examination of a witness: 'It would be very desirable, my lord, if some means were adopted to save us – if your lordship would be kind enough to press on these gentleman the necessity of brevity.'[87] In *Mathew v. Harty and Stokes*, a juror asked a witness if he was familiar with the passage from *Hamlet* that touched upon 'the law's delay', again provoking laughter.[88]

Related to the desire to entertain was the jury's assertion of power. In eighteenth-century England, the jury came to be viewed as a means of limiting or thwarting state power, and by the nineteenth century, 'perverse' verdicts in Ireland were commonly viewed as a means of protest on, for example, religious or political issues. But not all power struggles necessarily related to clashing political ideologies between juries and judges. Simple animosity towards an unpopular litigant, defendant, prosecutor, witness, judge or lawyer was sometimes apparent, or a jury might seek to establish its central role and expertise. Class considerations also featured in some jurors' assertion of power or superiority, particularly in special-jury cases. In the late eighteenth century and early nineteenth century, special jurors generally enjoyed significant respect, and may have considered themselves more as experts than mere laymen. How vocal and confident jurors were at trial probably also stemmed from their level of experience: the more often they served, the more vocal they became. For example, in 1829, following a riot at Borrisokane, Co. Tipperary, at which 2 persons were killed and 21 were wounded,[89] a number of trials took place in Clonmel. Some jurors served on multiple cases,[90] and it is clear that there was more juror participation in the later cases, suggesting that juror confidence grew as the assizes progressed.[91]

In *Cavendish v. Hope*,[92] discussed above, it was clear that the jury was engaged in a power struggle with the judge and lawyers – and, ultimately, the power in that

87 *Dowling v. Lawlor* (1854), pp 88–9.

88 S.N. Elrington and W.P. Carr, *Authentic report of the most important and interesting trial of Mathew v. Harty and Stokes before the right hon. the lord chief baron and a special jury, on Thursday December 11, 1851, and the following days* (Dublin, 1851), p. 44.

89 See *Constabulary, Ireland*, HC 1830–1 (167) viii, 403, pp 39–40.

90 E.g. the same jury tried the cases of *R v. Lalor and R v. Ledger (No. 2)*: see A. Brewster, *A report of the trial of John Ledger for firing at Michael Fell* (Dublin, 1830); and A. Brewster, *A report on the trial of James Lalor, for firing at John Dalton* (Dublin, 1830). Lalor consented to the same jurors being used, presumably because they had found Ledger to be not guilty.

91 By contrast, a number of jurors served on multiple trials at the 1806 special commission in the West – e.g. in *Hargedan*, four of the jurors had tried *Flynn et al.*, but while there was juror questioning in the earlier case, the jurors were silent in the Hargedan case the following day. See W. Ridgeway, *A report of the proceedings under a special commission of oyer and terminer and gaol delivery, for the counties of Sligo, Mayo, Leitrim, Longford and Cavan, in the month of December, 1806* (Dublin, 1807). Note that the judge in *Flynn* had commented, p. 241, that this was 'an intelligent and respectable jury'.

92 *Cavendish v. Hope* (1813).

case rested with the jurors. This case was an extreme example, but there were more subtle ways in which jurors could assert their status and importance within the trial. Participating in the questioning of witnesses and having their voices heard at trial undoubtedly had an empowering effect on jurors. Another example of a jury attempting to assert its power was in the case of *Angeli v. Galbraith*.[93] At the second trial of this libel action, when barrister James Whiteside was addressing the jury for the defence, he was interrupted by Isaac Butt for the plaintiff. When he wished to continue, the foreman of the jury interjected and the following exchange took place:

> *Foreman*: My lord, it might save the time of the court if I were to state that the jury have made up their minds, and that on the close of the plaintiff's case, before Mr Whiteside began his address at all. [applause]
> *Whiteside*: My lord, I give up [laughter] – I do not press that evidence.
> *Court*: It will be necessary, if that be your view, to heart the plaintiff's counsel.
> *A juror*: Our minds have been long since made up on the subject, my lord.
> *Foreman*: I thought it right to make the statement, in order to save the time of the court; there is no use in Mr Whiteside calling any evidence.
> ...
> *Foreman*: What I meant to convey was this: that we have not been moved in the least by Mr Whiteside's eloquence, although we were gratified in hearing it. When the plaintiff's case closed, our minds were made up, that they have made no case whatever.
> *Another juror*: There is no case whatever.[94]

Juries often directly addressed lawyers and judges, and this may also have been an exercise of power. For example, in *R v. Ledger (No. 2)*[95] at the aforementioned Clonmel assizes, the jurors interrupted Moore J.'s charge four times on points of evidence.[96] At William Smith O'Brien's 1848 high treason trial,[97] jurors interrupted or corrected Chief Justice Blackburne a dozen times, sometimes referring to their own notes, which were at odds with his.[98] Jurors also criticised or chastised lawyers for their verbosity,[99] and could be critical of lawyers for pursing a particular line of questioning, if, for example, they felt that they would have done things differently themselves. One can sense the frustration of jurors on lengthy trials, faced with repetitive testimony and uninspiring advocates.

Judicial tolerance was probably a factor influencing whether jurors spoke out at trials, with some judges appearing to have been particularly associated with talkative juries. For example, in the libel action *Brabazon v. Potts*, Hughes B.

93 *Angeli v. Galbraith* (1857). 94 Ibid., p. 350. 95 *R v. Ledger (No. 2)*.
96 Ibid., pp 365, 368, 369 and 374. 97 See pp 139, 158.
98 J.G. Hodges, *Report of the trial of William Smith O'Brien for high treason, at the special commission for the Co. Tipperary held at Clonmel, Sept. and Oct. 1848* (Dublin, 1849), pp 819–21, 861. See also *R v. Vance* (1790), p. 50, *R v. Spollen* (1857), p. 131; and *Angeli v. Galbraith* (1857), p. 199.

commented, 'I seldom stop jurors asking questions',[100] giving the impression that juror questions were not a novelty. One judge whose juries seem to have been particularly vocal was Lord Norbury. In the early nineteenth century, frequent and sustained questioning by jurors was a common feature of trials over which he presided.[101] A controversial judge, Norbury, who was chief justice of the common pleas for almost three decades, was known for his 'scanty knowledge of the law, his gross partiality, his callousness, and his buffoonery'.[102] He had a 'ribald' sense of humour and was 'remarkably belligerent'.[103] His coarse humour and frequent altercations with leading counsel meant that his courtrooms were often packed, providing entertainment for Dubliners. Jurors may have sought to play a part in this entertainment, and their questions appear to have added to the general uproar of Norbury's court.

On the other hand, a rowdy courtroom was not the only setting in which juror questioning flourished. Baron Downes, who was a quiet, serious man, also frequently allowed juror questioning in his courtroom. He was considered to be an able judge, 'respected for his dignity, impartiality, and learning'.[104] His courtrooms differed from those of Lord Norbury, and 'he contributed a good deal to such dignity as the immediate post-union Irish bench was able to muster'.[105] The practice of allowing jurors to ask questions also seems to have been well-tolerated by lawyers, and the reports show no evidence of counsel having serious objections to allowing it. Some barristers appear to have been more open to it than others.[106]

99 E.g. *Dowling v. Lawlor* (1854), p. 89. 100 *Brabazon v. Potts* (1862), p. 31.

101 E.g. the 1803 treason trials; Anon., *A full and accurate report of the trial, wherein Edward Whitley, esq. was plaintiff, and Brabazon Morris, esq defendant, for slander* (Dublin, 1807); Arthur B. Mosse, *Report of the trial of an action wherein Samuel Rosborough, esq. was plaintiff and Richard Frankling Gough, esq. was defendant. Before the right hon John Lord Norbury, chief justice of his majesty's court of common pleas in Ireland, and a special jury, the 25th day of Feb., 1810* (Dublin, 1810); *Cavendish v. Hope* (1813); *Higgins v. Higgins* (1813); Anon., *Crim. Con. Report of a trial in the court of common pleas on Saturday, December 14, 1816. John Hinds, gentleman attorney, plaintiff. Philip Perry Price Myddleton, defendant* (Dublin, 1816); *Birch v. Meredith* (1819); and William Draper, *Trial in the court of common pleas on the 9th and 10th of July 1816, an action for money had and received. Henry Gresson, attorney, plaintiff. Messrs. Finlay & Co Bankers, defendants* (Dublin, 1816).

102 W.N. Osborough, 'Toler, John, 1st earl of Norbury (1745–1831)' in J. McGuire and J. Quinn (eds), *Dictionary of Irish biography* (Cambridge, 2009).

103 R. Keane, 'Toler, John, first earl of Norbury (1745–1831)', *Oxford dictionary of national biography* (Oxford, 2004; online ed., Jan. 2008) [http://www.oxforddnb.com/view/article/27498, accessed 8 Aug. 2013].

104 P. Geoghegan, 'Downes, William' in *Dictionary of Irish biography* (Cambridge, 2009).

105 W.N. Osborough, 'Downes, William, First Baron Downes (1751–1826)', *Oxford dictionary of national biography* (Oxford, 2004; online ed., Jan 2008) [http://www.oxforddnb.com/view/article/7976, accessed 8 Aug. 2013].

106 E.g. at the trial of those involved in a riot at the Theatre Royal in 1822 a prosecution witness was questioned by a juror, and the attorney general (Plunket) remarked, 'I hope the juror will follow up the question?' Anon., *State trial. Court of king's bench. Monday, Feb. 3, 1823. The king, at the prosecution of the right hon William Conyngham Plunket, attorney general, versus Mathew Handwick, Henry Handwick, George Graham, William Graham, William Brownlow and James*

By contrast, Langbein describes a 'hardening' of counsel's attitude against juror questioning by the late eighteenth century in England.[107]

CONCLUSION

It is difficult to pinpoint exactly when Irish jurors began to evolve into more passive recipients of information, but it appears that by the late nineteenth century their zeal for questioning witnesses and speaking out at trial may have begun to wane. This is based on the dearth of reported instances of juror interaction from the late nineteenth century onward, although it is true that fewer detailed trial pamphlets were being published by this stage. Additionally, many categories of jury, such as the wide-streets jury and the jury of matrons, had disappeared, taking with them further opportunities for jurors to play active roles. The late nineteenth century saw sporadic episodes of juror questioning,[108] although by 1881 it was observed that for the most part, jurors were 'passive and silent'. It was acknowledged that a juror could of course 'ask questions; but as a rule, he sits perfectly still. He does not take notes of the rules of evidence, and if he tried to do so he would soon be hopelessly muddled.'[109] The many examples highlighted in this chapter illustrate that early nineteenth-century juries were dynamic, and, notwithstanding the general reluctance to engage in jury service, those who did participate tended to be enthusiastic and took their role seriously. This chapter also demonstrates some of the mutual respect between jurors and other actors in civil and criminal trials, which is arguably one of the major reasons why trial by jury endured even in difficult circumstances, a theme that will be returned to in chapter 14.

Forbes (Dublin, 1823), p. 39. (See also W.N. Osborough, *The Irish stage: a legal history* (Dublin, 2015), pp 197–8.) Judge Perrin then re-phrased the juror's question and asked it again. In a number of James Whiteside's cases, jurors asked questions, and he considered a witness to have been handed over to the jury once cross-examination was concluded. Later, presiding over the high-profile litigation between Reverend O'Keefe and Cardinal Cullen as chief justice of the queen's bench, he allowed jurors to ask questions, particularly of O'Keefe, and at one stage instructed a witness to answer a juror's question.

107 Langbein, *Origins*, p. 320.

108 *R v. Boyle*, *Cork Examiner*, 6 Dec. 1886.

109 Anon., 'Trial by jury', *I.L.T. & S.J.*, 15 (1881), 412.

CHAPTER THIRTEEN

Deliberations and verdict

THE VARIOUS RULES, PRACTICES AND procedures outlined in previous chapters brought the jury to its key function: the delivery of a verdict. Having considered the evidence, heard the testimony of witnesses and speeches from counsel, and possibly conducted a view, before they considered their verdict, trial juries (including mixed juries) and juries of matrons were 'charged' or 'given in charge' by the judge. It was seen in the previous chapter that jurors sometimes interrupted the judge's charge; but this was the exception; usually they paid attention. They then conducted their deliberations (with varying degrees of privacy, depending on the type of jury and the facilities available) and either delivered a verdict or informed the judge that they were unable to reach agreement. The traditional requirement that jurors' verdicts be unanimous often resulted in hung juries in difficult or sensitive cases, and judges had various means at their disposal to try to secure a verdict and avoid a retrial.

THE JUDGE'S CHARGE

In civil and criminal trials, after the presentation of witness testimony and other evidence, lawyers on both sides took turns addressing the jury. The jury then listened to the judge's charge, which included a summary of the evidence presented, as well as the judge's own views as to how the case ought to be disposed of. Other jury proceedings, such as commissions of lunacy,[1] similarly involved 'charging' the jury. At a coroner's inquest, either the coroner or the magistrate, if acting in substitution, charged the jury.[2] Judges' charges could be quite lengthy – for example, at the trial of Charles Stewart Parnell, Fitzgerald J. was reported as having addressed the jury for five hours, and the following day he picked up where he had left off.[3] Purcell described the judge's duty as being 'to sum up the evidence to the jury, at greater or less length, according to the extent of the evidence, or the difficulty or importance of the case'.[4] Judges' charges to civil and criminal trial

1 E.g. commission of lunacy regarding Margaret Watte, *Irish Examiner*, 13 July 1860

2 Constantine Molloy, *Justice of the peace for Ireland: a treatise on the powers and duties of magistrates in Ireland in cases of summary jurisdiction in the prosecution of indictable offences and in other matters* (Dublin, 1890), p. 363.

3 *Freeman's Journal*, 25 Jan. 1881.

4 Theobald Purcell, *A summary of the criminal law of Ireland* (Dublin, 1848), p. 203.

juries were often published in pamphlets as part of the proceedings,[5] or were reported at length in newspapers.[6]

Some judges were clearly of the view that their role was not to influence the decision of the jury, but merely to present a dispassionate summary of the evidence. Chief Justice Bushe commented in 1839: 'I never charge in such a way as to intimate my own opinion upon the facts of the case.'[7] Similarly, Chief Justice Morris in 1882 described the 'ordinary part of a judge in a criminal trial' as being 'to draw the attention of the jury to the chief points in the evidence, without expressing any opinion on the question of the guilt or innocence of the accused'.[8] Baron Deasy was asked in 1874 whether juries always ought to return verdicts in accordance with the judge's charge. 'Certainly not', he replied, 'I have sometimes differed with juries, but I have come round to the conclusion, after all, that they took a more commonsense view of the case than I did.'[9] This view of their role may not have been universal among Irish judges, as it was not unknown for them to indicate to jurors the verdict they expected, at least in civil cases. In 1874, James Hamilton, the chairman of Co. Sligo remarked that in civil cases, juries did 'just what the judges direct, and in that case we might as well have no jury at all. The verdict is the verdict of the judge.'[10] In criminal cases, the judge might not go so far, but could drop heavy hints indicating his view of the facts.[11]

What Green describes as 'the jury's war with the law' appears to have been tempered by deference towards individual judges.[12] Irish juries were often guided by the judge's charge. In 1848, for example, the *Freeman's Journal* referred to 'the great art' of Chief Justice Francis Blackburne;[13] following his charge to the jury at

5 E.g. Anon., *Report of the trial in the case of Thelwall v. Yelverton, before the chief justice and a special jury, on 21st February 1861, containing the letters, speeches of counsel, judge's charge and finding of the jury* (Dublin, 1861); Anon., *The whole of the trial, on an action brought by Judith Homan, spinster, against Richard Johnson, for non-performance of a marriage contract, in his majesty's court of exchequer, on Wednesday the 14th of February, 1787, before the right hon. lord chief baron Yelverton, and a special jury of freeholders of the county of the city of Dublin, with the pleadings of counsel on both sides, and the lord chief baron's charge to the jury* (Dublin, 1787); Anon., *Crim. con. A full and impartial report of that most extraordinary and interesting trial, with speeches of counsel and judge's charge: in the case wherein J. Hinds, esq. was plaintiff, and P.P. Middleton, M.D. defendant, in an action for damages for crim. con. with the plaintiff's wife: tried in the court of common pleas, Dublin, on the 14th and 16th December, 1816, before the right hon. Lord Viscount Norbery* (Dublin, 1816); T.R. Dunckley, *Hurst v. Whaley. An authorised report of the charge delivered by the right hon. Lord Chief Justice Doherty in the above case, on Tuesday, February 14, 1843* (Dublin, 1843).

6 E.g. *Freeman's Journal*, 1 Mar. 1862 (Hughes B.); *Kildare Observer*, 29 Jan. 1881 (Fitzgerald J.); *Kerry Evening Post*, 24 Dec. 1881 (Morris C.J.); *Irish Examiner*, 14 Dec. 1882 (O'Brien J.).

7 *Report on the state of Ireland*, HC 1839 (486) xii, 1, para. 11280.

8 *The Nation*, 15 Apr. 1882.

9 *Report on the Irish jury system*, HC 1874 (244) ix, 557, para. 2539.

10 *Report on the Irish jury system*, HC 1874 (244) ix, 557, para. 7.

11 See, e.g., the discussion by W.E. Vaughan, *Murder trials in Ireland* (Dublin, 2009), pp 254–5.

12 Thomas A. Green, *Verdict according to conscience: perspective on the English criminal trial jury, 1200–1800* (Chicago, 1985), p. xviii.

13 *Freeman's Journal*, 6 Jan. 1848.

the Limerick special commission, counsel were of the view that jurors found verdicts on the basis of his word.[14] '[C]ertainly', it was reported, 'the Limerick juries retained throughout a lively conviction of the guilt of many of the prisoners after the persuasive eloquence of the chief justice, and before a single proof was brought against them'. Similarly, it was said that Chief Justice Morris, a staunch Unionist:

> could bring jurors to endorse any view of a case he had himself adopted. On these occasions there was a kind of electric sympathy between the bench and the jury-box, for the judge was a kind of glorified juror himself. In his sound common sense, his unaffected plainness of language, his broad brogue, and his rough and racy humour was to be found the secret of his success.[15]

Vaughan notes that several other judges – including O'Brien J., Lefroy J. and Palles C.B. – were described as being influential over juries.[16]

RETIRING TO DELIBERATE

When the judge had delivered his charge, trial jurors usually – but not invariably – retired to deliberate.[17] According to Hayes, writing in 1842, in criminal trials:

> the evidence having closed on both sides and the jury having been charged by the judge at the assizes, or by the assistant barrister or chairman of the sessions, the issue paper is handed up, and the jury proceed to consider their verdict. If the evidence be long, or the jury not unanimous, at the moment, they retire to their jury room, to which no one is admitted but themselves.[18]

Coroners' juries often had nowhere they could retire to – for example, if an inquest took place in the cramped surroundings of a private home. The various categories of trial jury usually retired, as did the juries of matrons. Sometimes, however, trial jurors remained in the jury box to consider their verdict;[19] Purcell observed in 1848

14 *Freeman's Journal*, 15 Jan. 1848. In one case, the trial of William Ryan (Puck) for murder, the jury convicted without leaving the box.

15 M. Bodkin, *Recollections of an Irish judge* (New York, 1915), pp 122–3.

16 Vaughan, *Murder trials*, p. 257.

17 For a more detailed examination of jurors' experiences during the trial and deliberations see Niamh Howlin, '"The terror of their lives": Irish jurors' experiences', *L. & Hist. Rev.*, 29:3 (2011), 703–61.

18 Hayes, *Crimes and punishments*, ii, p. 449.

19 E.g. John Hatchell, *Report of the trial of an action wherein Nicholas Higgins, gent., was plaintiff and Thomas Higgins, gent. attorney, defendant. Before the right hon. John Lord Norbury, lord chief justice; and a special jury of the city of Dublin, in the court of common pleas, Ireland* (Dublin, 1813) (forgery; verdict for plaintiff); Anon., *A report of the trial of Edward Browne and others for administering, and of Laurence Woods for taking an unlawful oath* (Dublin, 1822) (guilty); J. Levy, *Home circuit. Mullingar spring assizes, 1838. The right hon. the attorney general versus John D'Arcy and others.*

that they would only retire to their room if the evidence presented was 'complicated or voluminous', or 'if on consultation in their box the jury cannot agree in a short or convenient time'.[20] The physical limitations of courtrooms and courthouses also affected the manner in which jurors conducted their deliberations. The layout of nineteenth-century courthouses varied,[21] and overcrowding was common, with court personnel, litigants, jurors and curious onlookers often filling these buildings to capacity.[22] While grand juries usually had their own room or chamber, where they not only deliberated but also heard testimony, there was not always a designated space for petty jurors in every courtroom. Describing manor courts, which were generally held in public houses in County Clare in the 1830s, a witness before a parliamentary committee remarked that jurors sat around a table, 'and the crowd would be leaning over them'.[23] He noted that 'when the jurors were consulting, they might go up stairs to another room'.[24] Courthouses built during the nineteenth century tended to incorporate designated jury rooms, as recommended to the Architectural Association of Ireland.[25] Brett indicates that there were separate designated rooms for petty jurors in several Ulster courthouses,[26] and other courthouses around the country also had designated rooms.[27] Where there was a separate jurors' room, this was generally directly accessible from the jury box, the idea being that jurors should not have to walk through the courtroom to upon retiring to consider their verdict.[28]

Before the chief justice of the common pleas (Dublin, 1838) (writ of intrusion; verdict for plaintiff); and *A report of the trial of Robert Robinson for bigamy; tried in the sessions house, Green-Street, at the commission of oyer and terminer, before the hon. Justices Mayne and Fletcher, on Wednesday the 24th of June 1812* (Dublin, 1812) (guilty). See also Máire Ní Cearbhaill, 'The bigamist of Ballinavin' in Liam Clare and Máire Ní Cearbhaill (eds), *Trouble with the law: crimes and trials from Ireland's past* (Dublin, 2007). 20 Purcell, *Criminal law*, p. 204.

21 See, for example, C.E.B. Brett, *Court houses and market houses of the province of Ulster* (Belfast, 1973); Billy Patton, *The court will rise: a short history of the old courthouse, Lifford, Co. Donegal* (Donegal, 2004); and Mildred Dunne and Brian Phillips, *The courthouses of Ireland: a gazetteer of Irish courthouses* (Dublin, 1999).

22 N. Garnham, *The courts, crime and criminal law in Ireland, 1692–1760* (Dublin, 1996), pp 104–7, notes that in the eighteenth century the assizes were of significant local importance – as well as the legal activities of the court, there was important local government business carried out, and sizeable crowds were attracted to the assizes town. Fairs, markets and auctions, as well as balls and social events kept the town busy and crowded for the duration of the assizes and beyond.

23 *Report on manor courts*, HC 1837 (494) xv, 1, p. 115 (Thomas Fitzgerald). 24 Ibid.

25 See J. Brett, 'County courthouses and county gaols in Ireland', *Irish Builder*, 17 (1875), 25–6.

26 These included Cootehill, Co. Cavan (p. 56), Clough, Co. Antrim (p. 30) and Londonderry (p. 17). A design for a courthouse at Ballyconnell, Co. Cavan, also included a petty jury room just off the main courtroom, although this plan was never executed: ibid., p. 13.

27 For example, Ballymahon, Co. Longford: Dunne and Phillips, *Courthouses of Ireland*, pp 46–7. Others included Carndonagh, Co. Donegal (pp 78–9), Castleblayney, Co. Monaghan (pp 90–1), Donegal town (pp 126–7), Moate, Co. Westmeath (pp 230–1), Nenagh, Co. Tipperary (pp 242–3) and Wexford town (pp 326–7).

28 Examples include the courthouses at Baltinglass, Co. Wicklow, built around 1810 (Dunne and Phillips, *courthouses of Ireland*, pp 52–3) and Listowel, Co. Kerry (ibid., pp 212–13).

An officer of the court was supposed to be placed at the door of the juror's box 'to prevent any one having communication with them'.[29] However, petty jurors were not always kept in strict isolation, especially in the less formal manor courts, where the jurors might be a 'sitting in the court mixing with the people, and … talking to each other'.[30] There are numerous reports of trials where jurors mingled and conversed with outsiders. For example, at the 1882 trial of Francis Hynes,[31] the jurors stayed overnight in a hotel and were seen in the hotel billiard room mixing with persons who were not on the jury.[32] In another case, it was reported that jurors were speaking to people who had congregated outside their window.[33] A newspaper account of the case gives an interesting and vivid account of the jury's confinement, which in that case was apparently on show for the general public:

> a large number of persons congregated under the window and a spirited fire of wit was kept up between them and the twelve gentlemen in durance … Roars of laughter were elicited at the oddness of the thing, and certainly it was a strange way of keeping watch and ward upon a jury.[34]

There were no consequences as regards the jury's verdict in the Hynes case. This sort of informality and mixing between jurors and other court actors was a common feature at quarter sessions and assizes. George Bolton, the Tipperary crown solicitor, observed that at the 1873 Clonmel assizes, 'the jurors, the prisoners and the witnesses were all staying together in the same class of public-houses and lodging-houses … I saw the jurors and witnesses in groups around the public-house doors.'[35]

Where there was a room to which jurors could retire to consider their verdicts, the standard of accommodation provided could be poor. Chief among the complaints of the Dublin Jurors Association[36] was the state of the jury boxes and jury rooms in Dublin courthouses. One member claimed that the accommodation in a particular jury room had been so bad that he had complained to the sanitary association. Conditions were said to be 'abominable', with poor ventilation, draughts, dirt and cramped seating common.[37] The *Freeman's Journal* agreed that jury boxes were 'the very perfection of misery'.[38] Things were not much better in the courtroom:

29 Leonard MacNally, *The justice of the peace for Ireland: containing the authorities and duties of that officer, as also of the various conservators of the peace*, 2 vols (Dublin, 1808), ii, p. 67.
30 *Report on manor courts*, HC 1837 (491) xv, 1, 81, para. 1479 (Philip Harding, Cork magistrate).
31 See p. 152.
32 Francis Brady, a hall porter, later testified, 'I remarked to the constable who was standing in the hall, "Is it not a very unusual thing for a jury to be mixing with other people; I never saw jurors in a public billiard-room before."' *Dublin commission court* (*Francis Hynes*, HC 1882 (408) lv, 167, p. 5).
33 *Ryder v. Burke* (1847) 10 Ir. L.R. 474.
34 *Galway Mercury*, 24 July 1847.
35 *Report on Irish jury system*, 1874, para. 1490.
36 See pp 12–13, 24–5.
37 *Freeman's Journal*, 25 June 1875 (F.W. Pim).
38 Ibid.

> [t]he boxes were almost as bad as the rooms and quite as uncomfortable. There was no place to stretch one's legs, and nothing to write upon except a scrubby bit of a desk that no trader in Dublin would see in his own office.[39]

Jurors also complained at having nowhere to wait in the courthouse before and between cases. Dublin jurors argued that '[t]here should be a good central waiting-room with a comfortable fire where the jurors could remain until they were called for and not be sent knocking about the courts or passages for days when not wanted'.[40] The secretary of the Waterford Jurors Association similarly complained that 'there is no place for them to sit down in, they have often to stand in the passages, and the fatigue is very great'.[41]

DELIBERATIONS

By the nineteenth century, trial juries were not supposed to be self-informing[42] – if a juror had personal knowledge about some details of the case he might be sworn as a witness to testify under oath.[43] Jurors were entitled to take into their room any document that had been presented as evidence,[44] and they could also bring their own notes.[45] Hayes wrote that it was in fact the solemn duty of 'the foreman, and such of the others as may be capable, to take notes of the evidence, to aid their recollection while deliberating on their verdict'.[46] No other papers or documents could be brought in. Lord Campbell warned in 1854 that care should be taken to

39 Ibid., 30 Jan. 1875 (Pim). 40 Ibid.

41 *Report on Irish jury laws*, HC 1881 (430) xi 1, para. 821 (T. Newenham Harvey).

42 Although it was long accepted that early juries relied primarily on their own knowledge and experience when deciding cases, scholars now disagree over the extent to which early juries self-informed: e.g. Edward Powell, 'Jury trial at gaol delivery in the late Middle Ages: the midland circuit, 1400–1429' in J.S. Cockburn and Thomas A. Green (eds), '*Twelve good men and true': the criminal trial jury in England, 1200–1800* (Princeton, 1988); Bernard William McLane, 'Juror attitudes towards local disorder: the evidence of the 1328 Trailbaston proceedings' in ibid.; J.B. Post, 'Jury lists' in ibid.; Daniel Klerman, 'Was the jury ever self-informing?' *Southern California L. Rev.*, 17 (2003), 123–50; and David J. Seipp, 'Jurors, evidence and the tempest of 1499' in John W. Cairns and Grant McLeod (eds), *The dearest birth right of the people of England: the jury in the history of the common law* (Oxford, 2002).

43 Anon., *The trial of Mary Heath, upon an indictment for perjury, before the lord chief justice Marley, and the justices of the court of king's bench in Ireland, Dublin, 1745*; and Anon.,*The trial of Thomas Lenergan, for the murder, by poison, of Thomas O'Flaherty, esq., at the king's bench, on Monday the 19th of November, 1781. To which is added his dying declaration. Likewise Thunderstruck's remarks on the nature of giving absolution to criminals under sentence of death; with Candour's apology to Thunderstruck* (Dublin, 1781).

44 *Report on jury laws*, 1881, p. 205. If they were given any extra papers by one of the parties, a verdict in his favour could be set aside.

45 E.g. J.G. Hodges, *Report of the trial of William Smith O'Brien for high treason, at the special commission for the Co. Tipperary held at Clonmel, Sept. and Oct. 1848* (Dublin, 1849), pp 819–21, 861.

46 Hayes, *Crimes and punishments*, ii, p. 448.

ensure that 'the jurors were not engaged in reading newspapers or fashionable novels',[47] suggesting that these rules may not have been fully complied with. Nevertheless, sometimes jurors did not rely exclusively on the evidence presented in court. A coroner's inquest in Dublin in 1878, for example, centred on the cause of a fire that led to the death of an inmate at the Richmond asylum. Several jurors informed the coroner that they had received letters regarding the state of the chimneys at the asylum, while another stated that there was a rumour that inmates were responsible for cleaning them. They were not admonished by the coroner.[48]

Each juror had a vote and all twelve had to agree unanimously to the verdict.[49] This had long been considered to afford accused persons 'the best possible method of trial'.[50] Houston observed in 1861 that the rule sprang from 'that maxim of our law, which declares that the accused shall always have the benefit of the doubt. If the case against him were such that it could not be proved to the satisfaction of the entire of the twelve men who had listened attentively to the evidence, a doubt in fact subsist, and he would be entitled to the advantage of it.'[51] The length of time jurors spent deliberating varied from case to case, and could have been anything from a few minutes to over twelve hours.[52] Of course, little is known about jurors' deliberations, or the means by which they achieved unanimity, save in the exceptional cases that ended up before the courts.[53] One such case was *Frazer v.*

47 *Hansard 3*, cxxx, 1345 (27 Feb. 1854) (HL). This had clearly been an issue in some recent case.

48 *Freeman's Journal*, 13 Mar. 1878.

49 J. Hope, *Dissertation on the constitution and effects of a petty jury* (Dublin, 1737), p. 33, suggested that jurors ought to cast their votes without engaging in any conversation or debate with each other. Inspired by the Greeks, he suggested that they cast their votes in secret using black and white stones

50 M. Hale, *Pleas of the crown; or, a methodical summary of the principal matters relating to that subject*, 8 vols (London, 1678), i, p. 33; W. Blackstone, *Commentaries on the laws of England*, 4 vols (17th ed., London, 1830), iii, p. 379. An English writer in 1821 defended the unanimous verdict as opposed to the majority verdicts allowed in Scotland and France: D. Booth, *Observations on the English jury laws in criminal cases with respect to the distinction between unanimous verdicts and verdicts by a majority* (London, 1821). A Scottish writer had vehemently defended the Scottish practice in a pamphlet published six years earlier: J. Campbell, *Considerations on the immoral tendency of a law requiring unanimity of juries* (Edinburgh, 1815). See also P. Duff, 'The Scottish criminal jury: a very peculiar institution' in Neil Vidmar (ed.), *World jury systems* (Oxford, 2000); and Ian D. Willock, *The origins and development of the jury in Scotland* (Edinburgh, 1966). See James Q. Whitman, *The origins of reasonable doubt: the theological roots of the criminal trial* (New Haven, CT, 2008), pp 142–4 for an alternative view of the unanimity requirement.

51 Arthur Houston, 'Observations on trial by jury, with suggestions for the amendment of our present system', *J. Dub. Stat. Soc.*, 3 (1861), 100–9 at 104.

52 For example, in *R v. Thompson, Belfast Newsletter*, 23 Mar. 1849, the jurors were confined for nineteen hours in total, while jurors in the case of *R v. Davison, Kerry Evening Post*, 18 Mar. 1865, spent twelve hours together. See *Capital offences (Ireland)*, HC 1865 (352) xlv, 323, p. 3.

53 P.J.R. King, '"Illiterate plebeians, easily misled": jury composition, experience and behaviour in Essex, 1735–1815' in Cockburn and Green (eds), '*Twelve good men and true*', p. 292. If a verdict was found to have been reached by means such as tossing a coin or drawing lots, it would probably be set aside: e.g. the English cases of *R v. Lord Fitz-Water* (1793) 2 Lev. 139; 83 E.R. 487; *Foster v. Hawden* (1793) 2 Lev. 205; 83 E.R. 520; *Fry v. Hordy* (1729) T. Jones 83; 84 E.R. 1158; *Vaise v.*

Burke, in which one of the special jurors was reported by the foreman as refusing to discuss the matters at hand when the jury retired for their deliberations. The main question before the jury was whether the plaintiff had been involved in a riot in the Phoenix Park. The juror, a Mr Hill, spoke in open court about his reasoning – it seemed he disagreed with the evidence in the case as to whether a riot had taken place. The solicitor general protested against what he called 'this catechising of a particular juror', but Pigot C.B. persisted in a close questioning of Hill. The juror pointed out that he had in the past served on other juries, and had witnessed jurors disagreeing; but never had he seen a juror 'called before the judge in this way'. When finally the jurors were sent back to their room, Hill expressed his displeasure at having been singled out by the foreman.[54]

A certain amount of bullying probably went on in the jury room. For example, at a Longford murder trial in the 1830s, the morning after the verdict was delivered, a juror wrote to both the chief justice and the crown solicitor claiming that he had not agreed to the acquittal but that the foreman had made him hold his tongue. The foreman denied this when questioned by Chief Justice Blackburne.[55] One strong-willed juror could make all the difference, as illustrated by this description of the trial of Fenian Pagan O'Leary:

> One of the jurors was living in Mullingar, in good business, and a rich man, and as soon as they retired into the jury room, somebody addressed this gentleman and said, 'We shall have no trouble in this case; it is clearly proved, and we shall not be delayed by it.' 'Oh', said this gentleman, 'the case is clearly proved; there is no doubt that the man has done all that they attribute to him, but I shall never find him guilty; he is a Fenian, and I will not convict a Fenian.' So they sat down, and remained there until they were kept long enough, and then they were discharged.[56]

Jurors' deliberations did not always remain secret, and we saw in chapter 11 that this could put them at risk. After the jury in *Frazer v. Burke* had been deliberating for about an hour, they complained that some police officers were eavesdropping in the passageway.[57] In cases where juries were unable to reach a verdict, the breakdown of their votes sometimes became common knowledge and was reported in the press. For example, in *R v. Delany*, a nuisance case involving a slaughterhouse near Sackville Street, 11 jurors were for an acquittal and one was

Delaval (1785) 1 T.R. 11; 99 E.R. 944; *Hale v. Cove* (1795) 1 Str. 642; 93 E.R. 753; *Philips v. Fowler* (1732) Bar. N. 441; 94 E.R. 994; *Parr v. Seames and others* (1732) Bar. N. 438; 94 E.R. 993; *Aylett v. Jewel* (1779) 2 Black. W. 1299; 96 E.R. 761; *Owen v. Warburton* (1805) 1 Bos. & Pul. (NR) 326; 127 E.R. 489.

54 *Freeman's Journal*, 17 Jan. 1873.

55 *Report on the state of Ireland*, 1839, paras 7864–71 (E. Tierney). The case was *R v. Rodden*.

56 *Reports on juries (Ireland)*, HC 1873 (283) xv, 389, para. 1464 (Battersby).

57 *The Nation*, 18 Jan. 1873. The report simply states that the registrar took steps to prevent this re-occurring, but gives no further indication as to what happened.

for a conviction.[58] The dissenting juror only made his position known when the foreman was in court about to deliver the verdict.[59] In *R v. Vignolles and Watson*, a case of assault by two magistrates arising from an election in Carlow, 9 jurors were for a conviction and 3 for an acquittal. However, the jury was discharged after one of its members was certified as ill.[60] In *R v. Weir*, a case of forcible abduction, 8 jurors were ready to convict without leaving their box, while 4 were unconvinced.[61]

NO REFRESHMENT

Once they had been charged by the judge, Coke wrote that the trial jury 'ought to be kept together in some convenient place without meat or drink, fire or candle'.[62] It would appear that the latter part of this injunction was less strictly observed than the former; Purcell observed in 1848 that '[t]he restriction as to candle-light has always been dispensed with on the retirement of the jury at night, when they require the inspection of documents which have been given in evidence'.[63] The unanimity requirement was one of the main factors behind the rule against refreshment, the idea being that men who were hungry would more readily reach a consensus.[64] They could partake of refreshment before retiring[65] – though sometimes they declined to do so.[66] Wide-streets juries were unlikely to have operated under these conditions, given that they did not deliberate under lock and key but sat at their leisure, in well-appointed rooms, on consecutive days. Other types of valuation and inquest juries may, however, have deliberated without refreshment. In any case, jurors often ignored the rule against refreshment, with such instances varying from the relatively innocent smuggling of sweetmeats or dried fruit, to the more questionable concealment of bottles of whiskey.[67]

A drunken juror was relatively uncommon, but not unheard of. At the infamous trial of United Irishman William Orr in Carrickfergus in 1797, for example, two

58 *Freeman's Journal*, 12 Aug. 1841. 59 A juror was withdrawn by consent.

60 *Freeman's Journal*, 14 Apr. 1838.

61 *Belfast Newsletter*, 23 Mar. 1838. The jury was discharged by consent.

62 3 Co. Inst. 227b. 63 Purcell, *Criminal law*, p. 204.

64 As Hope wrote in *Dissertation*, p. 11, they were 'to have neither meat, drink, fire, candle nor easement … till they can all think one way'. See J.H. Thomas, *A systematic arrangement of Lord Coke's first institute of the laws of England*, 3 vols (Philadelphia, 1826–7), iii, p. 537 (3 Co. Inst. 227b).

65 E.g. *Lessee John Hamilton O'Hara v. Henry Hutchinson Hamilton O'Hara* (1825), reported in P. Burke, *Celebrated trials connected with the upper classes* (London, 1851), p. 343.

66 See, for example, the trial of McClure, in *Reports of proceedings at the special commission (1867) for the county and city of Cork and the county and city of Limerick* (Dublin, 1871), p. 195.

67 See the English cases of *Welcden v. Elkington* (1578) 2 Plowd.; 75 E.R. 763 516; *Mounson v. West* (1588) 1 Leon. 88, 132; 74 E.R. 82, 123; *Richmond v. Wise* (1683) 1 Vent. 124; 86 E.R. 86; *Everett v. Youells* (1833) 4 B. & Ad. 681; 110 E.R. 612; *Cooksey v. Haynes* (1858) 27 L.J. Exch. 371; *Morris v. Davies* (1828) 3 Car. & P. 216, 427; 172 E.R. 393, 486.

jurors were said to have been intoxicated.[68] They subsequently swore affidavits that 'two bottles of very strong whiskey spirits' had been smuggled in through the window of the jury room. Despite this, and their recommendation to mercy, Orr was hanged.[69] After the reforms of the 1870s, complaints were made about poorer working-class jurors arriving to court drunk. Hamilton told the 1874 committee of a case where '[a] couple of the jury got drunk', and could not agree upon a verdict.[70] Several witnesses before the 1881 committee had similar tales to tell. One referred to a 'very large class in Tipperary' of 'persons who are consistently and habitually drunk'. He was of the view that such men were unsuitable as jurors.[71] A solicitor told a similar story of drunkenness from Co. Mayo, which had occurred 'a great number of years ago'.[72] This concerned a serious assault on a land bailiff on the estate of Sir Robert Bloss. The case in question was sent to the jury late on a Saturday evening, and a verdict could not be received until Monday morning. Apparently:

> at this time the juries when they retired to consider their verdicts, had access to wine and whiskey, and every sort of stimulant. They got a lot of it on the Sunday, and they managed to make this intemperate fellow so thoroughly drunk that on Monday morning, when they came to hand their verdict in, one stood on each side of him, and they walked him into the place where the issue paper was handed down, and he was in such a state that he could neither assent to, nor dissent from, the verdict. The verdict was a verdict of guilty …[73]

Jurors on coroners' inquests were also known to be intoxicated at times, and the holding of inquests in public houses no doubt exacerbated this. Even inquests held in courthouses could be problematic, however. At one inquest in 1870, the jurors returned after a half-hour's adjournment and 'one of the jurors exhibited unmistakable signs of having made "good" use of his time'[74] – he repeatedly stood up and muttered 'unintelligible expressions', shuffling about and trying to make conversation with the other jurors. He then lit his pipe and 'opened the door of the jury room where he continued in the enjoyment of a delicious smoke'. When the coroner finally noticed the juror's behaviour he directed a constable to remove him, but such was the uproar in the court that the officer could not hear him. The newspaper report stated that the juror, 'believing he was in some tap-room, struck the table in the jury room, and called for another round', and eventually fell asleep

68 Anon., *A brief account of the trial of William Orr, of Farranshane, in the county of Antrim, to which are annexed several interesting facts and authentic documents connected therewith* (Dublin, 1797), p. 22.
69 One of the jurors on the trial later reported being attacked near Larne: *Letter from George Casement to George Anson McLevirty*, 20 July 1798 (PRONI D562/3038).
70 *Report on Irish jury system*, 1874, paras 9–10.
71 *Report on Irish jury laws*, 1881, paras 2520–2 (Thomas Boyd).
72 Ibid., para. 3142 (William d'Arcy Dowling). 73 Ibid. 74 *The Nation*, 21 May 1870.

on the jury-room table, on top of the hats of his fellow jurors. Luckily, there were 15 jurors empanelled, so it was still possible to obtain a verdict of 12.[75]

Intoxicated jurors were dealt with in different ways, with judges in later cases taking a more interventionist approach. Testifying before the 1873 committee on the Irish jury system, Whiteside C.J. recalled a murder trial at which, on the second morning, it became obvious that one of the jurors was intoxicated.[76] He directed the jurors to withdraw and a doctor examined the juror, confirming that he was drunk on whiskey. The juror had smuggled the whiskey into the jury room, possibly disguised as medicine.[77] The doctor recommended several hours' repose before the trial could resume, but because this was a capital case, the jury could not be separated, so the sheriff was directed to take all twelve jurors for a few hours' rest. When the doctor was sent in again to examine the juror, he declared 'that the man was comatose', and was unlikely to have comprehended anything that was said in court all day. Whiteside C.J. did not have the time to restart the trial, so the case was left over until the next assizes, and the sheriff was ordered 'never to summon that drunken man again'.

At the Waterford quarter sessions in October 1879, a juror was found to be 'so far under the influence of drink as to be unable to discharge his duties', and was sent into custody for contempt of court.[78] In Sligo in 1858, a juror on a trial for indecent assault was fined £20 by Christian J. for being intoxicated.[79] In *Minahan v. Goulding*, tried at the Limerick spring assizes in 1878, a juror found to be intoxicated was ordered by Fitzgerald J. to file an affidavit the following day explaining his conduct.[80] In a rather extraordinary move, when the drunken juror was discharged in that case, counsel on both sides agreed to go on with only eleven jurors.[81]

Much also depended on who had paid for the alcohol or refreshment. If the jurors ate or drank at their own expense they were generally fined,[82] but if it was at the expense of one of the parties, before having delivered a verdict, the verdict could become void. Not all judges took a severe view of such transgressions, however. In *Harris v. Harris*,[83] one of the plaintiff's witnesses admitted that during

75 Ibid. 76 *Report on Irish juries*, 1873, para. 4230. 77 Ibid., para. 4293.

78 *Freeman's Journal*, 23 Oct. 1879. Afterwards, the foreman of the jury apologized on his behalf, explaining that his fellow juror had travelled a long distance the night before, and had had no sleep. The judge retorted that the juror ought not to have taken any drink at all, but the foreman explained that they had been drinking in rounds together, and that he himself was not drunk. However, the judge was unmoved and the offending juror remained in custody for twenty-four hours.

79 *Freeman's Journal*, 6 Mar. 1858. 80 Ibid., 13 Mar. 1878.

81 The following day, the jurors were discharged as they were unable to reach a verdict. *Freeman's Journal*, 14 Mar. 1878. The newspaper reports do not state whether the drunk juror appeared with his affidavit.

82 E.g. see the English cases of *Cooksey v. Haynes* (1858) 27 L.J. Exch. 371; *Richmond v. Wise* (1683) 1 Vent. 124; 86 E.R. 86; *Mounson v. West* (1588) 1 Leon. 88, 132; 74 E.R. 82, 123; *Welcden v. Elkington* (1578) 2 Plowd. 516; 75 E.R. 763; and *Everett v. Youells* (1833) 4 B. & Ad. 681; 110 E.R. 612.

83 (1869) I.R. 3 C.L. 294.

the luncheon break, he had treated two of the jurors to refreshments. He told them that he knew more about the case than he had stated in his testimony, and had to be re-examined, but the verdict was allowed to stand. Fitzgerald B. noted that it was 'very unpleasant' that the witness and jurors should have been communicating in such a manner, but pointed out that there was no indication that the witness was an interested party. He cited a recent case where the plaintiff drove home from court with one of the jurors before the trial had concluded, and the verdict had stood. Strong evidence of interference with the verdict was necessary.

By the mid-nineteenth century, judges were likely to exercise their discretion to allow the jurors to eat and drink while deliberating.[84] In *R v. Locke and McGarry*,[85] the jurors deliberated all night without reaching a verdict, and the following morning informed Perrin J. that they were 'suffering the effects of confinement and want of sustenance'. After a doctor examined the jurors and swore that this was indeed the case, the judge ordered the sheriff to give the jurors some breakfast.[86] Two years later, at the height of the Great Famine, when the time came for the jury in *Ryder v. Burke* to deliberate,[87] the judge commented that 'these were bad times to be fasting', and ordered that the jurors be served refreshments before retiring. A number of courthouses built in the early nineteenth century contained fireplaces in the jury room,[88] indicating a similar relaxing of the rule against fire. In 1852 the common-law commissioners recommended 'unhesitatingly' that jurors be furnished with 'every fitting accommodation, and with necessary refreshment'.[89] Otherwise, jurors, they said, would be 'tempted to escape from prolonged hunger and suffering by compromising his conscience and his oath'. Others echoed this sentiment.[90] The custom was described in the house of lords as 'barbarous',[91] and the rule against fire and refreshment was formally abolished in Ireland in 1876,[92] having been discontinued in England six years previously.[93] Interestingly, Molloy did not consider this abolition to have applied to coroners' juries, and wrote in 1890 that they were still to be kept without meat, drink, fire or candle.[94] The extent to which this reflected practice, however, is unclear.

84 See J.F. Plucknett & J.L. Barton (eds), *St Germain: doctor and student* (London, 1974), p. 29; J. Bingham, *A new practical digest of the law of evidence, inc. the juryman's complete guide* (London, 1796), p. 79.

85 (1845) 3 Cr. & Dix C.C. 393. See also *Ryder v. Burke* (1847) 10 Ir. L.R. 474.

86 By the mid-nineteenth century legal commentators were critical of the rule against refreshment; see Anon., 'Our jury system', *Dub. U.J.*, 32 (1848), 723, where it was described as 'an absurd and monstrous custom'.

87 (1847) 10 Ir. L.R. 474.

88 For example, Dunne and Phillips, *Irish court houses*, identify fireplaces in the jury rooms in Castleblayney, Co. Monaghan (pp 90–1), Donegal town (pp 126–7) and Moate, Co. Westmeath (pp 230–1).

89 *Royal commission on pleading* (1852–3), p. 710.

90 E.g. Anon., editorial (1854) 6 *Ir. Jur.* (o.s.) 229.

91 *Hansard 3*, cc, 1345 (27 Feb. 1854) (HC) (Lord Campbell).

92 Juries Procedure (Ireland) Act, 1876 (39 & 40 Vic., c. 78), s. 12. Jurors were to be allowed the use of a fire when out of court, and reasonable refreshment at their own expense.

93 The Juries Act, 1870 (33 & 34 Vic., c. 77), s. 23.

94 Molloy, *Justice of the peace*, p. 364.

NOT ALLOWED TO SEPARATE

In addition to being denied refreshment, trial jurors and coroner's jurors were traditionally not allowed to separate once they had retired, until they had reached a verdict.[95] The reality, however, was that jurors on occasion did separate, for one reason or another. For example, in *R v. O'Neill and Henderson*,[96] when the time came for the jurors to return to court, one of them was missing. He had retired with the others to the jury room, but had subsequently left. After an hour and a half, the sheriff returned with the absent juror, who had been found at Westland Row, claiming to have been under the impression that the trial was over. Brady C.B. ruled that there had been no mistrial, as there was no suggestion that the juror was tampered with, and suggested that the proper course would be to hold such a juror in contempt of court. In *R v. Wallace*,[97] the proprietor of the *Anglo Celt* was indicted for libel regarding an article about the Sixmilebridge massacre.[98] At the end of the first day of the trial, all the jurors rose simultaneously, left the box and returned to their homes. Defence counsel sent for the chief justice in his chambers, but it was too late. When the jurors returned the following day, the defendant objected to the trial continuing, but the jury delivered a verdict for the crown. The queen's bench later emphasised that the mere fact of separation was not enough to set aside the verdict.

Coroners' juries were also to be kept together after viewing the body and hearing the examination of witnesses and the coroner's summing up. Huband wrote that they 'should be kept apart by themselves and should not be allowed to communicate with any one until they have delivered their verdict'.[99] This may have proved difficult where inquests took place in public houses or private homes. In *R v. O'Brien and Bourchier*,[100] the coroner and his son, who was the registrar, remained in the room while jurors considered their verdict. The coroner explained that there was no other room to which he could retire, unless he went out onto the street. Quashing the inquest, May C.J. ruled that the jury ought to be left to themselves 'and not allowed to mix with others who might mingle in their discussions'.

If trial jurors deliberated late into the evening without a verdict, they were kept together overnight, either in the courthouse or in some other accommodation.[101]

95 See the aforementioned case of the entire jury having to take a rest together because one man was drunk. 96 (1843) 3 Cr. & Dix 146. 97 (1853) 3 I.C.L.R. 38; 5 Ir. Jur. 179.

98 This article stated that 'the men under the command of Captain Eagar of the 31st Foot were guilty of wilful and deliberate murder', and had 'butchered our fellow-countrymen in open day upon their native soil'. It was also claimed that 'the cowardly wretches of the 31st' had discharged their guns 'over a defenceless crowd'. The 1852 general election was described as 'one in which the landlords were unusually active and were opposed with unusual bitterness'. See J.H. Whyte, 'Landlord influence at elections in Ireland, 1760–1885', *Eng. Hist. Rev.*, 80 (1965), 739–59 at 750; and *Minutes of evidence on the Clare election petition*, HC 1852–3 (595) ix, 50.

99 Huband, *Treatise*, p. 254. 100 (1882) 17 I.L.T.R. 34.

101 E.g. *Return of persons for trial at last spring assizes*, HC 1833 (402) xxix, 407, 1. At the fourth trial

At Daniel O'Connell's 1844 trial, the attorney general suggested that the jurors might stay in a hotel during the trial, which was predicted to last several weeks. However, after several jurors made representations to the court as to the necessity of their being able to tend to their business affairs, the court ruled that they could return home in the evenings. Nevertheless, before they could deliver their verdict they were obliged to remain together overnight, and they stayed at the Green Street courthouse.[102] Jurors were occasionally kept in for a second night,[103] although this was unusual.

The standard of accommodation provided for jurors varied greatly. In the early part of the century, and in rural areas in particular, jurors were often accommodated in the courthouse, which they unsurprisingly disliked. In a case from 1860, jurors who had been deliberating for some four hours were informed by the judge that they would have to be locked up for the night if they did not reach a verdict. On hearing this, the jury hastily requested more time, and returned with an acquittal within forty minutes.[104] Similarly, in a case from Cootehill, Co. Cavan, in 1873, eleven jurors were in favour of a conviction for larceny of coal, while one, convinced that the defendant had asked for the coal, held out. The chairman of the quarter sessions told the jurors 'that I was very sorry for it, but I should have to lock them up until the morning, when the man said at once "I will agree" and they returned a verdict'.[105] One commentator in 1881 described the discomfort of damp beds,[106] and outside the main cities it may be presumed that the rooms available for the use of jurors were not luxurious. At the Montgomery murder trial in 1873,[107] there was an unusual instance of an outsider wishing to spend the night with the jury in the courthouse. When the judge had delivered his charge:

> [t]he sheriff, when about to lock up the jury, found to his astonishment that he had thirteen gentlemen to accommodate. Inquiry elicited the fact that a

of Sam Gray in 1843, the judge ordered that the jurors be provided with 'proper accommodation': *Freeman's Journal*, 17 Mar. 1843. At the fifth trial, the jurors were accommodated at a hotel: *Irish Examiner*, 21 July 1843.

102 *Affidavits and pleadings filed in the cause of The queen v. Daniel O'Connell and others*, HC 1844 (395) xliv, 225.

103 J.G. Hodges, *Report of the proceedings under the Treason Felony Act, 11 Vic., c. 12, at the commission court, Green-Street, Dublin, Aug. and Oct. 1848* (Dublin, 1848) (first trial of Kevin Izod O'Doherty).

104 *R v. Freyne, Irish Times*, 13 Jan. 1860.

105 *Report on Irish juries*, 1873, para. 3775 (James Robinson, chairman of the Cavan quarter sessions). By contrast, in *Angeli v. Galbraith*, the jurors could not agree but told the court that they did not wish to be discharged late at night because many of them lived a considerable distance from the courthouse. Instead, they were locked up overnight and discharged the following morning. William R. Furlong, *Action for libel. Report of the case of Angeli v. Galbraith, as tried before the lord chief justice at the Kildare summer assizes, 1856; and before the lord chief baron in the court of exchequer, at the after-sittings, Michaelmas term, 1856* (Dublin, 1857).

106 *Report on Irish jury laws*, 1881, para. 222 (Henry Arthur Blake, a Galway R.M.).

107 See p. 154.

> friend of one of the jurors intended to pass the night in their company. On the same day in the same town a case was nearly concluded when it was discovered that there were only eleven jurors in the box, the missing juror having quietly taken his seat in a remote corner of the court.[108]

If jurors retired on a Saturday night, they had to remain together until the following Monday, as no verdict could be received on a Sunday. In *R v. Spollen*, the jurors expressed some concern over whether they would be able to attend Sunday religious services, and Monahan C.J. told them that the sheriff would bring them to their 'several places of worship', as long as they did not communicate with anyone.[109] Similarly, at the trial of Daniel O'Connell, the jurors had not handed in a valid verdict by midnight on Saturday, and were kept together until Monday morning, with Crampton C.J. telling them that they could attend divine service en masse.[110]

Occasionally jurors in Dublin city were accommodated in high-end hotels, such as the Imperial[111] and Gresham[112] hotels on Sackville Street.[113] The sub-sheriff in the *Hynes* trial in 1883 remarked to some of the jurors that in times past they would have been locked up all night in Green Street,[114] suggesting that the use of hotels was a relatively recent development. The jurors in that case caused a national scandal when it was reported in the *Freeman's Journal* that they had been uproariously drunk and disorderly at the hotel.[115] This was a murder trial whose venue was changed to Dublin under the Prevention of Crime (Ireland) Act, 1882.[116] The editor of *United Ireland*, William O'Brien, described as 'Ireland's first investigative journalist',[117] had been staying in the same hotel and brought the jurors' antics to public attention. When Lawson J. discovered this, he notified the attorney general.[118] The jurors swore affidavits claiming to have been sober going

108 *Freeman's Journal*, 8 Mar. 1873.

109 Anon., *Trial of James Spollen for the murder of Mr George Samuel Little at the Broadstone terminus of the Midland Great Western Railway, Ireland, August 7th, 8th, 10th & 11th, 1857* (Dublin, 1857).

110 *R v. O'Connell and others* (1845) 1 Cox C.C. 411.

111 *R v. Hynes*: J. Frost, 'The case of Francis Hynes', *I.L.T. & S.J.*, 16 (1882), 432–4. See also *Dublin commission court (Francis Hynes)*, HC 1882 (408) lv, 167, 16.

112 *Attorney general v. The primate* (1837) 2 Jones 362; and *R v. Barrett* (1870) I.R. 4 C.L. 285.

113 Speaking after the special commissions of 1867–8, Molloy referred to the fact that city jurors could be accommodated in the Gresham Hotel, while country jurors trying a case in the city would not be allowed to leave the courthouse, as this would amount to leaving the county. C. Molloy, 'A central criminal court for the county and city of Dublin', *J.S.S.I.S.I.*, 4:34 (1867), 445–7 at 447. The Special Juries (Ireland) Act, 1825 (6 Geo. IV, c. 51), s. 2 provided that for special-jury cases where the venue was laid in a county of a city or of a town, the jury could come from the adjoining county.

114 *Dublin commission court (Francis Hynes)* (1882).

115 *Freeman's Journal*, 14 Aug. 1882.

116 45 & 46 Vic., c. 25

117 Felix M. Larkin, '"Green shoots" of the new journalism in the *Freeman's Journal*, 1877–1890' in Karen Steele and Michael de Nie (eds), *Ireland and the new journalism* (London, 2014), p. 13.

118 *Freeman's Journal*, 15 Aug. 1882.

to bed, though staff from the hotel testified otherwise.[119] Lawson J. fined Edmund Dwyer Gray, the proprietor and editor of the *Freeman's Journal*, £500 and sentenced him to three months' imprisonment for contempt of court.[120]

An increasingly sympathetic approach to all of these issues was evident from mid-century onwards, and there are examples of judges expressing concern over jurors' discomfort.[121] This sensitivity towards jurors' well-being was promoted not only by a desire that they be comfortable and well looked-after, but also a realisation that having verdicts delivered by exhausted, hungry jurors was almost tantamount to coercion, and reflected poorly on the administration of justice.

UNANIMITY

The issue of unanimous verdicts arose periodically throughout the nineteenth century. Trial juries had to return verdicts that were agreed unanimously. Juries where there were up to 23 jurors (such as grand juries and coroners' juries) still only required the agreement of 12, which left room for dissent. More broadly, majority voting was sufficient for the trials of peers in the house of lords, for courts martial and for Scottish trials. As Vaughan points out, '[i]f a majority was good enough to hang a Scot, to decapitate a duke, or to shoot an admiral, it should have been good enough for Ireland'.[122] However, there was considerable reluctance to extend the majority verdict to civil and criminal trials. In 1831 the royal commission on practice and procedure in the superior courts considered it to be 'essential to the validity of a verdict that the jury should be unanimous'.[123] In the mid-nineteenth century the common-law commissioners grappled with the issue of whether the unanimous verdict rule should be maintained.[124] They referred to the rule against refreshment as 'a species of coercion'. The unanimous verdict was, in the commissioners' view, to be retained; however, unanimity was not to be coerced by shutting the jury away, 'often in an inconvenient room, without

119 See generally *Dublin commission court (Francis Hynes)* (1882). It emerged from the evidence of several jurors that the sub-sheriff had authorized the purchase of alcohol.

120 *Freeman's Journal*, 17 Aug. 1882; *Pall Mall Gazette*, 17 Aug. 1882. See also Anon., 'Mr. Gray's imprisonment', *I.L.T. & S.J.*, 16 (1882), 432; and Gray Indemnity Committee, *The power of judges to punish for contempt of court, as exemplified by the case of the high sheriff of Dublin, 1882* (Dublin, 1882). Gray spent six weeks in Richmond gaol and his fine was paid by public subscription.

121 E.g. *R v. O'Connell and others* (1845) 1 Cox C.C. 411. In England, Abbott C.J. had pointed out twenty years earlier that 'it would have been most injurious to the cause of the defendants, that their case should be heard by a jury, whose minds were exhausted by fatigue': *R v. Kinnear* (1819) 2 B. & Ald. 462; 106 E.R. 434.

122 Vaughan, *Murder trials*, p. 166.

123 *Royal commission on practice and procedure*, HC 1831 (92) x, 375. The criminal law commissioners also discussed the possibility of majority verdicts in criminal cases in 1845: *Eighth report on criminal law*, HC 1845 (656) xiv, 161.

124 *Royal commission on pleading* [C-1626] HC 1852–3, xl, 701, p. 708.

accommodation, without fire, without refreshment, for several hours, sometimes for a whole night'.[125]

An attempt was made in 1854 to allow for majority verdicts in certain circumstances,[126] but ultimately failed. The *Irish Jurist* considered these developments 'startling', but ones which would not necessarily 'sap the foundations of trial by jury'.[127] Ultimately, the provision allowing for majority verdicts was rejected.[128] An attempt was also made in 1859 to introduce majority verdicts in Scotland.[129] Brown described it as a 'very moderate measure',[130] and asked '[w]hat great and mysterious advantages are contained in the sacred number twelve?' There appears to have been some appetite in Ireland for the introduction of majority verdicts, especially in criminal cases involving Whiteboy or Ribbonmen offences, where convictions were difficult to secure.[131] This support grew, with Houston, for example, pointing out in 1861 that in appeal cases, the decision of a majority of the judges was acceptable.[132] He also pointed out that 'the narrowest majority in parliament is sufficient to determine matters affecting the dearest interests of the community, life and property, peace and war'. He recommended that 'it would be judicious to increase the number on the jury, and to require a certain definite preponderance of votes to constitute a verdict'. Later in the nineteenth century, other commentators became critical of the unanimity rule,[133] which was not, however, abolished in criminal cases until the twentieth century.[134]

THE VERDICT

The nature of the verdict delivered depended on the nature of the jury and the circumstances of the case. In a criminal trial the verdict was 'guilty' or 'not guilty', and by the nineteenth century the 'beyond reasonable doubt' standard was

125 Ibid., p. 8.

126 E.g. *Common law (amendment) bill*, 1854, s. 17, HC 1854 (123) i, 473. See *Hansard 3*, cxxx, 1335–6.

127 Anon., editorial (1854) 6 *Ir. Jur.* (o.s.) 181. The *Irish Jurist* later called the existing practice of keeping jurors confined for long periods 'vicious'. (1854) 6 *Ir. Jur.* (o.s.) 229.

128 The Common Law Procedure Act, 1854 (17 & 18 Vic., c. 25), however, made jury trial optional for civil cases in the royal courts at Westminster, thereby allowing judges in those cases to determine questions of fact. See C. Hanly, 'The decline of civil jury trial in nineteenth-century England', *J. Leg. Hist.*, 26 (2005), 253–78.

129 *Trial by jury (Scotland)*, HC 1859 (47) ii, 915; and *Jury Trial (Scotland) Act amendment*, HC 1859 (2) i, 509.

130 J. Brown, *The dark side of trial by jury* (London, 1859).

131 (1858) 11 *Ir. Jur.* (o.s.) 94. 132 Houston, 'Observations', p. 105.

133 An unsuccessful bill was introduced in 1871: *A bill to assimilate the law of trial by jury in Ireland to that of Scotland*, HC 1871 (47) vi, 473

134 The Criminal Procedure (Majority Verdicts) Act (NI) 1971, s. 1, and the Criminal Justice Act, 1984, s. 25 allowed for majority verdicts of ten in criminal cases. See also the Criminal Justice Act, 1967, which allowed majority verdicts in all criminal trials in England and Wales and the Juries Act, 1974, s. 17.

well-established.[135] MacNally's early nineteenth-century treatise on evidence[136] is credited by Shapiro as having played a significant role in 'diffusing the beyond reasonable doubt language'. He had acted as defence counsel at the trial of Patrick Finney, one of the late-eighteenth-century Irish state trials, and had emphasised on numerous occasions that a jury entertaining a reasonable doubt was obliged to acquit.[137]

In a civil action, a jury could give a verdict for either party and decide on damages and costs. The jury of matrons gave a verdict of 'with quick child' or 'not with quick child'. Coroners' verdicts varied more, as they gave the cause of death. Valuation juries such as wide-streets juries gave a valuation instead of a verdict. Wide-streets juries sometimes gave a verdict of 'reasonable' or 'unreasonable' in relation to valuation claims. Traverse juries and juries appointed to assess damages simply returned a sum of damages.

In all trials, the foreman of the jury was given an issue paper to complete. When the jurors had agreed on a verdict, they returned to court, and he handed the issue paper to the clerk of the crown. The clerk then called out the list of jurors, each of whom had to answer to his name, before he asked them, 'Gentlemen, have you agreed upon your verdict? Who shall say for you?' To this they replied, 'our foreman', and the clerk went on to ask the foreman what the verdict was.[138] It would appear that the issue paper was handed back even where the jury disagreed,[139] or the case was withdrawn from them.[140] The foreman wrote the verdict on the paper and sometimes signed it, although this was problematic in cases of poor literacy – for example, the sub-sheriff of Dublin observed in 1874 that he frequently encountered jurors, including foremen, who could not sign their names or write 'guilty' on the issue paper.[141] At a Donegal trial in 1894, for example, the foreman wrote 'giltey' in a large, shaky hand,[142] and there are numerous examples of verdicts of 'gilty' or 'gulty'.[143]

The verdict could either be public or privy. The public verdict was delivered in court before a judge, while the privy verdict was delivered before a judge out of court. Coke explained that in civil cases, if the court had already adjourned for the evening, the jury could give their verdict to the judge, and thus be allowed to eat

135 See Barbara J. Shapiro, '"Beyond reasonable doubt": the neglected eighteenth century context', *L. & Humanities*, 8:1 (2014), 19–52, which notes the standard's first use at the Boston Massacre trials of 1770. See also Barbara J. Shapiro, '"To a moral certainty": theories of knowledge and Anglo-American juries, 1600–1850', *Hastings L. Rev.*, 38 (1986), 153–93. See also James Q. Whitman, *The origins of reasonable doubt: the theological roots of the criminal trial* (New Haven, CT, 2008).

136 Leonard Mac Nally, *Rules of evidence on pleas of the crown* (Dublin, 1802).

137 Shapiro, 'Beyond reasonable doubt', pp 46–7.

138 Purcell, *Criminal law*, p. 207.

139 E.g. *R v. Denis Murray*, Lifford quarter sessions, 19 Jan. 1892 *Donegal jury issue papers 1887–1908* (NAI, 1C-49–26).

140 E.g. *R v. James Breslin and James Mulhern*, Donegal quarter sessions, 5 Jan. 1893 (NAI, 1C-49–26).

141 *Report on the Irish jury system*, HC 1874 (244) ix, 557, paras 500–1.

142 *R v. Grace Bower*, Donegal spring assizes, 16 Mar. 1894 (NAI, 1C-49–26).

143 E.g *R v. Doherty*, Donegal spring assizes, 14 Mar. 1899 and *R v. Charles McHugh*, Lifford quarter sessions, 16 Jan. 1902 (NAI, 1C-49–26).

and drink.[144] The following morning, they could either confirm or alter their privy verdict, and in cases of inconsistency the verdict that was delivered in court was the one that stood.[145] The privy verdict was so called, according to Coke, because 'it ought to be kept secret and privy from each of the parties before it can be affirmed in court'.[146] There could be no privy verdict in cases of felony and treason,[147] but in cases of 'inferior misdemeanours' there was no requirement that the defendant be present.[148] A jury could not vary their verdict once it had been recorded.[149] Verdicts could also be general or partial. A partial or qualified verdict in a criminal case might, for example, find the accused guilty on one charge or count, but acquit him on another. This was sometimes used in cases with long indictments and multiple charges.

The form of the verdict could be either special or general.[150] Bingham explained at the end of the eighteenth century that jurors were to try issues of fact, and judges were to try issues of law.[151] According to Swaine, '[a]lthough a distinction between law and fact was firmly established by the sixteenth century, applying the division in practice was not always so easy'.[152] By the mid-eighteenth century, however, the difference 'had become absolutely distinct in law and practice'.[153] Coke warned that 'if [jurors] will take upon them the knowledge of the law in the matter, they may; yet it is dangerous; for, if they mistake the law, they run into the danger of an attaint; therefore to find the special matter is the safest way, where the case is doubtful'.[154] A general verdict covered legal as well as factual issues, whereas a special verdict was one in which the jury separated the legal question from the factual question. Typically, the jury would make a finding of fact and seek the court's advice as to the applicable law. An example given by Bingham was where a person was indicted for grand larceny. The jury could deliver a verdict that the defendant was guilty of larceny, but that the goods were worth less than £10, so the defendant was guilty of the lesser offence of petty larceny. MacNally wrote in 1802 that a special verdict might find that the accused was present at the perpetration of the charge in question, 'but does not find any particular act of *force* committed by him'.[155] This type of verdict could also be called a verdict at large: Coke wrote that it was so called because the jurors 'find the special matter at large, and leave the judgment of law thereupon to the court'.[156] The special verdict had to be removed by writ of *certiorari* to the court of queen's bench for consideration by the judges.[157]

144 Huband, *Treatise*, p. 783. See J. Bingham, *A new practical digest of the law of evidence, inc. the juryman's complete guide* (London, 1796), p. 81.
145 *Saunders v. Freeman and wife* (1816) 1 Plow. 208; 75 E.R. 321. 146 3 Co. Inst. 228a.
147 3 Co. Inst. 227b. 148 Purcell, p. 207. 149 3 Co. Inst. 227b.
150 See W.S. Holdsworth, *History of English law*, 12 vols (London, 1903–34), iii, pp 613–14; 3 Co. Inst. 227b. 151 Bingham, *New practical digest*, p. 77.
152 Warren Swaine, *The law of contract, 1670–1870* (Cambridge, 2015), p. 25. 153 Ibid., p. 28.
154 3 Co. Inst. 228a. 155 L. MacNally, *The rules of evidence on pleas of the crown* (Dublin, 1802), p. 527. 156 3 Co. Inst. 228a.
157 E. Hayes, *Crimes and punishments, or a digest of the criminal statute law of Ireland*, 2 vols (2nd ed., Dublin, 1842), ii, p. 921.

Under the common law, a jury had the right to bring a special verdict in all cases, both civil and criminal.[158] They could be advised by the judge to bring such a verdict, but he could not compel them.[159] Coke was of the view that the special verdict was the safest option open to a jury where they had any doubt over the case.[160] There was no particular form of words necessary for a special verdict, but Purcell warned that it should 'positively state the facts themselves *as facts*, and not merely set out the evidence adduced to prove them'.[161]

STATEMENTS ACCOMPANYING THE VERDICT

Sometimes juries accompanied their verdict with a statement or rider. Hayes refers to riders in a manner that suggests that they were relatively common in the mid-nineteenth century.[162] Although there was no legal requirement to do so, juries occasionally gave reasons for their verdict. This was more common in relation to acquittals than convictions. Such a rider might state, for example, that the jury believed the defendant acted in self-defence,[163] or that there was an 'insufficiency of the evidence',[164] or that shots fired were intended to warn and not to injure,[165] or that the injury or death may have resulted from another cause.[166] In civil cases, riders often related to damages,[167] with jurors justifying or explaining how they had arrived at a particular sum.[168] Jurors might also add general commentary on their view of the parties,[169] the judge,[170] the evidence,[171] the police[172] or issues such as contributory negligence.[173] Coroners' juries frequently added riders to their

158 3 Co. Inst. 227a. The Libel Act (33 Geo. III, c. 43), provided that juries in libel actions could deliver both general and special verdicts.

159 See the English cases of *Devizes v. Clark* (1835) 3 Ad. & E.; 111 E.R. 506 and *William Owen's case* (1752) 18 How. St. Tr. 1203.

160 3 Co. Inst. 228a. Examples of special verdicts were *Conway v. Brophy, Freeman's Journal*, 21 Feb. 1821 and *Illot v. Wilkes, Freeman's Journal*, 29 Jan. 1820.

161 Purcell, *Criminal law*, p. 208.

162 Hayes, *Crimes and punishments*, i, p. 452.

163 *R v. Lavel, Freeman's Journal*, 21 Mar. 1839. This case involved the murder of Francis Reynolds, chief officer of the Achill coast guard.

164 William Ridgeway, *A report of the proceedings in the cases of Thomas Kirwan, Merchant, and Edward Sheridan, M.D., for misdemeanours charged to be committed in violation of the Convention Act* (Dublin, 1811), p. 292.

165 *R v. Buchanan, Belfast Newsletter*, 8 Apr. 1831.

166 *Report on Irish jury laws*, 1881, para. 3864 (Bolton).

167 E.g. *Kinsella v. Hamilton, Irish Times*, 19 Apr. 1890.

168 E.g. *Smith v. Holbrook, Freeman's Journal*, 19 June 1845 and Anon., *Persecution of Protestants in the year 1845, as detailed in a full and correct report of the trial at Tralee, on Thursday, March 20, 1845, for a libel on the Rev Charles Gayer* (Dublin, 1845), p. 85.

169 E.g. Anon., *A special report of the trial of the issues in the case of M'Lain v. Enery, tried before judge Burton and a special jury of the county of Tyrone, at the spring assizes held at Omagh, in 1842* (Dublin, 1842).

170 *Ferguson v. Humphrey, Irish Times*, 7 Aug. 1871.

171 *R v. Fitzgerald, Irish Times*, 11 Nov. 1884.

172 E.g. *R v. Guston, Irish Times*, 11 Aug. 1883 and *R v. Larkin, Irish Times*, 2 Dec. 1881.

173 *R v. Sands and others, Irish Times*, 16 Oct. 1877.

verdicts regarding the apportionment of blame for the death in question,[174] or exhorting private companies to take steps to ensure greater public safety around things like canals,[175] cesspools,[176] rivers,[177] harbours[178] and railways.

The most common form of jury rider was the recommendation to mercy accompanying a conviction in a criminal case. Vaughan examines recommendations to mercy in the context of murder trials,[179] and McMahon has examined them in the context of sentence commutation more generally, identifying differences between England and Ireland.[180] The jury could recommend mercy in both capital[181] and non-capital cases, such as manslaughter,[182] stealing,[183] assault,[184] perjury,[185] and membership of secret agrarian societies.[186] Some recommendations were made without the jury specifying any grounds for mercy,[187] but others provided some insight into the jury's reasoning. The motivation for recommending mercy varied depending on the nature of the case. In some cases, juries were dissatisfied with the law or its application, or the evidence adduced at trial,[188] while in others they recommended mercy because they opposed capital punishment.[189] A jury might also be driven by compassion, and factors such as the prisoner's age and health were important.[190] As McMahon points out, the prisoner's good character and lack of prior convictions was also extremely relevant to Irish juries,[191] and there are numerous examples of jurors during this period explicitly stating this as a reason for their recommendation.[192] Jury recommendations to mercy indicate

174 E.g. inquest on Henry Jessop, St. John's Parish, Sligo, *Sligo Independent*, 8 Aug. 1902.
175 Inquest on Richard Duignan, Sallins, 3 Jan. 1891; inquest on Mary Donohue, Robertstown, 18 Nov. 1890; inquest on James Sales, Mylestown, Co. Kildare, 24 Dec. 1888 (NAI, 1C-02–6024).
176 E.g. inquest on Daniel Ryan, Killaloe, 23 Aug. 1885 (NAI, 1D-39–112).
177 E.g. inquest on Cornelius Keating, 24 Apr. 1916 (NLI, MS 41, 655).
178 E.g. inquest on Maura Gavin, Sligo, 10 Dec. 1892 (NAI 1C-31–95).
179 Vaughan, *Murder trials in Ireland*, pp 282–304.
180 Richard McMahon, '"Let the law take its course": punishment and the exercise of the prerogative of mercy in pre-Famine and Famine Ireland' in Sean Patrick Donlan and Michael Brown (eds), *The laws and other legalities of Ireland, 1689–1850* (Surrey, 2011).
181 E.g. William Sampson, *The trial of the Rev. William Jackson at the bar of the king's bench in Ireland for high treason, on Thursday the 23rd of April, 1795* (Dublin, 1795) and William Ridgeway, *A report on the trial of Walter Clare upon an indictment for high treason* (Dublin, 1803).
182 E.g. *R v. Crowley, Irish Examiner*, 25 July 1895, and *R v. French, Irish Examiner*, 16 Dec. 1892.
183 E.g. *R v. O'Neil and Agnew, Belfast Newsletter*, 1 Apr. 1828.
184 E.g. *R v. White, Irish Times*, 2 Dec. 1881.
185 E.g. *R v. Peacy, Freeman's Journal*, 16 July 1838.
186 E.g. Andrew Bourne, *Report of the trial had at the court-house, Green-Street, on the 23rd, 24th, 25th and 29th Days of June, 1840, of Richard Jones, who was charged with being a member of an illegal society* (Dublin, 1841).
187 E.g. William Ridgeway, *A report on the trial of Walter Clare upon an indictment for high treason* (Dublin, 1803) and J.G. Hodges, *The trial of William Smith O'Brien*, p. 886.
188 E.g. *R v. O'Neil and Agnew, Belfast Newsletter*, 1 Apr. 1828.
189 E.g. *R v. Wade, Irish Times*, 17 Dec. 1883.
190 E.g. *R v. Jackson* (1795), p. 29.
191 McMahon, 'Let the law take its course', p. 162.
192 E.g. Anon., *Commission of oyer and terminer: the trial of Thos. Edward Bellamy, for forgery; before the hon. baron George and the hon. Justice Finucane, at Dublin, the 5th of Nov. 1802* (Dublin, 1802).

an awareness among jurors of different levels of culpability that perhaps could not be reflected in the traditional verdicts of guilty or not guilty. They recommended mercy if particular motives could be ascribed to the accused,[193] or if they identified particular mitigating factors.[194]

Judges did not always comment, positively or otherwise, on juries' recommendations to mercy, but where they did provide a reaction, this was likely to be positive.[195] Judges often agreed with the jury's views,[196] although there are also examples of cases where judges disagreed with the jury's comments or recommendations.[197] Riders from trial juries had varying impacts depending on the nature of the case and the surrounding circumstances. Recommendations to mercy tended to have a significant impact on sentencing in Ireland, where rates of sentence commutation were relatively high. McMahon demonstrates that the share of capital cases in which a sentence of death was commuted rose from 45 per cent at the beginning of the century to over 90 per cent by 1840,[198] while in Vaughan's sample of 85 murder cases, almost one-third of juries recommended the prisoners to mercy.[199]

It is clear that some riders were elucidations of the jury's reasoning, while others may have been the result of compromise within the jury box. The unanimous verdict left little room for discord or disagreement, but a rider or recommendation to mercy may have helped to overcome these difficulties. The recommendation to mercy in a capital case, for example, might sweeten the pill for jurors who opposed capital punishment. Juries used riders and recommendations to sidestep the blunt tools of the guilty/not guilty, or plaintiff/defendant verdict.

GIVING THE 'WRONG' VERDICT

When jurors in civil actions were supposed to make findings from their own knowledge, it followed that they would be guilty of perjury if they gave a 'wrong' verdict. They were also liable to punishment by the writ of attaint,[200] the origins of which are uncertain.[201] This was 'a key medieval institution embodying both the legal and spiritual threats that menaced jurors'.[202] A party who felt aggrieved by the finding of the jury could sue out a writ of attaint, and twenty-four new jurors

193 E.g. *R v. Crowley, Irish Examiner*, 25 July 1895.
194 E.g. *R v. Quinlisk, Freeman's Journal*, 11 Mar. 1878 and *R v. French, Irish Examiner*, 16 Dec. 1892.
195 E.g. *R v. Thackaberrey, Irish Times*, 30 Mar. 1895.
196 E.g. *R v. M'Auliffe and others, Irish Examiner*, 19 Jan. 1882 and *R v. Turner, Freeman's Journal*, 9 Oct. 1821.
197 E.g. *R v. Harvey, Weekly Irish Times*, 21 Feb. 1891; *R v. Kennedy, Nenagh Guardian*, 12 Feb. 1887.
198 McMahon, 'Let the law take its course', p. 156.
199 Vaughan, *Murder trials*, p. 282.
200 Whitman, *Origins*, pp 141–4.
201 J.M. Mitnick, 'From neighbour-witness to judge of proofs: the transformation of the English civil juror', *American J. Leg. Hist.*, 32 (1988), 201–35 at 209.
202 Whitman, *Origins*, p. 141.

were sworn in to try the issue in dispute.[203] This was not merely a reconsideration of the facts in dispute, but 'a criminal trial of the first jury for perjury'.[204] If the first jury was found to have delivered a false verdict, 'in spite of their own better knowledge of the facts',[205] they were severely punished, losing their lands and goods and becoming infamous. This, says Plucknett, was 'only logical' at a time when the function of the jury was to relay its own knowledge of the facts.[206] The use of attaint declined in the fifteenth and sixteenth centuries as jurors began to be assisted by the production of evidence in court.[207] By the late eighteenth century it was rarely invoked.[208] There could be no writ of attaint in criminal proceedings, though there are instances of jurors being fined and imprisoned for their verdict in such cases.[209] The famous decision in *Bushel's case*[210] is credited with having secured the independence of the jury, by declaring the illegality of fining and imprisoning them an account of their verdict. Vaughan C.J. held that jurors were not bound to follow the direction of the court, and that the threat of attaint was enough to secure an honest verdict, without the risk of subsequent punishment in the star chamber[211] or elsewhere.[212] After *Bushel's case*, juries were considered to be independent from the bench. From the mid-seventeenth century on, new trials could be granted and the writ of attaint fell into disuse, finally being abolished in Ireland in 1833.[213] Verdicts in civil cases could be set aside if, for example, the judge was of the view that the verdict went against the weight of evidence.[214] Baron Deasy noted in 1874, however, that this was 'very difficult', and that the power was 'rarely exercised, unless it is a very flagrant case indeed'.[215]

Decisions by wide-streets juries could be appealed or challenged. For example, it will be recalled that in the 1790s when a party subject to a valuation of properties

203 Attaint jurors tended to be of higher social standing: Oldham, *Trial by jury*, pp 135–6.
204 T.F.T. Plucknett, *A concise history of the common law* (5th ed., Boston, 1956), p. 131.
205 Ibid. 206 Ibid. 207 Ibid., p. 132.
208 Bingham, *New practical digest*, p. 105, and Mitnick, 'Neighbour-witness', 210.
209 For example, *Wharton's case* (1792) Yel. 24; 80 E.R. 17. All of the jurors were 'committed and fined, and bound to their good behaviour', after acquitting the prisoners on an indictment for murder.
210 (1682) Vaughan 135; 124 E.R. 1006. See Thomas A. Green, *Verdict according to conscience: perspectives on the criminal trial, 1200–1800* (Chicago, 1985), pp 236–49.
211 The Irish equivalent was the court of castle chamber: Jon Crawford, *A star chamber court in Ireland: the court of castle chamber, 1571–1641* (Dublin, 2005).
212 Some scholars have questioned the impact of *Bushell*: e.g. John H. Langbein, 'The criminal trial before the lawyers', *U. Chic. L. Rev.*, 45 (1978), 263–316 at 297–8; Green, *Verdict according to conscience*, p. 239; and John H. Langbein, *The origins of adversary criminal trial* (Oxford, 2003), p. 324. Crosbie, however, argues that the case had contemporary relevance, both for ending the judge's power to fine and as part of the general reappraisal of the role of the jury: Kevin Crosbie, 'Bushell's case and the juror's soul', *J. Leg. Hist.*, 33:3 (2012), 251–90.
213 The Juries (Ireland) Act, 1833 (3 & 4 Will. IV, c. 91), s. 47. It had been abolished in England in 1825.
214 E.g. see W. Blackstone, *Commentaries on the laws of England*, 4 vols (London, 1791), iii, p. 387.
215 *Report on the Irish jury system*, HC 1874 (244) ix, 557, para. 2537.

on Cutpurse Row, New Row and Cornmarket disagreed with the finding of a Dublin wide-streets jury, a second jury was appointed in 1801 to conduct another valuation of the property.[216] A valuation by a wide-streets jury that was deemed excessively high was liable to be quashed by the wide-streets commission.[217] However, it was relatively unusual for valuations by juries to be subject to appeal, and most such valuations were considered final.[218] In fact, where such valuations were made by other persons, they were sometimes subject to appeal to a jury, whose verdict was final.[219]

In criminal cases, it was not until the twentieth century that full courts of criminal appeal were established in Ireland.[220]

NO VERDICT

Bacon wrote in the early eighteenth century that traditionally, 'a jury sworn and charged in a capital case [could] not be discharged (without the prisoner's consent), till they [gave] a verdict'.[221] This rule was generally adhered to, though there were exceptions. Sometimes criminal jurors deliberated for many hours without being able to reach agreement.[222] In civil cases a judge could not discharge a jury from giving a verdict on any material issue without the consent of the parties on both sides.[223] In order to effect this discharge, a practice developed of withdrawing one juror by consent;[224] this left the jury incomplete, meaning no verdict could be delivered.[225] This happened relatively regularly; for example, in 1863, in 88 cases a juror was withdrawn, out of a total of 2,601 civil cases, representing 3.3 per cent.[226] With the parties' consent, a jury could also be

216 Wide Streets Commission, *Extracts from the minutes of the commissioners appointed by act of parliament, for making wide and convenient ways, streets and passages in the city of Dublin* (Dublin, 1802), pp 62–3.

217 *Fifteenth report on salaries*, p. 540 (Sobieski Kildahl, solicitor).

218 See p. 68.

219 E.g. 23 & 24 Geo. III, c. 52, s. 37.

220 These were established in the Free State by the Courts of Justice Act, 1924 and in Northern Ireland by the Criminal Appeal (Northern Ireland) Act, 1930.

221 Matthew Bacon, *A new abridgement of the law*, 5 vols (London, 1736–66) iv, p. 269.

222 E.g. *R v. Barrett* (1870) I.R. 4 C.L. 285; Jebb C.C.R. 103 (five hours), and *R v. Fay* (1872) I.R. 6 C.L. 436 (seven hours).

223 E.g. the English case *Tinkler v. Rowland* (1836) 4 Ad. & E. 868; 111 E.R. 1010.

224 E.g. Anon., *Crim. Con. Report of a trial, in the court of common pleas, on Saturday, Dec. 14, 1816. John Hinds, gentleman attorney, plaintiff. Philip Perry Price Myddleton, defendant* (Dublin, 1816).

225 E.g. the English cases *Moulin v. Dallison* (1638) Cro. Car. 484; 79 E.R. 1018; *Sanderson v. Nestor* (1826) Ry. & Mood. 402; 171 E.R. 1063; *Everett v. Youells* (1832) 3 B. & Ald. 349; 11 E.R. 131; *Moscati v. Lawson* (1835) 4 Ad. & E. 331; 111 E.R. 811; and *Harries v. Thomas* (1836) 2 M. & W. 32; 150 E.R. 656. Unless the record stated otherwise, it was generally presumed that the parties had consented to the discharge of the jury: *Scott v. Bennett* (1868) I.R. 3 C.L. 217 (1871) LR 5 HL 234.

226 *Judicial statistics, 1863* [C-3418] HC 1864 lvii, 653, p. v. Jurors were discaharged without a verdict in 29 cases. The figures refer to cases in the courts of queen's bench, common pleas, exchequer and *nisi prius*.

discharged from giving a verdict on immaterial issues.[227] If a coroner's jury was unable to agree on a verdict within a reasonable time, the coroner could discharge them and empanel another jury.[228] This was generally done relatively quickly, as time was of the essence when it came to inquests.

A trial jury could also be discharged if one of its members fell ill during the proceedings.[229] A physician was generally sworn in to examine the ill juror, and in most cases, he swore that the juror's life was endangered, and that there was a high risk that he would die if not discharged. Sometimes this was due to, or exacerbated by, an existing condition, such as gout[230] or old age,[231] but in other instances it was brought about almost entirely as a consequence of the poor conditions under which the jurors were detained.[232] At the first trial of Kevin Izod O'Doherty in 1848, the jurors were kept in deliberations for two nights, and on the third morning Pennefather B. observed that '[u]nder all the circumstances, it does not appear to the court that they ought to endanger the lives of the jury by keeping them confined any longer'.[233] He added that human life 'cannot endure this kind of trial beyond a certain extent'. The attorney general pointed out that a certificate from a sworn doctor was necessary, but Pennefather was satisfied to proceed without one. He had it entered on the record that the jury had been locked up 'without food or easement; and it appearing to the court that they are exhausted by fatigue and labour, and that it would be dangerous to their health, if not to their lives, to keep them longer confined, the court does discharge them'.[234] The attorney general appeared to be nervous about proceeding in this manner, and pointed out that one of the jurors did in fact appear to be ill. The record was amended and the jurors were discharged. Claims of illness were sometimes conveniently made after a judge refused to discharge the jury on other grounds, and judges appeared to be quick to accept a physician's testimony about the risk to a juror's health. Sometimes the remaining eleven jurors were discharged and then re-sworn onto a second jury, along with one replacement for the sick juror.[235]

227 E.g. *Garvin v. Carroll* (1847) 10 Ir. L.R. 323; *Shea v. The queen and Dwyer v. The queen* (1848) 12 Ir. L.R. 153; *Tisdall v. Parnell* (1863) 14 I.C.L.R. 1; and *Cassidy v. Kincaid* (1865) 10 Ir. Jur. (n.s.) 176.

228 The Coroners (Ireland) Act, 1881 (44 & 45 Vic., c. 35), s. 6. None of the original jurors could sit on the second jury.

229 E.g. see Micheal McMahon, *The murder of Thomas Douglas Bateson, County Monaghan, 1851* (Dublin, 2006), p. 47, discussing the trials of Bryant Grant, Patrick Coomey, Francis Berr, John Maginnis, William McArdle and Edward Magennis.

230 E.g. *R v. Barrett, Connors and others* (1829) Jebb C.C.R 103.

231 E.g. *R v. Delany and Cheevers* (1829) Jebb C.C.R 106.

232 E.g. *R v. Dunne and others* (1838) Cr. & Dix Abr. 535; *R v. Lecken* (1844) 3 Cr. & Dix C.C. 174 and *R v. Newton* (1849) 3 Car. & K. 85; 175 E.R. 473. See also *R v. Leary and Cooke* (1844) 3 Cr. & Dix C.C. 212.

233 Hodges, *Report of proceedings under the Treason Felony Act*, p. 175.

234 Ibid., p. 176.

235 E.g. the English cases *Jeffrys v. Tyndall* (1624) Palmer 411; 81 E.R. 1147; *R v. Scalbert* (1794) 2 Leach 260; 168 E.R. 412; and *R v. Edwards* (1812) Russ. & Ry. 224; 168 E.R. 772.

Instances of criminal jurors being unable to reach verdicts were not unheard of. The unanimity requirement, of course, meant that a single tenacious juror could have a significant impact. In 1865, statistics were compiled indicating the number of instances over a twenty-year period in which juries had failed to agree verdicts in capital cases.[236] Nationally, there were seventy-seven, an average of less than four per annum. While this is a small proportion of the number of convictions per annum,[237] it is in fact quite a high proportion of capital cases; between 1854 and 1863 there were an average of 5.3 capital convictions per annum. Some of the accused persons in such cases were released on recognizances, while the majority were sent for retrial, usually at the next assizes. While some of the trials related to politically motivated acts of violence, others involved domestic killings, feuds or other forms of violence. It is also worth noting that in some counties, such as Cork, Dublin and Fermanagh, there were no instances of juries failing to reach a verdict in a capital case over the twenty-year period. In others, it was a comparatively frequent occurrence. Tyrone, for example, accounted for 14 of the 77 cases, while Armagh had 22 instances. While some of the cases in which jurors could not agree had a political or agrarian hue,[238] others were instances of domestic violence, for example.[239]

Hope wrote in 1737 that until jurors reached a verdict, 'they are all confin'd … nor can they be set at liberty, till the judge is out of the county'.[240] Jurors were occasionally transported to the county line if they had failed to reach a verdict by the time the judge was ready to depart at the end of the assizes. Bacon wrote that 'if they agree not before the departure of the justices of gaol-delivery into another county, the sheriff must send them along in carts, and the judge may take and record their verdict in a foreign county'.[241] This seems to have been used as an alternative to simply discharging the jurors if they were unable to reach an agreement. There was no official rule as to when this was done – much depended on the nature of the case, the public interest in obtaining a verdict and the judge's determination not to leave unfinished business in his wake.[242] The *Ulster Times*, for example, described in 1836 how, after a two-day trial in Queen's County, the prisoners were placed in a chaise, and the jurors in carts, and the entourage

236 See appendix two.

237 Capital convictions represented only 0.13% of total convictions: over the ten-year period from 1853 to 1864 there were an average of 4,000 convictions per year. *Judicial statistics, 1864* [C-3418] HC 1864 lvii, 653, p. xx.

238 E.g. *R v. Berry and Maginnis, Belfast Newsletter*, 9 Aug. 1852. Berry was executed for his part in the attempted murder of his landlord following a dispute over rent.

239 E.g. *R v. Thomson, Belfast Newsletter*, 23 Mar. 1849 (murder of wife); *R v. Sleeth, Irish Examiner*, 20 May 1863 (murder of husband).

240 Hope, *Dissertation*, p. 9.

241 Bacon, *A new abridgement*, iv, p. 269. Similarly, in *R v. Ledgingham* (1682) 1 Vent. 97, 104; 86 E.R. 67, 72, it was stated that if the jurors were unable to reach agreement before the departure of the judges, 'they are to be carried in carts after them so they may give their verdict out of the county'.

242 See the example given in O.J. Burke, *Anecdotes of the Connaught circuit* (Dublin, 1885), p. 163.

proceeded to the county boundary. The judge met the jury again at a nearby town, and they once again claimed that they had reached no verdict, and were finally discharged.[243]

The practice appears to have fallen out of favour by the mid-century.[244] An 1854 editorial in the *Irish Jurist* pointed out that formerly, 'a jury unable to agree were carted to the verge of the county', but that 'in our more polished age, a protestation on the part of the foreman, after the lapse of a few hours, as to the total impossibility of an agreement, usually induces the parties to a suit to consent to their discharge'.[245] In 1860, an Irish judge remarked that jurors who were unable to agree a verdict were no longer 'liable to be taken in a kish to the end of the county',[246] and the following year the Dublin Statistical Society referred to the 'barbarous' practice of carting as having been discontinued.[247]

CONCLUSION

As well as the possible risks to their persons and property for delivering an unpopular verdict, when one considers the physical conditions facing trial jurors, it is unsurprising that so many of them were reluctant to participate, as discussed in earlier chapters. Aside from their poor remuneration, however, conditions generally improved over the course of the nineteenth century, with practices such as carting phased out, prohibitions on refreshments abolished, and courthouse accommodation generally improved.

When it came to delivering their verdict, jurors had a number of options, from the delivery of a special or partial verdict, to the adding of commentary or recommendations to mercy. The frequency with which trial and inquest juries added riders to their verdicts once again highlights the relatively active role they still played in the nineteenth century.

243 *Ulster Times*, 31 Mar. 1836.

244 An 1854 *Irish Jurist* editorial pointed out that formerly, 'a jury unable to agree were carted to the verge of the county', but that 'in our more polished age, a protestation on the part of the foreman, after the lapse of a few hours, as to the total impossibility of an agreement, usually induces the parties to a suit to consent to their discharge'. Anon., editorial *Ir. Jur.* (o.s.), 6 (1854), 181. Seven years later, a paper published by the Dublin Statistical Society pointed out that the pressure on jurors to reach a unanimous verdict used to be 'much more violent than at the present time'. The paper stated that '[i]n modern times, happily, these barbarous practices, though not explicitly forbidden by the legislature, have been altogether discontinued; but two engines for enforcing unanimity are still in use, namely, starvation and imprisonment.' Houston, 'Observations', p. 104.

245 Anon., editorial, *Ir. Jur.* (o.s.) 6 (1854) 181.

246 *Irish Times*, 13 Jan. 1860.

247 Houston, 'Observations', p. 104. The practice had also ceased in England by that stage: in *Winsor v. The queen* (1866) 6 B. & S. 143; 122 E.R. 1150, Mellor J. declared it 'absolutely inconsistent with our modern ideas that a judge should carry a jury in a cart with him to the confines of the county, or round the circuit, and then turn them out'.

CHAPTER FOURTEEN

Conclusions

SCHOLARSHIP ON NINETEENTH-CENTURY Irish juries has usually focused on the problems encountered, and has concentrated on the criminal trial jury.[1] As McEldowney has pointed out, given the many problems facing the operation of the jury system in Ireland in the nineteenth century, the fact that it survived at all 'was a remarkable achievement'.[2] This has been the general tenor of studies of Irish criminal juries – that their survival is extraordinary. Johnson, for example, concurs with McEldowney's conclusions.[3] Vaughan, it will be seen, unpicks these statements somewhat, although his discussion is limited to criminal juries. There was corruption and, at times, apathy among the officials tasked with returning lists of jurors, many of whom enjoyed too much autonomy and too little accountability. In the early part of the century, information regarding who qualified as a juror under the law was often unavailable, leaving officials to guess who was likely to qualify. Discrimination was rife in the eighteenth century, as Catholics were prevented from sitting on many juries, and even when legal impediments to their serving were removed, some officials continued to exclude them from certain types of cases. Later, persons of particular political beliefs were left off juries, through the use of the stand-aside procedure. The frequent allegations of jury packing[4] during certain periods, although sometimes exaggerated, nevertheless damaged the reputation of the Irish jury system. Criminal juries acquitting in the face of clear evidence was perceived as a significant problem during times of unrest. It ought to be borne in mind, however that not all problems with Irish juries stemmed from the political upheavals of the nineteenth century. Complaints about the exclusivity and non-representativeness of juries went hand in hand with absenteeism by qualified jurors. This posed a major difficulty, and consequently judges frequently threatened to impose fines, and bystanders in courthouses were often used to fill juries. There were many reasons why jurors ignored summonses; the discomfort and inconvenience, the poor remuneration, the possibility of personal endangerment and the generally thankless nature of the task.[5] Jurors were known at times to

1 E.g. David Johnson, 'Trial by jury in Ireland 1860–1914', *J. Leg. Hist.*, 17:3 (1996), 270–91; John McEldowney, 'Stand by for the crown: an historical analysis', *Crim. L. Rev.* (1979), 272–83; David Johnson, 'The trials of Sam Gray: Monaghan politics and nineteenth century Irish criminal procedure', *Ir. Jur.* (n.s.), 20 (1985), 109–34; John McEldowney, 'The case of *The queen v. McKenna* and jury packing in Ireland', *Ir. Jur.* (n.s.), 12 (1977), 339–54; and W.E. Vaughan, *Murder trials in Ireland* (Dublin, 2009). 2 McEldowney, 'Stand by', 277.
3 Johnson, 'Trial by jury', p. 289. 4 See pp 147–56. 5 See pp 119–27, 158–69.

deliver perverse verdicts, inflated valuations and acquittals against the evidence. Bribery, drunkenness, ignorance and posturing were all facets of the jury system.

Much contemporary commentary on Irish criminal juries was negative, and negative viewpoints or stories often resonate most strongly. For example, an 1859 editorial in the *Belfast Newsletter* referred to the recent state trials held at Tralee. The evidence against one defendant was 'clear and unmistakeable' – yet he was acquitted. The paper noted that:

> In England or Scotland, upon such evidence, a jury would have found an English or Scotch prisoner guilty without leaving the box. But in Ireland we manage things better than that. A man engages in conspiracy or commits a murder in the full confidence that if not effectually screened by the sympathizing neighbours from the pursuit of the constables, there is still the chance of terrifying a witness or two or, at the worst, getting a staunch friend upon the jury.[6]

Many commentators emphasised the differences between English and Irish juries: for example, in evidence given to the 1852 committee on outrages, crown solicitor Sir Matthew Barrington commented that in England, 'every man aids the administration of justice, and the sympathy is with the injured person; in Ireland, every man of a certain class almost opposes the administration of justice, and the sympathy is with the prisoner'.[7]

All of this paints quite a dismal picture. However, if one takes a broader view of lay participation in the Irish justice system, the picture is less bleak. The system of lay participation was not entirely unworkable; during politically tranquil periods, both civil and criminal trial juries operated effectively and uncontroversially. In the context of a broader study of the nineteenth-century Irish criminal justice system, Vaughan re-examines Johnson's view of Irish criminal juries.[8] Johnson, it will be remembered, emphasised the problems inherent in the Irish criminal jury system, and described various 'stratagems' employed by the crown to circumvent these problems and secure convictions.[9] In Vaughan's view:

> One problem with Johnson's conclusions is that they rely on a small number of well-known cases. There is another problem, which is that they depend on conflating the crown's stratagems by assuming that their employment was uniform, ubiquitous and endemic throughout the whole period.[10]

He points out that Johnson's 'stratagems' tended to be used during particular periods of unrest. For example, before 1882 there were no special juries used on felony trials, and changes of venue in criminal cases were difficult to secure. The

6 *Belfast Newsletter*, 17 Mar. 1859.
7 *Report on outrages (Ireland)*, HC 1852 (438) xiv, 1, para. 4841. 8 Vaughan, *Murder trials*, p. 358.
9 Johnson, 'Trial by jury'. 10 Vaughan, *Murder trials*, p. 358.

vigorous use of the stand-aside procedure was not a significant issue until after O'Hagan's Act. Hung juries were not as common as one might have expected.[11] Vaughan also argues that Johnson's conclusions rest on a study of a relatively small number of high-profile cases. Such cases are not always representative of the vast majority. Moreover, the sensationalism around such cases meant that they were widely reported, analysed and derided in the press, pamphlets and other contemporary discourse. As such, the exceptional cases tend to dominate the sources and can lead to broad conclusions with a narrow base. By way of contrast, Vaughan focuses on convict reference files, which contain a broader range of cases. Complaints about juries were the third biggest category of complaints in these cases, representing 10 out of 63 cases examined. Vaughan considers this to be 'less than one might have expected'.[12] Furthermore, the main cause of complaint was the jury selection process and not necessarily the conduct of the jurors themselves: '[t]he fewness of complaints and their limited range suggests that the system worked much better than suggested by the criticism of contemporaries'.[13]

Vaughan's sample is small and his observations relate solely to criminal juries. However, his conclusions are borne out in this wider study of jury trials and lay participation in the Irish justice system. As has been demonstrated in earlier chapters, many of the other categories of jury, such as coroners' juries, market juries, and inquest and valuation juries, which have not traditionally attracted much scholarly attention, also managed to function well, despite instances of partisanship or corruption. It is vital that an evaluation of the impact and role of lay participation in the Irish justice system is not clouded by the problems that dogged the criminal jury system during periods of unrest. Jurors themselves, for the most part, took their role seriously, in line with Hayes' exhortation that it was 'the solemn duty of the jurors to pay strict attention to the proceedings'.[14] They questioned witnesses, viewed premises, scrutinised documents, evaluated evidence, took notes, engaged with lawyers and judges, paid close attention to what was said in court and arguably sought the truth in most cases. Even though the criminal jury could be dysfunctional at times, it was part of a broader, more successful system of lay decision-making. The wider context in which lay decision-making was used in Ireland also helps to explain the survival of the criminal jury. Vaughan notes that:

> The conduct of trials, characterised by the silence of the prisoner, the laws of evidence, the dominance of juries, do not suggest a country that was plagued by disorder. The Olympian calm of the judges suggest almost an academic engagement in matters of law enforcement.[15]

This book tends to support Vaughan's conclusion. Criminal juries and the criminal justice system generally operated satisfactorily, despite several tumultuous periods

11 Ibid., p. 357. 12 Ibid., p. 361. 13 Ibid., p. 362.
14 Hayes, *Crimes and punishments*, ii, p. 448. 15 Vaughan, *Murder trials*, p. 358.

during the nineteenth century. More broadly, the entire system of criminal and civil justice can be described as fit for purpose and well-regarded.

Just how did the Irish system of lay participation manage to survive the long nineteenth century? First, it ought to be pointed out that the idea of a jury verdict was clearly held in relatively high esteem by legislators and policymakers. The proliferation of different types of jury in the eighteenth century, to decide all sorts of matters – from land valuations,[16] to market infringements,[17] to sanity – indicates that the administration was generally comfortable with lay decision-making. Laypersons were drafted in to make decisions in a range of different contexts. The perceived problems with certain types of jury were acknowledged by lawmakers, and negative comments about juries were frequent during periods of unrest. For example, in the 1820s one MP commented that 'he would infinitely rather trust the life of a man to one of the judges of the land than to an Irish jury'.[18] In the 1830s, Earl Grey lamented that it was 'a melancholy fact, that there existed in Ireland a system of intimidation which … prevented juries from giving honest verdicts'.[19] Arthur Balfour remarked in 1887 that 'wherever party feeling ran high, Irish juries could not be trusted to give verdicts according to the evidence'.[20] However, for every politician who disparaged Irish juries, there were others who extolled them. Daniel O'Connell, for example, said in 1825 that the advantages of trial by jury were 'very great'.[21] The juries of Eniskillen, County Fermanagh were 'as conscientious a body as could be found in any part of the kingdom'.[22] The earl of Wicklow said in 1833 that '[i]t was a curious fact, but it was perfectly true, that among the institutions of Ireland, that which stood pre-eminently forward for its good working was the jury system'.[23] Chicester Fortescue, in 1868, remarked upon 'the admirable conduct of the Irish juries during the late political trials'.[24] The O'Connor Don, speaking in the context of disturbances in Westmeath in 1870, told the house of commons, 'It was not that the juries would not discharge their duties; he believed that notion to be a libel on Irish juries, and he believed that there had been no want of courage on the part of Irish juries in convicting offenders.'[25]

Why did lay decision-making become so popular with politicians and lawmakers? Lay decision-making in the twenty-first century is often portrayed as

16 E.g. Bog Act, 1715 (2 Geo. I, c. 12); Lighthouses Act, 1717 (4 Geo. I, c. 7); Mines Act, 1723 (10 Geo. I, c. 5); Inland Carriage Act, 1749 (25 Geo. II, c. 10).

17 E.g. Market Jury Act, 1787 (27 Geo. III, c. 46).

18 *Hansard 2*, xi, dcli–dclii (11 May 1824) (HC), M. Fitzgerald.

19 *Hansard 3*, xv, 1094 (22 Feb. 1833) (HL).

20 *Hansard 3*, 313, cclxxviii (1 Apr. 1887) (HC).

21 *Select committee on disturbances*, HL 1825 (200) vii, 501, p. 57.

22 *Hansard 2*, 11, dcxlviii (11 May 1824) (HC), General Archdall.

23 *Hansard 3*, xvii, 6 (2 Apr. 1833) (HL) Lord Ellenborough asked whether 'any complaint had been made of the recent practice with respect to the impanelling of Juries in Ireland? So far from that, the Juries there had conducted themselves in a manner to excite astonishment, and had given more courageous and better verdicts than could have been expected.' *Hansard 3*, xvii, 13 (2 Apr. 1833) (HL).

24 *Hansard 3*, 190, mdxcvii (13 Mar. 1868) (HC).

25 *Hansard 3*, 206, dccxxx (12 May 1871) (HC).

an expression of democracy. However, far from representing some sort of democratic ideal, in the late eighteenth century it was more likely to have been political pragmatism. Delegating decision-making to juries may have been a shrewd move when it came to matters such as property valuations, for example. These were generally carried out by men of substantial wealth, and thus could hardly be viewed as democratic in the representative sense. Moreover, such delegation also tended to ensure that decision-making power remained largely in the hands of the Protestant minority. Another factor may have been cost; lay juries often represented relatively good value for money. They were usually remunerated either poorly or not at all. Even the wide-streets juries, which were the best-paid Irish juries, were not paid nearly as much as the wide-streets commissioners. Valuation juries were an economical alternative to appointing and paying professionals to carry out the same functions. Lay jurors also had the advantage of being available to shoulder some of the administrative and judicial burdens of local government. Mayors, for example, could not realistically monitor and deal with all market issues, so it made sense to delegate these tasks to jurors. It was also a relatively straightforward matter to summon and assemble a panel of laypersons. By the time of the proliferation of lay decision-making bodies in the eighteenth century, the procedure and mechanisms for summoning panels of trial jurors already existed and were well-established with sheriffs. Vaughan describes the important role played by juries in the criminal justice system as 'unexpected'.[26] It is, however, less surprising when one considers the role of juries in the administration of justice more broadly. Jury decision-making had been entrenched in various disparate areas since the early eighteenth century.

Community acceptance was another crucial factor in the survival of the jury. Lay participation in the system of justice was popular among the Irish public. Despite the shortcomings of the various categories of jury discussed in this book, people generally acknowledged the legitimacy of jury decision-making. This was important for general acceptance of the law in the country. Lay decision-making permeated many aspects of life, from pregnancy to death. A land valuation or a determination of sanity carried out by lay persons may have been easier to accept than one conducted by state officials. Other reasons for community support for lay decision-making may have been less benign. There may, for instance, have been a generalised perception that juries were relatively easily manipulated. It was arguably easier to bribe or persuade a struggling Mayo farmer than a remote, well-paid judge, and the unanimity requirement meant that one needed only to convince a single juror in order to secure a favourable decision. It is unclear whether public support for juries was based on a perception of their relative impartiality, or, conversely, because they may have been easier to pack or sway. What is clear, however, is that there was strong public support for juries throughout this period. When proposals to suspend trial by jury were published in

26 Vaughan, *Murder trials*, p. 373.

1882, the *Freeman's Journal* warned that '[t]he real mischief is the effect [the bill] will have on the minds of the people, in weakening their already fragile confidence in the administration of justice'.[27] Later, it said: '[t]he simple truth is plainly this, that it is a very dangerous experiment to run extraordinary tribunals against the established moral procedures of law in this country'.[28] It has been seen that the judiciary had also recognised this public need for lay involvement in criminal cases.

Taking a more international view, the nineteenth century was the golden age of juries both in Europe and in the British empire.[29] It has been observed that '[i]n the late nineteenth century a jury was regarded as the *sine qua non* of the rule of law in every developed European country'.[30] The jury as the bulwark of liberty, interposing between the people and the state, was increasingly regarded as an essential aspect of any civilised system of justice.[31]

A final important factor that guarded against the collapse of the jury system in the nineteenth century was its popularity among the Irish judiciary. That is not to say that Irish judges were constantly in praise of Irish juries, and it is worth considering some of the negative judicial commentary directed towards lay decision-makers. Judges were known to criticise individual jurors or juries, most notably during turbulent periods. Juries that failed to convict were derided as obstinate, and several judges detailed to parliamentary committees instances of jurors who were too drunk, illiterate or poor to be considered worthy of their task. Monahan C.J. once spoke of jurors 'infesting the courtroom',[32] and it is at times clear from their interactions with jurors that judges were frustrated. Particularly from the 1870s onwards, many judges appeared increasingly dissatisfied with juries' conduct and the returning of 'perverse' or 'bad' verdicts. This is evident from both the content and the tone of their charges to petty juries. In 1833, Daniel O'Connell pointed out that 'it was the duty of the jury to check the judge, but juries came to be sometimes disliked when they performed that duty scrupulously'.[33] Similarly, Dodd commented in 1881 that if a verdict 'be not in accordance with what the judge thinks it ought to be, the jury often gets a left-handed compliment on their honesty and integrity'.[34] Some judges, such as James Anthony Lawson, were repeatedly critical of jurors.[35] For example, after Peter Barrett was abortively tried three times for attempted murder,[36] Lawson declared

27 *Freeman's Journal*, 12 May 1882. 28 Ibid., 15 May 1882. 29 See p. 3.

30 Tamás Antal, 'The codification of the jury procedure in Hungary', *J. Leg. Hist.*, 30:3 (2009), 279–97 at 297.

31 E.g. see James M. Donovan, *Juries and the transformation of criminal justice in France in the nineteenth and twentieth centuries* (Chapel Hill, NC, 2010).

32 *Report on juries (Ireland)*, HC 1873 (283) xv, 389, para. 2625. 33 *Hansard 3*, xvi, 345.

34 W.H. Dodd, 'Some grievances of jurors', *J.S.S.I.S.I.*, 8 (1879–85), 223–7 at 225. Tensions between judge and jury were not exclusive to Ireland. See M.J. Weiner, 'Judges v. jurors: courtroom tensions in murder trials and the law of criminal responsibility in nineteenth-century England', *L. & Hist. Rev.*, 7:3 (1999), 467–506.

35 This was the judge who had presided over the 1882 change-of-venue trials in Dublin, and who subsequently survived an assassination attack. 36 *R v. Barrett* (1870) I.R. 4 C.L. 285.

that it would be better to ignore the offence in question than to have justice receive such a public affront, 'because it is the most public manifestation that can be imagined of the impunity with which crime may be committed'.[37] Another example was at a Belfast murder trial in 1886. Having been informed by the foreman that the jurors were unable to reach agreement, Lawson J. said that they had 'wilfully made up their minds to disagree', and after a rather testy exchange, told the foreman 'if you believed the man fired the shot, you should find him guilty, and you can't believe anything else. Go back now.' The jury retired once more and were sent for after an hour. They told the judge that they still had not agreed, and he replied:

> I have said all I can to you. It is highly discreditable to the jurors of this county that in a case like this they cannot agree. A juror who would violate his oath under circumstances such as surround this case is a man I look upon as second in guilt only to the man whose case he has been investigating. I discharge you.[38]

Some judges were more critical of the jury qualification laws than of jurors themselves; several, for example, were opposed to the extensive categories of persons exempted from service.[39] A number of judges also questioned the merit of the property rating as the sole qualification for jurors, and suggested introducing 'a diversity of qualifications in order to get a good class of jurors',[40] including university degrees. Fitzgerald J. advocated the use of 'qualifications not dependent upon a personal rating … knowing that they would bring upon the list greater intelligence'.[41] He reasoned that this way 'you have at least *prima facie* reason to suppose that a person who has graduated at a university is a person of education and intelligence'.[42] Barry J. was similarly at a loss to understand why 'men of high education' might be excluded simply because they held no property.[43]

Nevertheless, in the face of these instances of negativity, there is also clear evidence of strong judicial support for lay decision-making, and of respect for juries. For example, at the close of a special commission in 1806, Baron George addressed the petty jury thus:

> Gentlemen, I find, that we shall have, upon this occasion, no more criminal trials. I think you extremely well deserve the thanks of the public, for the very great propriety with which you have conducted yourselves. You have supported the law, and the law will support you, if you be not wanting to yourselves.[44]

37 *Report on Irish jury laws*, 1881. 38 *R v. Walker, Freeman's Journal*, 18 Dec. 1886.
39 *Report on Irish jury laws*, 1881, paras 2982, 3246 (Fitzgerald).
40 *Report on juries*, 1873, para. 2786. 41 *Report on Irish jury laws*, 1881, para. 4227.
42 Ibid., para. 4228. 43 Ibid., para. 1404.
44 William Ridgeway, *A report of the proceedings under a special commission of oyer and terminer and gaol*

Some judges, as seen in chapter 12, were patient and tolerant when it came to jurors taking an active role in proceedings. James Monahan told the Statistical and Social Inquiry Society in 1865 that there was 'value' in the system of trial by jury, in which 'the bulk of the citizens, with minds unwarped by legal rules and unfettered by technicality, take their full share of the important duty of deciding the ultimate issue of the lawsuit'.[45] Notwithstanding the difficulties encountered after the passing of O'Hagan's Act in 1871, the judiciary, on the whole, continued to support the institution of the jury. As the *Irish Law Times and Solicitors' Journal* observed in 1881, judges and lawyers were 'all strongly prejudiced in its favour'.[46]

Alongside lofty respect for the institution of the jury and the ideal of lay decision-making, judges often took a humanitarian approach to the jurors themselves. An illustration of this is the Limerick case of *Gabbet v. Clancy and Dwyer*, where Ball J. ordered that members of the bar should give up their room so that the jury might have somewhere reasonably comfortable to spend the night.[47] The same judge displayed solicitousness towards jurors in the Tipperary case of *R v. Leary and Cooke*[48] a few years later. The jurors, facing a second night of being locked together, complained that their room was 'exceedingly damp'. Ball J. replied: 'Then gentlemen, take my room. It is exceedingly comfortable.'[49] In *R v. Spollen*, the jurors had to remain together on a Sunday and Chief Justice Monahan told them that the sheriff would conduct them to their places of worship, and afterwards for a drive in the park: 'you may be sure, gentlemen, the sheriff will do everything consistent with his duty to render your position as comfortable as possible'.[50]

Most of the judicial criticisms detailed above related to criminal juries; civil juries, and special juries in particular, were generally well-regarded by the judiciary, as is clear from some of the judge-jury interactions discussed here. There is also a wealth of humorous anecdotes recounting the lively interactions between the judiciary and the jurors.[51] Maurice Healy, for one, was under no illusions as to the general state of the Irish jury system: '[i]t must be admitted that there were some

delivery, for the counties of Sligo, Mayo, Leitrim, Longford and Cavan, in the month of December, 1806 (Dublin, 1807), pp 241–2

45 J. Monahan, 'The functions of grand juries in criminal cases', *J.S.S.I.S.I.*, 4:30 (1865), 218–27 at 223.

46 Anon., 'Trial by jury', *I.L.T. & S.J.*, 15 (1881), 412.

47 William O'Brien, *The fishery case. A report of the case Poole Gabbett, esq., a. Thomas Clancy and Thomas Dwyer, tried before Mr. Justice Ball, and a special jury, at Limerick summer assizes, 1841, and which occupied the court for over five days* (Limerick, 1841).

48 (1844) 3 Cr. & Dix C.C. 212

49 *Nenagh Guardian*, 27 Mar. 1844.

50 Anon., *Trial of James Spollen for the murder of Mr George Samuel Little at the Broadstone terminus of the Midland Great Western Railway, Ireland, August 7th, 8th, 10th & 11th, 1857* (Dublin, 1857).

51 See, e.g., Bodkin, *Recollections*; M. Healy, *The old Munster circuit: a book of memories and traditions* (London, 1939); J.R. O'Flanagan, *The Munster circuit: tales, trials, and traditions* (London, 1880); and O.J. Burke, *Anecdotes of the Connaught circuit* (Dublin, 1885).

very bad juries in Ireland'.[52] 'But', he added, 'the Irish juries, even when bad, had sometimes the mitigating grace that they added to the gaiety of the court'.

Certain judges were conspicuous in their support for juries. Baron Deasy was asked in 1874 whether trial by jury ought to be abolished, to which he replied '[c]ertainly not; on the contrary, I think it would be a great evil if there was any interference with it'.[53] An extremely vocal judicial supporter was John David Fitzgerald, who served as attorney general, solicitor general and a judge of the queen's bench.[54] He took a strong interest in Irish educational matters,[55] and was a champion of the national school system, which he thought to have the potential to affect profoundly the competence of jurors, particularly those newly qualified under the 1871 act. This system, he said, was 'bringing up an entirely new class of people'.[56] A decade later, he remarked that the jurors had 'been educated ... There is a great improvement and it arises from bringing them in connection with jurors of a higher stamp, and with the bar and the bench.'[57] He described the jurors of Cork, for example, as being 'remarkable for their intelligence, and for their reliability'.[58] However, in 1881, with the Land War and the Plan of Campaign exerting significant pressure on the criminal justice system, he warned that if juries continued to acquit prisoners, 'it would be necessary for the authorities to apply some remedy, and a remedy probably ending in a partial suspension of trial by jury'.[59] That is exactly how Balfour responded: the Crimes Act, 1882, as seen, provided for criminal cases to be tried in different counties and for certain cases to be tried without juries. The *Freeman's Journal* reported that 'the proposal stands condemned emphatically by the most eminent of the judges themselves'.[60] Similarly, the *Irish Law Times and Solicitors' Journal* reported that:

> at a meeting of the judges on Thursday the following resolution was passed unanimously: 'That, in the opinion of the judges of the superior courts, the immediate imposition upon them of the duty proposed by the prevention of crime (Ireland) bill would seriously impair the public confidence in the administration of justice in Ireland.' All the judges attended save the lord

52 Healy, *The old Munster circuit*, p. 228.

53 *Report from the select committee on the working of the Irish jury system, together with the proceedings of the committee, minutes of evidence, and appendix*, HC 1874 (244) ix, 557, para. 2538.

54 There were two judges named Fitzgerald in the superior courts, John David Fizgerald in the queen's bench, who was later elevated to the house of lords; and Francis Alexander Fitzgerald, a baron in the court of exchequer who never sought promotion or took an interest in politics.

55 He acted as a commissioner of national education from 1863 to 1889.

56 *Report on juries*, 1873, para. 3224.

57 *Report on Irish jury laws*, 1881, para. 4194. Similarly, Robert Ferguson said, para. 3339, that since the passing of O'Hagan's Act, he was 'more than once surprised at the amount of intelligence evinced by the verdicts of the jurors under the new system'.

58 Ibid., para. 4187.

59 Ibid., para. 4190. Although his words had been 'interpreted as words of menace, whereas they were words of warning only'.

60 *Freeman's Journal*, 12 May 1882.

> chancellor, Chief Justice Morris (who is away), Baron Dowse (who is ill), Mr. Justice Lawson (who is away), and the judges of the bankruptcy and admiralty courts.[61]

Baron Fitzgerald of the court of exchequer resigned on a point of principle over the proposed legislation.[62] While the *Freeman's Journal* lauded this move, it opined that it was scarcely necessary as the authorities were much less likely to resort to jury packing than juryless trials.[63] Members of the legal profession, many of whom similarly abhorred the legislation, were effusive in their praise of Fitzgerald for taking this step. Serjeant Hemphill remarked that 'the circumstances of his retirement were in keeping with his character and career',[64] and Serjeant Robinson noted that 'he gave up his position rather than act under a law which at the will of the executive might deprive people of trial by jury – of trial by their peers – which had long been a strong barrier between the liberties of the people and the prerogatives of the crown'.[65]

Finally, it is worth noting that while lay participation 'survived' the long nineteenth century, it constantly evolved during the period. At the turn of the twentieth century it was something quite different to what it had been in the eighteenth; as Cornish has observed, '[c]hange is by no means a novelty in the jury system'.[66] Swaine has also pointed out that '[t]he civil jury in 1670 was not the same body as the civil jury in 1770 or 1870'.[67] It is this adaptability, which, arguably, results in what Dzur describes as 'the continued relevance of the jury idea'.[68] Many categories of jury had disappeared by that stage: the market jury,[69] the jury of matrons,[70] the jury *de medietate linguae*[71] and the wide-streets jury,[72] for example. Other juries had seen their powers curbed or their use reduced: the lunacy jury, for example.[73] By and large, juries were less active – they appear to have asked fewer questions, and the view procedure was increasingly replaced by the use of maps and models.[74] The composition of juries changed significantly over the period, with restrictions based on religion abolished, and property qualifications broadened.[75] Jury procedure also changed over time, with increasingly

61 Anon., 'The administration of justice in Ireland', *I.L.T. & S.J.*, 16 (1882), 232. There was a report on the same page that stated that '[a]ll the judges and officials in Dublin are now guarded by policemen in plain clothes. Detectives are placed at the law and other public courts, and at the private residences of the judges'.

62 See V.T.H. Delany, *Christopher Palles, lord chief baron of her majesty's court of exchequer in Ireland, 1874–1916: his life and times* (Dublin, 1960), p. 90.

63 *Freeman's Journal*, 29 July 1882. See also *The Nation*, 10 June and 29 July 1882; and *Belfast Newsletter*, 21 Nov. 1882.

64 *Freeman's Journal*, 9 Nov. 1882. 65 Ibid.

66 W.R. Cornish, *The jury* (London, 1968), p. 10.

67 Warren Swaine, *The law of contract, 1670–1870* (Cambridge, 2015), p. 374.

68 Albert Dzur, *Punishment, participatory democracy and the jury* (Oxford, 2012), p. 107.

69 See pp 96–9. 70 See pp 83–8. 71 See pp 92–5. 72 See pp 64–70.

73 See pp 88–90. 74 See 176–7. 75 See pp 41–51.

prescriptive legislation removing much discretion from officials.[76] Overall, the jury fared better in the long nineteenth century than it did in the twentieth, which saw the decline of civil juries[77] and the increased use of juryless courts for certain types of criminal cases in both Irish jurisdictions.[78]

76 See pp 10–12, 27–9, 34.

77 See Bryan M.E. McMahon, *Judge or jury? the jury trial for personal injury cases in Ireland* (Cork, 1985); Sally Lloyd-Bostock and Cheryl Thomas, 'Decline of the "little parliament": juries and jury reform in England and Wales', *L. & Contemp. Problems*, 62:2 (1999), 7–40; Michael Lobban, 'The strange life of the English civil jury, 1837–1914' in J.W. Cairns and G. McLeod (eds), *'The dearest birth right of the people of England': the jury in the history of the common law* (Oxford, 2002); and Conor Hanly, 'The decline of civil jury trial in nineteenth-century England', *J. Leg. Hist.*, 26:3 (2005), 253–78. Hanly notes, p. 258, that 'Between the 1820s and the end of the 1840s, the attitudes of the legal profession towards the civil jury became increasingly hostile.' He further notes, p. 259, that 'by the early 1830s there is evidence that some lawyers were willing to dispense with the civil jury at least in smaller cases'. In Ireland, the Common Law Procedure Amendment Act (Ireland), 1856 (19 & 20 Vic., c. 102), s. 4, stated: 'the parties to any cause may, by consent in writing, signed by them or their attorneys, as the case may be, leave the decision of any issue of fact to the court, provided that the court, or a judge, shall, in their or his discretion, think fit to allow such trial'. The issue of fact could be determined and damages assessed by a judge or judges. The verdict 'shall be of the same effect as the verdict of a jury, save that it shall not be questioned upon the ground of being against the weight of evidence'.

78 In Northern Ireland, the recommendations of a commission led by Lord Diplock led to the passing of the Northern Ireland (Emergency Provisions) Act, 1973, which allowed for non-jury courts (known as Diplock Courts) for scheduled offences connected with the political agitation. See John Jackson and Sean Doran, *Judge without jury: Diplock trials in the adversary system* (Oxford, 1995); S.C. Greer and A. White, *Abolishing the Diplock courts: the case for restoring jury trial for scheduled offences in Northern Ireland* (London, 1986); and John Jackson, Katie Quinn and Tom O'Malley, 'The jury system in contemporary Ireland: in the shadow of a troubled past', *L. & Contemp. Problems*, 62 (1999), 203–32. In the Irish republic, the special criminal court was established under the Offences Against the State Act, 1939. The court was extensively used during what was known in Ireland as the 'Emergency' (Second World War). It operated briefly between 1961 and 1962, and during the 'Troubles', a government proclamation in 1972 created a special criminal court, which is still in existence. See Mary Robinson, *The special criminal court* (Dublin, 1974); F.F. Davis, *The history and development of the special criminal court, 1922–2005* (Dublin, 2007); and *Report of the committee to review the Offences Against the State Acts, 1939–1998 and related matters* (Dublin, 2002), chapter 9 (justice.ie/en/JELR/hederman%20report.pdf/Files/hederman%20report.pdf, accessed 13 Nov. 2016).

Cases considered in the analysis of juror interaction, chapter 12

Abbott v. Howard
Adams v. Dundas
Allen v. Donnelly
Angeli v. Galbraith
Arkins v. Brady
Attorney general v. Clotworthy Walkinshaw
Attorney general v. d'Arcy
Birch v. Meredith
Boyle v. McLoughlin
Brabazon v. Potts
Browne v. Blake
Bruce v. Grady
Bryan v. Fitzsimons
Burke v. O'Flaherty
Cavendish v. Hope
Charlton (doe d. Ralph) v. Allen, Ferguson and Dalzell
Clark v. Callaghan
Cloncurry v. Piers
Colles v. Kearney
Corporation of Dublin v. Herbert
Corporation of Dublin v. Tedcastle
Corporation of Dublin v. Thomas
Craig (Annesley) v. Anglesea
Dawes v. O'Connor
Donnolly v. Malone
Dowling v. Lawler
Doyle v. Brown
Doyle v. Fitzgerald
Duckett v. Staples
Egan v. Kindillan
Fitzgerald v. Kerr
Frazer v. Gamble
Gabbett v. Clancy and Dwyer
Gallagher v. Cavendish
Gayer v. Byrne
Gresson v. Finlay
Hardy v. Sullivan
Head v. Purdon
Hevey v. Sirr
Higgins v. Higgins
Hincks v. Turnly
Hinds v. Price Myddleton
Hodgens v. Mahon
Holmes v. Brophy
Homan v. Johnson
Hopkins v. Gowan
Howard v. Shaw
Hurst v. Whaley
Jones v. Corbett
Jones v. Minchin
Jones v. Sheehan
Kavenagh v. Kelly
Lloyd v. Trimlestown
Lyons v. Bingham
M'Kennon v. Hamilton
M'Lain v. Enery
Magee v. O'Gorman (1)
Magee v. O'Gorman (2)
Maley v. Fitzsimons
Mannin v. Edgeworth and Sheehan
Massy v. Headfort
Mathew v. Harty and Stokes
McCorkell and Rennie v. Marquis of Donegal
McGarahan v. Maguire

Minchin v. Allen
O'Keefe v. Cullen
Peakin v. Joynt
Persse v. Wood
R (Daly) v. Magee
R (O'Connor) v. Waring
R (Richmond) v. Magee
R (Westmeath) v. Connell and others
R (Wright) v. Fitzgerald
R v. Sullivan
R v. Alcock and Derenzy
R v. Beckham
R v. Begg
R v. Bellamy
R v. Bellew
R v. Bird and others
R v. Blaney
R v. Bond
R v. Brazil
R v. Brennan
R v. Bridgeman
R v. Browne
R v. Browne Hayes
R v. Burke and others
R v. Busby
R v. Byrne (1798)
R v. Byrne (1803)
R v. Byrne (1811)
R v. Byrne (1842)
R v. Carr and Connon
R v. Carroll
R v. Carty
R v. Casey
R v. Clare
R v. Crawley
R v. Delany
R v. Donnelly and others
R v. Donoghoe
R v. Doran
R v. Dowling
R v. Dry
R v. Duffy
R v. Dunn and Carty
R v. Early (John)
R v. Early (Martin)
R v. Edgworth
R v. Emmett
R v. Feighny
R v. Ferguson
R v. Finerty
R v. Finney
R v. Fitzgerald and others
R v. Fitzpatrick
R v. Fitzsimon
R v. Flaherty and Tierney
R v. Flynn
R v. Fogarty
R v. Forbes, Handwick and others
R v. Forde
R v. Gore
R v. Hanbridge
R v. Handwick and others
R v. Hargedan
R v. Heath
R v. Hodgens
R v. Howley
R v. Hurdy Gurdy
R v. Hurly
R v. Jackson
R v. James
R v. Jones
R v. Joyce (Myles)
R v. Joyce (Patrick)
R v. Kearney
R v. Keenan (1803)
R v. Keenan (1822)
R v. Kennedy
R v. Keon
R v. Kilfoyle
R v. Killen and McCann
R v. Kinch and Watson
R v. Kirwan (1803)
R v. Kirwan (1812)
R v. Kirwan (1852)
R v. Kirwan and Sheridan
R v. Lalor

R v. Lawless
R v. Ledger (1)
R v. Ledger (2)
R v. Lenergan
R v. Lidwell
R v. Lidwell & Prior
R v. MacIntosh
R v. MacPhadeen
R v. Mame
R v. Martin
R v. McCann
R v. McDonough and Kearney
R v. McHugh
R v. Mitchel
R v. Molloy
R v. Morris
R v. Napper Tandy
R v. Napper Tandy and Morris
R v. O'Brien
R v. O'Brien and M'Donagh
R v. O'Connell
R v. O'Connor and McKeon (1812)
R v. O'Connor and McKeon (1817)
R v. O'Connor and others
R v. O'Doherty (1)
R v. O'Doherty (2)
R v. O'Grady
R v. Orr
R v. Pearce
R v. Petcherine
R v. Pigott
R v. Ratigan and Connor
R v. Redmond (1803)
R v. Redmond (1890)
R v. Robinson
R v. Roche
R v. Rochfort
R v. Rooney and others
R v. Rourke
R v. Rowan
R v. Rowan Cashel
R v. Russell
R v. Ryan (1)
R v. Ryan (2)
R v. Sheares
R v. Sheridan
R v. Slevin, Devine and M'Kenna
R v. Spollen
R v. St Leger
R v. Stuart
R v. Timlin
R v. Vance
R v. Voss
R v. Warren
R v. Watson and Vignolles
R v. Wren
Rosborough v. Gough
Tandy v. Morris
Thelwall v. Yelverton
Tighe v. Jones
Whitley v. Morris
Wright v. Fitzgerald

Capital cases in which jurors failed to reach a verdict, 1845–65[1]

Case Name	Offence	County	Year
R v. William Locke and Hugh McGarry	Murder	Down	1845
R v. John Hamilton	Murder	Tyrone	1845
R v. Peter Magill	Murder	Armagh	1846
R v. Robert and William Stothers	Murder	Armagh	1846
R v. Henry Close	Murder	Armagh	1846
R v. Joseph Brown	Manslaughter	Armagh	1846
R v. Timothy Lalor	Attempt to murder	Queen's	1846
R v. Denis Kennedy, Dorry Carroll, Michael Treahy, James Scully, Timothy Lalor	Conspiracy to murder	Queen's	1846
R v. Bryan Seery	Attempt to murder	Westmeath	1846
R v. Hugh Quin and James Shoulder	Murder	Armagh	1847
R v. Terence Reilly, John Smith and John Farrelly	Murder	Cavan	1847
R v. Mary Conry	Murder	Galway	1847
R v. James Gibbons	Murder	Mayo	1847
R v. John Brien (Ardy)	Murder	Tipperary	1847
R v. Jane Patterson and William Loy	Murder	Tyrone	1847
R v. Arthur McCost	Murder	Tyrone	1847
R v. John Morris	Murder	Tyrone	1847
R v. Mary Ann Murphy	Murder	Armagh	1848
R v. James Boyle	Murder	Carrickfergus	1848
R v. James McEvoy	Soliciting to murder	Queen's	1848
R v. James Commons	Conspiracy to murder	Roscommon	1848
R v. Matthew Gara	Murder	Sligo	1848

1 Data summarized from Capital offences (Ireland). Return of the number of cases in Ireland, during the last twenty years, wherein persons accused of capital offences have been remanded to prison for re-trial, or have been set at large, in consequence of the inability of juries to agree to a verdict, HC 1865 (352) xlv, 323.

Case Name	Offence	County	Year
R v. Patrick Griffin, William Farrell, Michael English	Shooting at	Tipperary	1848
R v. Michael Maher, Edward Hart, Edward Burke, Honora Nagle, Michael Neale	Murder	Tipperary	1848
R v. Michael, John, Patrick, Felix and Peter Lynn	Murder	Tyrone	1848
R v. Hugh Thomson	Murder	Antrim	1849
R v. John Glyn	Murder	Galway	1849
R v. Mary Brown	Child murder	Armagh	1850
R v. John McAtavey and Patrick McNally	Murder	Armagh	1850
R v. William Graham and William Campbell	Stabbing with intent to murder	Armagh	1850
R v. Patrick Brady and Mary Woods	Murder	Cavan	1850
R v. John Keys	Murder	King's	1850
R v. James Phillips	Murder	Tipperary	1850
R v. Owen Kelly	Murder	Tyrone	1850
R v. James Johnson	Manslaughter	Armagh	1851
R v. Patrick Moylan	Shooting at	King's	1851
R v. Patrick Kieran	Murder	Louth	1851
R v. Francis Kelly	Murder	Monaghan	1851
R v. John Cody, John Cody, Jr., and James Carthy	Conspiracy to murder	Waterford	1851
R v. James McGahan	Manslaughter	Armagh	1852
R v. Francis Berry and John Maginnis	Attempted murder	Armagh	1852
R v. Mary Anne Trimble	Murder	Tyrone	1852
R v. John Walsh	Murder	Galway	1853
R v. Thomas Stockpoole	Murder	Clare	1854
R v. Bryant Grant and Patrick Coomey	Murder; conspiracy to murder	Monaghan	1854
R v. William McArdle and Edward Magennis	Murder; conspiracy to murder	Monaghan	1854
R v. Martin Healy	Murder	Roscommon	1854
R v. Thomas Graham	Soliciting to murder	Tyrone	1854
R v. William Tate	Murder	Tyrone	1854
R v. Brian Muckian	Murder	Armagh	1856
R v. Robert Hall	Shooting	Armagh	1856
R v. Thomas Byrne	Shooting at	King's	1856
R v. Bernard and James McAvry	Murder	Tyrone	1856

Case Name	Offence	County	Year
R v. Solomon and James Baxter, Steward Drugan, James Niblow, John Anderson, Robert Neely, John Baxter	Murder and conspiracy to murder	Tyrone	1856
R v. Robert Morrison and Thomas Callaghan	Manslaughter	Armagh	1857
R v. Susan Cole	Administering poison	Armagh	1857
R v. Patrick Connolly	Murder	Donegal	1857
R v. Patrick Flynn	Murder	Roscommon	1857
R v. Elizabeth Magrath, alias Baird	Child murder	Armagh	1858
R v. William Cormack	Murder	Tipperary	1858
R v. John Henry Alexander	Arson	Armagh	1859
R v. John Holden	Murder	Tyrone	1860
R v. Isabella Dixon	Murder	Tyrone	1860
R v. Thomas and William Humfrey	Murder	Armagh	1861
R v. John Webb	Shooting with intent to murder	Armagh	1861
R v. Matthew Phibbs	Murder?	Sligo	1861
R v. Agnes Connor	Murder	Antrim	1862
R v. Mary Sleeth	Murder	Armagh	1863
R v. Francis Bradley	Murder	Donegal	1863
R v. Peter and Michael Nugent, and Stephen Gorman	Murder	Tyrone	1863
R v. John Bodkin	Murder	Westmeath	1863
R v. Stephen McAnally	Murder	Armagh	1864
R v. Michael Morrisson	Murder	Mayo	1864
R v. William McNickle	Murder	Tyrone	1864
R v. Robert Davison	Murder	Antrim	1865
R v. Henry Laverty	Murder	Antrim	1865
R v. Patrick Collins	Shooting with intent to murder	Armagh	1865

Bibliography

PRIMARY SOURCES

Manuscripts and archives

DCA, WSC/Mins
DCA, PB/Mins
NAI, 1C-02–6024
NAI, 1C-7–127
NAI, 1C-12–87
NAI 1C-31–95
NAI, 1C-49–26
NAI, 1C-76–102
NAI, 1D-34–64
NAI, 1D-39–112
NAI, C.C.P 1C/76/100a
NAI, C.C.S/1862/223
NAI, C.C.S/1867/242
NAI, C.C.S/1870/197
NAI, C.C.S/1871/262
NAI, C.C.S/1877/448
NAI, C.C.S/1881/682
NAI, C.C.S/1890/1
NAI, CSORP/1819/914
NAI, OP/1832/549
NAI, OP/1833/14
NAI, OP/1833/579
NAI, OP/1844/122
NLI, MS 3103
NLI, MS 7584
NLI, MS 11,290
NLI, MS 11,421(1)d
NLI, MS 41,655
NLI, MS 44,529/8
PRO, 30/60/12
PRO, 30/60/7
PRONI, ANT1/1b/9
PRONI, ARM1/10/4/1
PRONI, ANT1/1b/1/4/33
PRONI, ANT/1/1b/1/4/34
PRONI, D562/3038
PRONI, D623/A/124
PRONI, T2519/4/1985

Newspapers

Aberdeen Weekly Journal
Belfast Newsletter
Bristol Mercury
Chute's Western Herald
Connaught Telegraph
Cork Constitution
Cork Examiner
Daily Express
Daily Mail
Dundalk Democrat
Finn's Leinster Journal
Freeman's Journal
Galway Express
Galway Mercury
Hibernian Journal
Irish Examiner
Irish Times
Kerry Evening Post
Kerry Sentinel
Lloyd's Weekly Newspaper
Londonderry Standard
London and Westminster Review
Manchester Times
Meath Herald
Morning Chronicle
Morning News
Nenagh Guardian
Northern Standard
Northern Whig
Pall Mall Gazette
Sligo Chronicle
Sligo Independent
The Nation
The Times
Tralee Chronicle
Ulster Times
Western Mail

Parliamentary papers

Report of the commissioners appointed to enquire into the conduct and management of the corporation for paving, cleansing, and lighting the streets of Dublin, HC 1806 (17) viii, 473

Report from the commissioners appointed to inquire into and inspect the condition and government of the state prisons and other gaols in Ireland, HC 1809 (265) vii, 577

Returns from the sheriffs of Dublin of writs lodged and fees received, HC 1818 (417) xvi, 429

The seventh report of the commissioners appointed to inquire into the duties, salaries and emoluments, of the officers, clerks, and ministers of justice, in all temporal and ecclesiastical courts in Ireland, clerks of nisi prius, or judges registers, HC 1819–20 (33) iii, 51

State of Ireland. Minutes of evidence taken before the select committee appointed to inquire into the disturbances in Ireland, in the last session of parliament, HL 1825 (20) vii, 1

Select committee appointed to examine into the nature and extent of the disturbances which have prevailed in those districts of Ireland which are now subject to the provisions of the Insurrection Act, HL 1825 (200) vii, 501

Minutes of evidence taken before the select committee of house of lords, appointed to inquire into othe state of Ireland, more particularly with reference to the circumstances which may have led to disturbances in that part of the United Kingdom, HL 1825 (521) ix, 249

Fifteenth report of the commissioners appointed to inquire into the duties, salaries and emoluments, of the officers, clerks, and ministers of justice, in all temporal and ecclesiastical courts in Ireland, HC 1826 (310) xvii, 29

Wide streets (Dublin) Accounts and papers; no. 1 to 8, inclusive, HC 1828 (81) xxii, 569

Nineteenth report of the commissioners of inquiry into the collection and management of the revenue arising in Ireland and Great Britain. Post-office revenue, United Kingdom: part II. Ireland, HC 1829 (353) xii, 1

Wide streets (Dublin). Returns of the number of inquests held under the statutes for the improvement of the city of Dublin; the names of persons who have served as jurors; and, the sum or sums of money paid to each, from the 1st Jan. 1820 to 1st Jan. 1830, HC 1830 (149) xxvi, 293

Fermanagh sub-sheriff. Copy of memorial of Francis McBryan and other prisoners, charged with the murder at Macken, to the lord lieutenant of Ireland, dated Enniskillen gaol, 1st Mar. 1830, complaining of the sub-sheriff of Fermanagh county, Ireland, HC 1830 (150) xxvi, 301

Constabulary, Ireland. A return of the number of persons who have lost their lives in affrays with or otherwise by the constabulary in Ireland; a return of the number of persons severely wounded in affrays with or by the constabulary in Ireland; a return of the names and number of persons employed in the constabulary force in Ireland, who have been killed or severely wounded in affrays with or otherwise by any of the people, HC 1830–1 (167) viii, 403

Royal commission on practice and procedure in the superior courts of common law, third rep., HC 1831 (92) x, 375

Report from the select committee on the state of Ireland; with the minutes of evidence, appendix and index, HC 1831–2 (677) xvi, 1

Court of exchequer, Ireland. A copy of the order made by the court of exchequer in Ireland on the 13th Nov. 1832, requiring the solicitors for the crown to pay five guineas to each of the four jurors summoned, but not sworn, on the trial, in the case of an information for intrusion by the attorney-general prosecuting for his majesty against the lord primate of Ireland and others, defendants, &c, HC 1833 (4437) xxxi, 463

Return of persons on the sheriffs' panel as jurors, in the county of Kildare, who were fined at the quarter sessions for the said county within the last twelve months, HC 1833 (602), (724) xxxv, 501, 503

Select committee on the right of Quakers to take their seat in parliament on their solemn affirmation: report, HC 1833 (6) xii, 137

Report from the select committee on medical education with the minutes of evidence, and appendix. Part I. Royal College of Physicians, London, HC 1834 (602) xiii, 1
Second report from the select committee appointed to inquire into the nature, character, extent an tendency of Orange lodges, associations or societies in Ireland, HC 1835 (475) (476) xv, xvi, 501, 1
First report of the commissioners appointed to inquire into the municipal corporations in Ireland, I [C-23–8] HC 1835 xxvii, xxviii, 51, 79, 199
Municipal corporations (Ireland). Appendix to the first report of the commissioners. Part III. – Conclusion of the north-western circuit, I [C-26, 29] HC 1836 xxiv, 297
Report from the select committee on manor courts, Ireland; together with the minutes of evidence, appendix and index, HC 1837 (494) xv, 1
Copies or extracts of reports of the commissioners appointed to inquire into the affairs of the island of Malta, and of correspondence thereupon, part III, HC 1839 (140) xvii, 753
Report from the select committee of the house of lords, appointed to enquire into the state of Ireland in respect of crime, and to report thereon to the house, HC 1839 (486) xi, xii 1
Jurors (Ireland). A copy of instructions given to crown solicitors on each circuit respecting challenge of jurors in crown cases, HC 1842 (171) xxxviii, 339
A return of the total population of England, Ireland and Scotland respectively, according to the census of 1841; accompanied by an abstract of the total number of persons in Ireland ascertained, by the Commissioners of Public Instruction, in 1834, to belong to each religious persuasion at the time of their inquiry, HC 1843 (354) li, 321
State trial (Ireland). Return to an address of the honourable the house of commons, dated 21 May 1844; for, copies of all affidavits and pleadings filed in the cause of The queen v. Daniel O'Connell and others, in the queen's bench, in Ireland, from the 10th day of Oct. to the 1st day of Dec. 1843; and also, from the 1st day of Apr. 1844 to the time when this return shall be complied with; together with copies of all indorsements (if any) made thereon, HC 1844 (395) xliv, 225
Eighth report of her majesty's commissioners on criminal law, HC 1845 (656) xiv, 161
First report of her majesty's commissioners for inquiring into the process, practice and system of pleading the superior courts of common law, HC 1851 (1289) xxii, 567
Bills of indictment (Ireland). Abstract of return from the clerks of the crown and clerks of the peace of the several counties in Ireland, of the number of bills of indictment sent up to the respective grand juries, between the 20th day of February 1850 and the 5th day of April 1851, HC 1851 (328) l, 317
Jury panel (Mayo). A return of the jury panel in the criminal court at the last assizes for the county of Mayo, stating the names of the jurors empanneled and sworn in the case of The queen versus Thadeus Derrig and others; the order in which the persons on said panel were called; the names of those ordered on the part of the crown to stand by, and the names of the counsel engaged in said prosecution, HC 1851 (235) l, 655
Report from the select committee on outrages (Ireland), HC 1852 (438) xiv, 1
Second report of her majesty's commissioners for inquiring into the process, practice and system of pleading in the superior courts of common law, second rep. [C-1626] HC 1852–3, xl, 701
Minutes of evidence taken before the select committee on the Clare election petition, HC 1852–3 (595) ix, 50
Fairs and markets commission, Ireland. Report of the commissioners appointed to inquire into the state of the fairs and markets in Ireland. Part II. Minutes of evidence, I [C-1910] HC 1854–5 xix
Third report of the postmaster general, on the post office, HC 1857 (2195) iv, 293
Informations and dying declarations in relation to cases of homicide, riot, illegal or party processions alleged at Derrymacash, in county of Armagh, July 1860, HC 1861 (315) lii, 505
Copy of the shorthand writers' notes of the trials at the last assizes at Armagh, arising out of the riots at Derrymacash, HC 1861 (315) lii, 315

Tyrone assizes (jury panel). Copy of the challenge to the array of the jury panel at the late Tyrone assizes, and of Mr. Justice Christian's ruling when quashing the said panel as returned by the sheriff, HC 1862 (232) xliv, 251

Judicial statistics. Part II. England and Wales. Common law – equity – civil and canon law [C-3418] HC 1864 lvii, 653

Judicial statistics 1864. Ireland. Part I. Police – criminal proceedings – prisons. Part II. Common law – equity – civil and canon law [C-8563] HC 1864 (52) lii, 657

Index to the report from the select committee on Africa (western coast), HC 1865 (412–I) v, 1, 499

Capital offences (Ireland). Return of the number of cases in Ireland, during the last twenty years, wherein persons accused of capital offences have been remanded to prison for re-trial, or have been set at large, in consequence of the inability of juries to agree to a verdict, HC 1865 (352) xlv, 323

Report of the oaths commission 1867 [C-3885] 1867 xxxi, 1

Report from the select committee on special and common juries, together with the proceedings of the committee, minutes of evidence and appendix, HC 1867 (425) ix, 597

Index to the report from the select committee on special and common juries, HC 1867–8 (401) xii, 677

Report of the royal commissioners for inquiring into the laws of naturalization and allegiance, HC 1868–9 (4109) xxv, 607

Select committee appointed to inquire into the state of Westmeath, and certain parts adjoining of Meath and King's County, and the nature, extent, and effect of a certain unlawful combination and confederacy existing therein 1871, HC 1871 (147) xiii, 547

First, second, and special reports from the select committee on juries (Ireland), HC 1873 (283) xv, 389

Report from the select committee on the working of the Irish jury system, together with the proceedings of the committee, minutes of evidence, and appendix, HC 1874 (244) ix, 557

Return of the number of jurors summoned at the spring assizes, 1879, in each county, county of a town, city, or town in Ireland, with the total number in each county, &c., HC 1878–9 (249) lix, 351

Report from the select committee of the house of lords on Irish jury laws, HC 1881 (430) xi, 1

Census of Ireland for the year 1881. Preliminary report with abstract of the enumerators' summaries [C-2931] HC 1881 xcvi, 159

Dublin commission court (Francis Hynes). Copies of any documents in the nature of evidence or memorials, submitted for the consideration of the Irish executive, with reference to the alleged misconduct of members of the jury, the verdict, and the sentence, in the case of Francis Hynes, HC 1882 (408) lv, 167

Report from the committee on privilege (Mr. Gray), HC 1882 (406) xii, 503

Criminal and judicial statistics, Ireland, 1888. Report on the criminal and judicial statistics of Ireland for the year 1888, with tables [C-5795] HC 1889 lxxxv, 241

Rule for guidance of crown solicitors in Ireland in relation to the impannelling of jurors, HC 1894 (33) lxxii, 29

Report of the departmental committee appointed to inquire into and report upon the law and practice with regard to the constitution, qualifications, selection, summoning, &c. of juries [C-6817] 1913, xxx, 403

Report of the committee to review the Offences Against the State Acts, 1939–1998 and related matters (Dublin, 2002) (www.justice.ie/en/JELR/hederman%20report.pdf/Files/hederman%20 report.pdf)

Parliamentary debates

The parliamentary register: or, history of the proceedings and debates of the house of commons of Ireland

Hansard's parliamentary debates, series 3–5

Dáil Éireann debates

SECONDARY SOURCES

Amar, Akhil Reed, 'Reinventing juries: ten suggested reforms', *University College Davis L. Rev.*, 28 (1995), 1169–94

Anderson, Stanley, 'Lay judges and jurors in Denmark', *Am. J. Comp. L.*, 38:4 (1990), 839–64

Anon., 'Change of venue and transfer of actions commenced in the chancery division', *I.L.T. & S.J.*, 17 (1883), 93

Anon., 'Directing jurors to standby in criminal prosecutions', *I.L.T. & S.J.*, 21 (1887), 72

Anon., 'Historical sketch of the British Medical Association', *British Medical J.*, 1 (1882), 847–85

Anon., 'Illegality of crown grants of public fisheries in Ireland', *Dub. Rev.*, 11 (1841), 356

Anon., 'Irish juries', *I.L.T. & S.J.*, 7 (1873), 284

Anon., 'Mr Gray's imprisonment', *I.L.T. & S.J.*, 16 (1882), 432

Anon., 'Mr Parnell's arrest', *I.L.T. & S.J.*, 15 (1881), 566

Anon., 'Our jury system', *Dub. U.J.*, 32 (1848), 717

Anon., 'Report of committee on suggestions for diminishing the excessive summoning of jurors in the county and city of Dublin 1874', *J.S.S.I.S.I.*, 6 (1870–9), 378–84

Anon., 'The administration of justice in Ireland', *I.L.T. & S.J.*, 16 (1882) 232

Anon., 'The bill to amend the law relating to juries', *I.L.T. & S.J.*, 6 (1872) 326–7

Anon., 'The Jury Act', *I.L.T. & S.J.*, 7 (1873), 167

Anon., 'Treasure trove', *I.L.T. & S.J.* (1894), 127

Anon., 'Trial by jury', *I.L.T. & S.J.*, 15 (1881), 412

Anon., editorial, *Ir. Jur.* (o.s.), 6 (1854), 181

Anon., editorial, *Ir. Jur.* (o.s.), 6 (1854), 221

Anon., editorial, *Ir. Jur.* (o.s.), 6 (1854), 229

Anon., *The book of oaths, and the severall forms thereof, both antient and modern* (London, 1715)

Anon., *The complete juryman; or, a compendium of the laws relating to jurors* (Dublin, 1774)

Antal, Tamás, 'The codification of the jury procedure in Hungary', *J. Leg. Hist.*, 30:3 (2009), 279–97

Bacon, M., *A new abridgement of the law*, 5 vols (London, 1768)

Baker, John (ed), *The Oxford history of the laws of England*, 13 vols (Oxford, 2004–10)

Ball, F.E., *The judges in Ireland, 1221–1921* (London, 1926)

Barton, T.H., *The practice of the civil bill court in Ireland* (Dublin, 1865)

Beattie, J.M., 'Scales of justice: defence counsel and the English criminal trial in the eighteenth and nineteenth centuries', *L. & Hist. Rev.*, 9:2 (1991), 221–61

Bennett, J.M., 'The establishment of jury trials in New South Wales', *Sydney L. Rev.*, 3 (1959–61), 463–85

Bentley, David, *English criminal justice in the nineteenth century* (London, 1998)

Berkowitz, J.S., 'Breaking the silence: should jurors be allowed to question witnesses during trial?', *Vanderbilt L. Rev.*, 44 (1991), 117–48

Bingham, J., *A new practical digest of the law of evidence, inc. the juryman's complete guide* (London, 1796)

Blackstone, William, *Commentaries on the laws of England*, 4 vols (London, 1791)

Bodkin, M. McDonnell, *Famous Irish trials* (Dublin, 1918)

Bodkin, M. McDonnell, *Recollections of an Irish judge* (New York, 1915)

Bolton, Albert D., *The Labourers (Ireland) Acts, 1883 to 1906* (Dublin, 1910)

Bonsall, Penny, *The Irish RMs: the resident magistrates in the British administration of Ireland* (Dublin, 1997)

Booth, D., *Observations on the English jury laws in criminal cases with respect to the distinction between unanimous verdicts and verdicts by a majority* (London, 1821)

Bourke, Edward J., 'The sinking of the *Rochdale and the Prince of Wales*', *Dub. Hist. Rec.*, 61:2 (2008), 129–35

Brady, J., 'Irish interpreters at Meath assizes', *Ríocht na Midhe*, 2:1 (1959), 62–3

Brett, C.E.B., *Court houses and market houses of the province of Ulster* (Belfast, 1973)

Brett, J., 'County courthouses and county gaols in Ireland', *Irish Builder*, 17 (1875), 25–6

Broderick, David, *Local government in nineteenth-century county Dublin: the grand jury* (Dublin, 2007)

Brown, J., *The dark side of trial by jury* (London, 1859)

Brown, M., & S. Donlan (eds) *The laws and other legalities of Ireland, 1689–1850* (Surrey, 2011)

Brown, Robert Blake, '"A delusion, a mockery, and a snare": array challenges and jury selection in England and Ireland, 1800–1850', *Canadian J. Hist.*, 39:1 (2004), 2–26

Brown, Robert Blake, *A trying question: the jury in nineteenth-century Canada* (Toronto, 2009)

Burke, O.J., *Anecdotes of the Connaught circuit* (Dublin, 1885)

Cairns J.W., & G. McLeod (eds), *'The dearest birth right of the people of England': the jury in the history of the common law* (Oxford, 2002)

Cairns, David, *Advocacy and the making of the adversarial criminal trial, 1800–1865* (Oxford, 1998)

Cameron, N., S. Potter & W. Young, 'The New Zealand jury', *L. & Contemp. Problems*, 62 (1999), 103–40

Campbell, J., *Considerations on the immoral tendency of a law requiring unanimity of juries* (Edinburgh, 1815)

Carleton, W., *Traits and stories of the Irish peasantry*, 2 vols (2nd ser., Dublin, 1832)

Chitty, J., *A practical treatise on the criminal law: comprising the practice, pleadings, and evidence which occur in the course of criminal prosecutions*, 4 vols (London, 1816)

Chitty, T., *Archbold's practice of the court of queen's bench*, 2 vols (London, 1845)

Clark, Michael J., 'General practice and coroners' practice: medico-legal work and the Irish medical profession, *c.*1830–1890' in Catherine Cox and Maria Luddy (eds), *Cultures of care in Irish medical history, 1750–1970* (Basingstoke, 2010)

Clinton, F.W., 'Structure of judicial administration and the development of contract law in seventeenth-century England', *Colum. L. Rev.*, 83:1 (1983), 35–137

Cockburn, J.S., & T.A. Green (eds), *Twelve good men and true: the criminal trial jury in England, 1200–1800* (Princeton, 1988)

Cockburn, J.S., *Calendar of assize records*, xi: *Home circuit indictments: Elizabeth I and James I: introduction* (London, 1985)

Comerton, E.A., *A handbook of the Magistrates' Courts Act (NI) 1964* (Belfast, 1968)

Connell, K.H., *The population of Ireland, 1750–1845* (Oxford, 1950)

Connolly, Sean J., *Religion and society in nineteenth century Ireland* (Dundalk, 1985)

Constable, Marianne, *The law of the other: the mixed jury and changing conceptions of citizenship, law and knowledge* (Chicago, 1994)

Corfe, T., *The Phoenix Park murders: conflict, compromise and tragedy in Ireland, 1879–1882* (London, 1968)

Cornish, W.R., *The jury* (London, 1968)

Counsel, E.P.S., *Jury packing in Ireland* (Dublin, 1887)

Cox, Catherine, *Negotiating insanity in the southeast of Ireland, 1820–1900* (Manchester, 2012)

Crawford, Jon, *A star chamber court in Ireland: the court of castle chamber, 1571–1641* (Dublin, 2005)

Cremona, J.J., 'The jury system in Malta', *American J. Comp. L.*, 13 (1964), 570–82

Crilly, Daniel, *Jury packing in Ireland* (Dublin, 1887)

Crosbie, Kevin, 'Bushell's case and the juror's soul', *J. Leg. Hist.*, 33:3 (2012), 251–90

Crossman, Virginia, *Local government in nineteenth-century Ireland* (Belfast, 1994)
Cullen, L.M., *An economic history of Ireland since 1660* (London, 1972)
Dann, B.M., '"Learning lessons" and "speaking rights": creating educated and democratic juries', *Indiana L. J.*, 68 (1993), 1229–79
Daunton, M.J., 'How to pay for the war: state, society and taxation in Britain, 1917–24', *Eng. Hist. Rev.*, 111:443 (1996), 882–919
Davis, F.F. *The history and development of the special criminal court, 1922–2005* (Dublin, 2007)
Dawson, John P., *A history of lay judges* (Cambridge, MA, 1960)
De Blaghd, E.P., 'Tim Kelly, guilty or not guilty?', *Dub. Hist. Rec.*, 25:1 (1971), 12–24
De la Torre, L., 'New light on Smollett and the Annesley cause', *Rev. Eng. Stud.*, 22:87 (1971), 274–81
Delany, V.T.H., *Christopher Palles, lord chief baron of her majesty's court of exchequer in Ireland, 1874–1916: his life and times* (Dublin, 1960)
Deosaran, R., 'The jury system in a post-colonial multi-racial society: problems of bias', *Brit. J. Criminology*, 21:4 (1981), 305–23
Dicey, A.V., 'How is the law to be enforced in Ireland?', *Fortnightly Rev.* (n.s.), 179 (1881), 537–52
Dodd, W.H., 'Some grievances of jurors', *J.S.S.I.S.I.*, 8 (1879–85), 223–7
Dodd, William H., 'The preliminary proceedings in criminal cases in England, Ireland, and Scotland, compared', *J.S.S.I.S.I.* (1878), 201–9
Donovan, James M., 'Magistrates and juries in France, 1791–1952', *French Hist. Stud.*, 22:3 (1999), 379–420
Donovan, James M., *Juries and the transformation of criminal justice in France in the nineteenth and twentieth centuries* (Chapel Hill, NC, 2010)
Donovan, Tom, 'Miscellanea: some records of Limerick assizes', *North Munster Antiquarian Journal*, 45 (2005), 151–4
Doyle, Aiden, *A history of the Irish language from the Norman invasion to independence* (Oxford, 2015)
Duff, P., 'The Scottish criminal jury: a very peculiar institution' in Neil Vidmar (ed), *World jury systems* (Oxford, 2000)
Duncombe, Giles, *Tryalls per pais* (London, 1655)
Dungan, Myles, *Conspiracy: Irish political trials* (Dublin, 2009)
Dunne, Mildred, & Brian Phillips, *The courthouses of Ireland: a gazetteer of Irish courthouses* (Dublin, 1999)
Dutton, Matthew, *The office and authority of sheriffs, under-sheriffs, deputies, county-clerks, and coroners in Ireland* (Dublin, 1721)
Dzur, Albert, *Punishment, participatory democracy and the jury* (Oxford, 2012)
Farrell, Brian, *Coroners: practice and procedure* (Dublin, 2000)
Ferguson, W.D., *A treatise on the practice of the queen's bench, common pleas and exchequer of pleas in Ireland, in personal actions and ejectments* (Dublin, 1841)
Fitzherbert, A., *The new natura brevium* (London, 1677)
Flower, C. (ed.), *Introduction to the curia regis rolls, 1199–1230 A.D.* (London, 1943)
Foot, Charles H., *The grand jury laws of Ireland* (2nd ed., Dublin, 1884)
Forbes, Thomas R., 'A jury of matrons', *Medical Hist.*, 32:1 (1988), 23–33
Forsyth, J.S., *A synopsis of medical jurisprudence: anatomically, physiologically, and forensically illustrated; for the faculty of medicine, magistrates, lawyers, coroners and jurymen* (London, 1829)
Forsyth, T.W., *History of trial by jury* (London, 1852)
Frost, J., 'The case of Francis Hynes', *I.L.T. & S.J.*, 16 (1882), 432–4

Gabbett, J., *A treatise on the criminal law: comprehending all crimes and misdemeanours punishable by indictment*, 2 vols (Dublin, 1843)

Galligan, Eamon & Michael McGrath, *Compulsory purchase and compensation in Ireland* (2nd ed., Dublin, 2013)

Garnham, Neal, 'Local elite creation in early Hanoverian Ireland: the case of the county grand jury', *Hist. J.*, 42:3 (1999), 623–42

Garnham, Neal, *The courts, crime and criminal law in Ireland, 1692–1760* (Dublin, 1996)

Geary, L.M., *The Plan of Campaign, 1886–1891* (Cork, 1986)

Gilbert, G., *The history and practice of civil actions, particularly in the court of common pleas* (2nd ed., London, 1761)

Golan, Tal, 'The history of scientific expert testimony in the English courtroom', *Science in Context*, 12:1 (1999), 7–32

Gray Indemnity Committee, *The power of judges to punish for contempt of court, as exemplified by the case of the high sheriff of Dublin, 1882* (Dublin, 1882)

Green, Thomas A., *Verdict according to conscience: perspectives on the criminal trial, 1200–1800* (Chicago, 1985)

Greer, S.C., & A. White, *Abolishing the Diplock courts: the case for restoring jury trial for scheduled offences in Northern Ireland* (London, 1986)

Griffin, Brian, 'Prevention and detection of crime in nineteenth-century Ireland' in N.M. Dawson (ed.), *Reflections on law and history* (Dublin, 2006)

Gross, C., *Select cases from the coroners' rolls, A.D. 1265–1413; with a brief account of the history of the office of coroner* (London, 1896)

Gross, Charles, 'The court of piepowder', *Quarterly J. of Economics*, 20:2 (1906), 231–49

Hackett, E.A., *The Irish grand jury system: with a note on the Irish poor law system, 1898* (London, 1898)

Hale, Matthew, *The history of the pleas of the crown*, 2 vols (London, 1736)

Hall, G.D.G. (ed.) *The treatise on the laws and customs of the realm of England commonly called Glanvill* (London, 1965)

Hamilton, E.C., *The Woodford evictions: report submitted to the committee of the Property Defence Association at their meeting on Thursday, the 21st Oct., 1886* (Dublin, 1886)

Hancock, W.N., 'The cost of adopting a complete system of public prosecution in England, as illustrated by the results of the working of the Scotch and Irish systems of public prosecution', *J.S.S.I.S.I.* (1878), 271–4

Hanly, Conor, 'The decline of civil jury trial in nineteenth-century England', *J. Leg. Hist.*, 26:3 (2005), 253–78

Harrington, Tim, *The Maamtrasna massacre: impeachment of the trials* (Dublin, 1884)

Harris, Leslie Gerald Eyre, *A treatise on the law and practice in lunacy in Ireland* (Dublin, 1930)

Hawkins, M., *Treatise of the pleas of the crown*, 2 vols (8th ed., London, 1824)

Hay, Douglas, 'The state and the market in 1800: Lord Kenyon and Mr Waddington', *Past and Present*, 162 (1999), 101–62

Hayes, Edmund, *Crimes and punishments, or a digest of the criminal statute law of Ireland*, 2 vols (2nd ed., Dublin, 1842)

Healy, M., *The old Munster circuit: a book of memories and traditions* (London, 1939)

Heathcote, Bernard V., *Viewing the lifeless body: a coroner and his inquests held in Nottinghamshire public houses during the nineteenth century, 1828 to 1866* (Nottingham, 2005)

Hempton, David, Religion and political culture in Britain and Ireland from the Glorious Revolution to the decline of empire (Cambridge, 1996)

Hickey, É., *Irish law and lawyers in modern folk tradition* (Dublin, 1999)

Holdsworth, W.S., *History of English law*, 12 vols (London, 1903–34)

Holloway, I., '*O'Connell v. The queen*: a sesquicentennial remembrance', *N.I.L.Q.*, 46 (1995), 63–71

Holton, Karina, 'From charters to carters: aspects of fairs and markets in medieval Leinster' in Denis A. Cronin, Jim Gilligan and Karina Holton (eds), *Irish fairs and markets: studies in local history* (Dublin, 2001)

Hooper, W., *The birth of the law of illegitimacy: a treatise on the law affecting persons of illegitimate birth, with the rules of evidence in proof of legitimacy and illegitimacy, and an historical account of the bastard in mediaeval law* (London, 1911)

Hope, J., *Dissertation on the constitution and effects of a petty jury* (Dublin, 1737)

Hoppit, Julian, 'Reforming Britain's weights and measures, 1660–1824', *English Historical Review*, 108:426 (1993), 82–104.

Houston, Arthur, 'Observations on trial by jury, with suggestions for the amendment of our present system', *J. Dub. Stat. Soc.*, 3 (1861), 100–9

Howlin, Niamh, '"The terror of their lives": Irish jurors' experiences', *L. & Hist. Rev.*, 29:3 (2011), 703–61

Howlin, Niamh, 'Fenians, foreigners and jury trials in Ireland, 1865–69', *Ir. Jur.*, 45 (2010), 51–81

Howlin, Niamh, 'Irish jurors: passive observers or active participants?', *J. Leg. Hist.*, 35:2 (2014), 143–71

Howlin, Niamh, 'Nineteenth century criminal justice: uniquely Irish or simply "not English"?', *Irish J. Leg. Stud.*, 3:1 (2013), 67–89

Howlin, Niamh, 'The politics of jury trial in Ireland', *Comp. Leg. Hist.*, 3:2 (2015), 271–91

Howlin, Niamh, 'Who tried Roger Casement?', *History Ireland*, 25:5 (2017)

Howman, R., 'Trial by jury in southern Rhodesia', *Rhodes-Livingstone J.*, 7 (1949), 41-66

Hoyle, Mark S.W., 'The mixed courts of Egypt: an anniversary assessment', *Arab Law Quarterly*, 1:1 (1995), 60–8

Huband, W.G., *A practical treatise on the law relating to the grand jury in criminal cases, the coroner's jury and the petty jury in Ireland* (Dublin, 1896, rev. ed. Dublin, 1911)

Humphreys, H., *The Prevention of Crime (Ireland) Act 1882, 45 & 46 Vict., cap. 25, with a review on the policy, bearing, and scope of the act* (Dublin, 1882)

Hunnisett, Roy Frank, *The medieval coroner* (Cambridge, 1961)

Impey, J., *The new instructor clericalis* (4th ed., London, 1788)

Ireland, R.W., 'Putting oneself on whose county? Carmarthenshire juries in the mid-nineteenth century' in T.G. Watkin (ed.), *Legal Wales: its past, its future* (Cardiff, 2001)

Jackson, Alvin, *Home rule: an Irish history, 1800–2000* (Oxford, 2003)

Jackson, J., & S. Doran, *Judge without jury: Diplock trials in the adversary system* (Oxford, 1995)

Jeary, J.H., 'Trial by jury and trial with the aid of assessors in the superior courts of British African territories, I–III', *J. African L.*, 4:3 (1960), 133–44; 5:1 (1961), 133–46; 5:2 (1961), 36–47

Jellett, H.P., *An outline of the practice of the superior courts of common law in Ireland in personal actions and ejectment* (Dublin, 1865)

Johnson, David, 'Trial by jury in Ireland, 1860–1914', *J. Leg. Hist.*, 17:3 (1996), 270–91

Johnson, David, 'The trials of Sam Gray: Monaghan politics and nineteenth century Irish criminal procedure', *Ir. Jur.* (n.s.), 20 (1985), 109–34

Johnson, Stafford J., 'The Dublin penny post: 1773–1840', *Dub. Hist. Rec.*, 42:3 (1942), 81–95

Johnston, W.J., 'The first adventure of the common law', *L. Q. Rev.*, 36 (1920), 9–30

Joy, H.H., *The admissibility of confessions and challenge of jurors in criminal cases in England and Ireland* (Philadelphia, 1843)

Kahn, E., 'Restore the jury? Or "Reform? Reform? Aren't things bad enough already?" I–III', *South African L. J.*, 108:4 (1991), 672–87; 109:1 (1992), 87–127; and 109:2 (1992), 307–18

Keeley, T.C.S., 'One hundred years of lunacy administration', *Camb. L. J.*, 8:2 (1943), 195–200

King, Thomas, 'Local government administrators in Carlow – from grand jury to county council', *Carloviana: J. Old Carlow Soc.*, 47 (1999), 77–8

Klerman, Daniel, 'Was the jury ever self-informing?', *Southern California L. Rev.*, 17 (2003), 123–50

Knox-Mawer, R, 'The jury system in British colonial Africa', *J. African L.*, 2 (1958), 160–3

Koch, Arnd, 'C.J.A. Mittermaier and the nineteenth century debate about juries and mixed courts', *Revue Internationale de Droit Pénal*, 72:1 (2001), 347–53

Kostel, R.W., 'Rebels in the dock: the prosecution of the Dublin Fenians, 1865–6', *Éire-Ireland*, 34 (1999), 79–80

Kucherov, Samuel, 'The jury as part of the Russian judicial reform of 1864', *American Slavic & East European Rev.*, 9:2 (1950), 77–90

Langbein, John H., *The origins of adversary criminal trial* (Oxford, 2005)

Langbein, John H., 'The criminal trial before the lawyers', *U. Chic. L. Rev.*, 45 (1978), 263–316

Langbein, John H., 'The English criminal trial jury on the eve of the French Revolution' in A. Schioppa (ed.), *The trial jury in England, France, Germany, 1700–1900* (Berlin, 1987)

Langbein, John H., 'The origins of public prosecution and common law', *Amer. J. Leg. Hist.*, 17 (1973), 313–35

Larkin, Felix M., '"Green shoots" of the new journalism in the *Freeman's Journal*, 1877–1890' in Karen Steele & Michael de Nie (eds), *Ireland and the new journalism* (London, 2014)

Larkin, Felix M., 'Lord Frederick Cavendish and the Phoenix Park murders of 1882', *Hist. Ire.*, 22:3 (2014), 28–31

LaRue, Lewis H., 'A jury of one's peers', *Washington & Lee L. Rev.*, 33:4 (1976), 841–75

Leckey, John L. & D. Greer, *Coroners' law and practice in Northern Ireland* (Belfast, 1998)

Levine, M., 'A more than ordinary case of "rape", 13 & 14 Elizabeth I', *Amer. J. Leg. Hist.*, 7:2 (1963), 159–64

Lilly, J., *A continuation of the practical register*, 2 vols (London, 1710)

Lilly, J., *The practical register*, 2 vols (2nd ed., London, 1745)

Lloyd-Bostock, Sally & Cheryl Thomas, 'Decline of the "little parliament": juries and jury reform in England and Wales', *L. & Contemp. Problems*, 62:2 (1999), 7–40

Logan, Patrick, *Fair day: the story of Irish fairs and markets* (Belfast, 1986)

Low, Alex, 'Sir Alfred Stephen and the jury question in Van Diemen's Land', *University of Tasmania L. Rev.*, 21 (2002), 72–119

Lyall, A., *Land law in Ireland* (3rd ed., Dublin, 2010)

Lyon Cross, A., 'The English criminal law and benefit of clergy during the eighteenth and early nineteenth century', *Amer. Hist. Rev.*, 22:3 (1917), 544-65

Lyons, F.S.L., *Charles Stewart Parnell* (London, 1977)

Lyons, F.S.L., *Ireland since the Famine* (London, 1971)

MacBride, Ian, *Eighteenth century Ireland: the isle of slaves* (Dublin, 2009)

MacKay, Lynn, *Respectability and the London poor, 1780–1870: the value of virtue* (London, 2016)

MacNally, Leonard, *The justice of the peace for Ireland: containing the authorities and duties of that officer, as also of the various conservators of the peace*, 2 vols (Dublin, 1808)

MacNally, Leonard, *The rules of evidence on pleas of the crown* (Dublin, 1802)

Maddox, N., 'A melancholy record: the story of the nineteenth-century Irish Party Processions Acts', *Ir. Jur.* (n.s.), 29 (2004), 242–73

Malley, George Orme, 'On the expediency of the total abolition of grand juries in Ireland', *J.S.S.I.S.I.*, 6:40 (1871), 11–19

McAree, N., *Murderous justice: a study in depth of the infamous Connemara murders* (Limerick, 1990)

McConville, Sean, *Irish political prisoners, 1848–1922: theatres of war* (London, 2003)

McCormack, W.J., *The parliamentary register of Ireland: history of the proceedings and debates of the house of commons of Ireland* (Bristol, 1999)

McDowell, R.B., 'The Irish courts of law, 1801–1914', *I.H.S.*, 10:40 (1957), 363–91

McDowell, R.B., *Ireland in the age of imperialism and revolution* (Oxford, 1976)

McDowell, R.B., *The Irish administration, 1801–1914* (1st ed., London, 1964)

McEldowney, John & Paul O'Higgins (eds), *The common law tradition: essays in Irish legal history* (Dublin, 1990)

McEldowney, John, 'Lord O'Hagan (1812–1885): a study of his life and period as lord chancellor of Ireland (1868–1874)', *Ir. Jur.* (n.s.), 14 (1979), 360–77

McEldowney, John, 'Crown prosecutions in nineteenth-century Ireland' in Douglas Hay and F. Snyder (eds), *Policing and prosecution in Britain, 1750–1850* (Oxford, 1989)

McEldowney, John, 'Lord O'Hagan and the Irish Jury Act 1871' (PhD, Cambridge University, 1981)

McEldowney, John, 'Stand by for the crown: an historical analysis', *Crim. L. Rev.* (1979), 272–83

McEldowney, John, 'The case of *The queen v. McKenna* and jury packing in Ireland', *Ir. Jur.* (n.s.), 12 (1977), 339–54

McGuire, J., & J. Quinn (ed.) *Dictionary of Irish biography* (Cambridge, 2009)

McKenna, P.J., 'On the criminal jurisdiction of quarter sessions in Ireland', *J.S.S.I.S.I.*, 1 (1856), 276–85

McMahon, Bryan M.E., *Judge or jury? The jury trial for personal injury cases in Ireland* (Cork, 1985)

McMahon, Michael, *The murder of Thomas Douglas Bateson, County Monaghan, 1851* (Dublin, 2006)

McMahon, Richard, '"The madness of party": sectarian homicide in Ireland, 1801–1850', *Crime History and Societies*, 11:1 (2007), 83–112

McMahon, Richard, 'Manor courts in the west of Ireland before the Famine' in D.S. Greer and N.M. Dawson (eds), *Mysteries and solutions in Irish legal history* (Dublin, 2001)

McMahon, Richard, 'The court of petty sessions and society in pre-Famine Galway' in Raymond Gillespie (ed.), *The remaking of modern Ireland, 1750–1950: Beckett prize essays in Irish history* (Dublin, 2004)

McMahon, Richard, 'The courts of petty sessions and the law in pre-Famine Galway' (MA, NUI Galway, 1999)

McParland, E., 'Strategy in the planning of Dublin, 1750–1800' in P. Butel and L.M. Cullen (eds), *Cities and merchants: French and Irish perspectives on urban development, 1500–1900* (Dublin, 1986)

McParland, E., 'The wide streets commissioners, their importance for Dublin architecture in the late eighteenth – early nineteenth century', *Bulletin Ir. Georgian Soc.*, 15:1 (1972), 1–32

McParland, E., *James Gandon: Vitruvius Hibernicus* (London, 1985)

Milne, Kenneth, *The Dublin liberties, 1600–1850* (Dublin, 2009)

Mitchell, James, 'The Catholics of Galway, 1708–13: a commentary on a report by Don Giovanni Donato Mezzafalce', *J. Galway Archaeological and Hist. Soc.*, 61 (2009), 79–106

Mitnick, J.M., 'From neighbour-witness to judge of proofs: the transformation of the English civil juror', *American J. Leg. Hist.*, 32 (1988), 201–35

Mittlebeeler, E.V. 'Race and jury in Nigeria', *Howard L.J.*, 18 (1973–5), 88–106

Mnookin, Jennifer L., 'Idealizing science and demonizing experts: an intellectual history of expert evidence', *Villanova L. Rev.*, 52 (2007), 763–802

Molloy, Constantine, 'Observations on the law relating to the qualification and selection of jurors, with suggestions for its amendment', *J.S.S.I.S.I.*, 4:39 (1865), 186–93

Molloy, Constantine, *Justice of the peace for Ireland: a treatise on the powers and duties of magistrates in Ireland in cases of summary jurisdiction in the prosecution of indictable offences and in other matters* (Dublin, 1890)

Monaghan, J., 'The functions of grand juries in criminal cases', *J.S.S.I.S.I.*, 4:30 (1865), 218–27

Moody, T.W., & W.E. Vaughan (eds) *A new history of Ireland, iv: Eighteenth century Ireland, 1691–1800* (Oxford, 1986)

Moore, E.J., 'Lord O'Hagan', *I.L.T. & S.J.*, 42 (1908), 255–6

Mullins, Bernard, *Observations upon the Irish grand jury system* (Dublin, 1831)

Napier, James J. & Herbert McVeigh, *The law of valuation (Northern Ireland and Irish Free State* (Belfast, 1935)

Nemytina, Marina, 'Trial by jury: a Western or a peculiarly Russian model?', *Revue Internationale de Droit Pénal*, 72:1 (2001), 365–70

Newark, F.H., 'Notes on Irish legal history', *N.I.L.Q.*, 7 (1946–8), 121–39

Newell, Joseph, *Inquest jurymen. An enquiry into the nature and duties of inquest jury-men, of the city of London, together with the by-laws of the common council, and the articles of charge. Also the law for regulating the election of constables, leet and annoyance jury for the city of Westminster, shewing the nature and duties of their office, and the general laws respecting defective weights nad measures for counties, liberties and divisions, of England and Wales* (London, 1825)

Ní Cearbhaill, Máire, 'The bigamist of Ballinavin' in Liam Clare and Máire Ní Cearbhaill (eds), *Trouble with the law: crimes and trials from Ireland's past* (Dublin, 2007)

Nichols, F.M., *Britton: an English translation and notes* (Washington, 1901)

O'Brien, Francis William, 'Switzerland questions the jury', *Saskatchewan L. Rev.*, 32:1 (1967), 31–44

O'Brien, R.B., *Dublin Castle and the Irish people* (2nd ed., London, 1912)

O'Callaghan, M., *British high politics and a nationalist Ireland: Criminality, land and the law under Foster and Balfour* (Cork, 1994)

O'Carroll, G., *Mr. Justice Robert Day (1746–1841): the diaries and the addresses to grand juries, 1793–1829* (Tralee, 2004)

Ó Cionnaith, Finnian, *Mapping, measurement and metropolis: how land surveyors shaped eighteenth-century Dublin* (Dublin, 2012)

O'Connell, M., *The correspondence of Daniel O'Connell*, 8 vols (vols i–ii Shannon, 1972; vols iii–viii Dublin, 1974–1980)

O'Connor, Roger, *A view of the system of Anglo-Irish jurisprudence and the effects of trial by jury when individuals consider themselves belonging to a faction rather than to the community* (London, 1811)

O'Donnell, I., & F. McAuley (eds), *Criminal justice history* (Dublin, 2003)

Ó Drisceoil, Diarmuid & Donal Ó Drisceoil, *Serving a city: the story of Cork's English market* (Cork, 2011)

O'Flaherty, Eamon, 'Ecclesiastical politics and the dismantling of the penal laws in Ireland, 1774–82', *I.H.S.*, 26:101 (1988), 33–50

O'Flanagan, J.R., *The Munster circuit: tales, trials, and traditions* (London, 1880)

O'Hagan, T., 'Legal, educational and social reforms in Ireland', in T. O'Hagan, *Occasional papers and addresses* (London, 1884)

O'Higgins, Paul, *A bibliography of Irish trials and other legal proceedings* (Abingdon, 1986)

O'Shaughnessy, Mark, 'The venue for trials, civil and criminal', *J.S.S.I.S.I.*, 4:30 (1865), 193–203

Oldham, James C., 'On pleading the belly a history of the jury of matrons', *Crim. Jus. Hist.*, 6 (1985), 1–64

Oldham, James C., 'Special juries in England: nineteenth century usage and reform', *J. Leg. Hist.*, 8 (1987), 148–66

Oldham, James C., 'The origins of the special jury', *U. Chic. Law Rev.*, 50 (1983), 137–211

Oldham, James C., *The Mansfield manuscripts and the growth of English law in the eighteenth century* (Chapel Hill, NC, 1992)

Oldham, James C., *Trial by jury: the seventh amendment and Anglo-American special juries* (New York, 2006)

Osborough, W.N., *The Irish stage: a legal history* (Dublin, 2015)

Otway-Ruthven, A.J., *A history of medieval Ireland* (London, 1980)

Oxford dictionary of national biography (online edition)

Palmer, N.E., 'Treasure trove and the protection of antiquities', *Mod. L. Rev.*, 44:2 (1981), 178–87

Parker, Graham, 'Trial by jury in Canada', *J. Leg. Hist.*, 8 (1987), 179–89

Patton, Billy, *The court will rise: a short history of the old courthouse, Lifford, Co. Donegal* (Donegal, 2004)

Phelan, Mary, 'Irish language court interpreting, 1801–1922' (PhD, Dublin City University, 2013)

Pihlajamäki, Heikki, 'From compurgators to mixed courts: reflections on the historical development of Finnish evidence law and court structure', *Revue Internationale de Droit Pénal*, 72:1 (2001), 159–74

Plucknett, J.F. & J.L. Barton (eds), *St. Germain: doctor and student* (London, 1974)

Pole, Adam, 'Sheriffs in Victorian Ireland' in Felix M. Larkin and N.M. Dawson (eds), *Lawyers, the law and history* (Dublin, 2013)

Pollock, F., & F.W. Maitland, *A history of English law before the time of Edward I*, 2 vols (2nd ed., Cambridge, 1898, repr. 1911)

Porter, Roy, *London: a social history* (London, 1994)

Purcell, T., *A summary of the criminal law of Ireland* (Dublin, 1848)

Reader, W.J., *Professional men: the rise of the professional classes in nineteenth-century England* (London, 1966)

Richardson, H., & G. Sayles (eds), *Select cases of procedure without writ under Henry III* (London, 1941)

Rix, Keith J.B., 'Expert evidence and the courts: 1. The history of expert evidence', *Advances in Psychiatric Treatment*, 5 (1999), 71–7

Robinson, Christopher, *A charge given to the grand juries of the county of the city of Dublin and county of Dublin: at a sitting of his majesty's commissions of oyer and terminer, and general gaol delivery, for the said counties, on Monday the 15th day of Dec. 1760* (Dublin, 1760)

Robinson, Mary, *The special criminal court* (Dublin, 1974)

Rosenthal, Lloyd L., 'The development of the use of expert testimony', *L. & Contemp. Problems*, 2 (1935), 403–18

Savage, J., *Fenian heroes and martyrs* (Boston, 1868)

Savitt, William, 'Rethinking the nineteenth-century French jury', *Colum. L. Rev.*, 96:4 (1996), 1019–61

Scannell, James, 'The inevitable demise of Thomas Bewley', *Dub. Hist. Rec.*, 61:2 (2008), 114–19

Schioppa, Antonio Padua, *The trial jury in England, France, Germany, 1700–1900* (Berlin, 1987)

Scully, Denys, *A statement of the penal laws which aggrieve the Catholics of Ireland: with commentaries* (2nd ed., Dublin, 1812)

Sellon, B.J., *The practice of the courts of king's bench and common pleas*, 2 vols (London, 1792)

Shapiro, Barbara J., ''Beyond reasonable doubt': the neglected eighteenth century context', *L. & Humanities*, 8:1 (2014), 19–52

Shapiro, Barbara J., '"To a moral certainty": theories of knowledge and Anglo-American juries, 1600–1850', *Hastings L. Rev.*, 38 (1986), 153–93
Shapiro, Barbara J., 'Oaths, credibility and the legal process in early modern England: part one', *Law and Humanities*, 6:2 (2012), 145–78
Sheridan, E., 'Designing the capital city' in J. Brady and A. Simms (eds), *Dublin through space & time* (Dublin, 2007)
Sloan, Robert, *William Smith O'Brien and the Young Irelander rebellion of 1848: the road to Ballingarry* (Dublin, 2000)
Smythe, Hamilton, *The office of justice of the peace in Ireland* (Dublin, 1841)
Spellissy, Sean, *A history of County Clare* (Dublin, 2003)
Spiller, R., 'The jury system in early Natal (1846–1874)', *J. Leg. Hist.*, 8:2 (1987), 129–47
Spring-Rice, Thomas, *An inquiry into the effects of the Irish grand jury laws: as affecting the industry, the improvement, and the moral character of the people of Ireland* (London, 1815)
Stebbings, Chantel, 'Protecting the property of the mentally ill: the judicial solution in nineteenth century lunacy law', *Camb. L. J.*, 71:2 (2012), 384–411
Stephen, J., *A digest of the criminal law* (London, 1877)
Stephen, J., *New commentaries on the laws of England*, 4 vols (New York, 1843)
Stephen, J.F., *A history of the criminal law of England* 3 vols (London, 1883)
Strauss, S.A., 'The jury in South Africa', *U. Western Australia L. Rev.*, 11 (1973–4), 133–9
Style, W., *The practical register* (2nd and 3rd eds, London, 1670, 1694)
Sullivan, A.M., *The dock and the scaffold* (Dublin, 1868)
Sullivan, Alexander, *The last serjeant* (London, 1952)
Swaine, Warren, *The law of contract, 1670–1870* (Cambridge, 2015)
Taylor, Greg, 'Jury trial in Austria', *New Criminal L. Rev.*, 14:2 (2011), 281–325
Thayer, J., *A preliminary treatise on evidence at the common law* (London, 1898)
Thomas, J.H., *A systematic arrangement of Lord Coke's first institute of the laws of England*, 3 vols (Philadelphia, 1826–7)
Thorne, S. (ed.), *Bracton on the laws and customs of England*, 4 vols (London, 1977)
Tidd, W., *The practice of the courts of king's bench and common pleas in personal actions and ejectment* (9th ed., London, 1828)
Townshend, C., *Political violence in Ireland: government resistance since 1848* (Oxford, 1983)
Traest, Phillip, 'The jury in Belgium', *Revue Internationale de Droit Pénal*, 72:1 (2001), 27–50
Trench, Fred, 'John Hatch and the development of Harcourt Street', *Dub. Hist. Rec.*, 62:1 (2009), 70–7
Tuke, Daniel Hack, *Chapters in the history of the insane in the British Isles* (Dublin, 1882)
Unsworth, Clive, 'Law and lunacy in psychiatry's "golden age"', *Ox. J. Leg. Stud.*, 13 (1993), 79–507
Van Caenegem, R.C., *English lawsuits from William I to Richard I* (London, 1990–1)
Van Caenegem, R.C., *Royal writs in England from the conquest to Glanvill* (London, 1958–9)
Vaughan, William E. (ed), *A new history of Ireland; v, Ireland under the Union, 1801–1870* (Oxford, 1989)
Vaughan, William E., *Landlords and tenants in mid-Victorian Ireland* (Oxford, 1994)
Vaughan, William E., *Murder trials in Ireland* (Dublin, 2009)
Vidmar, Neil (ed.) *World jury systems* (Oxford, 2000)
Viner, C., *A general abridgement of law and equity*, 24 vols (2nd ed., London, 1791)
Vogler, Richard, 'The international development of the jury: the role of the British empire', *Revue Internationale de Droit Pénal*, 72:1 (2001), 525–50
Waldron, J., *Maamtrasna: the murders and the mystery* (Dublin, 1992)

White, Jerry, 'City rivalries and the modernisation of eighteenth century London, 1720–1770', *Literatur in Wissenschaft und Unterricht*, 43:2/3 (2010), 83–102

Whitman, James Q., *The origins of reasonable doubt: the theological roots of the criminal trial* (New Haven, CT, 2008)

Whittaker, W. (ed., tr.), *The mirror of justices* (London, 1895)

Whyte, J.H., 'Landlord influence at elections in Ireland, 1760–1885', *Eng. Hist. Rev.*, 80 (1965), 739–59

Wide Streets Commission, *Extracts from the minutes of the commissioners appointed by act of Parliament, for making wide and convenient ways, streets and passages in the city of Dublin* (Dublin, 1802)

Williams, Glanville, 'Venue and the ambit of criminal law', *L.Q. Rev.*, 81 (1965), 276–88

Willock, Ian D., *The origins and development of the jury in Scotland* (Edinburgh, 1966)

Wilson, Adrian, *The making of man-midwifery: childbirth in England, 1660–1770* (London, 1995)

Wolf, Nicholas M., *An Irish-speaking island: state, religion, community and the linguistic landscape in Ireland, 1770–1870* (Madison, WI, and London, 2014)

Woodruff, Douglas, *The Tichborne claimant: a Victorian mystery* (London, 1957)

Table of legislation

ACTS

BILLS

RULES OF COURT

Table of cases

Index

compiled by Julitta Clancy

Irish Legal History Society

Established in 1988 to encourage the study and advance the knowledge of the history of Irish law, especially by the publication of original documents and of works relating to the history of Irish law, including its institutions, doctrines and personalities, and reprinting or editing of works of sufficient rarity or importance.

www.ilhs.eu